)B FAMILY

FAVERSHAM, KENT
–1788)

died 1839)

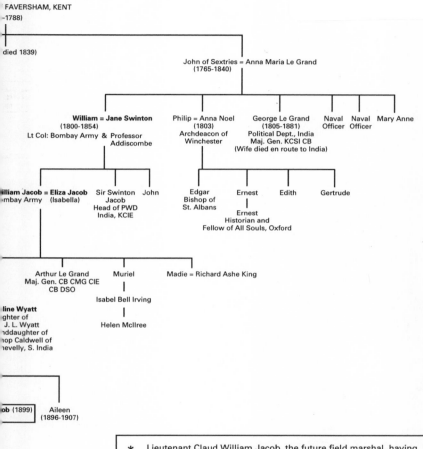

John of Sextries = Anna Maria Le Grand
(1765-1840)

William = **Jane Swinton**
(1800-1854)
Lt Col: Bombay Army & Professor
Addiscombe

Philip = Anna Noel
(1803)
Archdeacon of
Winchester

George Le Grand
(1805-1881)
Political Dept., India
Maj. Gen. KCSI CB
(Wife died en route to India)

Naval Officer   Naval Officer   Mary Anne

illiam Jacob = Eliza Jacob   Sir Swinton   John
mbay Army   (Isabella)   Jacob
Head of PWD
India, KCIE

Edgar
Bishop of
St. Albans

Ernest

Ernest
Historian and
Fellow of All Souls, Oxford

Edith   Gertrude

Arthur Le Grand   Muriel   Madie = Richard Ashe King
Maj. Gen. CB CMG CIE
CB DSO

Isabel Bell Irving

line Wyatt
ghter of
J. L. Wyatt
nddaughter of
hop Caldwell of
nevelly, S. India

Helen McIlree

ob (1899)   Aileen
(1896-1907)

(1928) = Rhonda McComas
utenant
N (retd)

Patrick

> *   Lieutenant Claud William Jacob, the future field marshal, having
> been commissioned in the Worcestershire Regiment, after two
> years in India joined the Thirtieth Bombay Infantry in 1884, and his
> brother Arthur Le Grand followed him in 1887. The battalion was
> officially the Third (Baluch) Battalion, and was popularly known as
> Jacob's Rifles, having been raised by John Jacob of Sind.
> Claud was one of twenty-eight male members of the Jacob family
> who, in the period 1817-1926, served in the East India Company's
> Army or, later, in the Indian Army. There were others who served
> in the Civil Service or the Public Works Department, and in the
> Wyatt family there were also soldiers and missionaries. Ian Jacob
> was the last 'Child of the Raj'.

From Churchill's Secret Circle to the BBC

The Biography of
LIEUTENANT GENERAL SIR IAN JACOB GBE CB DL

For John
with all best
wishes from your book
Ian Jacob.
28.9.91

Charles Richardson

Also from Brassey's

BAYNES

The Forgotten Victor:
The Life of General Sir Richard O'Connor

BRAMALL AND JACKSON

The Chiefs

DANCHEV

Establishing the Anglo-American Alliance:
The Second World War Diaries of Brigadier Vivian Dykes

KINNARD

Ike 1890–1990:
A Pictorial History

MEARSHEIMER

Liddell Hart and the Weight of History

MESSENGER

The Last Prussian:
A Biography of Field Marshal Gerd von Rundstedt

STAHLBERG

Bounden Duty:
The Memoirs of a German Officer 1932–45

IAN JACOB

From Churchill's Secret Circle to the BBC

The Biography of
Lieutenant General Sir Ian Jacob GBE CB DL

by
General Sir Charles Richardson GCB CBE DSO

BRASSEY'S (UK)

A Member of the Maxwell Macmillan Group
LONDON · OXFORD · WASHINGTON · NEW YORK

First edition 1991

UK editorial offices: Brassey's, 50 Fetter Lane, London EC4A 1AA
orders: Brassey's, Headington Hill Hall, Oxford OX3 0BW

USA editorial offices: Brassey's, 8000 Westpark Drive, First Floor, McLean, Virginia 22102
orders: Macmillan, Front and Brown Streets, Riverside, New Jersey 08075

Library of Congress Cataloging-in-Publication Data
Richardson, Charles, 1909–
From Churchill's secret circle to the BBC: the biography of Lieutenant General Sir Ian Jacob, GBE CB DL/Charles Richardson. – 1st ed.
p. cm.
Includes bibliographical references and index.
1. Jacob, Ian, Sir. 1899– . 2. Generals – Great Britain – Biography. 3. British Broadcasting Corporation – Officials and employees – Biography. 4. Great Britain – History, Military – 20th century. 5. World War. 1939–1945 – Diplomatic history. I. Title.
DA69.3.J33R53 1991 941.08'092 – dc20 91-10437

British Library Cataloguing in Publication Data
Richardson, Charles 1908–
From Churchill's secret circle to the BBC: the biography of Lieutenant General Sir Ian Jacob GBE CB DL.
1. Great Britain. Armies. Jacob, Ian
I. Title
355.331092
ISBN 0-08-037692-4

Printed in Great Britain by B.P.C.C. Wheatons Ltd., Exeter

DEDICATION

*This biography of a brilliant soldier
and trusty servant of the State is
dedicated to the Corps of Royal Engineers,
which fostered him in his early years.*

Contents

Acknowledgements	ix
Foreword	xiii
List of Illustrations	xvii
Chronology	xix
Glossary	xxvii
Introduction	xxxi
1. Child of the Raj	1
2. 'Peace for our Time'	16
3. Stumbling into War	27
4. Churchill at the Helm	45
5. With Churchill to Meet Roosevelt	59
6. 'All in the Same Boat Now'	81
7. Darkest Days	106
8. Conferring with Stalin	132
9. Planning for Victory	147

10.   On the Conference Circuit Again   172

11.   The Road to Victory   192

12.   A Second Career   217

13.   Director General of the BBC   233

14.   'Never Look Back'   263

Chapter Notes   284

Bibliography   287

Index   289

Acknowledgements

In the first place my thanks must go to Sir Ian and the late Lady Jacob who repeatedly received me at their home at Woodbridge where I was able to have many discussions with Sir Ian, then in his ninetieth year, and also meet other members of the family. Their encouragement and hospitality were greatly appreciated.

Of General Jacob's colleagues during the war not many remain. My gratitude is all the greater to those who have helped me depict my subject in those heroic times, particularly Mrs Maxwell, General Jacob's secretary, and Mrs Joan Bright Astley, Mr Mark Norman and Air Chief Marshal Sir Alfred Earle who worked in the Cabinet Office during that period; also to Sir John Peck, one of Churchill's Private Secretaries who helped me by correspondence from Eire, and to Lady Soames, who as a Junior Commander in the ATS accompanied her father across the Atlantic, and knew General Jacob well.

The path taken by General Jacob during his early career was not unfamiliar to me. I had followed much the same route: an Army family, with a father absent in France in World War I, Wellington College, the Royal Military Academy Woolwich, Sappers and Miners in India, World War II, a year in the Cabinet Office, and after retirement, experience in industry; but the BBC was unknown territory. I could not have attempted to write of that significant phase in General Jacob's life without the generous help of Leonard Miall, a distinguished member of the BBC, now retired and a research historian. His wide knowledge and wise advice, and the hospitality offered by him and his wife greatly smoothed my path. I have also enjoyed meeting other members of the BBC of that period, particularly Harman Grisewood, Frank Gillard, Maurice Farquharson and Oliver Whitley. I record my thanks also to Lord Briggs, the historian of the BBC, Mr Hussey, the Chairman of the BBC, and Mr Michael

Checkland the present Director General, and Mrs Jacqueline Kavanagh, the Written Archives Officer.

My friend from Eighth Army days, Sir Edgar Williams, who in his distinguished career at Oxford University was also editor of the *Dictionary of National Biography* for thirty-one years, was kind enough to read an early draft; he gave me much wise advice.

Many others have kindly contributed with information and recollections, including Colonel MB Adams, Honorary Secretary of the Association of King George the Fifth's Own Bengal Sappers and Miners, Brigadier EFE Armstrong, Major General WM Broomhall, Sir George Burton, Lieutenant General Sir John Cowley, the late Major General PH de Havilland, Dr Alex Danchev, Brigadier EW Denison, Sir Arthur Drew, Major General Sir Charles Dunphie, Major General WG Fryer, Mr Martin Gilbert, Lieutenant Colonel HSM Hogg, Brigadier RH Keenlyside, the late Brigadier Sir Geoffrey Macnab, Colonel A Murray, Major General Cosmo Nevill, General Sir Patrick Palmer, Lieutenant Colonel and Mrs Richard Probert, Mr John Profumo, Sir Frank Roberts, Sir Joshua Rowley, Lord Lieutenant for Suffolk, Lieutenant Colonel GA Shepperd, the late Brigadier CD Steel, Mr George Straschnov, of Geneva, the late Brigadier CEF Turner, General Sir Richard Vincent, and Sir Richard Way.

I express my gratitude also to the staffs of the following institutions: the Public Record Office, the Liddell Hart Centre in King's College London, the BBC Written Archives Centre, the Imperial War Museum (Photography Department), the libraries of the Ministry of Defence, the Royal Military Academy Sandhurst, the Staff College and the Institution of Royal Engineers.

I am grateful also to the Trustees and Secretary of the Army and Navy Club for making available to me the History of the Club 1837–1965, and to the Master and the Archivist of Wellington College.

In addition, I have to thank the following for permission to quote from their published work:

Cassell PLC—*John Jacob of Jacobabad* by LT Lambrick, *The Diaries of Sir Alexander Cadogan* by David Dilks and *The Second World War* vols I, II and VI by Winston S Churchill (with permission on behalf of the Winston Churchill Estate from Curtis Brown Ltd).

Collins Publishers—*My Early Life* by Winston S Churchill (with permission on behalf of the Winston Churchill Estate from Curtis Brown Ltd).

Macmillan Publishers Ltd—*Action This Day* by Sir John Wheeler-Bennett.

Hodder & Stoughton Ltd and WW Norton & Company Inc. (American rights)—*The Fringes of Power* by John Colville.

The Oxford University Press—*History of Broadcasting in the United Kingdom* by Asa Briggs.

The Random Century Group—*One Thing at a Time* by Harman Grisewood.

Foreword

THE Jacob family has left its mark on British military history. Jacobabad, Jacob's House, Jacob's Rifles, Jacob's Mountain Battery are names sufficient in themselves to underline the Indian connection. The father of Sir Ian Jacob, the subject of this book, was Sir Claud Jacob (1863–1948), who was commissioned in 1882 and followed the family tradition into Jacob's Rifles. Sir Claud, however, was destined for more than Indian fame; due for retirement in September, 1914, instead he soon found himself commanding a brigade in the Indian Corps in France. In 1915 he took command of the Meerut Division, and when the Indian Corps left the Western Front at the end of that year, General Sir Douglas Haig, commanding the First Army, applied for him to remain in France to command a British Division. In 1916 he advanced to command of II Corps, and Haig referred to him as 'an A1 Officer'. General Gough, his Army commander, considered him 'perhaps the soundest soldier in the British Army'. His reward was promotion to Field Marshal in 1926.

Sir Claud's son, Ian, bent the tradition but did not break it. When he took his commission, in June, 1918, it was into the Royal Engineers – just too late to play any part in the First World War beyond that of ADC to his father in the Victory March. But in 1920 he returned to the family parade ground, India, to join the Bengal Sappers and Miners. One hears all too little, in the general run of war literature and memoirs, of the Royal Engineers and their associates. What General Richardson has to tell us in the pages that follow about Ian Jacob in India is therefore doubly riveting – a close-up of the last stage of the Raj and also of some amazing work on the edge of the imposs-ible, which is always favourite territory for the Sappers. I, for one, would have wished for a good deal more of this part of the story.

But of course the next part could be guaranteed to elbow all else aside. Churchill, towering over the Western part of the Second World War, guiding it in his particular fashion and moulding important parts of it in his own image, enjoys a very special kind of limelight whether one altogether applauds him or not. Already firmly lodged in Staff duties before war broke out, Ian Jacob could well, like many others, have quietly faded into virtuous and industrious oblivion. But the coming of Churchill put paid to any idea of that. In Jacob, already at the centre of events in the Committee of Imperial Defence, closely linked to the Cabinet Secretariat, Churchill soon realised that he had found a virtually ideal assistant. The next few years were to be unforgettable, and perfectly summed up in Jacob's own greeting to his old 'Master' on his 90th birthday:

> 'Warmest congratulations from one whose finest hours were spent in your service.'

This began on 10 May, 1940. Prior to that, Jacob had had substantial dealings with Churchill in his capacity as First Lord of the Admiralty; 'service', in its full sense, began when the First Lord became Prime Minister. Simultaneously, he assumed the title of Minister of Defence – an empty phrase, since no such Ministry, as normally understood, existed. Nor did Churchill want one; all he required was what he called a 'handling machine', and for this he appropriated the Military Wing of the War Cabinet Secretariat, headed, as he tells us, by 'General Ismay, with Colonel Hollis and Colonel Jacob as his two principals'. The whole apparatus comprised about a dozen officers who now became 'the staff of the office of the Minister of Defence'. Ismay informs us that many of his friends told him 'that they would not have had my job for the world. I can only say, in all sincerity, that I would not have exchanged with any of them for a king's ransom.' It is another way of referring to what Jacob meant by 'finest hours'.

Under Ismay's vigilant eye and sensitive direction, the strange arrangement worked. Hollis and Jacob he describes as 'my trusted deputies', acting as what would now irreverently be called 'minders' in Ismay's absence, accompanying the Prime Minister when he set forth on the travels he so much enjoyed, and which refreshed his spirit after long spells of the gruelling working day that was his norm. As a later observer remarked:

> 'Churchill liked Jacob and he was used to him. He liked his strong and lucid intellect, his grasp of detail, his air of unruffled and unhasting efficiency. He admired, perhaps, Ian Jacob's character, so utterly different from his own, the stoic calm, the

absolute self-control, the mistrust of exaggerated and excessive emotion, and nothing too much of anything.'

It was a companionship of honour and affection and achievement among the high peaks of human endeavour.

All this is military history, and my warrant for writing about it is the military history that I have written during the last thirty years. But there is a tail in General Richardson's title: after the central matter (much fortified by selections from Sir Ian's diaries and letters), 'Churchill's Secret Circle', comes the third part of the book, 'To The BBC'. To call the change of subject anti-climactic is an understatement, but this is where I come in personally. I joined the BBC in time for the last stage of the war. I had the privilege of entering a group which, despite some striking dissimilarities, unanimously and unquestioningly considered itself an elite: RADIO NEWSREEL, under its brilliant creator, Peter Pooley. In 1944 and 1945 this daily programme, boasting 'hook-ups' across the world, drew heavily on the BBC's equally admirable War Reporting Unit to follow the Allied armies through D-Day, the fighting in the Normandy beach-head and all the way into Germany – and much else besides. Without the slightest consciousness of the fact, I was in a very real sense at the receiving end of the great plans with which Ian Jacob was concerned at a far loftier level.

I was also privileged to be in the BBC during the last years of its proud existence as a public corporation, with a mystique – you could call it a professional morality – setting it quite apart from commercial Radio. I have little doubt that we were pretty smug about this, but I have total doubt whether the extraordinary regiment of quite unregimented, perverse, creative, many-talented anarchists among whom I served was ever dull. And we were *all* (for practical purposes, *all*) possessed of the 'Public Service spirit'. It was Sir Ian's bad luck that his Director-Generalship coincided with the irresistable onset of Television, including Commercial Television, which undermined Public Service and ultimately everything the BBC stood for. And this, of course, was also something that he, too, stood for. I think I can speak for a great number of my amazing colleagues in saying that, even down to a distinctly low level, we recognised that 'Jake' did stand for this. After he had gone there were many who looked back on his tensure as that of the last of the real DGs.

London   JOHN TERRAINE
12 June 1991

List of Illustrations

PLATES

Frontispiece Ian Jacob
1. General John Jacob
2. Second Lieutenant Ian Jacob RE
3. Brandon Rectory (1908)
4. Winston Churchill with General Sir Claud Jacob, Cologne 1919
5. The Wedding of Ian Jacob and Cecil Treherne, 27 August 1924
6. The Ypres Salient, 1917
7. The Waziristan Circular Road
8. Jacob with his Brigade Commander, Port Said 1938
9. 'Peace for Our Time', Chamberlain Returns from Munich
10. Letter from Lord Hankey to Jacob 12 May 1940
11. Divine Service, Placentia Bay 10 August 1941
12. Churchill and Roosevelt in *Prince of Wales*
13. In the Admiral's Cabin in *Prince of Wales*
14. At the White House, Washington
15. Churchill with Auchinleck at Eighth Army
16. Churchill and Brooke with Montgomery at Eighth Army
17. Churchill's Directive to Alexander on his Assumption of Command in the Middle East 1942
18. Churchill and Stalin after the Banquet at the Kremlin, August 1942
19. Churchill in the Garden of the Cairo Embassy
20. Casablanca Conference 1943, the British Delegation
21. Casablanca, the United States Delegation
22. Churchill with Eisenhower and Alexander
23. Churchill with President Inonu and Marshal Chakmak, Adana, Turkey
24. Jacob Broadcasting from San Francisco, 6 June 1945

25. The San Francisco Conference, May 1945
26. Cairo, The Stansgate Mission
27. Sir Ian Jacob, Controller of European Services BBC with Dr Lili Hodacova
28. President of the European Broadcasting Union, Torquay 1950
29. 'Sir Ian Jacob, I presume?' The BBC Meets the ITA in the Jungle
30. Receiving the Marquess of Salisbury at Bush House
31. Answering Questions on Broadcasting with the 'Asian Club'
32. With Sir Alexander Cadogan, greeting M. Gabriel Delauney
33. A Rehearsal of Montgomery's Television programme 'Command in Battle'
34. An Audience with the Pope as President of the European Broadcasting Union, 7 December 1961
35. Some members of the Covent Garden Authority, 16 January 1967
36. Some Board Members of Fison's Ltd.
37. Ian and Cecil with Grandson Nicholas
38. Sir Ian and Lady Jacob in Retirement at the Red House.

MAP
The Waziristan Circular Road (page 12)

Chronology

27 September	1899	Born at Quetta, Baluchistan, now Pakistan.
	1901	At Brandon, Suffolk, placed in the care of his maternal grandmother, while his father and mother were on military service in India.
	1906	Entered Preparatory School as a boarder at Hunstanton.
	1913	Entered Wellington College, Berkshire, having won an Exhibition.
4 August	*1914*	*Britain declares war against Germany.*
June	1917	Enters Royal Military Academy Woolwich as a cadet.
December	1917	Visits his father Lieutenant General Sir Claud Jacob, Corps Commander in France.
6 June	1918	Commissioned Second Lieutenant Royal Engineers.
11 November	*1918*	*Armistice: World War I.*
28 November	1918	Joins Royal Engineers in France and Germany.
28 June	*1919*	*Treaty of Versailles.*
14 July	1919	Attends his father as ADC for Victory March in Paris.
6 December	1919	Promoted Lieutenant.
27 January	1920	Ordered to join King George the Fifth's Own Bengal Sappers and Miners at Roorkee, India.
	1921–1922	Regimental duty in Peshawar.
	1923	Engaged in the construction of the Waziristan Circular Road on the NW Frontier.

3 May	1923	Becomes ADC to his father, now Chief of the General Staff, India at Simla.
4 August	1923	Sails for England on conclusion of service in India.
September	1923	Becomes engaged to Miss Cecil Treherne, daughter of Major General Sir Francis Treherne.
4 October	1923	Enters King's College Cambridge to complete his engineering education.
27 August	1924	Marries Cecil Treherne
10 August	1925	Admitted Bachelor of Arts (Second Class Honours in the Mechanical Sciences Tripos).
	1926	Joins 12 Field Company at Aldershot.
September	1928	Appointed Company Commander and Engineering Instructor at Royal Military Academy Woolwich.
1 June	1929	Promoted Captain.
June	1930	Passes examination for entry to Staff College Camberley with record marks.
21 January	1931	Student at Staff College (two year course).
21 January	1933	Appointed Garrison Engineer Aldershot.
18 December	1934	Appointed General Staff Officer 3rd Grade in the Military Operations Directorate of the War Office.
1 July	1935	Promoted Brevet Major.
13 November	1936	Posted to Egypt as Brigade Major Canal Brigade.
6 June	1938	Promoted substantive Major.
29 September	*1938*	*Prime Minister Neville Chamberlain signs agreement with Hitler at Munich.*
2 November	1938	Having returned to England assumes the appointment of General Staff Officer Grade II as Military Assistant Secretary to the Committee of Imperial Defence in Whitehall.
1 July	1939	Promoted Brevet Lieutenant Colonel.
3 September	*1939*	*Britain declares war against Germany. Churchill becomes First Lord of the Admiralty.*
10 September	*1939*	*British Expeditionary Force sails for France.*
9 April	*1940*	*German forces invade Denmark and Norway.*
10 May	*1940*	*German forces invade Holland, Belgium and Luxembourg.*

10 May	*1940*	*Churchill becomes Prime Minister.*
14 May	1940	Promoted Lieutenant Colonel (unpaid).
3 June	*1940*	*Evacuation of British Army from Dunkirk completed.*
4 June	1940	Promoted (acting/paid) Lieutenant Colonel.
22 June	*1940*	*France signs Armistice with Germany.*
6 September	1940	Application to return to regimental duty is refused in the national interest.
13 September	*1940*	*Italian Army advances into Egypt and occupies Sollum and Sidi Barrani.*
3 November	*1940*	*British Forces are landed in Greece.*
6 December	*1940*	*Start of General O'Connor's operation COMPASS under General Wavell C-in-C Middle East.*
6 February	*1941*	*General O'Connor's forces capture Benghazi.*
27 February	*1941*	*Rommel with his Deutsche Afrika Korps makes contact at El Agheila.*
7 April	*1941*	*Rommel's offensive starts: he captures Halfaya Pass on 27 April. Tobruk besieged.*
21 June	*1941*	*Auchinleck succeeds Wavell as C-in-C Middle East.*
22 June	*1941*	*Germany invades the Soviet Union.*
3 August	1941	Accompanies Churchill in HMS *Prince of Wales* to meet President Roosevelt at Placentia Bay Newfoundland (Atlantic Conference: RIVIERA).
18 November	*1941*	*Start of Auchinleck's offensive: CRUSADER.*
7 December	*1941*	*Japan attacks United States' Navy in Pearl Harbour.*
12 December	1941	Accompanies Churchill in HMS *Duke of York* to meet President Roosevelt (ARCADIA).
24 December	*1941*	*Benghazi recaptured by British Forces.*
25 December	*1941*	*General Sir Alan Brooke succeeds General Sir John Dill as CIGS.*
January	*1942*	*Britain and United States establish the Combined Chiefs of Staff.*
21 January	*1942*	*Start of Rommel's second offensive.*
15 February	*1942*	*Singapore surrenders to the Japanese.*
27 April	1942	Promoted Temporary Colonel.
18 June	1942	Leaves London with Oliver Lyttelton, Minister of Production, for Washington, then joins up with Churchill and his advisers, and

		attends meetings of the Combined Chiefs of Staff to resolve Anglo-American strategy.
21 June	*1942*	*Fall of Tobruk, news of which reaches Churchill in the White House.*
2 July	*1942*	*Churchill wins vote of confidence by 475 votes to 25.*
24 July	*1942*	*Britain and USA reach agreement in London to launch GYMNAST (later TORCH) in the autumn.*
1 August	1942	Accompanies Churchill to Cairo, Teheran and Moscow to survey situation in Middle East after recent disasters and to confer with Stalin. Takes Prime Minister's letter of dismissal to Auchinleck, who is succeeded by Alexander, with Montgomery as Commander of Eighth Army.
15 September	1942	Commended by Churchill, he is appointed Assistant Secretary to the War Cabinet and promoted Acting Brigadier.
23 October	*1942*	*Battle of Alamein.*
8 November	*1942*	*Allied landings at Western end of Mediterranean (Operation TORCH).*
25 December	1942	Sent to Casablanca and Algiers to organise Conference between Churchill and Roosevelt (SYMBOL) and then accompanies Churchill to Turkey, Cyprus and Tripoli.
4 May	1943	Accompanies Churchill in '*Queen Mary*' for second Washington Conference (TRIDENT).
12 May	*1943*	*German Army surrenders at Tunis.*
9 July	*1943*	*British, Canadian and US assault troops sail for Sicily (HUSKY).*
5 August	1943	Accompanies Churchill to First Quebec Conference (QUADRANT).
3 September	*1943*	*Eighth Army lands in Southern Italy.*
8 September	*1943*	*Italy surrenders unconditionally.*
9 September	*1943*	*United States Fifth Army lands at Salerno.*
23 November	1943	Churchill confers with Roosevelt in Cairo (SEXTANT); they then fly to Teheran to confer with Stalin on 28 November (EUREKA). Major decisions were agreed about the disarmament of Germany, the

launching of OVERLORD and ANVIL
(landings in the South of France), the
participation of the Soviet Union in the war
against Japan and the post-war frontiers of
Poland.

6 June	*1944*	*British, US and Canadian forces land in Normandy (OVERLORD).*
8 June	1944	Made a Companion of the Order of the Bath.
10 August	1944	Accompanies Churchill on a visit to the Italian Front.
8 September	1944	On Churchill's recommendation, promoted Acting Major General.
9 October	1944	Accompanies Churchill to Moscow Conference (TOLSTOY).
4 February	1945	Attends Conference at YALTA (ARGONAUT).
25 April	1945	As UK Military Adviser, attends conference on United Nations at San Francisco.
8 May	*1945*	*VE Day (Victory in Europe).*
6 June	1945	Anniversary of OVERLORD D-Day. Broadcasts from San Francisco.
15 July	1945	Attends Potsdam Conference (TERMINAL).
26 July	*1945*	*Labour Party wins the General Election: Attlee becomes Prime Minister.*
6 August	*1945*	*Atomic bomb dropped on Japan.*
9 November	1945	Accompanies Prime Minister Attlee to USA and Canada for discussions on atomic weapons.
13 November	1945	Awarded the United States order 'Legion of Merit'.
14 December	1945	Accompanies the new Foreign Secretary, Bevin, to Moscow for a conference with Stalin.
1 April	1946	Attends War Crimes Trial at Nuremburg, invited by Lord Justice Lawrence.
3 April	1946	To Cairo as Military Adviser to Stansgate Commission.
1 July	1946	Retires from the Army with Honorary rank of Major General, and becomes Controller of European Services of the BBC.

11 August	1947	Appointed adviser to the panel of official War Historians, and joins the Royal Institute of International Affairs, later becoming Vice-Chairman.
February	1950	Elected President of the newly created European Broadcasting Union.
	1950	Invited to examine and report on the organisation of the War Office.
26 October	*1951*	*After Conservative Party wins the General Election, Churchill becomes Prime Minister.*
15 November	1951	Churchill requests Jacob (of the BBC) to examine the organisation of NATO.
27 March	1952	With Lady Jacob dines at 10 Downing St at Churchill's farewell to Ismay.
5 May	1952	Released temporarily by the BBC to be Chief Staff Officer to the Minister of Defence, and Deputy Secretary of the Cabinet, and is promoted Temporary (unpaid) Lieutenant General.
	1952	Churchill sponsors him for election to the Other Club.
1 December	1952	Becomes Director General of the BBC.
5 March	1953	Accepts the Presidency of the Southwark Cadet Corps and the Sherborne House Boys' Club.
13 April	1956	With his wife, stays at Windsor Castle as a guest of the Queen.
31 December	1959	Resigns from the BBC at the age of 60, and next day is gazetted as Knight Grand Cross of the Order of the British Empire.
4 January	1960	Joins the Board of Fisons Ltd as a non-executive director.
1 February	1960	Joins the Board of Electrical and Musical Instruments Ltd as non-executive director.
2 April	1960	Elected County Councillor of East Suffolk.
22 December	1960	Appointed Justice of the Peace, East Suffolk.
20 October	1961	Appointed Chairman of the Covent Garden Market Authority, charged with re-siting the market.
27 October	1961	Appointed member of the Pall Mall Committee of Lloyds Bank.

1 October	1962	Having prevented the demise of the Army and Navy Club, as Chairman lays the foundation stone of the new premises.
1 January	1963	The Minister of Defence invites Ismay and Jacob to examine and report on the central organisation of Defence.
1 August	1964	Member of the Royal Commission on the Police. Becomes Deputy Lieutenant for the County of Suffolk.
31 January	1965	With Lady Jacob attends funeral of Sir Winston Churchill among 'principal mourners'.
17 February	1965	As Chairman, receives the Queen at an evening reception at the Army and Navy Club.
20 May	1966	Appointed Trustee of the Imperial War Museum.
1 January	1969	Becomes Chairman of Burton Sons and Sanders Ltd of Ipswich, and subsequently executive Chairman of Matthews Holdings Ltd after a merger.
13 January	1970	Elected County Alderman for East Suffolk.
24 July	1970	Installed as Honorary Canon of St Edmundsbury Cathedral.
17 May	1971	At Edmonton and Calgary, Canada, is guest of honour at the annual banquets of the Churchill Society.
11 September	1971	Elected Chairman of the Suffolk Police Authority.
28 July	1974	Attends 90th Birthday celebration of Field Marshal Auchinleck.
27 August	1984	Diamond wedding celebrations at Woodbridge.
28 September	1989	Entertained to lunch by the Chairman and Board of Governors of the BBC to celebrate his ninetieth birthday on 27 September.

Glossary

ABDA	American British Dutch Australian (Area in the South West Pacific)
ADC	Aide de Camp
AFHQ	Allied Force Headquarters (in North Africa)
AOC-in-C	Air Officer Commanding-in-Chief
ARP	Air Raid Precautions
BGS	Brigadier General Staff
CAS	Chief of Air Staff
CB	Companion of the Order of the Bath
CBE	Companion of the Order of the British Empire
C-in-C	Commander-in-Chief
CID	Committee of Imperial Defence
CIGS	Chief of the Imperial General Staff
CNS	Chief of Naval Staff (or First Sea Lord)
COS	Chiefs of Staff
COSSAC	Chief of Staff to the Supreme Allied Commander
CSM	Company Sergeant Major
DCGS	Deputy Chief of General Staff
D-Day	(for OVERLORD) 6 June 1944. Invasion of North-West Europe.
DL	Deputy Lieutenant (The Queen's representative for the county)
DMI	Director of Military Intelligence
DSO	Companion of the Distinguished Service Order

EBU	European Broadcasting Union
GBE	Knight Grand Cross of the Order of the British Empire
GHQ	General Headquarters
GPU	Soviet secret police (forerunners of the KGB)
ITU	International Communication Union
JCOS	Joint Chiefs of Staff
JPS	Joint Planning Staff
KBE	Knight Commander of the Order of the British Empire
NATO	North Atlantic Treaty Organisation
OBE	Officer of the Order of the British Empire
ODC	Overseas Defence Committee
OIR	Organisation Internationale de Radio-diffusion
PDC	Chiefs of Staff Sub-Committee: Port Defence
PM	Prime Minister
RE	Royal Engineers
UIR	Union Internationale de Radio-diffusion
UNO	United Nations Organisation
VC	Victoria Cross
VCAS	Vice Chief of the Air Staff
VE-Day	Victory in Europe Day (8 May 1945)

CODE NAMES
Conferences

ARCADIA	1st Washington (December 1941)
ARCHER	USA and Canada with Prime Minister Attlee (November 1945)
ARGONAUT	Yalta (February 1945)
BRACELET	Middle East and Moscow (August 1942)
EUREKA	Teheran (November 1943)
OCTAGON	2nd Quebec (September 1944) (Not attended by Jacob)
QUADRANT	1st Quebec (August 1943)
RIVIERA	Placentia Bay (The Atlantic Conference) (August 1941)
SEXTANT	Cairo (November 1943)
SYMBOL	Casablanca (January 1943)

TERMINAL	Potsdam (July 1945)
TOLSTOY	3rd Moscow (October 1944)
TRIDENT	2nd Washington (May 1943)

Operations

BOLERO	Build-up of American forces in the United Kingdom for a cross-Channel operation
COMPASS	Wavell's first offensive in Cyrenaica, December 1940
CRUSADER	Auchinleck's Western Desert offensive, November 1941
DRAGOON (formerly ANVIL)	Allied invasion of Southern France, August 1944
HUSKY	Allied invasion of Sicily, July 1943
JUPITER	Allied plan to invade Northern Norway (not implemented)
OVERLORD	Allied invasion of Normandy, June 1944
ROUNDUP	Allied plan for final assault in North-West Europe (to follow SLEDGEHAMMER in late 1943) (not implemented)
SLEDGEHAMMER	Allied plan to land 6–8 divisions in North-West Europe in September 1943 (not implemented)
TORCH (formerly GYMNAST)	Allied invasion of North Africa, November 1942

Introduction

When Ian Jacob's father, a future Field Marshal, told him in 1914 'You must be a Sapper', the teenaged boy, from a family of distinguished soldiers long associated with India, embarked without hesitation on a military career.

But soon his life was to follow a very different pattern.

After a short visit in the closing stages of World War I, followed by active service as a Sapper officer on the North West Frontier of India, his intellectual prowess, tactical ability and athletic skills marked him out as an outstanding young officer. In 1931 he passed first into the Staff College, and this was followed by two years in the Operations Directorate of the War Office. In 1935 he was awarded brevet rank, and a year later became Brigade Major of the Canal Brigade in Egypt.

At the time of Munich, he returned to the United Kingdom to become Military Assistant Secretary of the Committee of Imperial Defence, with the brevet rank of lieutenant colonel. In that appointment, the appalling unpreparedness of Britain and the Empire was laid bare before him, and with great efficiency and stoic calm he applied himself to the preparation of the nation for war within the frustrating limitations of a peace-time government beset by indecision.

After the outbreak of war in 1939, he was appointed Military Assistant Secretary to the War Cabinet, serving with Ismay and Hollis in the triumvirate dubbed by Churchill as 'My Secret Circle'. 'My debt to its members was immeasurable' was Churchill's verdict after six years in which every initiative by the Prime Minister, by day or by night, had to be translated by members of the circle into urgent coordinated action.

As the principal controller of military information entering the War Cabinet, and as one of the three coordinators of government action,

Jacob occupied a key position from which to survey British warlike activity in all its forms, and observe closely the towering figure who directed it. Admiration grew on both sides, and Churchill declined to release him from Whitehall duties. On innumerable occasions, in transit by battleship or aircraft, in the United Kingdom, in foreign capitals worldwide or at military headquarters, Jacob was in close touch with the Prime Minister; he was present with him at conferences with Roosevelt in Placentia Bay, Washington, Moscow, Casablanca, Cairo, Quebec and Yalta, and on three occasions he attended meetings with Stalin. At many of these events, in addition to keeping the official record, he wrote a personal diary giving the candid impressions of a sophisticated observer.

With the advent of victory, to which he had greatly contributed as a government official rather than a fighting soldier, he faced a difficult decision: should he, as a temporary major general, return to the Army fold in competition with those whose military experience, though narrower, had been more relevant, or should he strike out on a new career? The Army authorities were not encouraging, and he chose the latter.

In 1946 he retired from the Army, and became Controller of the European Service of the BBC and, in 1948, Director of External Broadcasting. It was a crucial period for the Corporation: external broadcasting in war time, designed to enlist sympathy for the Allied cause and promote opposition to Hitler's tyranny, had now to be changed to a peacetime role operating under a strict budget in the novel conditions of the Cold War. Jacob's experience as a servant of the War Cabinet and his close wartime contacts with the Foreign Office, were valuable assets in the new assignment, which lasted for six years. His adaptation to the new role was much admired.

With the return of the Conservative Government in 1951, a call came from Churchill: 'Jacob you must come back!'. Sir Ian, promoted temporary Lieutenant General, was appointed by Churchill as Chief Staff Officer to the Minister of Defence, Field Marshal Lord Alexander, and Deputy Secretary of the Cabinet. Within a year, he returned to the BBC from leave of absence, and became Director General of the Corporation for a period of seven years. Once again, he was faced with major decisions in a critical period of growth dominated by the expansion of television and the advent of commercial competition.

Retiring from the BBC in 1960, he subsequently held many offices: Chairman of the Covent Garden Market Authority, Trustee of the

Imperial War Museum, Chairman of the Army and Navy Club, Director of Fisons and EMI, Chairman of Matthews Holdings, Regional Director for Inner London of Lloyds Bank, County Councillor of East Suffolk, Deputy Lieutenant, and Lay Canon of St Edmondsbury Cathedral.

Though in retirement, his advice was sought by the Government on organisational problems associated with NATO, the War Office and the Central control of Defence. Seldom has a regular Army officer had such a significant, varied and demanding career in the service of the nation. In many aspects of the nation's life his influence has been profound. Yet, perhaps as a reflection of his self-effacing modesty, his name is well-known only to those of his own generation or to those associated with him and his valuable work. History will come to show that Britain stands deeply in his debt.

1

Child of the Raj

In the province of Sind, near the great Sukkur Dam which holds back the flood waters of the River Indus, lies a city called Jacobabad, the city of Jacob. From that place, now in Pakistan, may be traced the story of Edward Ian Claud Jacob, who was born at Quetta, one hundred and fifty miles away on 27 September 1899. Like generations of Jacobs before him, he was a 'child of the Raj'. His career, at its inception true to type, was to take a strange course, acquiring an unusual lustre to be set alongside the reputations of many of his forbears, whose names have found an honoured place in the history of the British Raj. From 1817 onwards, for more than a hundred years, succeeding generations of the Jacob family had sent their sons to spend their lives with the East India Company and, after the Mutiny, in the service of the Sovereign. Twenty-eight Jacobs had followed that path.[1]

The origins of the family may be traced back to Edward Jacob of Faversham, in Kent, who was born in 1705. Two of his sons, John of Sextries and Stephen Long Jacob contributed between them five sons to the service of the Raj. One of them, Ian Jacob's great-grandfather William, born in 1800, after training at the East India Company's college at Addiscombe, sailed for India at the age of sixteen, and was commissioned in the Bombay Artillery.

William Jacob's brother, George Le Grand, went to India in 1821 as an Ensign in the Bombay Native Infantry and, after many campaigns, he moved into the Political Department of the Bombay Presidency. He was a student of the literature of India and made one of the earliest translations of the edicts of the Emperor Asoka. He retired as Major General Sir George Le Grand Jacob.

Of the same generation as William and George were their cousins Herbert, George and John. Herbert joined the Bombay Army and

1

served with distinction, becoming a Major General; but it was his younger brother, John Jacob who was to become a legend in his lifetime.

John, a cousin of Ian Jacob's great-grandfather William, born in 1812, at an early age used to organise mimic battles in the grounds of his father's vicarage, and was dubbed 'the Warrior' by his elder brother George. On John's eleventh birthday, George contributed for his brother a mock-heroic poem enclosed in a wreath of laurel:

Let all rejoice! – this mighty day gave birth
To one whose fame shall spread through all the earth,
And bursting through each opposition, shed
Its blooming honours on his glorious head.[2]

In his ironic assessment, George was not far wrong about young John.

At the age of fourteen, John set out from his home in Somerset for Addiscombe, intent on becoming an officer in the Engineers. He had already shown a talent for mathematics and mechanics, but due to an escapade in his last term he was excluded from the Engineers and, as second best, was commissioned in the Bombay Artillery on his sixteenth birthday.

His first ten years in India were spent in peace-time soldiering in the Bombay Presidency, where he made a great name for himself as a horseman. But always he longed for active service on the troubled North-West Frontier of India.

On 1 October 1838, the Government of India decided that a British Force should be stationed in Sind, and John Jacob moved to a base camp near the mouth of the Indus on 3 December 1838.

It was in Sind, an inferno of heat, dust and sandflies, and twice the size of Wales, that John Jacob was to make his name as a victorious leader and brilliant administrator. He was given command of the mounted troops in the Force, and greatly distinguished himself at the battles of Miani and Hyderabad. He was then made Commandant of the local forces, and Political Superintendent of the Frontier of Upper Sind. He set up his headquarters at a village called Kanghur, established irrigation, and founded a cantonment in the desert, well-watered and shaded with trees, which subsequently became the city known to this day as Jacobabad.

John Jacob was not only a skilful and determined soldier and administrator but also a thinker, inventor and agnostic. He criticised the lack of authority given to the Commanding Officers of the Bengal

Army, and deplored the limited responsibilities given to the Indian officer; however, he himself was fortunate in having a very free hand in organising his own force, which eventually comprised the Sind Irregular Horse, Jacob's Horse, an infantry unit known as Jacob's Rifles (later the 130th Baluch Regiment) and Jacob's Mountain Battery.

On 5 December 1858 John Jacob, aged only forty-five, died in his bed at Jacobabad. The grief of his British officers was intense, exceeded only by that of his Indian officers who had lost the patriarch of their clan; round the bier they could not restrain their tears.

In London there were tributes in the House of Lords, and references in all the principal newspapers including a discerning statement in the *Spectator*:

> He was one of those rarest spirits who love work – good true and noble work – for its own sake; who could and did refuse opportunities of distinction in order to cling to a post of which the world of newspapers knew little, but which he felt was the proper field of his labours . . . longer life could hardly have added more to his achievements than that noisy fame which he held so cheap.[3]

Five years after his death, there was born in India another Jacob, Claud William, who was commissioned in 1882, and two years later joined Jacob's Rifles. Seventeen years later, he would be the father of Ian. He was to have a great military career, culminating in the command of Second British Corps in France in World War I, followed in India by appointments as Chief of the General Staff, Commander-in-Chief Northern Command, acting Commander-in-Chief India, and promotion to Field Marshal. Later, he was to become Secretary to the Military Department of the India Office in Whitehall. He would become a close friend of Winston Churchill, supporting his stand over Indian constitutional development, and would be the last exemplar of the Jacobs of the Indian Army.

In 1894, Claud Jacob had married Pauline Wyatt a daughter and granddaughter of missionaries in Southern India. He had had to travel nearly two thousand miles to collect his bride and bring her back to Chaman, a small post on the Baluchistan frontier one hundred miles from Quetta. There was only one other woman in Chaman, and the quarters consisted of small rooms furnished principally with wooden boxes covered with cretonne. There were no shops, and the limited water supply did not permit gardens.

With her two babies, Ian and his sister Aileen, Pauline Jacob travelled around with her soldier husband, visiting frontier garrisons in the Zhob Valley, overlooked by bleak mountains. The climate was extreme, with summer temperatures of 100°F and often zero in winter with biting winds. There was, of course, no electricity or gas, and hence there were no fans, refrigerators or cookers.

The Jacobs travelled on camels, taking their own cow with them so that fresh milk could be provided for the children under Mother's tight supervision. For Pauline, this was a very different environment to the hot lush countryside of Southern India; happily, she was an energetic, extrovert and vivacious woman, and those qualities, backed by a good education, including attendance at a finishing school in Germany, sustained her without succumbing in any way to the mental and physical hardships and the sense of isolation of the Frontier, mitigated only by the weekly mail and infrequent leave back to England. Unselfish service to the Raj was in her blood. With two World Wars ahead of them, it was fortunate that Major and Mrs Claud Jacob with their two children formed a devoted family.

Now that the Raj has passed into history, the mystique of service in the Indian Army may require some explanation. What were the influences that summoned so many men, not always impoverished younger sons, from Britain to spend years of exile in a climate which was generally uncomfortable and often unhealthy? Why was it that, before the opening of the Suez Canal and later the advent of air travel, very long periods of family separation were cheerfully tolerated?

For the young bachelor there were obvious advantages: and some of those, who in earlier years had tasted that life, had retained vivid recollections of the luxury which had surrounded them. Winston Churchill, as a subaltern in the 4th Hussars, was one: he had recalled life at the turn of the century in these words:

> If you like to be waited on and relieved of home worries, India thirty years ago was perfection. All you had to do was to hand over all your uniform and clothes to the dressing boy, your ponies to the syce, and your money to the butler, and you need never trouble any more. Your cabinet was complete; each of these ministers entered upon his department with knowledge, experience and fidelity. They would devote their lives to their task. For a humble wage, justice and a few kind words, there was nothing they would not do. Their world became bound by the commonplace articles of your wardrobe and other small possessions. No toil was too hard, no hours too long, no dangers too great for their unruffled calm or their unfailing care. Princes could live no better than we.[4]

Even if in the twentieth century, the 'princely' life was not invariably available, there was always financial inducement in both pay and pension, a factor which was particularly relevant for members of British families who lacked resources from land or private income.

Moreover, for the young man in the Indian Army there was great scope for initiative while leading a very active life in unusual surroundings, and there were exceptional opportunities for sport. Above all, there was the attraction of leading tough soldiers, in minor operations of war, which tested military capabilities while avoiding the tragedy of serious casualties. It was the relationship in battle between the British officer and the Indian soldier that formed the central core of that mystique that drew generation after generation to the Raj and, once there bound them, like John Jacob, with emotional bonds which nothing less than a major crisis could sunder.

As the relationship between Britain and India evolved, Ian Jacob may perhaps have discerned that he belonged to an imperial dynasty whose members – military heroes, administrators and missionaries – had, for over a century, rendered exceptional service to the British Raj. The decision whether to follow that path was still many years ahead, and the first influence to be felt by young Jacob was that of the missionaries. With his mother in India, and his father increasing his reputation year by year on the North-West Frontier, he was placed at the age of two in the care of his maternal grandmother Isabella Wyatt, daughter of the great missionary, Bishop Robert Caldwell of Tinnevelly. She had married the Reverend JL Wyatt who had been the Bishop's suffragan in India, and was now Rector of Brandon in Suffolk.

Isabella had inherited many of the talents of her remarkable father, a man of deep piety and a pioneer in the scientific study of the Tamil language. From her experience in the Mission she had acquired a remarkable influence over children, and young Jacob with several other young children in the Rectory fell under her spell. Attendance at matins was compulsory; but afterwards the children were called upon to produce pictures of the characters described in the lessons which they had heard in Church. Granny Isabella was so affectionate and entertaining that this routine became an enjoyable game rather than a chore. After exercise in the large garden, there was usually a game of biblical 'happy families'. Before going to sleep, there were hymns at the piano, with the children playing realistically any of the actions described, of which 'Pull for the shore' was the favourite. During the day, while Granny Isabella was supervising household duties, young Jacob would toddle around behind her from room to room. These were named in sequence after the counties of England, and thus the names and locations were memorised by the young boy at an early age. Later, teams used to be drawn for charades and card games, but books were never allowed in bedrooms, and only religious books could be read on Sunday.

It was thus that Isabella's techniques, so successful in motivating the dark-eyed children of Southern India, were adapted to lead, educate, and discipline the many children in her care at Brandon. At the Rectory, laughter and singing were often to be heard, but in Granny Isabella's commanding presence scenes of temper were unknown. She was an excellent disciplinarian, and inculcated in young Ian strong self-discipline, a sense of duty, and a recognition of right and wrong.

In 1909, there was a tragedy in the household: Aileen, Ian's sister, contracted mastoid infection, and died at the age of eleven.

At the age of seven, Ian Jacob had been sent to a preparatory school at Hunstanton, a remote place on the coast of the Wash. He did not enjoy it: he did not like the headmaster, and found the school oppressive. Perhaps the change from Granny Isabella's imaginative régime was too sudden a contrast. However, during those formative years, Ian had not been entirely divorced from parental influence; on various occasions his mother had preceded her husband to England and had stayed on for a few months after he had returned to India.

Young Jacob's future career was now at the forefront of his parents' minds. He was their only surviving child, and might be expected to follow the path trodden by generations of Jacobs. He himself had fancied a career in the Royal Navy, but with his father in the Meerut Division, fighting in France, the Army now beckoned, and Ian was content to become a soldier.

But what sort of soldier? Should he follow his ancestors into the Indian Army? Here father intervened with very definite views, based not on any intuition of the changes which in thirty years would profoundly alter the Indian Army, but on other considerations. He advised Ian to join the British Army, and so avoid years of separation from his children, and become a Sapper; only in the Royal Engineers with their extra pay of two shillings a day could he live on his pay.

Thus Ian Jacob, by now showing signs of considerable intelligence, was directed towards a Corps which traditionally attracted cadets with agile brains. Moreover, the Royal Engineers and the Indian Army had a special relationship, which offered exceptional advantages to a child of the Raj.

Young Jacob's life now began to follow a more normal pattern, in which his mother was to play a prominent part, while his father was earning a great reputation in the mud and blood of Flanders. His mother moved to London, and had no difficulty in adjusting to the life of the metropolis after the stark conditions of the North-West Frontier. Her intelligence and vivacity gained her many friends: when both father and mother were present it was mother who did all the talking.

Their son, now in his last years at preparatory school, was not only intelligent but was also a good games player and athlete. With entry into the Royal Engineers as the target before him, academic performance became very important, and to the joy of his parents he won an exhibition to Wellington College, and entered in 1913.

He was to enjoy his years at Wellington, despite the onset of World War I, which created serious problems. Dr Vaughan, the Master, had to write in 1914 to Lord Derby, Vice-President of the Governors, asking for authority to waive all notice in the case of those boys who might have unexpected opportunities to get into the Army at once. Some of the masters were volunteering for immediate service, wherever they might be accepted.[5]

On 2 September 1914, ten days after the battle of Mons, the school reassembled early in tense excitement; thereafter, for a considerable period, all games were cancelled, and each afternoon was spent on military training. The term ended with a memorial service for the Old Wellingtonian dead. The atmosphere of mingled patriotism and tragedy must have deeply affected the junior masters, many of whom were urgently called away, but it seemed to make little impression on boys belonging to army families: most of them, including Jacob, took it all in their stride. They were more interested in the improvements being introduced in their living standards, many long overdue.

Cultural activities at this period were underdeveloped, particularly the appreciation of music, although Dr Vaughan soon changed that situation, thanks to the arrival of a new master, George Dyson, a future 'Master of the King's Musick'. But Ian Jacob, deprived then of that life-long benefit, had to develop his appreciation of music at a much later date.

The tutor of Ian's dormitory, the Hopetoun, had left hurriedly to go to the war, and Dr Vaughan initially filled the gap. He was a big man in every sense of the word and achieved much for Wellington, but Jacob was to have an unfortunate experience with this daunting figure. He had completed a test in trigonometry and had reached the correct answer: cosine thirty degrees. In the test, the boys were allowed to have their mathematical tables with them, but instead of looking it up, he asked the boy next to him for the answer. The invigilating master immediately accused Jacob of cheating, and sent him to report to Dr Vaughan who, sweeping aside all explanations as mere prevarication, gave him six strokes of the cane.

Fortunately for Jacob, a replacement tutor soon arrived, a Mr Larmour, who formed an easier relationship with the intelligent boy, and encouraged him to read serious books, particularly those with an historical theme such as Kingslake's 'Crimea' and Prescott's 'Conquest of Mexico'.

Jacob's ability as a games player became evident at an early stage, and when he left Wellington he had been a member of the first eleven at cricket and of the second fifteen at rugger. He had also been Head of Gymnasium, a Corporal in the Officers Training Corps, joint head of the Hopetoun and a school prefect. He and his fellow prefects had enjoyed unique opportunities for leadership in the unusual wartime conditions, which had diluted the supervision of masters; and Jacob's achievement must have greatly pleased his father, now in France during a period of terrible stalemate.

In June 1917, three months short of his eighteenth birthday, Ian passed eighth into the Royal Military Academy Woolwich, familiarly called 'The Shop'. The twelve-month course for cadets, devised under wartime pressure, was very crowded, and had been compiled with little imagination. A ten-hour day of great exertion under tight discipline ended with the absurd arrangement of two hours of lectures to the cadets, many of whom by then were physically exhausted. Jacob did not enjoy it.

At Christmas 1917, there was a holiday of ten days, and Gentleman Cadet Jacob was fortunate to be able to join his father in France, at Headquarters Second British Corps, behind the Ypres Salient. The Salient was an appalling wilderness. Outside the ramparts of the ruined city, as far as the eye could see, there were shell holes filled with water and stumps of trees with here and there a ruined building. Scattered around were men scraping places to live in, putting down duck boards and levelling out areas for horse lines, guns and stores. But this scene of devastation had little emotional effect on Ian Jacob: he was already developing the calm detachment which, later, would serve him well.

For Christmas day, his father arranged a treat. Jacob was taken up in an aircraft of the Army Cooperation Squadron, Royal Flying Corps. In a two-seater aircraft, a RE8 (Reconnaissance Experimental, 8) which the cadet understood to be 'reasonably reliable', he looked over the side of the fuselage and surveyed that unique scene of horror, made even more surreal by a light fall of snow. It was his first taste of air flight, of which in succeeding years he would have a surfeit.

Returning to 'The Shop' for his last term, and having many a tale to tell, Jacob was made an Under-Officer, the first stamp of approbation in his adult career. His Company Commander, an infantryman aged thirty-eight was universally regarded as a 'dead-beat', because he wore medals from the Boer War and was sloppily dressed. He must have found Under-Officer Jacob, who was neat, alert, sensible and modest, of great use to him in commanding the company; but their relationship never developed beyond the official level.

From the Royal Military Academy, Jacob passed out fourth in the order of merit, out of ninety-eight cadets who left the Academy. He was also awarded most appropriately, the Pollock Medal, which had originally been given by the British inhabitants of Calcutta to be awarded to the most distinguished cadet passing out from Addiscombe, but had been transferred to the Royal Military Academy in 1875.

On 6 June 1918, Jacob received his commission in the Royal Engineers; immediately he was posted to the School of Military Engineering at Chatham for a shortened course to fit him for the limited engineering tasks that would face a junior officer in the war in France.

Five months later, the Armistice was signed on 11 November 1918, and Jacob joined a Field Company in Germany. The highlight of his two years of regimental duty was taking part in the Victory March in Paris on 14 July 1919, as ADC to his father.

General Jacob and his wife returned to England in 1919, and the General then left once more for India to become Chief of the General Staff, a remarkable appointment for a man who had never been to a Staff College. Ian Jacob went to Aldershot to learn about horse management and, at the beginning of 1920, sailed for India to join King George the Fifth's Own Bengal Sappers and Miners at Roorkee, about a hundred miles north of Delhi.

For a child of the Raj, even though Ian Jacob had been a baby when he had left in 1902, service in India must have seemed both to him and his father the inevitable climax of a long period of preparation. On arrival at the Sapper and Miner headquarters, young Jacob naturally received an enthusiastic reception, and there was an interesting reaction by the Indian Officers. The Subedar[6] Mir Din, produced from his pocket a letter, and explained to Jacob that it was from his friend Subedar Ali Dost of the 106th Hazara Pioneers, the regiment raised by Ian's father:

'The letter says: why is the *Chota* Jacob Sahib[7] not coming to us?'

The tradition of a son going to his father's regiment was as strong in the Indian Army as in the British, and the Subedars were not to know that *burra*[8] Jacob Sahib had for good reason deflected his son elsewhere. Often their foreknowledge of arrivals, departures and future postings seemed uncanny.

Jacob was soon introduced to the special delights of service in India: big game shooting, moving on elephants through the jungles of the Himalayan foothills, the morning flight of duck, polo on the ponies of the Sapper Field Squadron, and the attractions of Simla, where he stayed with his parents in the CGS's splendid bungalow.

During a Christmas leave, he was able to go with his parents to stay at Bikaner with the Maharajah, whose duck shoot was world-famous. Among the guests was Clemenceau, the 'Tiger' of France who, having finished his work at the Versailles Conference, was touring India; he remained indoors wearing his grey cotton gloves.[9]

Before returning to Delhi, they also paid a quick visit to Jaipur, where Ian Jacob's great uncle Sir Swinton Jacob had been State Engineer. He had built Bikaner's Palace and had restored many buildings at Jaipur.

However, a subaltern's life in India in the 1920s was not devoted exclusively to pleasure – far from it. Jacob at a very early age was often put in command of units of which the permanent commanding officers were temporarily absent; he had to organise the various engineer tasks they were allotted, plan and supervise the training of his sappers, and manage the disciplinary aspects of his command, which sometimes involved presiding at a Summary Court-Martial in which the proceedings had to be conducted and recorded in Urdu. Jacob soon became a proficient speaker, like his father who, in addition, had learnt the languages of the Frontier tribesmen.

He found that once confidence had been established with the Indian sappers they were delightful men to serve with. The British officers knew them all by name and a good deal about their homes. At their head was a fine Subedar who was a Hindu, Ram Rup Singh, a strongly built man from the United Provinces. He could tell wonderful stories of deeds in Tibet and elsewhere at the turn of the century. He had fought all through the war in France and Mesopotamia, and had won an Indian Order of Merit as well as the Indian Distinguished Service Medal. The Sikh Jemadar was a fine tall man with an excellent record in the war and, like most Sikhs, with a sense of humour.

Very soon, Jacob was to serve in the frontier area which had been the principal stamping ground of many of the Jacob family down the ages. In the spring of 1921, 3 Field Company, in which he was serving, was ordered to Peshawar. Brian Robertson, son of Field Marshal Sir William Robertson, and a Captain with a DSO and MC from France, came to command the Company known as 'the Field Marshal's Company' as it also included Robert John Napier, the son of Field Marshal Lord Napier of Magdala. As bachelors, Jacob and Robertson, later to become Lord Robertson of Oakridge, occupied the same bungalow, and this led to a friendship which was to last over fifty years.

Close by the Cantonment in Peshawar was the Grand Trunk Road, immortalised in 'Kim', which ran from Delhi, through Lahore and on to the Khyber Pass, leading into Afghanistan. Afghanistan was separated from the territory administered by the Government of India by a Tribal Zone in which control was not fully exercised, although the main valleys, such as the Khyber and the Kurram, were garrisoned by permanent militia units under British officers.

In 1919 and 1920, an expedition had fought its way into the heart of Waziristan, occupying Wana on 22 December 1920, after which it had been garrisoned. But the Mahsuds, defeated, impoverished, sullen and exhausted, were ready nevertheless to rise again if opportunity offered, and the Government decided to occupy their country permanently. A fortified camp was to be established at Razmak, to be connected to the railheads near the Administrative Boundary by the construction of the 'Waziristan Circular Road', the most useful engineering work ever accomplished on the North-West Frontier.

In 1923 Jacob played his part in constructing the road, and years later described his experience:[9]

> It was a fact of tribal life and of the barren mountainous country in which the tribes lived that fighting, looting and blood feuds were regarded more highly than humdrum work, and indeed there was so little cultivable land that it was impossible to find enough work for everyone. To help the situation, the Government paid subsistence subsidies to the tribes, enrolling them as Khassadars, or irregular levies, and punishing them from time to time by marching into their territory. This system tended to break down when any religious leader emerged in Waziristan or, indeed elsewhere on the Frontier, and stimulated the tribes into concerted action. This had happened in 1919 and 1920, and even the

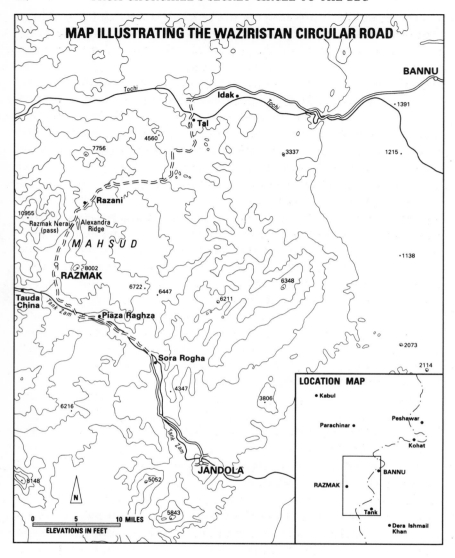

MAP ILLUSTRATING THE WAZIRISTAN CIRCULAR ROAD

BANNU

Tochi

Idak ●

Tochi

● 1391

● Tal

4560

7756

● 3337

1215 ●

● Razani

10955

Razmak Nerai (pass)

Alexandra Ridge

M A H S U D

● 1138

8002

RAZMAK

6722 ●

● 6447

6348

Tauda China

Tank Zam

● Piaza Raghza

6211

6216

● Sora Rogha

● ● 2073

4347

2114 ●

3806

LOCATION MAP

● Kabul

Tank Zam

Parachinar ●

Peshawar ●

Kohat ●

8148

5052

JANDOLA

BANNU

RAZMAK ●

N

5843

Tank ●

0   5   10 MILES

ELEVATIONS IN FEET

● Dera Ishmail Khan

most disciplined militia bodies rose up here and there, and
murdered their officers.

It was decided that a more suitable way of dealing with the
Mahsuds and Wazirs would be to open up their country by building a metalled road right through their territory and by stationing
a strong garrison at Razmak. It was expected that the work provided by the road building and the improvement in communica-

tions, would create a new spirit among the tribes and make them more open to the influence of the outer world. Moreover, the existence of the road would make it easy for the troops to arrive at any point where trouble arose.

Before the road could be built, its route would have to be surveyed and marked out, and then troops must move forward to cover the engineers and contractors who would build it. Political officers had also to summon the tribal leaders to a 'jirga', and explain what was going to happen and try to secure their cooperation, or at any rate their acquiescence. All these preparations were put in hand in the autumn of 1922 when 3 Field Company had been in Peshawar for nearly 18 months. Millis Jefferis, a sapper who had been with me at The Shop, was sent up to Waziristan with a small party of sappers to conduct the survey of the Northern part of the road from Idak to Razmak. A better choice for a dangerous and skilled engineering job could not have been made, and we were all delighted when at the end of operations he was awarded the Military cross.

We entrained on 11 November 1922 and were moved to Bannu, where we took to our feet. Our normal tools were carried on our mules as usual, but our tents and baggage were loaded on to about 100 camels, our first line transport, and off we set.

On the second day we reached Tal. As there was no room for us inside the little fort or the existing camp, we had to make our own. This was not just a question of pitching tents; the whole camp had to be surrounded by a dry stone wall about four feet high, and outside that a barbed wire entanglement. These precautions were necessary because no-one could ever tell whether a party of tribesmen would try and force their way in and steal rifles and kill a few people. The more serious occurrence was sniping at night; but this might build up to more intense action if the tribes really wanted to oppose an advance into their country.

Every day we marched out from camp and were engaged in completing the marking out of the road. Behind us came contractors with steam rollers and road metal to complete the surface. Before long it was decided to move us on to Razani, which had been occupied by a brigade, and to put us to work on the much more difficult stretch of about five miles from there up to the Razmak Plateau.

Before leaving Tal, a little incident took place which illustrated the normal outlook of the Senior Indian Officers at that time. An

Indian Field Ambulance had arrived at Tal, and had camped just outside our perimeter. The Unit was commanded by an Indian captain of the Indian Medical Service and he was the only officer. He came into our camp and asked Brian Robertson whether he could join our Mess: Brian answered 'certainly', and gave orders accordingly. The next morning, I was talking to our Subedar Ram Rup Singh and he said to me: 'Sahib, is it true that an Indian Officer is going to join your Mess?'

'Yes' I said, whereupon he replied:

'What a disaster! But these things happen in war'.

We left Tal on 17 January and marched to Razani, where we settled in for a stay of some weeks. We were soon fairly comfortable though we had frequent snow and frost. The ground at Razani was not too hard so we could dig ourselves in. The men were in 160-pound tents, about ten to a tent and they lay feet inwards on each side.

To guard the rifles a small trench was dug lengthways, so that when the men lay down it passed along under their waists. The rifles were laid in this little trench so that no-one could move a rifle without waking up the men under whom it lay. The alternative to this was to chain the rifles together, but we thought that our scheme was better because no keys or locks had to be found in a hurry if there was an alarm. As it turned out we found that our system was by no means foolproof. One night some Pathans must have got through the wire and over the wall without being seen by the sentry, and must then have dragged a rifle out without waking anyone. There was no alarm, but in the morning it was found that three rifles were missing. To lose a rifle on the Frontier was a matter of shame, and we were very upset by this occurrence. No amount of investigation provided any further clue, and we just had to live under the disgrace.

Our first task at Razani was to construct a pilot track about eight feet wide suitable for men, mules and camels, right up the valley on to the top of the Pass . . . In less than a week the track was ready and on 23 January the advance of the 7 Infantry Brigade was ordered to take place. The Brigade was accompanied by 4,000 mules and 1,200 camels carrying the numerous stores required for establishing a permanent camp at Razmak . . .

A few days later the Brigade moved out from Razmak to deal with some tribesmen who were collecting in a village under a big mountain not far off. We could hear the mountain guns firing, and this had an interesting significance for my men. One of the Indian officers had said to me that he wondered whether a medal would be granted for this little campaign; he said that it was generally believed by the men that the medal was given only if the artillery fired at least five rounds in earnest. There was thus great satisfaction when the noise of considerable gun fire was heard!

In due course, Jacob received the Indian General Service Medal, in peacetime always a proud moment for any young officer, even if sometimes he might question whether he had faced sufficient danger.

Before leaving the area, he paid a visit to the 106th Hazara Pioneers, and to his joy met Subedar Ali Dost. The occasion was a family reunion, as the battalion was under the command of Lieutenant Colonel Ernest Wyatt, his mother's brother, who had followed his father and his uncle, Lieutenant Colonel Arthur le Grand, in that post.

News now arrived that he was to return to England to complete his engineer education, which had been cut short by the war. This involved a short course, once more at Chatham, followed by going up to Cambridge to take the Mechanical Sciences Tripos. The prospect of returning to England was not wholly welcome to the 'child of the Raj', involving as it did the loss of all the attractive features of life in India, and a long farewell to its splendid soldiers. Jacob's three and a half years' service, mostly under Brian Robertson, a first class commanding officer, had been an instructive and rewarding experience, well-suited to a young man finding his feet and eager to exploit every opportunity whether of service or of recreation. With so many family links with that country he had felt very much at home there. However, it was time to 'settle down', and he had plans to do so.

He spent his last three months as ADC to his father in Simla, widening his outlook by accompanying the Chief of the General Staff on his tours of inspection. Then at Bombay on 4 August 1923, after a cheerful dinner at the Yacht Club with a friend who had been with him in the cricket eleven at 'The Shop', he sailed in the SS *China* for the long voyage home. It would be thirty-six years before he would see India again – a continent which would be transformed by political developments already looming on the horizon.

2

'Peace for our Time'

Lieutenant Jacob, a tanned, athletic figure in tropical uniform show-ing the ribbon of his first medal, stepped from the SS *China* on to the shores of England at the end of August 1923. He was almost twenty-four, and there was an air of maturity about him. He soon received orders to report to Chatham after five weeks' leave, and then enter King's College, Cambridge. After two short visits to relatives, he went to stay with Major General Sir Francis and Lady Treherne at their home, The Red House, in Woodbridge, Suffolk.

General Sir Francis Treherne KCMG, of the Royal Army Medical Corps, had been the senior medical officer in General Claud Jacob's Meerut Division in France. In India the two families had known each other well, and Ian Jacob had corresponded regularly with the Tre-herne's daughter Cecil, a friend since teen-age. Soon after he had arrived in Woodbridge, they became engaged. Long engagements were normal in those days, so they decided they would marry after Ian's first year at King's; the wedding would take place in Wood-bridge on 27 August 1924, with Major Brian Robertson as best man. The marriage would prove a very happy one, lasting well over sixty years.

Although Lance Corporal Adolf Hitler was writing *Mein Kampf* in prison, all was peace in Europe, and Ian thought he was lucky to be at King's, a small and beautiful college in the very centre of Cambridge. He had agreed with another Sapper, Ouvry Lindfield Roberts, who was also engaged to be married, that they would both go to King's; so they shared lodgings almost opposite the Main Gate. Ouvry Roberts, who later would rise to high rank, was also a very good games player; they both played for King's at cricket, tennis, rugger and hockey, for which Roberts got a blue. They both settled down happily to enjoy the life at King's and in particular the games. As for the academic side,

Jacob, having looked at the syllabus and the nature of the Tripos examination, decided that first class honours were out of his reach, but that he ought to be able to achieve a second. In this he may have underestimated his capabilities.

For the second year, Jacob and his wife were installed in a small house which was found for them by Granny Isabella, and in May 1925 he achieved his second class honours and took his BA. Soon afterwards a son was born.

The Jacobs and Roberts then went back to Chatham for further technical training in military engineering and survey, and from there Jacob was posted to 12 Field Company in Aldershot. He found that his commanding officer seemed tired of soldiering, and preferred shooting, and a quiet life. When the combined training season arrived in August, it was the major's custom to go off to Scotland to shoot grouse, leaving Jacob in charge. He was in no way upset by this: in fact he enjoyed it.

After two years at Aldershot, Jacob, who had passed his promotion examination with distinction, received a letter dated 25 March 1928 from the Senior RE Instructor at the Royal Military Academy suggesting that he should apply to become an instructor there. Jacob with his wife joined the Academy in August 1928. The Commandant was Major General de Pree, and one of the RE Instructors was Major CJS King (known as 'The Monarch'), a very able officer, who would rise in the Second World War to become Engineer-in-Chief. Also on the staff was Major Cameron Nicholson who, as a boy in the Hopetoun at Wellington, had admired Jacob's performance at rugger; the two families became great friends. The Jacobs now had two sons, John and William, and the Nicholsons a son and two daughters.

Remembering his suppressed criticisms of the Academy when a cadet, Jacob was glad to find that the syllabus had been reorganised. Although the discipline was still strict, the dead brutality of the place had gone, and relations between officers and cadets were good.

Jacob had sufficient leisure to study for the entrance examination for the Staff College, where there were only four vacancies for the Royal Engineers with more than fifty sapper officers competing. Assisted by a 'crammer', as was usual in those days, he passed in top with record marks, and received the congratulations of General Sir Bindon Blood, the Chief Royal Engineer, on his 'brilliant success'.

Before leaving 'The Shop' for the Staff College, he had the good fortune to be present at the funeral of Marshal Foch in Paris in 1929.

His father was one of the five field marshals in the impressive delegation. Jacob commented afterwards that the event

> demonstrated the difference between such ceremonial occasions as managed in England and in France. There was more spontaneous grandeur in Paris, but it was mixed with near chaos. In England everything is completely organised, whereas in France much is left to chance, and occasionally impatience bursts forth.[1]

By the end of 1929, Jacob was beginning to stand out amongst his contemporaries. The Waziristan campaign had taught him a lot: how to get the best out of his men, how to organise them both tactically and for engineering work, and how to anticipate the actions of an enemy whose endurance and inborn cunning made up for his lack of heavy weapons. At King's, he had extended his mental powers, and at the Royal Military Academy he had continued the process. To the extent that examinations can be only a guide to success in the military arts, he had demonstrated in Staff College and promotion examinations that he was outstanding in his ability to sift a complex problem to its core, and apply mature judgement to its solution. He had also had the benefit of moving, if only on limited occasions, in high military and governmental circles; in that regard, to have as a father a field marshal who was well-known in Whitehall had been no disadvantage. Lastly, he had a devoted wife who was prepared to play a full part in supporting her husband's career. Socially he was an asset, and he could mix in any society. Although he had inherited some of his father's reserve, he could talk intelligently on any topic, however profound, and participate with skill in almost any game. He was a good shot, and played well at bridge and poker, a game he had learnt in 1919 from an American doctor from California in the Field Company's Mess in the Army of the Rhine.

Jacob joined the Staff College Course in January 1931. The Commandant was Sir John Dill, with Colonel (later Field Marshal Lord) HM Wilson as Chief Army Instructor. There were many students who would soon shine in war – Slessor, Brownjohn, Kirkman, Nicholson, Simpson and Rees – but it was Horrocks who stood out. His performance in the Olympic Pentathlon in Paris in 1921 had won admiration, and his wide experience, intelligence and charm were allied to an extrovert personality which dominated the scene. Soon, he would be marked down by Montgomery as potentially a first-class commander, and in 1942, before Alamein, would be summoned to command a Corps in Eighth Army. Montgomery then confided to his staff: 'Jorrocks is coming: very good, very good, *enthusiasm.*'

A facet of life at Camberley in 1931, which surprised Jacob, was the extravagant cult of the horse. After nearly four years spent in India, he was no mean horseman himself, and had achieved some success in point-to-points, but he was amazed that the horse should hold such an exalted place in the ethos of the Staff College, fifteen years after the tank had made its first appearance on the battlefield. Although it could still be argued that a good man 'across country' would be a good man in battle, with an eye for the tactical use of ground, to make the Drag Hunt in the winter of 1931 a compulsory activity twice a week seemed to Jacob to be archaic. Moreover, the kudos attached to the activity was such that the Chief Instructor barely spoke to anyone who was not a member of the Drag Staff. With the mechanisation of the Army taking place, albeit slowly, was it not time that junior officers should devote their thoughts to a study of the tank and the role of an armoured or mechanised division, a subject which had been researched in the nineteen twenties? But such an interest would not of course lend itself readily to supporting activity of a kind that was socially acceptable; for some time yet to come, intimate contact with the internal combustion engine, with its association of oily spanners and dirty fingernails, would still be considered beyond the pale in fashionable circles.

In retrospect, Jacob was also critical of the light work-load placed upon the students. Exercises, in his view, should have been conducted with more realistic conditions, and should have lasted longer. He summed up his two years' experience in these words:

> One certainly derived a great deal of value from the company of one's fellows, and one was well-trained in the duties of the Staff, but there should have been rather more driving, and less jolly fun.

Nevertheless he himself had exploited the 'jolly fun' to the full, particularly in the hockey team and on the cricket field, where he had headed the batting averages. Needless to say, he was also interested in his future career, but the technicalities of engineering had never much appealed to him, and his ambition was to become involved with the General Staff, in which many Sappers excelled. Towards the end of the Staff College Course, Sir Maurice Hankey, Secretary of the Cabinet and of the Committee of Imperial Defence (CID), came to Camberley to give a lecture, accompanied by a Sapper officer, Lieutenant Colonel GN Macready, who was an Assistant Secretary of the Committee. Hankey and his Committee of Imperial Defence were well-known to Jacob's father, and the idea of an appointment there had been passed by his father to Ian, who now took the opportunity of discussing it with Macready. It was left that when a vacancy occurred, he would be considered for it. Hankey too was a friend from Indian days of the Field Marshal, who was now Constable of the Tower in London.

In the summer of 1931, the Field Marshal and Lady Jacob, accompanied by Ian and Cecil, visited Lord and Lady Inchcape at Glenapp Castle in Scotland. Ian wrote an ironical account of the visit pouring scorn on the pompous ostentation of the proceedings, and showing surprise that his host should live the life of a rajah.

In January 1933, Jacob finished the Staff College course, and the Commandant, General Sir John Dill, congratulated him, saying that he hoped that one day Jacob would become a brigade major. That appointment, rare for Royal Engineers, was the prime target for all keen officers, but would not come Jacob's way until 1936; meanwhile he was posted once more to Aldershot as Garrison Engineer. There he had to cope with the fickleness of the General's Lady over the colour of her drawing room walls and, even more challenging, the problem of installing a lavatory seat to suit the contrasting postures of the General and of Lord Derby, the massive Secretary of State for War who was due to visit the Command – problems typical of the crosses which Garrison Engineers often had to bear: their relevance to war was hard to detect.

In December 1934, however, his career took a more promising turn: he was appointed General Staff Officer, Grade III in the Military Operations Directorate of the War Office, a section concerned with Coast Defence, Air Defence and Internal Security at home and abroad. The main preoccupation of the major and two captains involved was with the Air Defence of Great Britain. Jacob's colleague, the other captain, was a gunner, Noel Martin; whom he would meet again later in very different circumstances.

For those responsible for the defence of the nation, the nineteen-thirties were a confused and difficult period, due in large part to the operation of the Ten Year Rule, which was based on the assumption that there would be no major war in Europe for ten years. It had first been introduced by the Cabinet in 1919 to provide a basis for controlling defence expenditure. Ironically, in 1925, Churchill, as Chancellor of the Exchequer, had defended the economies that he had imposed on the Naval Estimates by arguing that the ten year period was still valid; however he conceded that the validity of the basic assumption should be re-examined every year. This decision was formalised in 1928 when the Committee of Imperial Defence (CID) was charged with responsibility for reviewing annually the validity of the Rule. Not until 1932 did the CID recommend its abandonment, but even then no plan was drawn up to remedy the manifest deficiencies in Defence.

In 1933, some of those political groups, which were still pursuing the chimaera of disarmament, began to adopt a more realistic attitude. The rearmament of Nazi Germany, at that stage covert, was well known to Churchill and his friends; Duff Cooper, the War Minister, on holiday in Austria, had written to Churchill that the Germans were preparing for war 'with more enthusiasm than a whole nation has ever before put into such preparation'.[2]

In November, Lord Londonderry circulated a memorandum to the Cabinet on German rearmament which gave a horrifying estimate of the size of the Luftwaffe to be expected by 1936. Nevertheless Ramsay Macdonald, the Prime Minister, told his colleagues that to expand the Royal Air Force to meet the Luftwaffe's expansion would 'bring trouble'. However, in February 1935, by which time Jacob was firmly installed in the War Office, Ramsay Macdonald agreed at the request of Churchill, Austen Chamberlain and Professor Lindemann to examine the possibility of setting up a special sub-committee of the CID to deal with research in air defence. This was a great step forward, as the sub-committee, pressurised by Churchill and Lindemann, would eventually provide the impetus which would result in radar.

In July 1935, Jacob, now thirty-five, was promoted to Brevet Major. In the same list, appeared the names of two future field marshals: Harding and Templer. In ability and experience at that time, Jacob was fully their equal.

Throughout the two years that Jacob had spent in the Operations Directorate of the War Office – years which Churchill would later categorise as 'the years that the locust hath eaten',[3] he was aware that the preparations which the nation was making for a war which week by week was becoming more and more likely, were totally inadequate. Although he had won high praise for his work, and had been complimented on his 'outstanding ability, clear and logical thinking, ability to express himself exceptionally well either in speech or writing,' it was with a sense of relief that he prepared to sail to Moascar in Egypt in the autumn of 1936, to become Brigade Major of the Canal Brigade.

At that time the Army in Egypt consisted of a horsed Cavalry Brigade, an Infantry Brigade in Cairo and another in the Suez Canal Zone with headquarters in Moascar, a regiment of obsolete Vickers tanks, the 1st Brigade Royal Horse Artillery, a Field Regiment Artillery, 46 Field Company Royal Engineers and administrative troops. There was also a small contingent of the RAF. Of the three battalions in the Canal Brigade, two were in Moascar close to Ismailia, and the other was in Alexandria commanded by Lieutenant Colonel 'Boy' Browning.[4]

During the previous year, Italy, under Mussolini, had invaded Abyssinia; and the most imminent threat to the British position in the Middle East and the security of the Canal now came from Mussolini's expansionist policies. An offensive operation against the Egyptian frontier by Italian troops in Cyrenaica was always a possibility. A more distant and less likely threat was the further aggrandisement of Mussolini's Empire by operations in the South from Italian Somaliland. There was a further possibility of having to reinforce British Troops in Palestine, where there was sporadic unrest between Arabs and Jews.

An infantry brigade was an unfamiliar military group to Jacob, but he soon made himself conversant with their routine, and rapidly mastered their problems. During the hot weather, when the individual training of the infantry was carried out, Jacob could be seen riding his grey charger before breakfast, keenly observing progress; this was followed by office work until lunch time, and sport in the late afternoon.

Meanwhile at home, the two Jacob sons, John and William, were making good progress, and short leave in England, by ship through the Mediterranean, thence by train to Calais was manageable. But there were clouds on the horizon. Edward VIII's infatuation with Mrs Simpson was not a welcome subject for discussion within an international community; more serious was the progressive darkening of the European scene. This was very troubling to an officer who knew so much about the possible threats and the inadequate measures being taken in Whitehall to meet them. But he was now concerned with more mundane matters; he quickly succeeded in introducing more realism into brigade training by persuading his Commander to carry out annually an 'all arms' exercise of a week's duration, instead of the customary thirty-six hours exercise, which lacked realism.

Jacob was again unfortunate in having a Commander whose qualities were patently inadequate to meet the potential dangers that threatened Egypt in 1937. It was a year of uneasy peace: the Abyssinian affair had been finished, and Hitler with an army which had now become very large, thanks to conscription, had reoccupied the Rhineland and had marched into Austria. In fact, to any realistic observer, it was clear that Europe was on the brink of war. Yet the Canal Brigade, charged with the prime responsibility of safeguarding Britain's Line of communication to her oilfields in the Persian Gulf and to her sources of military manpower and raw materials in India, Malaya, Australia and New Zealand, was in the hands of a leader known locally as 'the Squire of Moascar' who, after two easy jobs, had lost the capacity for sustained work. He took a great interest in amenities for the troops, and in the completion of the Garrison Church, and he seemed to have fallen in love with the desert: after ten minutes in the office he would be driven out alone along the Canal or into the desert and was seen no more. Jacob had to support this unpredictable character, and his letters home to the Field Marshal and to his mother refer frequently to the problem.

Initially he could not make up his mind about the Brigade Commander, but 'time would show'. Then, in a Brigade exercise, he found him 'a bit anxious and inclined to get excited'. Although 'he had many good soldierly qualities, and plenty of personality, he continually flies off here and there, and is not easy to work with in many ways, and difficult to pin down, . . .' But Jacob soon felt he had him 'taped', and they 'got on very well together'. Later, after four months' collaboration, and a more ambitious exercise which went well, Jacob wrote confidentially to his father:

> . . . he is not a great hand at training and is a bad speaker, but he has the knack of sending units away in a good frame of mind, and people like serving under him. He is an absolute gentleman, and I am very fond of him. I fear he is a spent force mentally and smokes and drinks more than is good for him. The real difficulty is of course that, being new to the game myself and not being an infantry man, I think that the units do not get the guidance in training that they should get, because the Brig really hasn't any idea in his head. Next year will be different, as I shall know what is what, and shall be able to screw him up to the mark beforehand . . .

A brigade commander 'past his prime' was by no means unique in the Army of 1937, and it would take a Montgomery to weed them out after inevitable disasters. However, the battalion commanders of the Canal Brigade, as assessed by the mature, observant Brigade Major, were very good, particularly 'Boy' Browning the 'absolute boss' of the 2nd Battalion Grenadier Guards in Alexandria, and Lieutenant

Colonel Jack Whittaker, who followed him with the 3rd Battalion Coldstream Guards. Whittaker wrote to him as follows:

> ... A line to thank you and all the Brigade Staff for all the help you gave us while under your immediate command. One did so appreciate the general atmosphere of friendliness and efficiency, and all my officers commented (with surprise) on the brigade staff being apparently all out to help and make the wheels go round smoothly. And this was I know so largely due to the way you and the Staff Captain tackled things and foresaw our needs and difficulties ...

In the spring of 1937, the Jacobs decided to take their summer leave at home to coincide with the boys' holidays. Cecil went ahead and Ian followed. After a splendid holiday, he returned ahead of her by train to Venice, thence to Alexandria by an Italian boat. He was travelling tourist, and his companions at dinner were a Jew, on his way to sell furs in Egypt, who spoke English and German, and a Swiss lady who spoke only German and French; Jacob with his English and French found that a general conversation presented some difficulty. In the First Class the atmosphere was much livelier: there were about sixty *Mousquitieri del Duce* enjoying a cruise to Alexandria. Jacob recorded them as 'a tremendously hearty and arrogant bunch' and speculated grimly on their future fate in the war 'which was certainly coming'.[5]

Returning to Moascar, he began to think about the brigade exercise scheduled for February 1938. Realism would be difficult to achieve because of the lack of modern equipment. The infantry battalions now had trucks instead of horsed wagons, but there were no anti-tank guns, no anti-aircraft artillery and still only the one regiment of ancient Vickers tanks, seldom seen outside Cairo. The RAF were represented by three reconnaissance planes and three old transport aircraft. Nevertheless the exercise, which lasted a week, turned out to be a considerable success.

Jacob's tenure as brigade major would soon be ended, and he began to speculate on his future employment. He had not served regimentally with the Royal Engineers since 1927, so he expected to be posted to a Sapper unit somewhere in the Middle East. Meanwhile he and his wife arranged to take a month's leave to go home to see the family. Just before sailing, he was surprised to receive a letter from the War Office asking whether he would be in London shortly, because someone important wanted to see him. On arrival in London, the important person turned out to be Sir Maurice Hankey. Hankey told Jacob that he was about to retire, and that Colonel HL Ismay, the Deputy Secretary of the CID was to succeed him as Secretary, and that Sir Edward Bridges was to become Secretary of the Cabinet. He went on to say that there was a vacancy in the post of Military Assistant Secretary of the CID, as another Sapper, Lieutenant Colonel Vyvian Dykes was finishing his time; Jacob had been recommended for the job, and would he like to join in November 1938?

Jacob leapt at the chance. He was particularly impressed by Ismay, known as 'Pug' to all his friends, who was 'a striking looking officer' originally in an Indian Cavalry regiment, 'tall, well set-up, perfectly dressed and with a charming manner'. Ismay was yet to climb to the pinnacle of fame which later he would achieve; but at this meeting his charismatic personality already had a pronounced effect on Jacob. It was to be the beginning of a most fruitful and happy association, which both would cherish to the end of their lives.

Jacob then arranged to meet one or two of the Assistant Secretaries and sense the atmosphere at their offices in Richmond Terrace, and he quickly came to the conclusion that with Ismay at their head it was in this organisation beyond all others that he would wish to serve. Not only was the friendly, informal ambience very apparent, but also there was a pronounced feeling of urgent efficiency, so much so that he secretly wondered whether he could measure up to the standards that were set. However, greatly excited by the prospect, but sobered by the darkening international scene, he returned by train and ship to Moascar, leaving his wife in England.

By the end of August 1938, his plans for returning to England were finalised: he would sail in the *Nevassa* due to reach Southampton on 16 September. He wrote home to his mother a short letter:

> This will be my last from Egypt, unless some hitch arrives at the last moment to prevent my sailing on Thursday. Events certainly look as if they are drifting to a crisis, though why the entire world should be torn up on account of a million or two of Sudeten Germans I can't think.
> ... I must stop because I have a thousand things to do. I am so looking forward to getting home, and I can only hope Hitler will have a little sense. It is all so blighting, and from our point of view so meaningless. I am thankful I am not Prime Minister. Whatever happens, I don't think we should declare war instantly, but I suppose we must be dragged in sooner or later. ... The French here are decidedly windy, though one can feel that their opinion has hardened greatly in the last few months, and they are much more willing to fight than they were. However, let us hope that it will all blow over!

Meanwhile, Hitler's plans to achieve the domination of Europe progressed inexorably, and on 15 September 1938, Chamberlain flew to Munich to 'negotiate' with him at Berchtesgarten. By 21 September, the sacrifice of Czechoslovakia was accomplished by a process amounting in Churchill's words to the complete surrender of the Western Democracies to the Nazi threat of force.

A hitch now occurred in Jacob's plans: two hours before leaving for Alexandria he was recalled to Moascar. Although very unwelcome, this development could have hardly have surprised him. That evening he wrote to his mother and father 'it makes a bit of an anti-climax when you have said goodbye to everyone, and there you are the next day. I shall slip away without saying a word next time.' He was booked next on the *Neuralia*, due in Southampton on 8 October.

His final letter to his mother and father was sent on 27 September 1938, his thirty-ninth birthday. At 0015 hours that day he had issued the order to mobilise. There was no sleep that night, but he completed his letter:

> It is of course only precautionary for the defence of the Canal, but I must say the outlook looks very black, and the whole thing looks much too much like 1914, with the added burden that we know the kind of thing we are in for this time. My sailing has of course been stopped like everyone else's in this part of the world, and Egypt is like a fortress putting itself into a state of defence as fast as it can. Of course if Italy remains neutral we are in no danger here; but if she does not, we can expect some excitement, though I don't think much of her chances! I can't believe Musso could be such an idiot. However, by the time you get this, we shall know which way the cat is going to jump.
>
> I am very worried about you sitting in London, and I hope you will clear out in good time before the war comes, if it does come. I am afraid you are in much greater danger than I am. England suddenly seems to have got much further off, and one feels so powerless to do anything even to advise one's family. We have just got to face the future calmly whatever it may bring.
>
> I am afraid the downfall of Germany, when it comes, will be terrible. Perhaps Hitler will draw back even now from the brink. I only hope the Sudetens get wiped out to the last man, woman and child in the struggle, and Hitler along with them.
>
> Well Mum, you know my feelings for you both, and whatever happens to any of us, we have the great joy of knowing that there has never been a happier or more united family: God bless you both. Ever your loving son, Ian.

Three days later, while Ian Jacob was mobilising in Moascar, Chamberlain returned to London from his second visit to Hitler and, waving a piece of paper in the air, exclaimed:

I believe it is peace for our time.[6]

PLATE 1. General John Jacob, from a silver statuette presented to the British officers of the Scinde Horse by the Indian officers of the Regiment (*National Army Museum*).

PLATE 2. Second Lieutenant Ian Jacob RE, aged 19.

PLATE 3. Brandon Rectory (1908). Ian seated with croquet mallet with Granny Isabella Wyatt (*on his left*). Ian's mother (*second from right, back row*). Rev JL Wyatt in clerical dress (left).

PLATE 4. Winston Churchill, Secretary of State for War, accompanied by General Sir William Robertson, greets General Sir Claud Jacob, Cologne 1919 (*IWM*).

PLATE 5. The wedding of Ian Jacob and Cecil Treherne, 27 August 1924. (*Back L–R*) Rev JL Wyatt, General Sir Claud Jacob, Ian Jacob, Major General Sir Francis Treherne and Major Brian Robertson. (*Front L–R*) Mrs JL Wyatt, Cecil Jacob, Lady Treherne and Lady Jacob. *Bridesmaids* Anne Taylor, Jean Bannister and Barbara Jarrett.

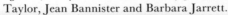

PLATE 6. The Ypres Salient as seen by Gentleman Cadet Ian Jacob from the air, Christmas 1917 (*From a painting by War Artist Sir David Cameron*) (IWM).

PLATE 7. The Waziristan Circular Road (*Institution of Royal Engineers*).

PLATE 8. Major Ian Jacob with his Brigade Commander, Brigadier Brooks, and Group Captain Coleman RAF awaiting the arrival of the Earl and Countess of Athlone, Port Said 1938 (*Photo Radio*).

PLATE 9. 'Peace for our Time'. Chamberlain returns from Munich, 30 September 1938 (*IWM*).

3

Stumbling into War

On 7 October 1938 Jacob at last sailed for England to join the Committee of Imperial Defence at Richmond Terrace in Whitehall. The troopship *Neuralia* was no longer available, but he was given a berth in the liner *Aquitania*, which had been hastily requisitioned in England and despatched to the Mediterranean with naval reservists and stores. She was now at Port Said awaiting the return passage to Southampton.

Fortunately, the onset of war is often relieved by comedy. This case was no exception. With some amusement, Jacob had observed his Brigadier at Ismailia Airport, in his chosen mobilisation dress of dungarees and sandals, welcoming General Ironside, faultlessly attired in uniform, and the Ambassador, Sir Miles Lampson, accompanied by his English butler, impeccable in a morning coat. Again, in the *Aquitania*'s Rembrandt Suite, usually booked by millionaires, a private soldier was discovered propped against the satin bedhead, teacup in hand and naked to the waist, who commented that he had been surprised at the berth he had been allocated, but had found it 'very comfortable'.

Jacob reported for duty in Whitehall in November 1938. Instead of the simple problems of a group of units preparing for war, he would now be concerned with the complex problems of an entire nation and indeed Empire. These had to be considered by high level committees, and their decisions fed into the Government's machine by carefully phrased minutes and memoranda. His first priority was to learn about the workings of the Committee of Imperial Defence.

The CID, set up in 1904 had resulted from the Esher Committee, which had recommended that a permanent advisory body should be established, with the Prime Minister as Chairman and sole statutory member; he would summon other appropriate experts as required.

Co-ordination of Imperial Defence was to be fostered by the creation of an Imperial General Staff with a Chief of the Imperial General Staff (CIGS) at its head.

From 1904 until the outbreak of World War I, the Committee had become increasingly active. Sub-committees had been established, the most important of which were the Home Defence Committee, and the Overseas Defence Committee. The CID had concentrated on administrative preparedness for war by the production of a War Book, which had set out in detail the measures necessary for an orderly transition from peace to war. Little thought had been given to strategy or to the conduct of operations, and there had been no overall naval and military plan of action.

Before World War I, the arrangements had been haphazard: there were no minutes of Cabinet Meetings, and the dissemination of decisions had been largely the work of Hankey. When Lloyd George had set up his first War Cabinet in 1916, Hankey had become its Secretary, and had introduced the orderly methods that had so successfully evolved in the Committee of Imperial Defence.

Once war had broken out in 1914, the CID, being an advisory body, had gone into abeyance, and it was not until 1919 that it had resumed its work, when it was resuscitated without any change in its constitution. In 1923, following the creation of a third Service, the Royal Air Force, the Chiefs of Staff Committee had been established to harmonise the higher direction of the fighting services, give unified strategic advice to the CID, and co-ordinate the plans and operations of the three Services in war. The essential feature of the whole of that organisation, as of the CID itself, was that co-ordination and co-operation were secured by bringing together the responsible officers from the Ministries and not by the appointment of special advisers divorced from the constitutional chain of command.

Jacob joined the CID as an Assistant Military Secretary. The family house at Farnborough was let, so he rented a house in Camberley near the station; commuting to London was easy, and General Treherne and his wife kept the Red House at Woodbridge warm for them; Ian and Cecil frequently visited them there, particularly during the boys' holidays.

Jacob's predecessor, Vivian Dykes, a man of great ability and common sense, was due to start as an instructor at the Staff College Camberley, where his remarkable talent for mimicry would happily supplement his other great qualities. He spent a week or two handing over to Jacob, and initiating him into the mysteries of life in close contact with ministers and the chief functionaries, civil and military, of government.

By this time, the office of the CID formed part of a combined office with the Cabinet Secretariat and Sir Edward Bridges, as Secretary of the Cabinet, was the overall head of the office. General Ismay, though ultimately subordinate to Bridges, was in command of the military portion of the combined office; he was assisted by Colonel LC Hollis, a Royal Marine, who was Secretary, Chiefs of Staff. Ismay looked after all the military committees from the Chiefs of Staff Committee downwards. He was Secretary CID, but Bridges also attended CID meetings, not only because of the quantity of civil work that fell under the heading of preparation for war, but because many items dealt with by the CID had to be submitted to the Cabinet for final decision.

Initially, Jacob was not directly concerned with the Chiefs of Staff Committee; his principal responsibility was as Secretary of the Overseas Defence Committee. The Chairman was Sir Cosmo Parkinson, the Permanent Under Secretary of State for the Colonies, and its job was to act in relation to the Colonies as the agent of the CID. It prepared instructions on administrative measures required on the outbreak of war: it examined Colonial defence schemes, and received reports of the annual inspections of local forces. Even after the Munich crisis, correspondence had to be clothed in formal language, and Jacob frequently found himself 'having the honour to request . . .'

To a military eye, the Cabinet Secretariat was a strange organisation: the curious duality of the arrangements might have presented difficulties if the civil and military chiefs had been men eager to stand on their dignity. But Jacob soon found that with men of the high character, loyalty, and devotion of Bridges and Ismay, difficulty was reduced to a minimum, with both sides working together harmoniously as a team.

It took him a little time to get to know all the Assistant Secretaries, as each had his own committees to look after, and there was no Mess or canteen in which to meet.

In moments of great stress, which were not infrequent, Ismay would order in a hamper from a restaurant, and they would sit round it, eating and continuing their work on the drafting of a report. Jacob gradually got to recognise the field that each covered, and obtained their advice which, he found, they were most willing to give to a newcomer.

There was no elaborate hierarchy; Jacob was responsible to Ismay direct, and had no subordinates other than a very good clerk. There were no men to do the donkey-work or to brief a superior officer. Each Assistant Secretary was expected to do his own work, aided by his Committee Clerk and his stenographer. This was an excellent arrangement which fostered speed and efficiency.

Jacob, still a major, had much to learn. The first thing he had to do was to read the key documents which had been approved in recent years by the CID, including the reports of the Defence Requirements Committee, which had been set up in 1933 to prepare a programme for meeting the nation's worst deficiencies. There were also appreciations drawn up by the Chiefs of Staff of the world strategic situation, and the discussions and decisions of the CID itself. Then it was necessary to discover how a secretary became of real value, and did not remain a mere handler of committee papers.

There had recently been added to the machinery of government a new Minister: the 'Minister for the Co-ordination of Defence'. Sir Thomas Inskip had been appointed to this office in March 1936. He had no Ministry as such, but was served by the staff of the 'Office of the Cabinet and Committee of Imperial Defence'. The duty of keeping the Minister informed and helping him to carry out his co-ordinating function was thus superimposed upon the previous work of the office, and they all contributed to the task, as called upon by Bridges and Ismay. The Minister's functions were ill-defined and he was in a difficult position.

Having found his feet within the office, Jacob had to make contacts in the appropriate Government Departments: but progressively he had to go much wider, because he had often to deal with Ministers and the Chiefs of Staff on business before the CID itself, if Ismay so wished. The essence of the system was that each member of the team had direct access to everybody from the Prime Minister downwards; this arrangement added greatly to the effectiveness of their work, and to the contribution they could make to the speedy conduct of business.

For this system to work, officers chosen for the Secretariat had to be able to establish confidence in their integrity and trustworthiness, work with speed and accuracy, and know how to approach the different levels and mentalities with which they had to deal. They had quickly to acquire a thorough knowledge of the governmental machinery, and discover what could and could not be done successfully. Far from being just pushers of paper, they had to learn how to drive the work forward: for it was a tradition in Ismay's 'band of brothers' that regardless of the time at which a meeting closed, the minutes would be on his table at 9 am the next morning.

The success of this 'inner circle', which included men of great talent but very disparate personalities, was due primarily to Ismay's leadership. Jacob, whose admiration for him grew throughout Ismay's long career, wrote thirty years after their first encounter:

> He had a striking pair of grey eyes, under arched eyebrows, a wide mouth and a broad nose. The nickname 'Pug' certainly expressed the general impression of his face . . . He had a brain which was naturally quick and had been cultivated not only by his staff training but by his contact with keen men. He was a very hard worker, with amazing mental and physical endurance, but combined all this with a capacity to break away and enjoy himself. He was a born host, loved good living, and had the strength of personality to fit into any society. He had no trace of vanity, though he had a proper sense of ceremony and honour due to those who deserved it. He was quite fearless both physically and morally, and was incapable of subservience of any undesirable kind. His loyalty both to his seniors and to his juniors, was absolute. It extended to ministers no matter what their politics might be, and no matter what he might privately think of their qualities, and despite his natural sympathy for the aristocratic system in which he had grown up. His ambition was entirely honourable and had no element of jealousy or self-seeking. In the very best sense of the word he was a gentleman, and inspired in all those who worked for him the same spirit of loyalty that he so outstandingly possessed. . . .[1]

Jacob found that Ismay was a true decentraliser; he never allowed protocol to stand in the way of speed and efficiency of work. He never insisted that everything destined for the Chiefs of Staff or the Prime Minister must pass through him. Hollis and Jacob could deal directly with anyone, so there were no bottlenecks. The result was entirely successful. It made no difference which of them dealt with a piece of work, and except on the highest plane they were to a great extent interchangeable, though they knew exactly when they should step back and leave Ismay to act. On many occasions during the war, when the Prime Minister or the Chiefs of Staff went abroad, Ismay or Hollis or Jacob could be sent, or stay at home to 'mind the shop' without any reservations. Such an arrangement was only possible with a man who had the facility of inspiring his assistants with his spirit, and the unselfishness to waive all questions of personal status.

It is not surprising that Joan Bright Astley, one of the women in the organisation who rendered great service, described the ethos of the place in similar words:

> All of them were gentlemen: members as it were of the same club.[2]

John Colville, one of Churchill's private secretaries, wrote:

> They soothed the exasperated, and prodded the indolent.[3]

Early in December 1938, the first major question that came Jacob's way concerned the Army. The Secretary of State for War, Hore-Belisha, had submitted a paper to the Committee of Imperial Defence, seeking authority for six measures, the total cost of which was estimated at about £80m. They were designed to improve the power and readiness of the Regular Field Force and of those Territorial Divisions which would provide the first reinforcement of any contingent sent to fight overseas. The Secretary of State had argued that, if war came, a Field Force would have to be sent abroad, and it was urgent, therefore, to manufacture the equipment for it. This paper was considered at a meeting of the CID shortly before Christmas, and received a cold welcome.

The policy of the Government at that time was based on the supposition that, if war broke out against Germany, action would be limited to the defence of Great Britain, together with such offensive operations as could be carried out by the Royal Navy and the Royal Air Force. There was no plan to send an Expeditionary Force to the Continent, and expenditure by the War Office on equipment required only for that purpose was not authorised. Hore-Belisha's paper was an attempt to break out of this unreal situation; but it was evident that several senior Ministers were strongly opposed to anything which carried with it the recognition for the need for a continental campaign. 'We want no more Passchendaele's' was one exclamation Jacob heard. 'The role of the Army should be confined to the defence of Great Britain.' The Secretary of State made no headway, and had to agree that his paper should be remitted to the Chiefs of Staff Committee for examination and report.

Jacob had been in charge of the paper from the Secretarial point of view, and therefore became responsible for its further progress; so he attended an early meeting of the Chiefs of Staff Committee at which it was taken. The Chiefs were becoming seriously concerned at the Government's continued refusal to take seriously the probability of military operations on the Continent. The ruling factor was the situation *vis-à-vis* the French. If war broke out with Germany, and the French were threatened with attack, they would naturally expect maximum support from their ally. If they found that the British did not intend to fight on land at all, not because they had some other strategy to offer, but simply because they would not face the casualties, they might well think that it would be better to make terms with the enemy. The Chiefs of Staff decided that the only way of carrying conviction to the Cabinet and of inducing them to authorise a large and rapid expansion of munitions' production for the Army, would be by presenting them with a careful memorandum on the role of the Army, starting from first principles. The Secretariat was directed to draft this memorandum, and the job fell to Jacob.

He began by setting down the various ways in which a war against Germany could be lost. The first was by losing command of the sea. The second was by failing to prevent annihilating attack from the air, which would bring about the same situation in Britain as would follow loss of command over sea communications. The third was by allowing France to be overrun by the German Army. Not only would Britain's principal ally be destroyed in that event, but the capture by the Germans of the whole European coastline from Holland to Spain would most certainly prepare the way for one of the first-named calamities to follow. It was therefore essential for survival that every possible measure should be taken to bring strong support to the French on land. Air and sea defences, including strong anti-aircraft defences, must not be neglected, but it would be equally fatal to leave the French Army to fight alone. The paper then reviewed the situation of the Services and their rearmament programmes, and made recommendations as to the improvements that should at once be authorised for the Army.

Jacob realised that all this was far too late; there was not enough time to make good the neglect of so many years' duration, and the British Army was still far too small and still lacking in the decisive categories of equipment. It had not a single armoured division, and it had no anti-tank guns worthy of the name. The paper after being improved and 'polished' by Ismay and Bridges, went before the Chiefs of Staff, who approved it for submission to the CID.

Meanwhile an event had taken place which had a more profound effect on the Government than any arguments on paper. On 11 January, Chamberlain, the Prime Minister, and Lord Halifax, the Foreign Secretary paid a visit to Mussolini in Rome. Their object was to try to ensure that the Italians would not enter the war on the side of Germany. In Rome they did not make much impression, but on their way home they passed through Paris and saw M Bonnet, the French Prime Minister. It was only then that they awoke to the realisation that, if there was no firm undertaking to send a British Expeditionary Force to France on the outbreak of war, the French would not fight. Chamberlain returned to London, and in the course of the following few weeks, authorised the Army's requirements not in full, but to a degree that would allow a more realistic programme to be built up.

The increasing threat of war gradually produced changes in Richmond Terrace. The CID, which had originally met quarterly and then monthly, began to meet daily. The size of the staff in the Secretariat did not increase, but the feeling of urgency and the pressure of work were magnified, and Jacob found himself drawn increasingly into the work of the Chiefs of Staff Committee, whose meetings became almost daily events.

The three Chiefs of Staff at that time were Admiral of the Fleet Sir Dudley Pound, General Lord Gort and Air Chief Marshal Sir Cyril Newall: of these, only Pound would remain in office for long. Gort with his great fighting reputation and VC from World War I, had been appointed in 1937 by Hore-Belisha who had decided to dig down below the obvious successors to a younger fighting soldier. Jacob regarded it as a peculiar selection, because Gort had no pretensions to be a staff officer, and had never served in the War Office. It soon became apparent that he had little inclination towards wider strategical issues, and that his real ceiling was as the commander of a brigade. One day, walking up Whitehall he had asked Jacob if he read military history; Jacob had replied that he had studied it during the years spent in preparing for the Staff College examination, and at the Staff College, but had had little time for it recently. Gort said that he always tried to read military history for two or three hours a day. In Jacob's view this was a curious activity for a CIGS.

Newall, the Chief of the Air Staff, was not highly regarded by Jacob and people of his standing. He had a supercilious expression on his face; however, Jacob thought that perhaps he was a better man than appeared on the surface.

Pound had come fortuitously to the job of First Sea Lord owing to the death of his predecessor in 1938. To Jacob he appeared to be a man who knew everything that was happening at sea, and had strong ideas about what should be done. Like many sailors he tended to do too much himself. Because he was a keen sportsman, he liked to work late at night, a habit which later was to ease his relationship with Churchill, who would do a great deal of business with him direct.

Jacob, an observant secretary at many meetings, was unimpressed by some members of the War Cabinet. Lord Halifax, though high-minded and conscientious, seemed to have a singularly negative approach to affairs; he seemed to believe that provided any positive action were avoided, things would gradually turn in Britain's favour. Jacob thought Sir John Simon, the Chancellor of the Exchequer, a cold man, cautious and uninspiring. Sir Samuel Hoare, though more positive, did not inspire confidence. Chamberlain himself, as Chairman of the War Cabinet, was self-confident, alert and business-like; but at heart he was disinterested in and unfamiliar with military affairs. At a time when the Government needed a dynamic chief executive to drive forward its preparations for defence, Chamberlain was not the man for the job.

Jacob thrived on work and responsibility, but the sense of impending calamity destroyed the pleasure of working in surroundings of such absorbing interest and living once more at home with his family. Moreover, on every hand, there were doubts about the determination of the Chamberlain Government to profit from the respite of Munich. In the years ahead, Jacob would always look back on that time as the most disagreeable phase of his entire service.

In January, when Churchill was on a visit to France, it had been announced that Admiral of the Fleet Lord Chatfield was to succeed Sir Thomas Inskip as Minister for Co-ordination of Defence. Jacob felt that this appointment served only to demonstrate the half-hearted spirit of the time. Lord Chatfield was a sailor of great experience and repute: to place such an excellent officer in the position of the minister for co-ordinating defence was a move which perhaps would strike the uninitiated as a sign of determination to press ahead with military preparation. But those who were aware of the realities of Government could hardly be deceived. For such an important position in the Government, it was a politician of high quality, not a serving officer, that was required. First, he must know how to convince his colleagues and win their wholehearted backing for what he must do. Secondly, he would have to carry his plans through Parliament, and make an impact in the country. None of these things would come easily, if at all, to a military leader accustomed all his life to receiving and giving orders. Moreover when this military man, turned politician, would be a member not of the Commons but of the House of Lords, and when, by accepting the post, he would apparently take on great responsibility but be given no executive power, the chance of achieving any striking result would be minimal. However, the arrangement suited Chamberlain, because the new Minister would not be in a position to force him to go beyond what he, as Prime Minister, thought sensible, and that was a rate of preparation for war which would not damage peace-time industry, nor overstrain the economy, nor provoke the Germans.

Jacob, like many people, had expected that Chamberlain might at that moment have replaced Inskip with Churchill, who was separated from the Government, and for long had uttered warnings which Ministers were not able altogether to ignore. To have brought him back into the fold and to have made him Minister of Defence, with adequate powers, would have shown the world that the British Government had woken to the situation, and were determined to yield no further. The policy of appeasement would have been clearly abandoned. However, it was very late to introduce a radical change in the military machinery of the Government, which Jacob had observed closely from his central position. It was inconceivable to him that Churchill would have accepted the appointment had it not carried with it a large measure of direction over the whole field of military affairs. He would not have been content with the mere co-ordination of the work of the CID, and of the Service Ministers, who under Inskip had retained unimpaired their full responsibilities and powers. He would have insisted on executive power, and this would have been difficult to accept in a peacetime Cabinet in which all Ministers held an individual and collective responsibility to Parliament. Jacob envisaged much opposition and friction, which would probably have vitiated the advantages which eventually might have accrued.

However, Chamberlain with his new Minister installed, and aware that war was almost certain, now began to take a succession of hesitant steps. Staff conversations with the French were resumed, though the British were restricted to the offer of a force which in the first instance was to consist of only two divisions. Jacob, always a realist, felt that the French could hardly be stiffened in their resolution when they were appraised of the size of the British contribution. It was also agreed that an Anglo-French Supreme War Council, headed by the two Prime Ministers, should be established at the outset of war. Measures were put in hand, under Hollis, to create an underground War Room protected against air attack, and skeleton preparations were made to set up an alternative seat of Government if necessary.

March 1939 was a month of terrible anxiety. On the fourteenth, after the German invasion of Czechoslovakia, Hitler proclaimed his protectorate, and thus prepared the way for his onslaught on Poland. Chamberlain, to the surprise of Churchill and some of his followers, then gave the historic guarantee of British support to Poland 'in any action which threatened Polish independence'. At the end of the month, it was announced to Jacob's surprise that the Territorial Army was to be doubled in size. This move was at that stage a paper transaction unsupported as yet either by volunteers or equipment.

In April, Germany absorbed Bohemia and Moravia, and Italy

invaded Albania – a useful springboard for a future attack on Greece. In answer to this aggression Hore-Belisha succeeded in making Chamberlain introduce conscription, despite the repeated pledges against such a step which had been given in the past. Moreover, a Ministry of Supply was at last established, nearly three years after Churchill had first recommended it to Inskip.

In July 1939 Jacob, nearly forty years of age and still a major, despite the heavy responsibilities he was carrying, was made a brevet lieutenant colonel. He had been at the centre of military affairs for nine months, but was far from satisfied with what the CID had accomplished under Chamberlain's chairmanship. Admittedly, air raid precautions and schemes for the evacuation of children were progressing well, but such administrative arrangements were much easier to make than strategic plans for the opening phase of the war. It was in that area that great weaknesses still existed.

The Armed Forces, and particularly the Army, had been allowed to deteriorate for so many years that the partial measures put in hand in the period of so-called re-armament had not been sufficient to restore the position. The strategy to be followed on the outbreak of war was therefore defined as gaining time to build up strength. At sea, no great difficulty was foreseen; although the Germans were likely to resort to unrestrictive U-boat warfare from the start, and would probably try to disrupt ocean routes by using pocket battleships as commerce raiders, their overall strength was not sufficient to challenge successfully the combined fleets of France and Great Britain. In the air, the position was more complicated. Fighter Command was building up its strength, though not fast enough. Bomber Command was small, and still armed with twin-engined aircraft which were clearly obsolescent. In any case, it was thought by the Air Staff that, initially, Britain would be the losers in a bombing war, and that it would be advantageous to avoid any action which would bring, in retaliation, an all-out air offensive against industry, ports, and other semi-military targets. The policy adopted was that there was to be no bombing of any target on the mainland of the Continent which was not strictly related to military operations.

On land, there was the commitment to send an expeditionary force to France in accordance with the staff conversations that had been held in the Spring. Four Divisions was the maximum force that could now be rapidly got together. There was no armoured division and there were no effective anti-tank guns. There were few trained reserves, and if continuous fighting were to start immediately, there would very soon be critical shortages of warlike equipment and ammunition.

The War Office, had not taken decisions about several key types of equipment, and particularly about tanks, anti-tank guns, and weapons for engaging low-flying aircraft. The British, who had invented the tank, had produced, in the nineteen twenties, what for those days was quite a good model. A specimen armoured force had been assembled on Salisbury Plain in 1930, and had been tested; a manual with an up-to-date exposition of an Armoured Division and its composition and mode of operation had been written, and the Germans, having procured a copy from a spy (Baillie-Stewart, the notorious 'Officer in the Tower'), had founded their formations upon it. From then on, in the British Army, there was stagnation. Except for the slow and cumbersome Valentines and Matildas and some ill-protected and unreliable Cruiser tanks, nothing was produced. The armoured force was dispersed after its trial period and never re-assembled.

Another important question which had exercised the CID as war approached was that of higher direction, both political and military. Three decisions had been reached: the immediate creation of a War Cabinet: the intention to place the British Expeditionary Force under the overall command of the French: and the creation of a Supreme War Council. Jacob found that nothing else had been settled or even discussed. Moreover, the British Forces were still controlled in separate compartments – the Admiralty, the War Office and the Air Ministry. It had not occurred to anyone at that time that a unified system of control from the Chiefs of Staff in London to theatres of operations would be a necessary arrangement in modern warfare.

Finally, as the crisis mounted, the Soviet Agency, Tass, announced on 21 August that Ribbentrop, Hitler's Foreign Minister, was flying to Moscow to sign a non-aggression pact with the Soviet Union. In Richmond Terrace, this development removed all doubts that war was certain. On 1 September, Germany attacked Poland and the British guarantee came into effect. Chamberlain immediately set up his War Cabinet, but without any representatives of the Labour Opposition, who were not prepared to serve under his leadership. Two days later, Churchill was welcomed back to the Admiralty as First Lord, and on 3 September war was declared.

Five days later, Sir Cosmo Parkinson, Permanent Under Secretary of the Colonial Office wrote to Jacob announcing that the Overseas Defence Committee had 'gone into hibernation'; he then thanked him for his 'admirable work' and said how much all those in the

Colonial Office, who had been concerned with Defence, had valued his help.

Jacob, released from his commitments to the CID and now on the staff of the War Cabinet, would soon find himself drawn into even more critical activities.

When August arrived, with storm clouds over Poland, and with a British and French mission in Moscow holding long-drawn out discussions with the Russians, it was decided that the staff should take a fortnight's leave in two batches. Jacob was fortunate to be in the first of them and enjoyed a splendid fortnight at Woodbridge. At the end of his leave, he returned to the office, and the second batch, which included Ismay, went off. The Chiefs of Staff were also scattered. On 21 August, as soon as the Moscow non-aggression pact between Russia and Germany was announced, Jacob was summoned to 10 Downing Street, and told by the Prime Minister to recall from leave Ismay and the Chiefs of Staff. From then onwards, there was a continuous flow of meetings, as the War Book was put into effect.

On 3 September, the day war was declared, the Chiefs of Staff held a meeting in the underground War Room at Storey's Gate. The meeting ended, and Jacob with Ismay and Hollis, emerged into King Charles Street to walk back to Richmond Terrace. As they came out, the air raid siren sounded, and people were to be seen hurrying away from Downing Street where crowds always gathered at moments of crisis. They all assumed that the expected heavy raid was about to take place, and when they arrived at Richmond Terrace they descended to the basement which had been turned into a shelter by supporting the ceiling with heavy timbers. They were not there long before the 'all clear' sounded and they resumed work, wondering what had happened. The air raid warning had been a false alarm, and they had another that same evening. Again, they gathered down below, and, a few minutes later, Hollis told Jacob: 'A German U-boat has sunk the *Athenia* off the coast of Ireland, and the liner was full of Americans'. It was clear that unrestricted U-boat warfare was starting at once. Horrified though he was by this attack upon unarmed civilians, Jacob could not help hoping that American ideas of neutrality would be rudely shaken in consequence.

On the day that saw Britain and Germany at war, normal Cabinet Government ceased and Jacob attended the first meeting of the War Cabinet. The most exciting piece of business was the receipt of news that the German Fleet was moving from its North Sea bases and appeared to be making for the Kiel Canal. Could the RAF be permitted to launch an attack on the ships from low altitude in spite of the restrictions, then current, on offensive action? Permission was given, and an officer from the Admiralty rushed off to give the order. This was the first offensive act of the war. The attack was made from low altitude by Wellingtons and Blenheims and was almost entirely unsuccessful; on their way home, a number of the bombers were lost, shot down by fighters against whom the unescorted bombers had little defence.

The expected heavy air raids on London did not occur, and the country settled down into a curious half-and-half situation. Poland was rapidly destroyed, but elsewhere on land nothing seemed to be happening. The French occupied the Maginot Line and the extension of the Line North-Westwards behind the Belgian frontier, though this extension had not been fortified in advance. The British Army disappeared to France, where General Gort, previously CIGS, assumed command of the British Expeditionary Force; in Whitehall he was succeeded by General Sir Edmund Ironside. The Territorial Army was embodied, and the air defences stood by continuously; a new phenomenon, barrage balloons, flew in their hundreds over London, whence large numbers of children had been dispersed to other parts of Britain. At sea, the Royal Navy conducted their operations efficiently, but for the most part silently. The British people found the situation strange: they were certainly not living a normal peace-time existence, yet nothing warlike seemed to be happening. Jacob felt that the situation had its dangers: in such an atmosphere how could maximum efforts be stimulated through the nation?

He and Cecil adjusted their private life to suit the needs of wartime. They gave up the house at Camberley, and took a flat at Nell Gwyn House in Chelsea. The Red House was still available for weekends; they had had their leave there in the summer with a hired yacht on the river. At their schools, the boys were reasonably safe: John at Sherborne, and William at Rottingdean.

The Government too had settled down to a new routine. The War Cabinet met daily, and the Chiefs of Staff had their own meeting earlier, so that they could go to the War Cabinet having digested the day's news, and having discussed in a preliminary fashion any problems that had arisen. Jacob and his colleagues considered that the War Cabinet under Chamberlain's chairmanship was a well-conducted body; the agenda and supporting papers were methodically circulated in advance, and duly considered at the meeting. Yet in some strange fashion nothing seemed to happen. There was no obvious sense of urgency or drive. Although suitable as Chairman in peace-time, the Prime Minister was not equipped to be a powerful war leader. True there was little that could be done to impart urgency and drive to operations. The Navy required no spur that could not be provided by Churchill their First Lord. The Army was building up and training, and the Royal Air Force was doing the same. There was still an enormous leeway to make up in trained forces, in equipment, and in ammunition and stores of every kind, and it was here that the absence of drive was most apparent. The newly-formed Ministry of Supply was not yet equal to the task required of it: Mr Burgin, the Minister, did not have the personality to galvanise a ministry charged with an urgent and difficult task, nor was he well informed about the factors involved in war production. Jacob realised that it was more difficult to work up intense activity when nothing seemed to be happening, and when most people in their heart of hearts hoped that perhaps nothing ever would happen. Obviously it was not in Chamberlain's character to provide the spark which was so grievously missing.

There were further difficulties during this period of the twilight war due to the continued existence of the Minister for Co-ordination of Defence, and the personalities of the Ministers involved. Even in that period of spasmodic, small scale operations, it became increasingly obvious to Jacob that ineffectiveness must result if the Prime Minister continued to delegate to subordinate Ministers the conduct of grand strategy.

Moreover there was a lack of balance in the ministerial machine. The four wheels of the Governmental coach had to be of the same size if it was to roll forward smoothly. To install Churchill at the Admiralty in a subordinate position to Chatfield at the centre, and to match him on a level with Hore-Belisha at the War Office and Kingsley Wood at the Air Ministry, seemed to Jacob to be asking for trouble. Hore-Belisha, who could have contributed a great deal, was dismissed in January 1940 because of the difficult relations which had developed between him and senior officers in France and in the War Office. The various parts of the Government's machine had clearly not been selected for harmonious running: in consequence, the Military Co-ordination Committee had a stormy and unproductive life.

As to Churchill, there had been much opposition to him among senior Conservatives and, whereas in the co-ordinating role he might have threatened Chamberlain's position, the idea of 'Winston back at the Admiralty' offended no one, and had the romantic tinge that the public liked. That he might prove too big for his slot in the machine would thus have to be accepted. The result was an increasingly dangerous disharmony, which Jacob viewed with dismay.

Churchill had plenty of opportunity as First Lord of the Admiralty to accustom himself to directing the war at sea, as he had done in World War I; for the lull that, unexpectedly, had followed the declaration of war had not extended to naval operations. This fact was sometimes obscured by the lack of communiqués, the apparent absence of any activity of the Army in France, and the welcome anti-climax at home. There was admittedly no early likelihood of a challenge to Britain's command of the sea from German surface forces; but from the start, the Royal Navy had to meet the menace of unrestricted submarine warfare, and the probability of raiding cruisers loosed upon the Atlantic sea routes. The Expeditionary Force had been safely transported to France and its line of communications across the Channel safeguarded; and throughout the oceans, measures to initiate a naval blockade and to ensure the steady movement of our own shipping had been taken. All these problems had been familiar to Churchill, and he had fallen easily into the daily and nightly routine of naval control, exercised, as in the past, by the Admiralty.

He also played a very full part in the War Cabinet, though the circumstances were uncongenial and frustrating. To him it was particularly baffling to be at war with an enemy who made no move in the main theatre of operations, while paradoxically British strength was so woefully deficient that no initiative by them was possible. Jacob observed that each event that occurred began with a carefully-prepared situation brought about by the Germans, followed by a hastily improvised allied reaction.

Very soon it became evident to Jacob that Churchill's capacity was such that he would find plenty of time for matters beyond the concerns of the Admiralty. His long experience, and particularly his memories of World War I, made it possible for him to interest himself in the whole spread of Government activity. He began to circulate to his colleagues memoranda on all kinds of subjects, and these were not calculated to endear him to the ministers into whose field of responsibility he was trespassing. With him, thought led at once to action, which took the form of a written memo, inquiring, suggesting, urging; no minister distributed a greater volume of words, or dabbled in a wider range of subjects.

In the Military Co-ordination Committee, Jacob found that

Churchill did not hesitate to enquire into the affairs of the other two Services, and in so doing to go much further than his colleagues thought to be right or proper. Undignified squabbles and exasperation were the result. From time to time, Chamberlain took the Chair himself at the Committee; but when he was not there, it was evident that Churchill was so much the most experienced and commanding figure present that the position of his colleagues was made very difficult. Being lesser men, they resented Churchill's interference, and were less able to cope, lacking his advantages in personality and experience. They were reluctant to submit to direction by Churchill whom they regarded as an equal colleague, and resented his fiery efforts to drive things along. In this situation Churchill did not show up well, appearing to Jacob to be opportunist and changeable.

The position was just as frustrating to Churchill as it was to his colleagues, though for a different reason. They wanted to be left to get on with the build-up of their forces and run their departments as they were accustomed to do in peacetime, and they objected to this bull in a china shop who poked his head into everything, and harried them in a disagreeable manner. Churchill, on the other hand, found himself trying to impart energy and drive into the war effort, and to use his great talents on a scale for which they were fitted, while serving in a comparatively junior post. He could not be satisfied unless he was in supreme control, and he would feel no disquiet when the time came for him to assume that position.

The inadequacy of Government machinery for controlling operations was starkly exposed in the Norwegian campaign of April 1940. Planning before that date had repeatedly been frustrated by the need to secure the agreement of neutral Norway to any precautionary action. When, finally, mines were laid in the Norwegian leads, the activity was found to coincide with the unexpected German invasion.

Immediate counter-measures became necessary, but both the planning and execution of them were hindered by the lack of a central command system: there was no single commander responsible for all Norwegian operations, nor was there a tri-service headquarters in the area. Further confusion was caused by the unilateral actions of the Admiralty, and by Churchill's insistence on receiving operational signals direct without staff intervention. Thus the Cabinet frequently found itself examining an operational situation based exclusively on naval signals, unsupported by Army and Air counterparts; the Army and Air Ministers did not adopt a similar system, while the Minister for Co-ordination of Defence and the Prime Minister received no signals at all.

It was not surprising that, throughout the disastrous period of the campaign, Churchill's behaviour brought reminders to Jacob of Churchill at Antwerp, Churchill and the Dardanelles, even Churchill at Sidney Street. The First Lord seemed to keep his eyes too close to that part of the scene where operations seemed to be most lively. He was disinclined to take a little extra time to allow well-conceived plans to be made. Brave and pugnacious he certainly was, but to Jacob at this time he seemed not at all balanced or wise. Few could foresee how this star would shine when established in the right quarter of the firmament.

Fortunately, failure in the Norwegian Campaign was not of vital importance. Jacob consoled himself that it had not lost the war. Defeat was not due solely to lack of a proper system of command and to the absence of a capable prime minister; the enemy had held the initiative and had carried out his offensive plans successfully, unhindered in any way by moral scruple.

The occupation of Norway was a great gain to the enemy, as was found later when convoys to Archangel had to be run. However, some very valuable lessons were learnt in the War Cabinet before much more devastating operations took place. Disaster prepared the way for a change of government and for the acceptance of a prime minister of different calibre, who would also seize the reins of war as Minister of Defence.

On 10 May, Hitler launched his long-awaited attack on Holland and Belgium, and the twilight war was ended.

4

Churchill at the Helm

On that same evening of 10 May, after 'an avalanche of fire and steel' had rolled across the Dutch frontiers supported by an overwhelming onslaught from the air, Churchill was summoned by the King and asked to form a Government. By 10 pm that night, the new Prime Minister had sent to the Palace the names of his National Government, including Eden at the War Office, and Chamberlain as Lord President of the Council and Leader of the House of Commons. Churchill himself assumed the office of Minister of Defence without attempting to define its scope and powers.

Great changes would now ensue in the War Cabinet Office, and Jacob, who had been a familiar figure to the erstwhile First Lord of the Admiralty, could reasonably expect that much of the frustration of the twilight war would be lifted. He was now a highly esteemed officer in the talented band led by Ismay. His capacity for concentrated work was recognised as exceptional; and both his equals and superiors knew that any problem put to him would be addressed in depth with great thoroughness, leading quickly to the production of a manifestly sound solution, which would be presented in faultless language, either verbally or on paper. Under pressure from the many crises, which habitually occurred in the Office from which the nation's war effort was directed, his coolness under stress had been closely observed. Hankey on ceasing to be a member of the War Cabinet wrote to thank him for his 'most efficient help', ending his letter with: 'You are a true son of your father, and that is very high praise'.

Jacob did not suffer fools gladly, and some of his colleagues would have been happier if the Lieutenant Colonel's seemingly severe personality had been varied by flashes of extrovert charm; but just as his father, the Field Marshal, had been regarded as self-effacing, his modest son, whose every energy was concentrated on winning the war, could spare little time artificially to sweeten relationships. Nevertheless, if his demeanour at work was austere, there were many who, having looked more deeply, would value his friendship for countless years after the rigours of war had ceased.

But now the whole of Jacob's life was centred on the war. Cecil had left London for Woodbridge to look after her elderly father and mother; there she immediately launched herself into war work with the Red Cross, and canteens for the troops. Ian based himself in his father's flat in Ovington Court and, when late slept in the War Room complex. He usually had a quick lunch at the Army and Navy Club and, if time permitted, played there a rubber of bridge or a game of squash, before returning to the office.

The news that Churchill was Prime Minister was received with mixed feelings. There were some in Parliament, and in the most senior posts in the official hierarchy, who received it with relief and high expectation. They knew more of Churchill than did Jacob and his colleagues, and could distinguish the qualities that fitted him to lead the nation at a time of great danger. At a lower level, Jacob at that time formed the view that Churchill's actions were those of an energetic but undisciplined mind. In particular, he had seen the disarray that these methods had created during the Norway Campaign. Hence, Jacob's first reaction was that the new Prime Minister would create chaos in the governmental machine, would upset all his colleagues, and that the future would be a long succession of bitter disputes.

However, he soon began to appreciate that, although Churchill cared little for organisation or for methodical working, he had perfected a personal technique for inspiring and leading his colleagues and obtaining the maximum effort from all of them. The methodical but uninspiring chairman had gone; the driving, if unorthodox, chief executive had taken over. Long after the war, Jacob wrote: 'I well remember the misgivings of many of us in the War Cabinet Office. We had not the experience or the imagination to realise the difference between a human dynamo when humming on the periphery and when driving at the centre.'[1]

That the chaos was largely reduced to order was primarily due to the clear-sightedness of General Ismay. He succeeded in connecting the central dynamo, which might otherwise have run itself to bits and damaged all around it, to the carefully organised machinery of military control, which was already in existence waiting for someone to lay hold of it and use its full potential. What Ismay did on the military

CHURCHILL AT THE HELM

side, Bridges did on the civil. Surprisingly soon, the whole Government machine was adjusted to the new driving force and began to operate with ever-increasing efficiency, if with considerable heat.

The existence within the War Cabinet of a Military Staff, fully appraised of the current situation, enabled it to act immediately as the office of the Minister of Defence: it secured for him the necessary information, handled his military correspondence and telegrams and followed up his instructions and minutes. This staff was very small; including General Ismay, there were with Jacob a further six officers, though there were a few other staff officers engaged in special duties which set them apart from the central work of the office of the Minister of Defence. The essence of the arrangement, which was rigidly adhered to, was that the Minister should be served by a small 'handling machine', the same indeed that had served the Chiefs of Staff Committee and its subordinate bodies such as the Joint Planning Staff. The Minister of Defence did not create a Ministry. All the executive work was performed by those officers from the Chiefs of Staff downwards who held the appropriate responsibility in their own departments.

Thus Jacob and the other members of the office of the Minister of Defence had no executive responsibility, and were not advisers to the Chiefs of Staff or to the Minister on strategy or plans. It was indeed of vital importance that they should not usurp any of the powers or duties of those who held the responsibility for execution and were in the direct chain of command. If they had done so, they would very soon have created friction and mistrust, and their usefulness would have come to an end. They were able, however, to do much to facilitate the work of the inter-service staffs: they could prevent overlapping and suggest ways in which problems should be handled and, from their wide and growing experience of the central core of Government, they could be of great help to their committees and to the departmental staffs. It was fortunate that the office of the Minister of Defence had at its head a man of the quality of General Ismay who saw so clearly the essentials of smooth working, and who set such an example of selfless devotion in serving the interests of the Minister and of the Chiefs of Staff Committee.

For the first month of his administration, Churchill lived and worked in the Admiralty, while Chamberlain prepared to move out of No 10. This had created a difficulty which might have had serious consequences if Ismay had not been fully alive to it.

While installed at the Admiralty, Churchill could hardly be seen to be detached from the role he had been playing during the previous eight months, and it was difficult for visitors to feel that they were entering not a Service Department but the central point of Government. There was inevitably a certain lack of order, and it was much too easy for the lines of communication to get crossed. Ismay's solution to this difficulty was to remain at the Prime Minister's side or in his ante-room continuously, keeping a grip on the military activities that took place; thus he could steer into the right channel the stream of requests for information, demands for immediate action, and proposals for the development of the military effort. He could also ensure that the responsible officers were summoned either for meetings called by the Prime Minister or for questioning. This procedure called for great endurance and tact, particularly as it was difficult for Ismay to mobilise the full support available from his own office which remained at Richmond Terrace. He succeeded, nevertheless, in making the Prime Minister realise that he had, in existence, a highly organised military framework in actual operation day or night. The essential process of establishing mutual trust and confidence between the Prime Minister and the Chiefs of Staff and the War Cabinet Staff gradually began. As the procedure evolved, it resulted in the recognition by the Prime Minister of Ismay and his small military staff as the 'Office of the Minister of Defence'.

It was not long before Jacob began to receive, from the Prime Minister's Office in the Admiralty, minutes typed in double spacing on quarto paper with the famous red tag projecting above the top of the paper, bearing in black letters the phrase 'Action this day'. There were other tags of lesser urgency, but it was this one which remained for ever in his memory.

Another traffic, even more continuous, developed in the shape of military telegrams from Commanders-in-Chief abroad, which the Minister of Defence insisted on receiving at once, even though they were addressed to one of the Chiefs of Staff or to the Chiefs of Staff Committees as a body. It very quickly became clear that a special centre was required in the office of the Minister of Defence to handle this traffic, to register it, and to furnish or secure replies to the minutes received. Ismay charged Jacob with the formation of this centre, and gave him the responsibility of handling the PM's military correspondence. Jacob established what was known as the Defence Registry, and he remained responsible for it throughout the war.

Handling the Prime Minister's minutes was by no means an easy task: Churchill paid little attention to organisation or to levels of responsibility, nor was he always right in his assumption of whom to address on a particular subject. Hence, although a minute had to be passed straight on to the addressee, Jacob would have to take steps to see that the answer came from the responsible source, which could well be someone different. Moreover the intensity of concentration of the Prime Minister's mind was such that he often fired off minutes on the same topic at close intervals, and some of the sequence of which might be addressed to a civil authority, and thus would not pass through Jacob's hands. Close working relations had to be established with the PM's private secretaries if the staff was to serve him properly with appropriate speed.

Jacob was deeply impressed by the remarkable spirit infused into their daily routine by General Ismay, and his method of conducting affairs. Tenaciously and continually Ismay saw the needs of his exacting master, and spared no trouble to ensure that, regardless of how tiresome they might be, Churchill's requests should be complied with. Yet Ismay was in no sense a 'yes-man'. He never gave way when he judged that a principle was at stake, and he would do his utmost to prevent the Prime Minister from insisting on a course which he felt would be harmful or dangerous. He would fight equally hard for the Prime Minister's wishes when they were being opposed on grounds of their inconvenience or their unimportance. He was thus splendidly equipped to stand between the Prime Minister on the one hand and the Chiefs of Staff on the other, understanding both, and easing the inevitable friction between strong-willed men engaged in work of extreme importance. He assumed that each member of his staff was inspired by the same devotion to the task as himself, and thus he was able to treat them with complete confidence and without formality.

Churchill's chief task on coming to power was to deal with the appalling military situation that was developing in North-West Europe. The advance of the Allies into Belgium had gone forward deceptively smoothly, but a few days later it had been brought to a standstill when the German Armies, in great strength, had broken through the French front between Sedan and Dinant on the Meuse. By this unexpected stratagem, the essential hinge of the Allies' defensive plan had been struck away, and almost immediately a desperate cry for help came from the French Government: the Prime Minister, Reynaud, told Churchill by telephone 'the battle is lost'.

Then came the terrible sequence of events which Churchill had to master while his Government was barely formed and his own position hardly established. When the crisis burst on them on 15 May, Jacob who, as one of the Secretaries, had attended the first meeting of Churchill's War Cabinet on 13 May, was much impressed by the Prime Minister's controlled reaction. Churchill decided immediately to fly to Paris to learn at first hand what was happening: he took with him Ismay and the new CIGS, Dill, who had succeeded Ironside. From Reynaud they learnt that the French had no reserves to counter-attack the German divisions pouring through the gap at Sedan. Disaster was imminent.

On the return of Churchill to Whitehall, it was reassuring to Jacob that there was little apparent dismay: all possible action was to be pressed forward to make the best of the dire situation, and it seemed that no chain of circumstances, however daunting, could shake Churchill's spirit, or make him doubt his ability to master events. Perhaps the hard knocks given and received, which had always been a natural part of Churchill's life, gave him the strength and confidence to withstand any blow that fate could deliver. No doubt his long experience of war and of high office, and his tumultuous years in Parliament, had also hardened his fibre, and inured him to disappointment and to failure. At sixty-five, Churchill seemed to the forty-year-old Jacob to be at the height of his mental powers and possessed with the physical endurance of a young man, while his capacity for work was phenomenal.

Jacob observed the pattern of the Prime Minister's régime as it became established; the surprising element in it was the hour's sleep that he took each afternoon, not necessarily immediately after lunch but at some convenient time between 2.30 pm and 6 pm. The effect of this sleep was to enable him to work a thirteen-hour day, seven days a week and month after month. A typical day in his 91 hour week would be five hours work from 8 am to 1 pm, and four hours from 4 pm to 8 pm, followed by another four from 10 pm to 2 am.

Living in the specially created flat on the ground floor of his office in Storey's Gate, Churchill allowed himself little or no time for private life. There were few if any fixed points in his day; business was transacted in writing, and he avoided interviews as much as possible, and seldom allowed staff officers or secretaries to bring papers in and discuss them with him. Jacob understood that political discussions sometimes took place, and he was aware that one or other of the Chiefs of Staff was summoned from time to time, but in general the Prime Minister avoided time-wasting talk. He dealt with papers at any time of the day or night, without anyone being present except a stenographer. When interested in some topic, he would pursue it, leaving other work to pile up. He liked to concentrate his effort and build up a drive behind a project, thrusting aside any diversion until everything had been done. There was no procrastination when action was afoot, and he was always on the watch for possible obstruction by officials.

During inevitable lulls in active operations, his machinery was apt to race, and he immediately began to seek ways in which further action could be stirred up. His pugnacious spirit demanded action and he wanted the enemy to 'bleed and burn' everywhere at all times. However, at this early stage of his administration, there was no lack of action, and it was as much as even Churchill could do to cope with the catastrophic developments in France.

It was not long before the Prime Minister and Minister of Defence impinged on Jacob's daily duties, as he was responsible for feeding the PM with information, for passing on to him important telegrams, for dealing with his minutes on military subjects and for co-ordinating replies. Ismay and Hollis tended to be absorbed in matters arising from or moving towards the Chiefs of Staff.

The Chiefs of Staff Committee met every morning at 10.30 am. Whereas, before Churchill's advent to power, these meetings had often been routine and had seldom led to further meetings, and certainly had not resulted in papers and reports being sent in to Chamberlain, things were now much more lively. Often there would be a minute written that morning by the PM in bed to be urgently considered; sometimes the meeting broke up to resume later; and often a meeting of the Defence Committee was called before or after dinner. Hence it became necessary to strengthen and concentrate the Cabinet Office Staff dealing with the Chiefs of Staff business. Ismay was always present as an additional member, Hollis was the Secretary, and he was backed up by two assistant secretaries who did no other committee work except for the servicing of the Vice-Chiefs.

By this time, the Defence Committee had been split into the Defence Committee (Operations) and the Defence Committee (Supply). The latter became Jacob's particular responsibility and, although no hard and fast rule ever applied, his work tended to lie generally in the field where military and civil agencies were both involved. At different times in the War, he was Secretary of the Atlantic Committee, the Munitions Assignment Board, the 'Tank Parliament', the Cabinet Committee on manpower, the Joint War Production Staff, and the Post-War Committee for Europe. He was also apt to be the link between the military machine and the Foreign

Office, the Ministry of Production and the Ministry of Labour. There were, of course, numerous channels of direct contact between the civil ministries and the Service Departments which did not involve the Cabinet Office at all, but when there were important matters which affected several interests and which came to the notice of the PM, Jacob was usually the focus for action on them. He kept in very close touch with the Chiefs of Staff, and often attended their meetings and those of the Defence Committee (Operations), because it was a principle of the Cabinet Office that the load could be adjusted as required. He was also available, as required, either to travel, or to stay and 'mind the shop', when conferences were afoot.

In the summer of 1940, the PM sought by every possible means to stimulate the flow of munitions and to get arms from America. It was in this task that his drive and his unorthodox method seemed to Jacob to be so valuable. Churchill did not confine himself to the orthodox channel; he did not leave it to Ministers to get on with their duties undisturbed. Like Lord Beaverbrook, who was busy creating chaos while hastening the flow of fighters, the PM bombarded everyone who seemed to have any degree of responsibility for the matter in hand. The minute with the red label, the meeting called late at night and followed up with more minutes, instilled in the recipients a feeling of insecurity which had a startling effect. Some of Jacob's colleagues thought that the PM attended too much to details which should have been left to lesser people, but they were nevertheless aware that if they did not do their utmost to meet the PM's demands another minute would arrive on their desks, or on the desk of their superior. Jacob often heard his colleagues complain that it was silly to create such a commotion when plans had already been laid and things were coming along nicely, but they knew perfectly well that the heat was on them in a way they had not previously experienced, and that results would be publicly revealed.

On his own initiative, the PM had set up a little unofficial research department to develop anti-tank weapons. Jacob was delighted that this was headed by Major MR Jefferis MC, the Sapper who had so successfully carried out the reconnaissance of the Waziristan Circular Road in 1922: he was a first-rate, imaginative officer who had come to Churchill's attention by developing a mine for use against barges on the Rhine and on the German canals. The unit was under the wing of Professor Lindemann, whom Jacob came to know for the first time during this period. Although Jacob found that 'the Prof' occasionally hit a winner, he came to regard him later as a 'licensed gadfly'.[2]

In handling munitions production problems, Jacob had to cope with Churchill's devastating method of argument. On one occasion having presented to him the Ministry of Supply's plan for tank production, showing the dates several months ahead when each batch would reach armoured units, Churchill's first query was: 'Why are you proposing to produce one thousand obsolete tanks?' This startling comment was of course a half-truth, in that by the date that the last batch would enter the service, the first batch, supplied many months before, might well be approaching obsolescence, taking into account the limited rate of production and the speed with which technological improvements might emerge in war. However, the proper question for Churchill to have put was: 'Why cannot the rate of production be increased?' – for which of course, the national resources at that time were insufficient.

Churchill's method of arguing, developed perhaps in politics, was to place strong emphasis on one particular sore point, and disregard many of the surrounding factors. The result was that the person addressed did not know whether to defend the particular point seized upon, or deal with the disregarded factors in order to get the correct emphasis restored. Churchill would continue the attack, and the unfortunate victim might often relapse into confused silence. Jacob found that the only remedy was a vigorous reply, even a counterattack, followed by a clear and accurate statement of the entire case. Those capable of such a rejoinder had no difficulty in holding their own, and earned the Prime Minister's respect. Those who did not found him most unreasonable, and failed to win his esteem.

During the remaining weeks of May 1940, Jacob, who had many friends and contemporaries in the BEF, lived through the appalling events of the Belgian Army's surrender, the retreat to Dunkirk and the victorious onward march of the German Army towards the Channel Coast. For him at his desk in Whitehall, and for the British people as a whole, sole comfort lay in Churchill's magnificent speeches of defiance; these raised Jacob's spirits, despite his anxieties at the difficulty of translating eloquent defiance into hard military achievement.

On the morning of 30 May, Lieutenant General Pownall, Gort's Chief of Staff, came to London to report on the arrangements for evacuation from Dunkirk, which had started two days before. Jacob was present as secretary of that grim Defence Committee Meeting and he recalled later:

> The Prime Minister questioned General Pownall and listened to the plans. No one in the room imagined that they would be successful if the German armoured

divisions supported by the Luftwaffe pressed their attack; the perimeter would be broken as it thinned out, and there would be carnage on the beaches. Churchill never gave a sign of weakness. Nothing but encouragement and resolve showed in his face or his voice.

'We felt' Jacob added, 'that he would like to be fighting on the beaches himself.'[3]

On 2 June, by which time 222 naval vessels and 665 other ships had been involved in the successful evacuation, it was decided that only night operations should continue, and on the next day evacuation ceased. The Chiefs of Staff then turned their attention to the problems of the French, and particularly a request from Reynaud for the return to France of three British divisions that had been evacuated, and for British fighter squadrons to operate from French airfields.

Jacob, who was present at that meeting, recalled that, regardless of advice given by the Air C-in-C, Air Marshal Dowding, Churchill had never contemplated denuding the United Kingdom of the fighter strength it needed. The problem was how much could be spared without weakening too greatly the British defences. Unfortunately the Prime Minister and the Chiefs of Staff kept receiving conflicting statements as to the number of aircraft available, but eventually the decision was taken at a Defence Committee Meeting on 8 June, which Jacob attended, to inform the French that no further aircraft could be spared.

On 14 June, the German Army entered Paris, and on the 22nd the French Government signed an armistice with Germany.

In the United Kingdom, step by step, the British Army, saved from Dunkirk, was being re-equipped, redeployed and re-trained to face the prospect of invasion. The priority now shifted to coast and air defence, the subjects for which Jacob had had responsibility in the War Office in 1934. Meanwhile Churchill continued his efforts to obtain munitions from the United States. During the summer months when, in addition to air bombardment by the Luftwaffe, invasion was expected at any time, Jacob was heavily engaged in defence matters outside the purview of Army Commanders but close to the interests of the Prime Minister. The subjects of his reports included the construction of trenches, even on agricultural land, to act as obstacles against enemy landings by troop carriers – a subject of great controversy with civilian ministries – the examination of tides and phases of the moon to determine the most likely times of an enemy invasion, studies of the incidence of fog which it was thought might be of great assistance to an invading enemy, daily reports to the PM on the state of enemy preparations for invasion, daily reports of supplies received or expected from the United States, plans for the move of the War Cabinet and other officials to their protected headquarters at Dollis Hill, statements on the production of anti-aircraft weapons and of special radar stations inland from the coast, and the development of aerials for the control of searchlights by night. In addition to these duties, Jacob was often called upon to escort the Prime Minister on visits of inspection.

Despite the intensity of effort that now involved everyone in Whitehall, humour was not entirely lacking, particularly in the case of John Peck, one of Churchill's private secretaries who had a gift for the ridiculous. While in the Cabinet War Room he produced most realistically the following minute:

Action this Day
Pray let six new offices be fitted for my use, in Selfridges Lambeth Palace, Stanmore, Tooting Bec, the Palladium and Mile End Road. I will inform you at 6 each evening at which office I shall dine, work and sleep. Accommodation will be required for Mrs Churchill, two shorthand typists, three secretaries and Nelson*. There should be shelter for all and a place for me to watch air raids from the roof. This should be completed by Monday. There is to be no hammering during office hours, that is between 7 am and 3 am.

WSC

*The Black Cat

John Colville, another secretary to the PM, confided in his diary that the document had 'entirely convinced Morton, Jacob, Seal, Ismay and others of its authenticity – which goes to show the state of attrition to which all these moves and constantly changing plans had reduced the PM's entourage.'[4]

Despite the Blitz and the black-out, London continued to function. Jacob was at Ovington Court with his father during some of the worst of the raids. At Woodbridge the golf course was obstructed with barriers of tubular scaffolding to deter enemy gliders. It was an unsuitable place for the boys' summer holidays, but fortunately the Jacobs were lent a house in Oxfordshire by some friends.

Jacob thrived on work, but nevertheless in September 1940 he became restless. There was a growing feeling that the danger of invasion would soon subside. Moreover many of his friends and contemporaries who had survived the Dunkirk operation were now engaged in active operations elsewhere: others had been killed and yet others had achieved fame. He felt it was time to break away from the bureaucratic régime of Whitehall and become an active Sapper once more. So in a carefully phrased letter, he applied to Ismay to be released to regimental duty:

> *Gen Ismay*
>
> This is an application for my release to regimental duty. I shall have completed two years in the office in October, but this would not have caused me to ask you to let me go if it were not for other reasons. These are:
>
> (a) My present job is barely enough to keep me busy and is getting less and less on the military side of the house. The PM's mail does not take long to deal with, because nearly all the important items go immediately into the COS machine, and I have nothing further to do with them. The rest of my work for the PM is on the Defence Committee (Supply) which has spasms of intense activity, and longer periods of calm during which there is only a routine collection of figures to be done. It is largely a civil job.
>
> (b) I am now entirely out of the COS orbit. The ODC gets less and less to do as the operational theatres of war expand round the world, and the PDC does not occupy much time, reckoned over a period.
>
> (c) I missed the last war by a week, and I am not at all anxious to be out of the Army for the period when active operations on land are taking place. Unless I get back to the Army fairly soon, I shall be so out of touch that I shall be a liability rather than an asset to any formation to which I am posted. If I could do six months regimental work this winter, I might be of some use to the Army next summer.
>
> I am most unwilling to cause you any inconvenience, and I realize that the smooth working of this office is of more importance than personal feelings; but it does seem that an opportunity has now presented itself for me to be released without any dislocation. What I would suggest would be that I should be permitted to tell AG7 that I am available for a command on or after 1 October. My work could then either be passed on to a successor, or be farmed out amongst the others according as you thought best.
>
> I couldn't want for a pleasanter job than this one, but I feel that I am taking the right course in asking you to let me go, and hope you will be able to consent.
>
> *EIJ* 3/9/40
>
> The letter was passed to Colonel Hollis, who minuted to Ismay: . . . We should all feel the breeze very keenly if Jacob is allowed to go. I can, I think, off-load a certain amount (I have purposely avoided doing so hitherto). It was not intended that Ian should be 'outside the Chiefs of Staff orbit' – far from it.
>
> Suggest he should stay anyway until Xmas.
>
> LCH 5/9/40

Ismay then replied to Jacob's application as follows:

> We discussed this today, I entirely sympathise with your feelings, but I do not think that it would be in the national interest for you to revert to regimental duty at present. Let us review the position in two or three months.
>
> HL Ismay 6/9/40

Jacob reconciled himself to continuing in the service of the Prime Minister who, years later, would write of his Secretariat as follows:

> At the head stood General Ismay, with Colonel Hollis and Colonel Jacob as his two principals, and a group of specially selected younger officers from all three Services. This Secretariat became the staff of the office of the Minister of Defence. My debt to its members is immeasurable. General Ismay, Colonel Hollis and Colonel Jacob rose steadily in rank and repute as the war proceeded and none of them was changed. Displacements in a sphere so intimate and so concerned with secret matters are detrimental to continuous and efficient discharge of business.[5]

In October, a month after Jacob's application 'to go to the war' had been refused, Italian forces invaded Greece, but initially were repulsed. However, German forces then occupied Romania and prepared to enter Bulgaria. Churchill, encouraged by the Greek resistance turned his attention to the possibility of confronting the Germans in the Balkans – 'the soft underbelly of the Axis' – and of bringing Turkey and Yugoslavia into the war. Thus the idea was born of supporting Greece by sending British forces, to be withdrawn from North Africa, where Wavell's operation COMPASS, with General O'Connor in command, was being planned as a five-day raid against the Italian forces in Cyrenaica.

COMPASS, launched on 9 December 1940, succeeded beyond all expectations; after brilliant operations against weak Italian resistance, O'Connor's forces captured Benghazi and reached El Agheila on 8 February 1941. However, the formations withdrawn from the Western Desert which had sailed to Greece on 5 March to support the Greek Army failed to withstand the German attack, and were withdrawn after heavy losses on 26 April, to undertake the defence of Crete.

In Whitehall, Jacob was privy to many of the discussions which had led to the decision to weaken the Western Desert Force in order to support Greece. Despite the political advantages that might be claimed for it. Jacob, like most of the Defence Staff, had been astonished that Wavell, C-in-C Middle East, had never called for a purely military appreciation, but had accepted the practicability of the plan on military grounds. Jacob regarded it as a dangerous diversion.

The outcome was disastrous both in Greece and in the Western Desert. Rommel with his Deutsche Afrika Corps had arrived in Tripolitania in February 1941, and in March advanced eastwards against the British forces now gravely weakened by the diversions to Greece.

By the Spring of 1941, Yugoslavia and Greece had fallen to the Axis Powers, and at the end of May British forces were evacuated from Crete after heavy losses. In June, Hitler launched his long-awaited invasion of the Soviet Union.

After the disaster of Crete, the failure in June of Wavell's operation BATTLEAXE against Rommel, and the mounting threat to Egypt, Churchill decided to replace Wavell with Auchinleck, the C-in-C India. Wavell, after carrying a very heavy load for two years, was sent to India as C-in-C. Churchill had great expectations of Auchinleck: Jacob recalled the Prime Minister holding out both his hands as if he had a fishing rod in each, and saying: 'I feel I have a tired fish on this rod, and a very lively one on the other'.

Soon, more extensive operations would be developing worldwide and Jacob, when not at his desk in Whitehall, would find himself engaged on a larger stage.

5

With Churchill to Meet Roosevelt

Hitler's attack on the Soviet Union on 22 June 1941 produced for Britain the bonus of a new ally, however awkward, in the East: while in the West, the United States, which from the beginning had sought to provide maximum assistance within the limitations of nominal neutrality, now had to face a further extension of the war. In Churchill's negotiations with each of these allies, Jacob would soon be called upon to play an important part.

Churchill had always anticipated that, sooner or later, the United States would be drawn into the war. Immediately after the Dunkirk defeat, in a speech to the House of Commons on 4 June 1940, he had affirmed that Britain would never surrender, and had declared that even if the British Isles were subjugated, the struggle would be continued by the Empire guarded by the British Fleet 'until in God's good time the New World with all its power and might, would set forth to the rescue and liberation of the old'.[1]

Pursuing that policy, he had established by correspondence a unique personal relationship with President Roosevelt, reviving their association in World War I by using the title 'Former naval person'. Stimulated by that relationship at the top, much had already been done to obtain vital munitions – aircraft of all types, army equipment and the historic transfer of over-age destroyers to maintain Britain's capacity to continue the war while under air bombardment and submarine attacks against her sea communications.

A purchasing Committee under an industrialist, Arthur Purvis, had been set up in Washington as early as December 1939; and in October 1940 an agreement had been signed by Sir Walter Layton, Director General of the Ministry of Supply, with General Marshall the American Chief of Staff, for the provision of equipment for ten British Divisions.

Moreover, in January 1941, a delegation led by Rear Admiral Bellairs had been sent to Washington to frame a combined global strategy in the event of war spreading to the United States and the Pacific. Agreement had been reached that first priority should be given to the defeat of Hitler, and powerful American aid in the Battle of the Atlantic had followed. Permanent Anglo-American staff Missions had then been established in Washington. Most important of all these developments, was the passing by Congress on 9 March 1941 of the Lend-Lease Bill.

By the summer of 1941, the British War Cabinet was facing a series of very critical problems: strong enemy pressure, not yet mastered, in the Battle of the Atlantic: the unsatisfactory situation in North Africa after the failure of Wavell's BATTLEAXE offensive: the implications of Japanese activities in the Far East: lastly, difficult relations with the Soviet Union, and the extent of aid to be rendered to them in their desperate struggle against the Wehrmacht.

Towards the end of July, Harry Hopkins, Roosevelt's intimate friend and special envoy to Britain, who had by now established exceptionally warm relations with Churchill, told him in the garden of 10 Downing Street that the President wished very much to meet him, perhaps at sea in some unfrequented anchorage. Churchill accepted the invitation immediately, and at once obtained the permission of the King to absent himself from the United Kingdom, and the endorsement of the Cabinet. Placentia Bay in Newfoundland was chosen for the rendezvous, and Sunday 3 August was set as the date of departure of a large delegation from the United Kingdom.

The Prime Minister's party comprised the Chiefs of Staff, with Sir Alexander Cadogan the Permanent Under Secretary of the Foreign Office, Professor Lindemann, now Lord Cherwell, Colonel Hollis, Mr JM Martin, Churchill's principal private secretary, Commander Thompson, Lieutenant Colonel Jacob and Inspector Thomson. The Service staffs comprised Brigadier Dykes, now Director of Plans in the War Office and five other officers.

The story of Churchill's meeting with President Roosevelt in HMS *Prince of Wales* moored with USS *Augusta* in Placentia Bay is best told in the words of Jacob's diary which he kept daily from 3 to 19 August 1941. His enjoyment of the occasion is reflected in a letter dated 8 August sent to his wife as they approached Newfoundland. He commented:

I am afraid I can't tell you a thing, but we have had an excellent trip so far
and, what is more, good weather. . . . The Old Man is in great form and has had
a real holiday. He has actually been playing backgammon. . . . Dumbie (Dykes'
nickname) and Jo (Hollis) are in good form. This is a fine 'house' we are in, and
no mistake. . . .

The diary begins:

Sunday, 3 August 1941
The start of the journey was at Marylebone Station, where a
special train was standing at No 4 Platform; at 10.30 am . . .
various members of the party arrived in good time except Dumbie
Dykes. The train was due to start at 12.30 pm, and at 12.24 we
were anxiously awaiting Dumbie's arrival; a minute later he
turned up, and when questioned as to what had happened to him
he passed it off lightly with the well-known remark, 'Send no
money!' . . .

The only people there to see the train off were Lady Cadogan
and Lawrence Burgis. The latter regretfully parted with a couple
of sixpences to Jo and myself as the result of a foolhardy bet that
the Prime Minister would be taking Mrs Churchill with him on
the trip. The engine of the train had the auspicious name of
'Sansovino': we felt that all augured well for the expedition.

At 1.30 we arrived at Wendover, the station for Chequers,
where we found the Prime Minister and his personal party waiting on the platform. The Prime Minister dressed in his 'siren suit',
came aboard in terrific form. CAS and Pug were there to see us
off. Five minutes later were off.

Lunch was served at once, all the food in the world having been
collected. The PM sat with the CNS, CIGS and Sir Alexander
Cadogan.

Just as lunch was finishing, the PM suddenly jumped up in his
place, put his head over the back of his seat and said, 'Prof, what
is 24 times 365?'. Out came the Prof's slide-rule, and after considerable delay the answer was given as nearly 9,000. 'Well' said
the Prime Minister, '9,000 bottles of champagne are not too bad. I
can look back on a well-spent life. Prof, what size swimming bath
would that amount of champagne fill?'. More slide-rule, 'Well it
could easily get inside this compartment'. 'Ho', said the Prime
Minister, 'I do not think much of that. I shall have to improve on
that in the future'.

About 4 o'clock the Prime Minister went off for his sleep and the party began to settle down. . . . Dinner was served at 8, and surpassed even lunch. The food produced was of a kind we had not seen for weeks – in fact, travelling in this kind of train seems to be one long meal.

Monday, 4 August

Scrabster, which we reached at 10 am, is a tiny little harbour sheltered from the South West, but with sufficient water for destroyers to come alongside. The party had therefore to be conveyed in drifters to the two destroyers waiting in the offing. . . . We passed through the double boom guarding the Southern entrance to the Flow, and then turned the corner of Flotta Island to find the *King George V* and *Prince of Wales* lying not far apart with the *Euryalus* and *Curacoa* somewhere astern. HMS *Dorsetshire* was exercising in the middle of the Flow. We transferred to the *Prince of Wales* at 12.15 pm, and the Prime Minister almost immediately left for the *King George V* to lunch with the Commander-in-Chief.

Harry Hopkins had arrived before us by air from Moscow. It seems he had succeeded in bringing quite a fair supply of vodka and caviare with him in the flying boat. One of his first acts was to send a cable to President Roosevelt asking him to be sure to bring to the meeting place a good stock of ham, lemons, fruit and wine, as these would be very much appreciated on board.

We got under way at 4.30 pm, and Tommy reported that the things about which he had been anxious had arrived safely, namely 90 grouse for President Roosevelt. The only thing missing was the Prime Minister's globe.

Captain Pim, of the Upper War Room of the Admiralty, has fixed up a first rate miniature war room on board, in which the position of all the convoys and the latest war situation maps are displayed.

The Prime Minister has the Admiral's quarters, which are very well laid out and roomy, but as they are right over the stern there is considerable vibration. The staff have offices and cabins just forward of the Admiral's quarters.

We were all struck by the fine and jolly aspect of the ships' companies, both of the destroyers and of the *Prince of Wales*. We have naturally been hearing from the latter a good deal about their action with the *Bismarck*, during which the ship sustained a certain amount of damage and about 40 casualties. All the ship's company seem very pleased with their share in events, and feel that they benefited from their practical experience. The ship is commanded by Captain Leach, who has a great reputation among all ranks. The *Prince of Wales* seems altogether a happy ship.

At 8.45 pm the Captain announced to the whole ship's company by loudspeaker that the Prime Minister, accompanied by the Chiefs of Staff and Sir Alexander Cadogan, was on board and that he was going to Little Placentia Bay, Newfoundland, for a conference with President Roosevelt.

After dinner we had a cinematograph show in the Ward Room, at which the Prime Minister was present, wearing the Mess Dress of the Royal Yacht Squadron. The film was *Pimpernel Smith*, which he quite obviously enjoyed very much. He had not done a stroke of work during the day and was in a thoroughly good temper. [*He was greatly enjoying reading Captain Hornblower RN.*] . . . .

Tuesday, 5 August

The Prime Minister slept until 9.30 am in a cabin near the Bridge. The Admiral's quarters, which are right aft over the screw, are not very comfortable at sea, both on account of the motion of the ship and of the vibration. Consequently, the Prime Minister's party are using the Warrant Officer's Mess, which is on the port side of the main deck. The Admiral's dining room consists of two rooms, one quite large with two long dining tables capable of seating 60 or 70 people, the other smaller and fitted with a small bar at one end, an electric fireplace and a few chairs and settees. There is not room for everybody to sit down at once, but this does not matter much because all meals are at movable hours . . .

The Chiefs of Staff met at 10.30 am, and Jo and I were present. They seemed in quite good shape, but no more inclined to rattle through their business than they are on land. During the night a telegram had arrived, mostly filled with political stuff which did not get a very good reception. The second telegram, contained the morning news summary, and was short and to the point. Though still keen on hearing news, the Prime Minister on board ship seems quite content to forget about what is going on elsewhere and simply to enjoy himself, so we have not been at all troubled.

After lunch we had time for a bit of a 'shut eye', and resumed our meeting at 4 o'clock, by which time the ship had settled down to steady going and everyone was feeling all right. We had tea in the course of our meeting and the Prime Minister joined us in very skittish form. He asked the Chiefs of Staff what they were doing, and said it did him good to see them working. He then moved into the other half of the room where he and Harry Hopkins settled themselves down to listen to the wireless. I think this must be the first Chief of Staffs meeting held to the accompaniment of Bruce Belfrage's dulcet tones. We stopped work at 7 o'clock, very little business having been done.

After dinner we had another cinema show, this time *Comrade 'X'*, which was evidently a favourite film of the Prime Minister's as he displayed great enthusiasm throughout. There was also a short film taken of Harry Hopkin's arrival in Moscow. It depicted him getting out of his aeroplane and being greeted by some Russian, accompanied by General Mason Macfarlane the military attaché.

Wednesday, 6 August

The Chiefs of Staff had their usual meeting at 10.30 am, lasting until lunchtime, and continuing again at 4 pm.

The clocks were put back half an hour three times during the day – at 2 pm, 5 pm, and 7 pm – and this seemed to make the afternoon frightfully long. However, we made up for it by having two teas, one before the Chiefs of Staff meeting started, and one in the middle of it! The business done at these meetings was practically nil. However, the Chiefs are having a very good rest and it is, I am sure, doing them good.

The Prime Minister wandered about on deck and spent a lot of time in his cabin on the Bridge, but joined the party in the Warrant Officers' Mess at teatime. A regular feature of the Chiefs of Staff afternoon meetings now is the work being done in one half of the room at the same table as the teacups, while the Prime Minister and Harry Hopkins and the Prof listen to the wireless or carry on a conversation in the other half.

The telegram system seems now to be working well; we have received a number of messages at convenient times containing the kind of news required. One of these telegrams gave us the news that the Prime Minister's trip had leaked out. The Germans, in their trans-ocean broadcast, gave a report, said to have emanated from Lisbon, that the Prime Minister and President Roosevelt were going to have a meeting in the near future somewhere in the Western Hemisphere. Mr Attlee, Lord Privy Seal in London enquired what he was to do about it. The Prime Minister did not seem worried in the least, and he is secretly rather hoping the *Tirpitz* will come out and have a dart at him. We have been maintaining wireless silence most of the voyage, so that the output of telegrams from this end has been practically nil.

The Prof is a grand sight strolling leisurely up and down the deck in a yachting cap which, in the Army expression, is 'asleep'. He frequently succeeds in buttonholing one of the Chiefs of Staff for a long discussion of figures, just when the latter particularly wants to go off and have a sleep. He is, therefore, not entirely popular.

Thursday, 7 August

The Chiefs of Staff met at 10.30 am to consider the Far East, the meeting lasted an hour and three quarters. Hardly a word was uttered the whole time. CNS insisted on slowly reading right through the report of the American-British-Dutch Staff Conversations at Singapore, underlining nearly every line. He was quite undeterred by the occasional questions asked by the CIGS, questions which ranged from 'What is the food like in the Ward Room?' to 'What kind of aeroplanes have the Japanese got?'. However, by lunchtime the underlying process was finished, and the meeting was able to break up with a clear conscience. It was decided not to meet again until the following day.

Friday, 8 August

We are continuing at about 14 knots as we are well on our way and do not want to arrive too early.

A lot of the day has been taken up with rehearsals for the ceremonial which is to take place when the President comes on board. He will come over the side on the starboard side of the Quarter Deck, and a Marine Guard of Honour of about 100 men with band will be drawn up facing the ladder. The Prime Minister, the Captain, and the Chiefs of Staff will greet him; the Guard will present arms and the band will play 'The Star Spangled Banner'. Our party and the rest of the ship's officers will be drawn up on the after part of the Quarter Deck facing forward. When the guard has sloped arms again, it turns aft and marches off to the port side of the Quarter Deck. We then turn right and move forward in single file, all the officers down to and including Commanders are introduced and shake hands with him, and the remainder of the officers then march past in single file, saluting him with the left hand. All this procedure is necessary because the President is unable to walk sufficiently far to inspect the Guard and come aft to see the officers. The President will then be taken below by the Prime Minister, and special arrangements have been made for his conveyance in some kind of chair.

The programme is quite unknown at present. All that is certain is that the Prime Minister will call on the President and the President will call on the Prime Minister, but whether they will be accompanied by their Chiefs of Staff, or whether the Chiefs of Staff will go separately, will not be known until we reach harbour and there is an opportunity to consult the wishes of the Americans.

The Chiefs of Staff met once during the day, at noon. There is little more they can do now until the meetings start.

After dinner, we had the film *Lady Hamilton*. This is a fine film, excellently acted, ending with the Battle of Trafalgar and the death of Nelson. It is a favourite of the Prime Minister's, who has seen it five or six times. ... At the end of the film the Prime Minister turned to the audience in the Ward Room and said:

> I thought this would be of particular interest to you, many of whom have recently been under fire of the enemy's guns on an occasion of equal historical importance. Good night.

The Prime Minister certainly knows how to express things in a nutshell.

Saturday, 9 August

We woke to find ourselves approaching the entrance to Placentia Bay . . . .

Placentia Bay is surrounded by low wooded hills and there is little or no habitation. There is a very small village called Argentia on the Eastern side of the Bay, and further away near the entrance is the little town of Placentia itself. It is here that the USA are constructing buildings etc for the base they have leased from us. It looks nice country for walking over, but I doubt whether we shall get any opportunity to land. We steamed slowly in, and as we passed each anchored ship the men drawn up on the Quarter Deck were called to attention. There were several destroyers and other small craft, and then finally the cruiser

Tuscaloosa, the battleship *Arkansas*, and the cruiser *Augusta* with the President on board.

As we drew opposite the *Augusta* the guard presented arms and the Band played 'The Star Spangled Banner'. A similar ceremony was happening on board the *Augusta* and we could hear 'God Save the King' across the water. The Prime Minister stood with the Chiefs of Staff and others at the after end of the Quarter Deck, and through glasses we could see President Roosevelt under an awning just below the Bridge of the *Augusta* about 300 or 400 yards away. Almost immediately the Chief of Staff, Admiral King, who commands the Atlantic Fleet, came on board accompanied by another Naval Captain. We had been speculating beforehand as to whether the Americans would regard Placentia Bay as their own harbour or one of ours. Apparently, it is the custom in the Navy to fly an ensign on a launch only in a foreign harbour. We immediately saw that the large 'Stars and Stripes' at the stern of the launch bringing the two Captains, that the Americans still regarded the Bay as a British harbour although the small US base had been established there.

The news gradually trickled round that the Prime Minister would shortly call on the President and stay for lunch, accompanied by the Chiefs of Staff, but that the President would not be coming on board the *Prince of Wales* today. Accordingly, about 11 o'clock, the Prime Minister and his party were piped over the side, and went across to the *Augusta*. [*His first act on arrival was to present to the President a letter from King George VI.*]

Dykes, Schofield, Hollis, Goodenough and myself followed almost immediately in another launch. The Quarter Deck of *Augusta* is amidships under an awning, and we found ourselves greeted by Captain Wright, commanding the ship, and a guard of Marines looking extremely smart in their dark blue coats and light blue trousers and white caps. We were taken straight to the Ward Room and given coffee. All US ships are completely 'dry', and, as one of the American officers said 'The American Navy visits the British Navy in order to get a drink, and the British Navy visits the American Navy in order to get something to eat'. We sat and chatted with various officers of the staff of Admiral King and of Admiral Stark. Shortly after 12 o'clock, we were taken up to the Captain's cabin where we had a very good fork lunch. The Prime Minister lunched alone with the President, and the whole of the remainder of the party, including Mr Sumner

Wells, Admiral Stark, Admiral King, General Marshall, General Arnold, our Chiefs of Staff and Sir Alexander Cadogan, had the fork lunch together.

After lunch, the First Sea Lord had a discussion with Admiral Stark and Admiral Turner, the American Director of Naval War Plans. Meanwhile, CIGS and VCAS went off with General Marshall and General Arnold and the Staff Officers on both sides to the *Tuscaloosa* for a meeting; Jo and I went over too, and we all sat down in the Captain's cabin in an informal manner. General Marshall asked CIGS and VCAS to give their views about the present war situation. The other officers present were General Burns and Colonel Bundy of the US Army. When CIGS and VCAS had finished their statements, General Marshall gave us a very interesting account of the internal situation in America as it affected the Army. He pointed out that everything they were giving to us was at the expense of their own Army, which was woefully short of equipment with which to train. He mentioned the difficulty they had in sending any modern equipment to their outlying possessions; in fact, his remarks might have been made almost word for word by one of our own Chiefs of Staff two years ago when we were being pressed to send things to France, and to equip all the small nations, at a time when we had nothing even for ourselves.

I was very much struck with General Marshall, who is a young-looking man with a very open manner, and who appeared to have a very thorough grasp of his subject. He did not give any indication of their own views of the strategy of the war, but when the meeting broke up Jo, Dumbie and myself went into an adjoining cabin with Bundy and continued a very interesting discussion, in the course of which he showed us the draft of a Paper they had drawn up for the President, setting out their idea of the phases of American participation in the war. We had a cup of tea, and then, at about 5 o'clock, we left the *Tuscaloosa* and returned to the *Prince of Wales* where we found the Chiefs of Staff already back.

In the evening the Prime Minister and the three Chiefs of Staff went to dinner on board the *Augusta* after which the Prime Minister addressed an assembly of 20 or 30 American officers on the war situation. None of us went over, so what exactly occurred is not known. Meanwhile, we finished up our notes on the day's proceedings, and managed to get to bed at a reasonable hour.

Looking back on the day's events from the point of view of the work done, I have received certain impressions. First of all, it is quite clear that the American Navy and Army authorities have not got together and thought out a joint policy; for example, the views on the Far East expressed to the First Sea Lord by Admiral Stark and Admiral Turner were quite different from those expressed to the CIGS by General Marshall. Admiral Stark attaches very little importance to the Far East and imagines that we can afford to see it all 'go west' without bothering ourselves unduly. They appreciate the importance of the Indian Ocean in so far as it leads them to believe that we should fight in the Middle East, but they do not understand that we cannot possibly be indifferent to the fate of Australia, New Zealand and India. Their chief concern is that as little as possible of the US Fleet should be drawn into the Far East, and they seem to think that the war can be won by simply winning the Battle of the Atlantic.

General Marshall, on the other hand, favours reinforcing the Philippines so as to constitute a serious check to Japanese southward expansion. He appreciates the importance of Singapore, but we do not yet know what his views are about the Middle East.

A further illustration of their lack of cohesion is that each of them emphasised the bad effect the giving of first priority to heavy bombers would have on their own programmes; as far as we can judge they each had an exaggerated idea of its effect. They clearly regarded the air as something subsidiary to their own particular concerns, and do not appreciate the importance of acting offensively against Germany.

The next impression I got was that they were much more concerned with production and equipment questions than with strategy. This perhaps is natural at a time when they can hardly visualise active American operations on account of acute shortage of equipment. It is going to be difficult, however, to arrive at an agreed strategical concept of the war in the present talks if the American Chiefs of Staff maintain their attitude.

Sunday, 10 August

A really lovely morning; just like a summer's day in the west of Scotland; soft breeze, sun behind thin clouds, and a beautiful shimmering grey look on the waters, and the green rocky hills all round. There was great activity getting everything ship-shape for the joint service at 11 o'clock on the Quarter Deck. A large part of the ship's company and 100 or more American sailors from other ships were drawn up on each side of the Quarter Deck with the Petty Officers under the four guns of the after turret, and the officers aft facing forward. A special desk with the British and American flags draped on it was set up for the use of the Chaplains. The Marine Guard of Honour and Band were drawn up opposite the starboard gangway and, just before 11 o'clock, the President came alongside in a destroyer. He was greeted by the Prime Minister and by a salute, and then he walked aft to a position in front of the Officers, where he and the Prime Minister sat side by side, the latter in his uniform of the Royal Yacht Squadron, the President wearing a blue double-breasted suit and being without a hat. It is a very great effort for the President to walk, and it took him a long time to get from the gangway to his chair, leaning on a stick and linking his arm with that of one of his sons, who is acting as his ADC. The President is quite normal down to the hips, but his legs are evidently rather wasted and he has not much control over them. We heard that this was the longest walk that the President had ever taken since his illness many years ago. The Marine Band came aft and took up a position in front of the Petty Officers facing the Chaplains, and the Service began. The order of the Service and the hymns were chosen by the Prime Minister. The latter were 'Oh God our Help in Ages Past', 'Onward Christian Soldiers', and 'Eternal Father Strong to Save'. At the conclusion of the Service 'God Save the King' and the 'Star Spangled Banner' were played, and the ships companies then marched forward.

The President and the Prime Minister remained chatting in their chairs for half an hour or so, and then the President was taken in a wheeled chair for a tour of the Upper Deck and saw one of the turrets training its guns. Meanwhile, everyone else went below and then, at about a quarter to one, we went into the Ward Room where the President was seated and we were introduced to him and shook hands. It is hardly necessary for me to describe the President's face, which is exactly like his photographs, but I thought he looked much better and less care-worn than I had expected. It is a fine, strong face, particularly when seen in profile, and he has a very genial smile. Two of his sons were present, one on whose arm he leaned, and the other Franklin Roosevelt Junior, an Ensign in the Navy – a very fine looking chap too. Sumner Wells looks exactly as if he had stepped out of a film; he is the kind of man you always see in the films as the business lawyer.

Before lunch it had been the intention that the Chiefs of Staff should have a short meeting with the American Chiefs of Staff at which to hand over our future strategy paper. However, this went by the board as Admiral Stark and General Marshall decided to go back to their ships with the President and the Prime Minister having made short speeches. The President was immediately wheeled over the side into the destroyer, and the ship's company of the *Prince of Wales* assembled on the forecastle to give him Three Cheers as he steamed off. It was arranged that the First Sea Lord should go over and see the President at 5 o'clock, and that CIGS and VCAS should follow him and see the President at 6. In the meanwhile, the First Sea Lord had a seance with Admiral Turner on naval topics.

When the President had gone, [*taking with him a British draft of the Atlantic Charter*] the Prime Minister announced that he had an urge to set foot on shore, and he asked the Commander to call away a picket boat. The Prime Minister went off, accompanied by Cadogan, 'the Prof', Harriman, [*and others*]. They went to a small shingly beach, and landed and walked about on the rocks, and the small wooded hills running down to the beach. Soon after 4, the clouds blew up and a strong shower of rain soaked the party to the skin. However, they got back about half past four having apparently enjoyed themselves. [*Churchill had collected a bunch of flowers.*]

All the afternoon, parties of officers and ratings from the American ships kept coming over and being entertained and shown around. Colonel Bundy came over shortly before tea, and had a very long discussion with Dykes and myself on all kinds of questions connected with the possible American intervention. The Americans are busy trying to draw up a scheme of the forces which they should ultimately raise, and the possible theatres in which they might be utilised. They are tentatively aiming at an Army of four million men, and we did our best to point out to Bundy that this was possibly a wasteful use of manpower and manufacturing capacity; it hardly seems conceivable that large scale land fighting could take place on the Continent of America, and shipping limitations would make it quite impossible for large forces to be transferred quickly to other theatres. We also had a useful discussion on our Chiefs of Staff organisation and theirs, and tried to pave the way towards the acceptance of our idea that the ultimate requirements for winning the war should be worked out jointly by their staff and ours on the basis of our Future Strategy Paper. Our talk lasted right up to dinner time, when Bundy went off to dine with CIGS and VCAS, who were having a small party in the after cabin. The First Sea Lord dined with Admiral Stark, and the Prime Minister dined with the President.

The day had been almost entirely wasted from the point of view of joint discussion. We have been here two days and not yet succeeded in getting the opposite sets of Chiefs of Staff together round a table. We have thus given away the strength of our position, which lies in the fact that our three Chiefs of Staff present a united front on strategical questions, while it is quite clear that theirs do not. We have played into their hands by allowing the discussions to proceed in separate compartments. Perhaps we shall have better luck tomorrow. No-one has any idea of what the Prime Minister has been saying to the President.

Monday, 11 August

The Prime Minister called the Chiefs of Staff together at 9.30 this morning, and gave them an account of his conversations with the President. At 11 o'clock, Admiral Stark and General Marshall, accompanied by General Arnold, Admiral King, Admiral Turner, Commander Sherman and Colonel Bundy, came over for a meeting with the Chiefs of Staff on our Future Strategy Paper, copies of which had been sent over to them the day before. The meeting was fairly satisfactory, but unfortunately did not get further than half way through the Paper. The result of this was that the last section, containing our broad ideas of how to set about winning the war, had so far not been discussed. Perhaps another opportunity will occur tomorrow.

The dominating personality on the American Naval side is clearly Admiral Turner, a tallish man with iron-grey hair, rimless glasses, and a humourless face. He seems a man of strong character and decided views who is quite incapable of compromise. He is quite ready to express his views both on naval and land matters. You could never imagine him asking anyone's advice on any point.

Admiral Stark who is a little white haired man with bright eyes and a hooked nose, is a much more engaging personality, and generally seems to talk sound sense. He is probably under Admiral Turner's thumb.

General Marshall, who speaks very well, again entirely confined himself to the equipment side of the matters discussed, and let fall no remarks of any kind on strategical issues. His main concern, and indeed the main concern of both American Services seems at present to be the priority question. They feel that we have put forward inconsistent demands, and each Service feels that his own concerns are not receiving the priority they deserve. They are also worried about the effect of the Russian demands for equipment on the supplies which they want for themselves and those which they will be able to give us.

General Arnold, who is the head of the Army Air Corps, took no part in the discussion. He is a thick-set white-haired cheerful individual, but I have had no opportunity of judging his capabilities.

Summing it all up, the American Navy is entirely pre-occupied with naval matters, and seems to think that the war can be won by our simply not losing it at sea. The American Army sees no prospect of being able to do anything for a year or two, and thus is completely taken up with equipment problems.

The lunch broke up at 1 o'clock and everybody separated to lunch in various directions. CIGS arranged to go over to see General Marshall at 4 o'clock, though what the topic of conversation is to be we do not yet know.

The Governor of Newfoundland arrived by train at Placentia and came on board to lunch with the Prime Minister. The news also came from Lord Beaverbrook that he had arrived in Newfoundland by air, so no doubt he will be putting in an appearance later on today.

Streams of American Officers have been coming over again today, and it is very interesting to see their outlook. From what I have heard, there has not been a single enquiry from anyone of them about the ship, its capabilities and equipment, or its part in the *Bismarck* action. They do not appear in the least interested in the progress of the naval war. It is of course possible that they think it wrong to make such enquiries, or think that questions might be embarrassing, but the fact remains that they seem to be much more concerned in getting a few drinks and in having a good time and getting back on shore. They certainly do not show the smallest inclination to try to pick up any hints or to learn any lessons.

The Ward Room is flooded with American magazines which have been kindly given us by the American ships' officers. There is a wide assortment including *Time, The Saturday Evening Post, Colliers' Weekly, Life,* etc. There are papers on Hollywood, on baseball, and on Bible prophecy. I have not found a single reasonable article on the war from the British point of view. There are a few articles describing the German capture of Crete and emanating from German sources. A good illustration of the type of comment is from a paragraph in one of the papers referring to the replacement of General Wavell by General Auchinleck. Having pointed out that General Wavell was being demoted on account of his failures in Greece and Crete, the only thing it could find to say about General Auchinleck was the following, 'General Auchinleck is best known for his failure to hold Narvik for Britain.'

Not a single American officer has shown the slightest keenness to be in the war on our side. They are a charming lot of individuals, but they appear to be living in a different world from ourselves. The war certainly seems very remote over here, even to us who are so desperately interested in it.

Dumbie has just come back with the CIGS from his interview with General Marshall. He says that although the talk lasted for $2\frac{1}{2}$ hours it was almost entirely on the equipment side as it affected the American Army. The only strategic topic touched upon by General Marshall being the situation in Brazil, where the Americans fear a Nazi coup. It would do General Marshall, Admiral Stark and Admiral Turner a power of good if they could come over and spend a month in London.

[*By the end of 11 August some good progress had been made. There had been some useful talks between Cadogan and his opposite number Sumner Wells: and Roosevelt had agreed, after hearing Hopkins' report of his talks with Stalin, to give immediate aid to the USSR. Churchill then drafted a signal to Stalin, suggesting an Anglo-American Mission should be sent to Moscow to settle the munitions problem conjointly with the United States. 'Naval Plan 4' for US Navy patrols in the Atlantic was also agreed. A very severe warning, drafted by Churchill was sent by Roosevelt to Japan in the hope of deterring further encroachments in the SW Pacific; and action by the United States in the Canary Isles and Azores to deter German action against Spain was also agreed.*]

Tuesday, 12 August
There had been a rumour that we were to stay another two days so as to await replies to certain telegrams which the Prime Minister had sent home to the Cabinet. [*This was the draft of the 'Atlantic*

Charter' which had been an important topic of conversation between the President and the Prime Minister.] However, the reply from London arrived in the middle of the night, which enabled the Prime Minister to settle things satisfactorily with the President this morning. There must have been some pretty smart work in London because, according to our calculations, there would not have been more than two hours between the receipt of the telegram and the dispatch of the reply. The reply arrived about 1 o'clock in the morning, and Jo took it up to the Prime Minister in his cabin near the Bridge; he found him just getting into bed, and talking to the 'Prof'. On hearing that the telegram was the reply from London, he said to Jo, 'Am I going to like it?', rather like a small boy about to take medicine. However, all was well, as Jo was able to answer him that he would like it.

[*Jacob then describes the next morning as 'a scene of absolute chaos'. 'Going back to sea' had gone to Admiral Pound's head, and he became deeply involved with the Captain over all the details of their homeward journey. Meanwhile, forgetting that he had a staff to serve him, he had personally attempted to organise a meeting of the British and US Chiefs of Staff. Misunderstandings ensued, and the resulting confusion was increased by the unexpected arrival on board of Lord Beaverbrook, complete with doctor and valet. Finally Hollis, in the hearing of the Prime Minister addressed Admiral Pound as CNS, and was sternly rebuked for referring to the First Sea Lord in such terms.*]

The Diary continues:

At 11.30 we got down to business, and actually had the best meeting of all those which had taken place over here. The Americans were unanimous in stating their view that our present arrangements for telling them what we wanted them to provide are unsatisfactory. They think it is up to us to pass our demands on a proper strategical plan, and to lay down orders of priority to which the Americans can work. This, they say, is not at present happening. It is, of course, very easy to state this rather obvious ideal; it is very much harder to carry it out. It could only be done if our requirements were put over to the Americans by the Service Joint Staff Mission. This at present is impossible because the Army have to notify their demands to the Ministry of Supply, and the Air Ministry to the Ministry of Aircraft Production. It is these two Ministries which then make demands on the USA. A further complication is the use of the political channel for Supply demands, and as long as this channel is open, each Service will try to make use of it to push what it considers essential. However, now that the matter has been put bluntly by the Americans it may be possible to have it put right when we return. The stumbling block will probably be the fact that Lord Beaverbrook is now on his way to Washington with the power to act for all Departments on Supply matters. What kind of spanner he will throw into the works God alone knows . . .

Looking back on the three days, I think the Prime Minister can be well satisfied with the results. I have not said much about what he had been doing with the President, because strictly speaking, it has not been my immediate concern. Apart from the great value which is bound to be derived from a personal meeting, the Prime Minister has secured certain solid achievements. These are:

(a) A Joint Declaration, 'The Atlantic Charter', shortly to be issued, and containing a statement of the ideals which the Americans and ourselves hope to achieve after the war;

(b) An undertaking from the Americans to deal with the question of the Azores on an invitation from Dr Salazar;

(c) An undertaking by the President to issue a stiff warning to the Japanese that any further southward move on their part will cause the United States to take measures that may lead to war;

(d) The release by the Americans of a further 150,000 rifles.

The Chiefs of Staff, too, though they have not reached any specific agreements, have derived the advantage of personal contacts with their American opposite numbers, and have gained an insight into the American point of view and American difficulties which they would never have got without the meetings.

The only unsatisfactory feature of the whole business has been the realisation that neither the American Navy or the Army go much on the heavy bomber. The Navy are much more concerned with flying boats and naval aircraft, and the Battle of the Atlantic; the Army are more concerned in getting what they require for their own Air Force; and neither of them seems to realise the value of a really heavy and sustained aerial offensive on Germany. They are altogether too defensive-minded and doctrinaire. In the case of General Marshall, I think the reason he takes so little part in strategic discussion is that 60 per cent of his day-to-day job is work which in our case would be carried out by the Secretary of

State for War, i.e. appearing before Congressional committees and similar bodies, and justifying demands for manpower and alterations in military service Acts. He is much too much caught up on the Adjutant-General's side of the Army. No doubt this will change when their manpower situation is freed from the present handicaps under which it suffers, and when there is plenty of equipment for the American Army and Air Force.

The American Navy is naturally much nearer the war than their Army, particularly as Plan No 4, which means the taking over of convoys up to Iceland, is shortly to come into effect, but since naval co-operation is still entirely in the defensive field, the whole of the US naval thought appears to be tinged with a defensive bias. Fundamentally, I suppose, it all springs from the American doctrine that their job in life is to defend the Western Hemisphere; they have never had to contemplate aggressive or even offensive action against anybody, and their military thought suffers accordingly. This is quite natural, and we have suffered too from a parallel situation in our Army. Up to the war we have for twenty years thought little about how to win big campaigns on land; we have been immersed in our day to day imperial police activities, and this largely accounts for our slowness to realise the potentialities of combined Army and Air action in the battle. We are overcoming these difficulties, and no doubt the Americans will do the same when they are brought face to face with real problems.

Wednesday, 13 August

Early this morning, the captain broadcast a message to the ship's company in which he announced that we were going home via Iceland; that the Germans no doubt knew we had been to Newfoundland and were probably aware of our having sailed; and in these circumstances he asked the crew to be particularly 'on their toes' against the possibility of submarines and aircraft opposition.

The day was quite uneventful, with no meetings or other activities. I spent the morning going through the Minutes of Meetings we had held and Papers we have produced, with a view to extracting any points to go into our report. After tea, Dumbie and I had a tour of the Bridge, Mess Decks, Galleys, Bakery etc under the guidance of Schofield.

Thursday, 14 August

Another uneventful day, with a grey sky and a cold wind, the Prime Minister who had caught a cold, spent the day in bed, and there were no meetings or other activities.

Friday, 15 August

Soon after mid-day the Chiefs of Staff met to consider a Draft report which we had prepared for them, giving an account of the meetings for the benefit of the Cabinet.

[*Their report ended with this summary: 'We neither expected or achieved startling results. The American Chiefs of Staff are quite clearly thinking in terms of the defence of the Western hemisphere and have so far not formulated any joint strategy for the defeat of Germany in the event of their entry into the war. Nevertheless the personal contacts with our American colleagues will prove of the greatest value for our future collaboration. We have, we think, convinced the Americans that our policy in the Middle East is sound. They, in turn, have made us understand their difficulties. A most distressing revelation is the reduction in heavy bomber and Catalina allocation to us. This we consider a serious matter. We are also concerned at the small number of Catalinas allocated to the United Kingdom during the next few months.*]

At 8 pm we passed through a very large homeward bound Halifax convoy. It was steaming in about 12 columns each with about six ships in it, each column being about 500 yards from the next. A 'Town' class destroyer was out in front, and corvettes were on each flank. The convoy was proceeding at 6 knots and we roared through at 23, flying a signal 'Pleasant voyage, Churchill'. When we had passed right through we swung round through 180 degrees to port and passed back through the other end of the convoy so that the signal could be seen by everyone. It was a wonderful sight to see these seventy-two ships ploughing their way slowly across the ocean. All kinds of ships were included – tankers, tramps of all kinds, even some small liners, and three of the latest catapult ships which mount Hurricanes on catapults ready to go off and engage the Focke-Wulfs. Each ship as we passed dipped its ensign to us, and the crews all waved. We must have been a fine sight to them, and I expect they wished they could make their way home at our speed.

[*The period 16–19 August on the voyage home was spent with the Prime Minister on his visit to Iceland, and on the evening of the 19th, the party reached King's Cross. After the usual greetings to the Prime Minister and the scramble by Press photographers, Jacob set out for home, bearing from Iceland a large cheese and two pairs of stockings for his wife.*]

In his realistic way, he summed up his impressions of the Atlantic Meeting as follows:

I think the general opinion in our party would be that the Americans have a long way to go before they can play any decisive part in the war. Their Navy is further ahead than their Army, both in thought and in resources. Both are standing like reluctant bathers on the brink, but the Navy are being forced to dip one toe at a time into the shark-infested water. Their ideas however, have not got beyond how to avoid being bitten; they have not yet reached out to thoughts of how to get rid of the sharks. The President and his entourage are far ahead, and intend to keep pushing forward until the time comes when the Germans can no longer disregard American provocation. The sailors and soldiers only hope that moment won't come before they can gather together some respectedly armed forces with which to fight.

On his return to London, Churchill told his War Cabinet that the American naval officers present had not concealed their keenness to enter the war. In this he took a different view from Jacob, a sharp and trenchant observer, who had drawn his impressions from more junior officers.

However, there was no doubt in anyone's mind that the intimate relationship which Churchill had established with the President would be of immense benefit to Britain. The Prime Minister had taken great pains in preparing for the encounter, so much so that Harry Hopkins had commented:

You'd have thought he was being carried up to the heavens to meet God.[2]

Jacob was well aware that the Prime Minister had recognised to the full that the President was not only Chief Executive of the United States but also Head of State. Hence the letter from King George VI to the President, introducing Churchill, which had been presented at their first meeting. In his letter the King had commented:

I am glad you have an opportunity at last of getting to know my Prime Minister. I am sure you will agree that he is a very remarkable man . . .[3]

For his part, Churchill felt that he could convince Roosevelt of the wisdom of any course he wanted to pursue by written memoranda and by conversation. Roosevelt's parting message was of immense encouragement to the Prime Minister and his cabinet colleagues. The President had declared:

We will wage war but not declare it, and we will become more and more provocative. If the Germans do not like it they can attack American forces![4]

Churchill told the Cabinet that the President was obviously determined that the United States should come in, but 'clearly he was skating on pretty thin ice in his relations with Congress' . . .[5]

On his return to London, the Prime Minister could not speak openly in these terms to the British people; so to those who realised that without American entry into the war no end was in sight, there was disappointment unrelieved by the lofty sentiments of the Atlantic Charter. But Jacob himself, party to all the secrets and prone neither to euphoria nor despair, viewed the future with sober optimism.

Treasury Chambers,
Whitehall, S.W.

12th May, 1940.

My dear Jacob,

Now that I have ceased to be a member of the War Cabinet I want to thank you very warmly for the most efficient help that you have given me in the various matters in which we have been concerned. You are a true son of your father, and that is very high praise.

Good luck to you. On no account must you reply.

Yours ever
Hankey

Lt.-Colonel E.I.C. Jacob, R.E.

PLATE 10. Letter from Lord Hankey to Jacob, 12 May 1940 (*Reproduced by kind permission of the Second Baron Hankey*).

PLATE 11. Divine Service in HMS *Prince of Wales*, Placentia Bay, Newfoundland 10 August 1941 (*IWM*).

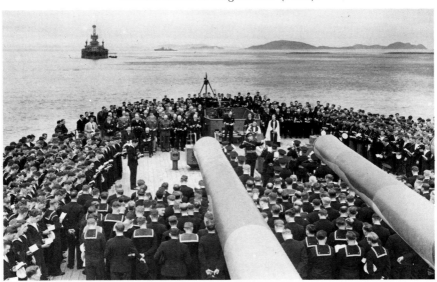

PLATE 12. Churchill and Roosevelt in *Prince of Wales* (*IWM*).

PLATE 13. In the Admiral's cabin of HMS *Prince of Wales*. (*L–R*) Hollis, Dill, Pound, Freeman and Jacob (*IWM*).

PLATE 14. At the White House, Washington. (*L–R*) Pound, Churchill, Dill, Portal and Jacob (*Jacob papers*).

PLATE 15. Churchill with Auchinleck at Eighth Army (*IWM*).

PLATE 16. Churchill with Brooke and Montgomery at Eighth Army (*IWM*).

Most Secret

BRITISH EMBASSY,
CAIRO.

Directive to General Alexander
Commander in Chief in the Middle East

_____

1. Yr prime & main duty will be to take
or destroy at the earliest opportunity the German-
Italian Army commanded by Field Marshal
Rommel together with all its supplies &
establishments in Egypt & Libya.

2. You will discharge or cause to be discharged
such other duties as pertain to yr Command
without prejudice to the task described in
paragraph 1, wh must be considered paramount
in His Majesty's interests.

WSC.
10. Aug. 42.

10.8.42

PLATE 17. Churchill's directive to Alexander on his assumption of
command in the Middle East, 10 August 1942 (*Jacob papers*).

6

'All in the Same Boat Now'

On 20 August 1941 Jacob picked up the threads once more in White-hall. At the Atlantic Meeting he had been kept up-to-date on major developments in London, but after an absence of sixteen days there was a considerable backlog of information to be digested.

Meanwhile, what had they brought back with them from the Atlantic Meeting? A profound friendship had been struck between the British Prime Minister, with all the reins of war-making in his hands, and the President, who in his understanding of the realities of war was ahead of most of his officials. However, his ability to take action was frustrated by the lack of a coherent executive organisation, and was further limited by a cautious and reluctant Congress. It was in that Congress, half of whose members were isolationists, that on 12 August the House of Representatives had passed by only one vote the bill to extend selective service, without which the American Army would have disintegrated. Between the British Chiefs of Staff and their opposite numbers a tentative understanding had been established on strategy and on the production and distribution of munitions, but much further work would be needed to clarify the arrangements.

To both Britain and the United States the intentions and capabilities of their new ally, the Soviet Union, were far from clear; the only immediate result of the Russians joining in the struggle against Hitler had been the diversion to them of precious American munitions intended for Britain which, of necessity, had been provided to meet the appalling menace of Hitler's advance on Moscow.

The boundaries of the war had already been extended by the need to secure the Abadan oilfields and open up a supply route to the Soviet Union additional to the hazardous convoys to Murmansk; and even while the Atlantic Meeting had been in progress, Attlee in London, on Churchill's instructions, had been examining with the 'second eleven' in the War Cabinet the implications of war with Persia, should that Government not comply with a joint British and Soviet demand for an access route.

Meanwhile, Stalin – in the desperate crisis facing the Russian Army – had started in August to make impossible demands for a 'Second Front' in the Balkans, and had later suggested, with a total lack of realism, that twenty-five to thirty British divisions be landed in Archangel or sent through Persia, where joint Anglo-Russian control would very shortly be established. A Supply Mission under Beaverbrook and Averell Harriman, together with Ismay, had later sailed by cruiser to Archangel, but had received from Stalin in Moscow a very frosty reception; and Ismay had been unable to open up any strategic discussions with the Soviet generals.

In the Middle East, still the only theatre of war in which British Forces were fighting the Germans on land, the launch of Auchinleck's operation CRUSADER was repeatedly put back. It was designed to relieve Tobruk, and in Churchill's expectations to advance even as far as Tunis; his impatience with his 'lively fish' was repeatedly expressed in stern telegrams and it was with dismay that he had finally to accept 18 November as D day for the operation.

However, on the credit side, there were further concrete demonstrations of help from the USA in the shape of naval protection of British convoys from Halifax, Nova Scotia, and the provision of shipping to move two British divisions to the Middle East as reinforcements. In Britain itself, a great increase in military power had now been built up, the threatened stranglehold on Atlantic convoys had been diminished, and the bombing offensive against Germany had been stepped up.

Churchill himself, always intent on the offensive, was looking to exploit Auchinleck's expected success by advancing to Tripoli and then developing that campaign even further to the West, by some sort of amphibious operation.

On the evening of Sunday, 7 December, Churchill was at Chequers with US Ambassador Winant and Roosevelt's Special Representative Averell Harriman when they heard on the radio of the Japanese attack on the US Fleet in Pearl Harbor. After obtaining confirmation by telephone from the President, Churchill immediately decided that he must meet him and his advisers to review war plans and the supply problems associated with them. Roosevelt's comment on the phone: 'We are all in the same boat now' had set just the tone that Churchill had looked for, and he sent an urgent inquiry to the President on

9 December suggesting a meeting; meanwhile the War Cabinet had authorised the immediate declaration of war against Japan. The President agreed at once to a meeting in Washington.

On 10 December, two days before his departure, the Prime Minister, while opening his boxes in bed, had answered the telephone and heard from the First Sea Lord that the battleships *Prince of Wales* and *Repulse* had been sunk, while sailing to attack Japanese Forces disembarking in Malaya.

From the start of that tragic story Jacob had watched its development. In December 1939 the Dominion Prime Ministers, who had come to London for a meeting, had been assured once again that if a Japanese attack developed in the Pacific, a fleet would be sent East, based on Singapore. If necessary, this would be at the expense of Middle East defence, which would be left to the French. As the war developed, it became clear that this assurance could not easily be fulfilled. The fall of France had left the Royal Navy alone in European waters; the balance of power there had been affected by losses and, with France out of the war, Indo-China became an easy prize for Japan. Nevertheless steps had to be taken to build up an Eastern Fleet as promised.

The Prime Minister at that time had thought that the Japanese would never be so foolish as to make war on the British and the Americans together; if they did, they would be bound to lose. However, as an insurance, he had felt that a couple of modern capital ships and an aircraft carrier, based somewhere in the South Pacific, would pose the same kind of threat to Japanese communications in SE Asia as had the *Bismarck* to British communications across the Atlantic. He had therefore proposed that three ships should be assembled at Singapore, the *Prince of Wales* and the *Indomitable* joining the *Repulse* already there. From Singapore, they would disappear in the vast area of the South Pacific, and could take a favourable opportunity to strike if the Japanese moved South.

Pound, the First Sea Lord, had disliked this proposal: he had wanted to take time to build up a substantial fleet based initially on Trincomalee and Kilindini, which could move when the time came to Singapore. After considerable discussion, it was finally decided to sail the *Prince of Wales* and the aircraft carrier as far as Cape Town, and on their arrival a decision could be taken as to whether they should proceed, and if so to what destination. Pound had done his best to oppose the Prime Minister's wishes, but in the end he had had to give way. The ships had sailed, but unfortunately at that moment the aircraft carrier had been damaged and could not join them. The two capital ships had reached the Cape, and Jacob had not been aware that their further move Eastwards was discussed: perhaps the Prime Minister and First Sea Lord had decided between them. At all events, they had sailed for Singapore. Jacob was convinced that Pound had intended that they should move off from Singapore if war came to the Pacific. It was never intended that they should linger near Malaya within range of heavy air attack. However, mistakes were made, and Admiral Tom Phillips, the C-in-C, acted precipitously: the Japanese attack fell on Malaya and the ships were sunk. It was a devastating blow to Churchill but an even greater tragedy for Pound, who henceforth carried the responsibility on his own shoulders. Jacob never heard him at any time utter a single word about the loss.[1]

The Staff of the Defence Office had been warned to leave for Washington on 12 December in the new battleship *Duke of York*, and Jacob had immediately got to work at high speed preparing agenda. The delegation was to be even larger than that for the Atlantic meeting. Winant and Harriman were to accompany the Prime Minister. Lord Beaverbrook the Minister of Supply was to go (with three representatives from his Ministry) and the Chiefs of Staff: Sir Dudley Pound, Field Marshal Sir John Dill and Sir Charles Portal, who had relieved Newall. Included also were Captain Lambe, Deputy Director of Naval Plans, Major General GN Macready, Assistant CIGS, Brigadier Dykes, Director of Army Plans, Air Commodore WF Dickson, Director of Air Plans, and Mr MJ Dean from the Air Ministry. Brigadier Hollis went with Jacob, who was now holding the acting rank of Colonel.

Before leaving, Jacob sent a quick note to his wife:

> Just a line to say goodbye . . . today has been so hectic that I have not had time to write. I hope to be back for your birthday . . . It is sad that I shall miss John, but I shall look forward to the latter part of the holidays. I wish they would arrange these trips in term time.
>
> All my best love darling. Take care of yourself and have a happy Xmas.

Jacob's diary of the Washington Conference begins on 12 December 1941:

> Once again we found ourselves setting out in the Prime Minister's special train, at 10.30 pm from Euston. The main addition to the party this time was Lord Beaverbrook and his retinue. Lord Beaverbrook had his private saloon on the train, and had a dinner party there before the train started. It was generally given out that the party was to be headed by Lord Beaverbrook and the Prime

Minister was going to see him off. So well was this fiction maintained, that after we sailed, some people were amazed when told that the Prime Minister was on board. Lance Bombardier Mary Churchill of the ATS came to see us off, and she and Mrs Hill, the stenographer, were the last to leave the ship when we sailed.

I was dog tired after two very hectic days of preparation for the trip, which came at the end of a fortnight during which I had had no day away from the office. I therefore slept like a log in the train.

Saturday, 13 December

After a good breakfast on the train, we stepped out at Prince's Pier, Gourock, where the arrangements for going aboard HMS *Duke of York*, were simple and soon over.

The *Duke of York* is a sister ship to the *Prince of Wales* and *King George V*: there is hardly any difference in characteristics. It was hard to remember that it was not the *Prince of Wales* which we were once more to travel in, and harder still to realize that the great ship which we had so much admired was now at the bottom of the sea. Every day on board brings home the bitterness of that blow.

We were met by Captain Harcourt, and soon shown to our cabins. Mine is in very nearly the identical spot as that I occupied before, though it is more roomy. The ship is fitted as a Fleet Flagship, and thus has more spacious accommodation aft than the *Prince of Wales*, which was fitted as a Squadron Flagship only. The Prime Minister, Lord Beaverbrook, and the First Sea Lord have cabins in the Bridge superstructure, and the rest of the party are aft. Jo Hollis and I are not far apart, and have our office in the same position as before. The Wardroom is the same shape, but better supplied with settees and chairs. The Prime Minister's party, which this time includes Jo, has again taken over the Warrant Officers' Mess, so that the Warrant Officers are also with us in the Wardroom. The Mess Staff seem to cope wonderfully with the numbers.

We got under way at noon, and made off with our three destroyers down the Clyde. After lunch, we soon got down to work with the Chiefs of Staff, to settle the programme which would have to be accomplished before we reached the other side. After tea, I had a game of bridge with General Macready, Lord Beaverbrook and Mr Harriman. I held wonderful cards! Dinner was at 7.30 and we fell straight back into the routine of our previous voyage with a film afterwards.

Sunday, 14 December

The sea remained very rough all day, and all the ports and doors on the upper deck remained closed. The Chiefs of Staff met again at 5.30 pm.

Monday, 15 December and Tuesday, 16 December

The sea gradually moderated during Monday, but it was not until Tuesday that I was able to have my first walk on the Quarter Deck. The lack of fresh air in rough weather is the worst part of the business. Our routine has been much the same every day, with usually a meeting after ten and a film after dinner. We have a very pleasant party, Charles Lambe, Dumbie Dykes, and Dickson being all good fellows. The Ministry of Supply party are also quite an amusing lot, and the vagaries of Lord Beaverbrook provide constant amusement.

Wednesday, 17 December

We dropped our destroyer escort near the Azores, and are now out of the usual submarine area and should be able to count on the width of the ocean to ensure seclusion. We have not sighted a ship since we sailed. The Chiefs of Staff met at 5.30, and again after the film. The latter was the most exasperating meeting, starting at 11.30 pm and ending at 2.15 am. During most of the time, no work was done and Jo and I felt thoroughly disgruntled at the end of it.

The news from Libya continues to be good, and there has been a series of encounters west of Gibraltar between the escort of one of our convoys and German U-boats. Three of the latter have been sunk. The Far East is causing great anxiety, and the forces in Malaya seem to be hard pressed. We are going to have much unpleasantness in that part of the world. One feels curiously detached on a voyage like this. It is hard to keep track of the date and the day of the week, as all seem alike. There are no newspapers and letters, and only fragmentary wireless news bulletins, as we are beyond the range of the BBC Home Service.

There has been some talk of our flying on from Bermuda to save time. Our progress during the first few days has been so slow on account of the bad weather that the Prime Minister is eager to press on. However, the project has been dropped.

Thursday, 18 December

The Chiefs of Staff had a long meeting this morning with the Prime Minister and Lord Beaverbrook. The discussion was mainly about the way to handle the forthcoming talks in Washington, and was satisfactory from our point of view provided our ideas are adopted. The Chiefs of Staff met again at 5.30 in the Whale's cabin. We have called the First Sea Lord the 'Old Whale' or the 'Whale' ever since the day, early in the war, when discussion turned to a meeting on the defences of Scapa Flow. General Ironside, who was then CIGS, was arguing with Sir Cyril Newall, the CAS, about the responsibility of the defences, and finally said, turning to the First Sea Lord, 'Well, anyway, it is this old whale who will have to lie in harbour there.'

Friday, 19 December

We had another meeting this morning, first between the Chiefs of Staff and the Directors of Plans, and then with the Prime Minister and Lord Beaverbrook. Not much business done.

Throughout the voyage the weather was bad, and it also succeeded in ruining all the beautifully arranged plans for our arrival, by making us late into Chesapeake Bay.

Monday, 22 December

We awoke on Monday morning to find ourselves sailing steadily towards land in mild sunlight, and in a smooth sea. The entrance and approach to Chesapeake Bay are shallow, and we had to take on a pilot to steer us through the minefield by a devious route.

With the pilot two US Naval Officers and Major Maude of the British Mission came aboard. They had been tossing about in the little pilot boat ever since 7 am until about 10 am when we came into view. They showed us the most complete and carefully worked out plans for our arrival, but as we had already wrecked them, we could do nothing but await fresh orders resulting from the feverish interchange of signals in progress between the ship and the White House. It seems that the President was in a great state of excitement over the possibility of danger to the Prime Minister if his route were known, so he had ordered a complicated arrangement under which the Prime Minister and his entourage were to transfer to a destroyer at Hampton Roads, just inside the mouth of the Bay, and were to be whisked up the Potomac River to a secret landing place, whence they would be spirited away to the White House.

The success of the President's plan, however, depended upon our reaching Hampton Roads fairly early in the forenoon, so as to allow for the rest of the journey in daylight. The Prime Minister would then have reached the White House comfortably in time for dinner. However, we did not reach Hampton Roads until nearly 4 pm, by which time we had received fresh orders to the effect that the Prime Minister and his party were to disembark with their hand luggage and go by naval aeroplane from Norfolk to Washington. The rest of the party were to entrain at Phoebus, a point between Chesapeake Bay and the Roads, in a special train for Washington.

From that moment everything went well. By 7.45 pm we were all settled down, in a special railroad car of the Vice-President of the Baltimore and Ohio Railroad, to hard boiled eggs, salad, coffee and fruit. A game of bridge whiled away the time for General Macready, Sharpe, Macmullen and myself, and it did not seem long before we reached Washington, though the clock said 1.15 am.

We were met at Washington by various members of the Mission, Coleridge the Secretary, on whom had fallen the nightmare of making the arrangements, Bill Thornton the Air Attaché, and others; we found a fleet of cars and lorries drawn up waiting to whisk us off to our hotels. Jo and I went with Richard Coleridge to the Wardman Park Hotel, where the latter had fixed us up with an ideal suite.

Thursday, 23 December

Our first day was a pretty good sample of what was to come. Jo had to hurry off down to the White House to see the Prime Minister, and got involved in a meeting between the latter and the Dominions representatives in Washington. Later we managed to get off to lunch with the Coleridges in their small house. They find living very expensive indeed, as prices are higher in Washington than anywhere in the world.

After lunch we went back to work, and at 5.30 there took place the first meeting between the Prime Minister and the President and their Chiefs of Staff at the White House. Jo and I went down to attend it, and had a good deal of difficulty getting in. We were stopped at the door of the Cabinet Room, the usher telling us that our names were not on the list, and the President never had note-takers in his meetings. We held our ground, and eventually we were admitted, a make-weight on the other side being also inserted in the shape of Captain Beardell, the President's ADC, and Brigadier General Watson. Neither of these contributed anything to the party or took any notes, but I suppose their presence in the background was felt to counterbalance ours. The first meeting took a general run over the course, and enabled the Prime Minister and President to air their views on the war. The meeting set various tasks to be carried out by the Staffs. The President is a most impressive man, and seems to be on the best of terms with all his advisers. By the side of the Prime Minister he is a child in military affairs, and evidently has little realisation of what can and what cannot be done. He does not seem to grasp how backward his country is in its war preparations, and how ill-prepared his Army is to get involved in large scale operations.

To our eyes, the American machine of Government seems hopelessly disorganised. To illustrate this from the first meeting: on the following day the US Chiefs of Staff met ours in their first formal meeting at the Federal Reserve Building. There was no Agenda and the first thing Admiral Stark, who was in the Chair, did was to run through the notes he had made on the previous day's meeting. General Marshall had also dictated, on his return to his office, his idea of what had happened. We of course had our minutes prepared, and it was a complete waste of everyone's time to go all over the ground again. Not to mention the waste of effort on the part of those Chiefs of Staff who had themselves to put down an account of the meeting. We found this utter lack of system extended right throughout.

When we arrived in Washington, we were met by Brigadier General Raymond Lee, until very recently the US Attaché in London. He told us he had been detailed to organise a Secretariat for the conversations. We were glad to hear this, but we were a bit taken aback when he gave us a list showing what he was arranging. He was to be Secretary General. There were assistant secretaries, an adjutant, a protocol officer, a liaison officer, and various minor functionaries. But there did not appear to be any naval contact, and we soon found that although, nominally, the Navy were coming in on the party, they were quite separate in reality, and had a secretariat of their own under Admiral Turner, their Director of Plans. Throughout the visit, we kept on finding that papers sent by us to the US Secretariat never got into the hands of the Navy at all. The American ideas on organisation and ours are wide apart, and they will have first to close the gap between their Army and Navy before they can work as a real team with us.

We soon realised that the way to achieve results with the Americans is to give up all idea of proceeding in an orderly way in accordance with our own machinery, and to deal direct with individuals. One man going direct to General Marshall, or to General Arnold, will achieve much more than any discussion with their Chiefs of Staff in session. CAS got on to very good terms with Arnold and fixed things up with him on the supply of aircraft very satisfactorily. On the other hand, the Combined Chiefs of Staff meetings, right up to the end, never achieved anything. There was never a settled agenda, and every kind of red herring was pursued. We thought we had achieved a considerable triumph when we got our general strategy paper agreed, almost without amendment, by the US Chiefs of Staff. I am pretty sure, however, that it is regarded as an agreeable essay to which all can play lip service, while each American Service follows its nose and does the job which seems to stick out at the moment. If you want ideas to bear fruit, you must sell them to individuals, who will then push them through. Americans are like we were in the days of Jacky Fisher and Kitchener – personalities each pushing their own ideas, and no real co-operation. We now see how much we owe to Hankey.

The Americans have no 'War Book'. They do not appear to have thought out and laid the foundations for the vast amount of administrative action which should follow automatically on the outbreak of war. Such things as control of shipping, enemy aliens, ARP and censorship are being improvised, e.g. Mayor La Guardia of New York is the ARP organiser for the States! As to shipping, their condition was well described by General Somervell, the Director of Movements in their War Department, when talking about shipping for various projects which were being planned for early execution. He said: 'Right now we are in the zone of hysteria'!

It seems that the Navy and Army do their movements quite independently, grabbing ships as they find convenient. When faced with planning a complicated series of moves like those with which they are now faced in the Pacific and the Atlantic, the result is chaos. They will get all right, but they have a hell of a lot to learn.

On the evening of our first day we had a large dinner given by Stimson and Knox at the Carlton Hotel – a very good dinner too. I sat between Lieutenant General McNair, Chief of Staff to General Marshall at GHQ and General Moore their Director of Staff Duties or its equivalent. I found the former a very good listener, unlike most Americans, but he gave the impression of being a real back-number. They all speak highly of him, so he may have been lying low, but I think their ideas of a good general are not quite the same as ours. Theirs seem much too old.

Thursday, 25 December

The Americans go in thoroughly for Christmas. Christmas trees are everywhere, and holly wreaths are hung up on the outsides of the front doors. The White House had a huge illuminated Christmas tree in the porch, and others outside. It all seemed a bit unreal to us, who were so far from our own homes and who were working at high pressure. The President and the Prime Minister went officially to Church, surrounded by bevies of G-men, armed with Tommy-guns and revolvers. Church was immediately followed by a meeting, and we were kept as busy as we could be for the rest of the day. Jo and I finally broke away at 8 pm, to go to dinner with Lord and Lady Halifax in the British Embassy.

Sunday, 28 December–Wednesday, 31 December

The Prime Minister, accompanied by CAS, Jo, and Francis Brown went off to Ottawa on Sunday, 28 December, and returned on Wednesday night. From all accounts they had both a useful and enjoyable time. I found my hands pretty full in Jo's absence, as of course all our domestic work, and work with the US Chiefs of Staff went on much as before, and in addition we had to keep the Prime Minister informed. We were in the middle of drafting the directive for the Supreme Commander in the new ABDA [*American, British, Dutch, Australian*] Area in the South West Pacific, and drawing up the machinery which should serve him and his affairs. The suggestion for unified command in the South West Pacific came from General Marshall, with whom unity of command is a bit of a parrot cry, dating back from his experiences in Pershing's Staff in the last war, and the benefits which he felt were derived from the appointment of Marshal Foch. When the idea was first put forward there was almost universal opposition, and the Prime Minister expressed his doubts about the wisdom of such a system. The US Navy were also against it. General Marshall, however, had backing from the President, whom he had convinced that unity of command would be the only solution to the Far East problems, and that nothing could be worse than having several commanders of different nationality, especially in a theatre where interests were divergent. Marshall then had an hour with the Prime Minister, and won him round, mainly by proposing that the Supreme Commander should be General Wavell. This very naturally put a different complexion on the affair, as it was hard for the Prime Minister to refuse to back a principle which was undoubtedly attractive in theory, and which was to be applied in a way which recognised the pre-eminence in the field of choice of a British General.

General Marshall, with the President and the Prime Minister in agreement, had achieved his object. It did not take long for the British Chiefs of Staff and the American Navy to come into line, though the former urged strongly that the commander should be an American. They foresaw inevitable disasters in the Far East, and feared the force of American public opinion, which might so easily cast the blame for these on to the shoulders of a British General. However, these fears were overruled, and the principle was accepted and strongly recommended to London, where the War Cabinet could do nothing but accept a *fait accompli*.

On his journey to Ottawa, the Prime Minister sent off telegrams to the Australian and New Zealand Prime Ministers explaining the new system, and to General Wavell offering him the post. The President undertook to explain it all to the Dutch. All accepted the principle, but when it came to the machinery for controlling the Supreme Commander we immediately got into difficulties with both the Dutch and Australian Governments. In his original telegram to Mr Curtin the Prime Minister had referred to a 'Joint Body' which would be the machinery in Washington for the higher control of ABDA matters. The Dutch also saw this phrase. They both saw this joint body as some kind of special and new politico-council which would direct the war from Washington, and they naturally put in a claim to be represented on it.

When we came to look into matters, it was very soon apparent that no separate body could deal with ABDA matters in isolation.

Any big problem – and only big problems would be referred back by the Supreme Commander, who had wide powers – must be viewed as part of the whole war situation. For example, a demand for reinforcements could only be judged by those who were fully aware of the position in the other theatres of war. When this fact was realised, it was clear that only the combined US and British Chiefs of Staff could control the Supreme Commander, and that their advice would be submitted as usual to the Prime Minister and the President, and not to any representative political body.

It would of course be necessary to consult the Dutch and Dominion Governments on any of the matters which would arise. The question was whether this consultation should take place in London or Washington. Logically it should be done in London, where the Dominion Governments were habitually consulted, and where the Dutch Government was situated. Both the Australian and Dutch Governments stuck out for representation in Washington where they saw possibilities of playing the Americans off against the British. We firmly resisted that arrangement, pointing out that there would be delay and confusion if the Dutch and Australians were officially consulted in two places at once, and that their view would get full value in London. The controversy was still unresolved when we left Washington. It was in no way permitted to delay the establishment of the Supreme Commander, and General Wavell reported himself as ready to assume command on 15 January, with Headquarters at Bandoeng, Java.

Throughout the time of our visit to Washington the Prime Minister received a series of most exasperating telegrams from Mr Curtin, the Prime Minister of Australia. The Australian Government have throughout the war taken a narrow, selfish, and at times craven view of events; in contrast to the Prime Minister of New Zealand who, though at times naturally critical of failures, has throughout been a tower of strength. 'That dear old man', as the Prime Minister calls Mr Fraser, is as honest and straightforward as you make them.

The Prime Minister has been most forbearing in his replies to Mr Curtin, realising that an exchange of abuse and recrimination gets no one anywhere, and knowing that the Australians have at least some cause for alarm.

I feel that the Prime Minister's treatment of Mr Menzies, who had resigned the Premiership in August 1941, is somewhat to blame. The PM has never really understood the Far East problem, and has deliberately starved Singapore in favour of home and the Middle East, without paying enough attention to the feelings of Australia. His policy was undoubtedly right, but he should have taken great pains to make Australia understand what was being done, and give them the impression that he was really taking them into his confidence. I am afraid we shall have a lot of bother with Australia as a result.

Thursday, 1 January 1942

New Year's Day was a great day for me. First of all, Richard Coleridge came into my office on New Year's Eve and said that we had had a peculiar telegram from Stirling asking him to 'tell Jacob not to forget the Navy' I could not understand this at all, and reviewed the various telegrams I had drafted recently thinking that perhaps I had been omitting the Naval aspect of some matter. Richard then went off to fetch the telegram: we found that it read 'Tell Jacob to take a fatherly interest in the Navy'. It then dawned on me that this was William Stirling's cryptic message telling me that William had passed into Dartmouth. This was wonderful news, and I felt absolutely delighted.

On New Year's Day, however, I got a wire which read: 'Following for Jacob from combined family, your colleagues and Defence registry. Very many congratulations on honour. You should in addition take interest in Admiralty estimate – more congratulations.'

From Martin and Jo I gathered that the first part of this message referred to a CBE, which I had been given in the New Year's Honours. The second part, I soon grasped, meant that William had got a scholarship to Dartmouth, so that success was complete in every direction. A fine beginning to the New Year. My only regret is that I shall not be home in time to see William go off to Dartmouth in his new uniform.

On this 'great day' Jacob wrote to his wife:

> 'I have just got back from work and it has just turned midnight. So the New Year has begun. May we be as fortunate in this year as we have been in the past. I am sure we shall be as united a little family as always. I only hope we shall be together more often than lately. . . . I miss you and think of you and the boys so much.'

He then told her of William's success and of his CBE – 'very satisfactory, because Lieutenant Colonels usually get OBEs, so it is a little above the general run. . . . We are having a terrific time here, nose absolutely glued to the grindstone. Very interesting but too much of a rush. One cannot do one's work with the correct accuracy and polish when one is dashing madly from meeting to meeting, and trying to keep six balls balanced in the air. [*To his colleagues Jacob, of course, was renowned for doing just that.*]

A week later he wrote: 'Jo and I have seen a lot of the PM of course, and the atmosphere has been excellent, a great change from the Atlantic Meeting trip when our presence was more or less ignored! He is in very good form, and has certainly done wonders here. He and his opposite number seem to get on like a house on fire.'

Thursday, 1 January 1942 (Continued . . .)

Personalities are of much greater importance in the American Government than they are nowadays in England, because the American machine is in a backward state of development compared with ours. The British Governmental machine is like a motor car or even a train. Provided a reasonably efficient driver is in charge, it will go. The American Government is not a machine at all. The various parts are not assembled into a working whole. The President is in the position of a patriarch, with a rather unruly flock, and depends on the actual men who actuate or influence the various sections of that flock. The patriarch also relies to a great extent on sheepdogs, who are his stand-by, but are regarded with fear and suspicion by his sheep.

The contrast between the entourages of the Prime Minister and the President is illuminating. The former has a Private Office and a strong Government Secretariat. He has his own familiar spirits, such as Professor Lindemann and Major Morton; but the activities of these are closely circumscribed, and can only take effect in the form of advice to the Prime Minister personally. The machine is strong enough to keep on the rails, and to ensure that the decisive say is in the hands of those who hold the responsibility.

The President, on the other hand, is served with no machine. He has no properly constituted Private Office, though he has various secretaries and the White House Ushers. He has no Government Secretariat at all, and apparently no means of recording and disseminating decisions. The Cabinet appears to be a body of little account, and rarely meets. The result is that the President tends to deal with individual men, whose place in the general scheme of Government is anomalous, in that they have power without responsibility.

The chief of these is Harry Hopkins, a frail anaemic man of great honesty and courage, who lives permanently in the White House and is the President's constant companion. Dumbie calls him 'the disused prawn', and the name certainly describes his lanky figure, bent back, and rather fish-like expression. He has no official appointment, though he has been nominated to various functions connected with Lend-Lease administration and the Office of Production Management. However, he is a real friend of Great Britain, and it is a mercy that we have such a man as the President's chief familiar. Hopkins is usually to be seen in his bedroom, or floating about the central passage in a magenta dressing gown and pyjamas, at any rate in the morning. He suffers from pernicious anaemia, but manages to keep a hold on affairs, and his influence is gradually extending over the field of war activities. He is on good terms with the heads of the Services, but they secretly distrust his activities, and resent his presence as the power behind the throne.

Another queer character is Bill Donovan. He is an honest-to-God American lawyer, with a great fighting record in the last war. The President has put him in charge of a kind of super intelligence organisation, which is designed to give him the low-down of events in all fields all over the world. Donovan has built this up in a big way, and has a very large staff. Apparently he works quite independently of the Service intelligence organisations, and I personally doubt whether he is on the right lines. Certainly some of the undigested reports from his representatives which he has put in front of the President do not reflect credit on his methods.

Other examples of the President's peculiar method of working are the personal representatives he sends about the place, such as Bullitt in the Middle East. These report to him direct, and to our way of thinking are irresponsible meddlers.

The President himself leads a most simple life. He moves about the White House in a wheeled chair. His study is a delightful oval room, looking South and is one of the most untidy rooms I have ever seen. It is full of junk. Half-opened parcels, souvenirs, books, papers, knick-knacks, and all kinds of miscellaneous articles lie about everywhere, on tables, on chairs, and on the floor. His desk is piled with papers; and alongside his chair he has a sort of bookcase also filled with books, papers, and junk of all sorts piled just anyhow. It would drive an orderly-minded man, or woman, mad. The pictures on the walls are fine, mostly prints or paintings of ships. There are also good bookcases round the walls, and the furniture is not bad. But the effect is ruined by the rubbish piled everywhere. It is rather typical of the general lack of organisation in the American Government.

They are, of course, much hampered by their constitution which was expressly designed to prevent any rapid and high-handed action by officials, though giving almost dictatorial powers to the President in times of emergency. For example, the Chiefs of Staff, and not the Secretaries of State, have to spend hours appearing before Congressional Committees who are free to ask them any questions they like. There is no proper Civil Service, and this militates against order and method. However, if they decide to do a thing, and put a strong man in charge, they go through with it in a big way.

Admiral King, the new Commander-in-Chief of all American Naval Forces, is a very dominating personality. He quite over-shadows Admiral Stark, many of whose functions he has taken over. At our meetings with the US Chiefs of Staff, Stark, with the title of Chief of Naval Operations, took the Chair. But he would not go a yard without being sure of King's backing. Admiral 'Betty' Stark was christened 'Tugboat Annie' by Dumbie, and that about hit him off. He is a little man, with a perky face, and looks as if he ought to be Captain of Showboat. His functions now are long term planning, and administration of the Navy.

Admiral Turner the Director of Naval War Plans, is a sort of discontented camel. A man of strong personality, and domineer-ing habits, he had Stark under his thumb. His utterly rigid mind was most unsuited to working in a Joint Planning Committee, of which by virtue of his rank and position he was Chairman. 'Take', he could understand, but 'give', was not in his vocabulary. It appeared that Admiral King took a jaundiced view of Turner's activities, and whenever the latter opened his mouth at a com-bined Chiefs of Staff Meeting, King jumped down his throat. This had a very good effect, and Turner became much more amenable as time went by.

One of the people of whom I saw a good deal was M Monnet. [*This was the young Jean Monnet who, after the war, would play an important role in the evolution of the European Community.*] He was originally in charge of the French contracts for war material bought in the United States. When France collapsed, he remained in Washington and helped with the taking over by us of the French contracts, and became a sort of 'Minister without Portfolio' on the British Supply Council. He had always been regarded with suspicion by our Military Mission, who are doubtful of the loyalty of a man who has no particular allegiance to anyone, and seems to have contacts with everybody of any importance. He has not joined the Free French, and is a real cosmopolitan. Air Marshal Harris is particularly against him, and urges his removal. The civilians regard him with respect, as he is a man of great brainpower, very clever in negotiation, persistent and determined, and with clear and far-sighted views. In any case, he has been in all our secrets for over two years, so it seems a bit late to think about removing him.

I found him very acute, and with a grasp of the American situation, and of how we should act to get the most out of it, which was unequalled by anyone else I met. He got into close touch with me early on, and I saw a good deal of him. I dined twice at his house, where I met Brand, the Head of our Food Mission, Salter the Head of our Shipping Mission, and Morris Wilson the Head of the Supply Council. We kept in close touch on all the machinery matters that affected various parts of the Mission, and the collaboration which should continue with the Americans when the Arcadia party had left. He had a number of friends in the War Department, and was able to say how the Americans would react to our proposals. His chief desire was that we should succeed in setting up a small body composed of Dill, Marshall and King, to conduct the strategy of the war; Marshall to hand over his day to day work to a Vice-Chief, rather as in our system at home. He did his best to work for this, but the various divergent pulls exerted by the Prime Minister, Lord Beaverbrook, the Military Mission, Dill himself, and the President and Hopkins, delayed any settlement of this point until after our departure.

Monnet's other desire was to see the machinery for making allocations of war weapons set up on a purely military base. On this, too, the Prime Minister and Lord Beaverbrook were too much for us. The usual cock-eyed arrangement under which Beaverbrook and Hopkins would manage the business was decided upon. This will give us endless difficulty in the future.

Monnet, is of course, a man who likes to work entirely behind the scenes. He knows what he thinks should be done, and his ideas are usually correct and in advance of those of other people. But he has to rely on other people to push them through. This leads him into a maze of telephoning, lobbying, interviewing, and indirect pressure which is not always successful, and makes slower and more direct people regard his activities with suspicion. Not being in an executive position prevents him from acting otherwise.

To get back after this digression to the day's work in Washington. The meetings with the President and the Prime Minister usually took place at 5 or 5.30 pm, in the President's study. The President sat at his desk, with the Prime Minister in a chair on his left hand side, and the rest of the company perched on chairs and sofas in a rough semi-circle facing him. No tables or anything, and very awkward for looking at maps or taking down notes. Quite an informal atmosphere. Once or twice, we met in the Cabinet Room in the Executive office, which was much more convenient except there was no room for the secretaries at the table. The first meeting was attended by the President's Aberdeen terrier 'Falla', who suddenly started barking, and had to be ejected, just as the Prime Minister was in the middle of an oration. I cannot think he liked it much!

Jacob then describes an incident which unwittingly could have seriously upset the harmony between the British and United States staffs. At a meeting of the British Chiefs of Staff with the Prime Minister presiding, the President had unexpectedly appeared in his wheel chair, and had mentioned his anxieties about the problems of Manila. He suggested that both Staffs should consider them, and the PM with the British Chiefs of Staff agreed. The President then mentioned two other naval subjects, sent for Colonel Knox for one of them, and asked him to examine it in the US Navy Department. He then left.

Jacob and Hollis then phoned the US Secretariat saying that they had some important points to put to them, and requested that a US officer should come over. Jacob gave the officer a note setting out the points which the President had raised. Later, Hollis told Jacob that there was a 'regular flutter in the dovecots, and that they had dropped a brick, but he could not understand how'. The Prime Minister had told him that they had issued minutes containing a directive by the President and this had given offence: 'they must realize that the President had to be treated with ultra respect and they had been guilty of some kind of *lèse majesté*.'

Jacob was puzzled at first, but then recalled his note, which apparently had been passed to General Marshall, who had referred to it as a 'Directive from the President', and shown it to Mr Stimson, the Secretary for War, who at once 'had got on his high horse'. The Americans, not realising that the purpose of the note was simply to tell them of a meeting at which no American Staff were present, had taken it to be an order by the President transmitted to them by the British, and this they had naturally resented.

Fortunately, by the evening, 'the storm in a teacup had blown over'.

Thursday, 1 January 1942 (Continued . . .)

Another amusing incident of quite a different type took place quite early on during our visit. Mr Jones, Jo Hollis' Personal Assistant, a most excellent man in every way, and the mainstay of the Office, had the most peculiarly pompous over-correct way of speaking. He never could get a straightforward sentence out. If you asked him where Brigadier Hollis had gone, instead of saying 'I am afraid I don't know', he would say 'I fear it is not within my knowledge where the Brigadier may be at this moment'. A master of circumlocution, in a stilted tone of voice, but the most accurate, loyal, and efficient chap you could come across.

Soon after we arrived, he drew me aside and said that he hoped I would forgive him mentioning the point, but if, when I was over at the White House, I could find occasion to ring up the Annex and ask him to bring over a secret paper urgently, he would be very grateful, as by that means he would be enabled to see the inside of the White House. I said I would certainly do so.

The very next day Mr Jones met me in the passage in a state of intense excitement, with difficulty suppressed, and proceeded to unburden himself. It seemed that Jo had done just what Mr Jones had asked me to do; he had gone to see the Prime Minister at the White House, and had had to ring Jones quite genuinely to bring a paper which was wanted urgently for the Prime Minister. Jones rushed off in the car, and got successfully into the White House, and delivered the paper to Jo in the little room off the Prime Minister's bedroom, where the Private Secretaries had their abode. He noticed that the Prime Minister was in the bathroom. Jones then came out into the passage and stood looking about for a few minutes, when what should he see coming towards him but the President in his wheeled chair, unaccompanied by anyone.

Jones stood rooted to the spot, and the President addressed him saying:

> 'Good morning. Is your Prime Minister up yet?'
> 'Well, Sir', said Jones, 'It is within my knowledge that the Prime Minister is at the present moment in his bath.'
> 'Good' said the President, 'then open the door'.

Jones accordingly flung open the bathroom door to admit the President, and there was the Prime Minister standing completely naked on the bath mat.

> 'Don't mind me', said the President, as the Prime Minister grabbed a towel, and the door closed.

Jones' day was made. Not only had he seen the inside of the White House, but he had spoken to the President and seen a meeting between him and the Prime Minister in quite unique circumstances.

Soon after the Prime Minister returned from Ottawa (which he had visited immediately after Washington) he decided to go away for a few days on his own. He was not ready to return to England and felt that his continued presence in the White House might be irksome and liable to cause suspicion in the minds of the officials of the Services and the members of the Cabinet, who might think he was trying to establish too intimate a connection with the President. It was accordingly arranged that a bungalow in Florida, not far from Miami should be lent to him. The place was very secluded, and right on the edge of the beach so that privacy could be assured, and the Prime Minister could nip down and bathe from his front door.

The Prime Minister accompanied by Sir Charles Wilson, John Martin, and Commander Thompson, left Washington on Monday, 5 January, and returned on Saturday, 10 January. A daily courier carried papers and telegrams down to keep him in touch with the situation, and when necessary he could telephone to Francis Brown or Jo, and indeed he quite frequently did so. In his absence, the work went on as usual, but each of the three Chiefs of Staff took the opportunity to go off for a day or two with their opposite numbers to see something of the US Forces. Jo and I seemed to be as busy as ever, coping with COS work, telegrams and meetings.

After the return of the Prime Minister from Florida, everyone was feverishly active trying to get things squared up before departure. The outstanding point of greatest importance was the machinery for continuing the collaboration which had made such a good start. We found the American Chiefs of Staff rather reluctant to discuss this question. I think the reasons for this were, first, the doubt in their minds about what the position of Sir John Dill was to be, and secondly the fact that their own organisation was still rather at sixes and sevens, and they were not sure how they could arrange it to fit into ours.

The Prime Minister had decided to leave Dill behind as his personal representative. He also wanted him to be the Head and focus of the Mission. He had never liked the idea that whenever any problems were to be discussed there must be present a triumvirate of the three Services. He wanted to see Dill dealing direct with Marshall and King. At the same time he wanted to be able to use him as his representative with Hopkins or the President.

Sir John did not want to be the leading member of the Mission, *primus inter pares*, as he put it, nor did the Mission. For a long time they had felt the need for a Head who would be over both Civil and Military Missions, and co-ordinate their work. They felt that the British Supply Council spent much of their time butting in on the military sphere, and would tend to do so still more as the business of securing American equipment for British contracts, or even Lend-Lease, dwindled away in favour of allocation according to strategical needs. The Mission had already made efforts to get a Ministerial Head appointed, on the lines of the Minister of State in the Middle East, but they had failed, and they now saw their chance of achieving their object by getting Dill set up as a head over all Missions. They pushed this project hard at a meeting of our Chiefs of Staff, and persuaded Dill to accept the idea by suggesting that he should have Sir Henry Self to act as his Civil right-hand man in dealing with the Civil Missions, about whose work he was naturally very ignorant.

The Chiefs of Staff put this proposal to the Prime Minister, who did not in the least understand what it meant, organisation not being his strong point. The Prime Minister, however, seemed to like the proposed lay-out and Lord Beaverbrook said he had no objection, and then the fun started. Someone told Self to go ahead, and before we could turn round we found him establishing himself in a room in our Office, and saying what was to be what. The Civil Missions, who have not been consulted, reared up on their hind legs, and bearded the Ambassador. Behind the scenes Monnet was continually in my Office trying to impress me how hopeless the proposal was, and that Dill should confine his attention to the military field, where there was a real necessity for a single Head to deal with Marshall and King, as three big men who would direct the strategy of the war. I very much agreed with him, and so did Jo, who saw great dangers from installing a civilian as Head of Dill's office. Moreover we both of us knew that Dill would be incapable of holding down the job of controlling the Civil Missions, and would be a straw blown about in the wind.

The Ambassador played a peculiar role in the affair. He was seen by all the chief protagonists in turn, and each put his own view of what the organisation should be. The Ambassador succeeded in agreeing with all of them.

The controversy about Dill's position was still at its height when our Chiefs of Staff at last met the American Chiefs of Staff on the subject of future collaboration. The latter stated quite plainly that they did not like the idea of having a soldier who at one moment would be dealing with them, and at the next would be going over their heads and dealing with Hopkins and the President. Either Dill should be the honest-to-God Head of the Military Mission, or else he should be a purely political figure.

Our Chiefs of Staff informed the Prime Minister of this, and I do not know what took place behind the scenes then. We came away still not knowing what Dill's functions were to be. The question was not settled until a fortnight later, when the Prime Minister at last signed Dill's directive. This was in two parts. The first, which was the open directive, appointing him Head of the Military Mission. The second, which was a kind of confidential Annex, appointed him the Prime Minister's personal representative. Neither mentioned in any way his relations with the Civil Missions, so we assumed that he had no duties towards them other than the natural duty as Head of the Military Mission of keeping in contact with them. Nevertheless, Self was appointed as his Civil right-hand man, though what his functions will be I cannot imagine. Time will show.

Jacob now became heavily involved in the preparations for departure. Security, planned by the Head G-man of the White House, loomed large, but Jacob was able to damp down the G-man's ardour. Eventually all went more or less according to plan, despite Beaverbrook's influence 'which was all on the side of impatience'. On 18 January, Jacob went on board HMS *Duke of York*, where he received a note from Hollis: 'In a world of Bedlam, I have at last established that the PM is going by air, and I am to go with him. *Bon Voyage*'.

After an uneventful sea voyage, Jacob arrived in the Clyde, transferring in the middle of the night to the special train which reached London on the afternoon of 25 January 1942.

The achievements of the Washington Conference may be sum-marised as the setting up of the Combined Chiefs of Staff, with Dill as the British Head, preparations for a combined United States–British expedition to North Africa in 1942 (code-named SUPER-GYMNAST at this stage, and later TORCH), the dispatch of two American divisions to Northern Ireland, the setting up of Wavell's command of American, British, Dutch, and Australian forces in the South Western Pacific: vast expansions in production programmes achieved by Beaverbrook, and lastly the signing of a 'United Nations' declaration. The twenty-six signatories pledged to employ their full resources, military or economic against members of the Tripartite Pact and its adherents, and agreed not to make a separate armistice or peace with the enemy.

The Conference was also marked by disasters: the fall of Hong Kong on Christmas Day 1941, and the lack of decisive success in Auchinleck's battles at Sidi Rezegh and Gazala. Worse was to follow.

After eight days of well-earned idleness, Jacob was back in Eng-land, where he would have to adjust to a new régime in the Chiefs of Staff Committee with the advent of Dill's successor, General Sir Alan Brooke. The removal of Dill to Washington had left Jacob with mixed feelings, as he had had warm relations with him since those Staff College days in 1931. Jacob and his friends had viewed him then as a future CIGS, but some doubts had arisen when they had observed him on manoeuvres. Dill had seemed to them to live on his nerves, and could rarely sleep under stress. Nevertheless Jacob had been astounded that Dill had not been chosen as CIGS in 1939, instead of Ironside, who seemed to him to be totally miscast for the role.

Jacob had first met Ironside as a divisional commander in Alder-shot in 1933. Tall, massive and with iron-grey hair, he was an impressive military figure. He was a great talker, and his reminiscences were fascinating. He had had an adventurous career, including campaigns in Persia and Archangel where, virtually, he had not been answerable to anyone. However, he had never served in the War Office nor had he acquired the technique of using a staff. Jacob would never forget some of Ironside's remarkable rejoinders in the Chiefs of Staff meetings:

> Newall (Chief of the Air Staff): 'When does the Gulf of Bosnia freeze over?'
> Ironside: 'In April: I have walked across it on the ice'.
> Newall: 'What sort of country is Thrace?'
> Ironside: 'Splendid country for tanks. I have walked all over it.'

From his days in intelligence, Ironside had acquired many languages including French. Jacob had admired his handling of the French generals in the disasters of 1940: the CIGS had not been averse to picking them up and shaking them to restore their morale. However, as the professional head of the Army, his whole method of operating had seemed to Jacob to be too 'hit or miss' to be endured for long. He had to be moved, and had been appointed to Home Command, thus making way for Dill, at that time his deputy.

During the six months that had followed Dunkirk, it had become increasingly clear that Dill could not cope with Churchill's methods of work and with his ideas, which so often seemed to him unsuitable. Dill was often right, but it was a continual battle, often taking place at very late hours, which Dill found trying. As the war progressed, he seemed to Jacob to have lost much of his fire, and he had been particularly inert when they had sailed for the Atlantic Meeting. It was before the Washington meeting that Brooke had been appointed as Dill's successor. As we have seen, Churchill wanted a thoroughly trustworthy man to be his link on military matters with the President and General Marshall, and had therefore resolved to leave Dill in Washington. This proved to be a most fortunate decision. Removed from the strain of running the war, Dill, a great gentleman, rapidly became a close friend of Marshall who was in the same mould. Dill did great service in interpreting the thoughts of the British Chiefs of Staff to the Americans and vice versa, and as time went on, Marshall treated him as a member of the American team.

Churchill was fortunate that he had thus installed two men of the highest calibre in tasks which suited them – Dill in Washington and Brooke in Whitehall. Jacob would now have the opportunity of observing Brooke, a CIGS whom Ismay would later assess as the best of the eight with whom he had been associated. In two months' time, the Prime Minister would appoint Brooke Chairman of the Chiefs of Staff; and meetings of that body would thereafter be conducted with remarkable dispatch, much to the approval of Jacob who, very quick himself, was a stickler for the rapid and orderly transaction of business.

7

Darkest Days

Jacob rejoined his wife in England at the end of January 1942. They, like many others, had had to split up, and Cecil at the outbreak of war had moved to her father's old home in Woodbridge where her mother and father were living. Ian, in London, had a bedroom in his father's flat in Knightsbridge, which had survived the Blitz without a pane of glass being broken; when required for late night duties he would bed down either in the shelter under Richmond Terrace or in a bedroom which later became available in the War Room premises in Great George Street. After a while, he and Cecil decided that there was no sense in being parted, and they rented a furnished flat near Sloane Square, using the Red House at Woodbridge for occasional weekends. William, the younger son, having won his scholarship, was at Dartmouth, and John, the elder, who had been at Sherborne and destined for the Army, had decided to join the Navy because, unlike the Army, they were still giving regular commissions.

Back once more in the Defence Office after Arcadia, the Washington Meeting, he could feel more optimistic about Anglo-American co-operation. Nevertheless, combined strategy was as yet unresolved, and there were far too many competing operations still in the air: exploitation of the expected British success in Libya (Operation GYMNAST), a joint Anglo-American assault in 1942 on a limited scale in North-West Europe at Cherbourg or Brest (Operation SLEDGEHAMMER), an operation in Norway (JUPITER) regarded by the Defence Staff as impracticable, but repeatedly resurrected by Churchill, preparations for the final assault in North West Europe in 1943 (BOLERO), defensive operations in the Indian Ocean and the Far East to limit the damage being inflicted by Japan, and continued aid to the hard-pressed Russians despite the naval losses incurred. However, the overruling principle 'Defeat Hitler first' was being loyally followed by the United States.

Had Jacob known the succession of disasters that would follow in the next eight months, his optimism might have turned to despair. Very soon, Auchlinleck's operation CRUSADER, on which so many hopes had rested, turned to disaster with the evacuation of Benghazi; this would be followed by the withdrawal of the Eighth Army to the Gazala position. In the Far East, disasters in Malaya which were not unexpected, reached a shattering climax with the surrender of Singapore on 15 February; the Australian Prime Minister saw fit to protest to Churchill at this 'inexcusable betrayal'.

On 19 February, Churchill, who had successfully fought off a vote of censure in January with a majority of 464 to 1, decided to make changes in his War Cabinet: Sir Stafford Cripps was made Lord Privy Seal and Leader of the House of Commons, and Mr Attlee, who had for some time been *de facto* the Prime Minister's deputy, was officially confirmed in that position, and also given the responsibility for Dominions Affairs; Oliver Lyttleton was installed as the new Minister of Production. Jacob, on whom the responsibility for handling the Supply side of Defence still rested, was to have many dealings with the new Minister.

In March came the surrender to the Japanese of the Dutch East Indies, threats to the security of Ceylon due to the unhindered operations of the Japanese Navy, and a desperate situation in Malta, beset by the Navies and Air Forces of the Axis Powers. At the end of May, Rommel attacked Eighth Army's position and, all too soon, this would result in another British withdrawal. The Russian Front was still in peril, and a German threat was developing through the Caucasus to North Persia.

However, across the Atlantic, the United States had begun to rouse itself to war. As a counterpoise to Jacob's criticisms at the Atlantic Meeting of the lack of interest displayed by individual Americans in the British at war, prodigies of organisation and munitions production were now taking place on a vast scale. Churchill, in a speech after the war, given to the United States Chiefs of Staff, would describe these activities as 'a wonder in military history'.

The United States had by now become the arsenal of the united nations fighting Germany and Japan, but the business of planning the production of munitions and allocating the harvest was beset by difficult problems, strategical, technical and diplomatic. Jacob in London, and Dykes in the Combined Chiefs of Staff in Washington, kept up a flow of personal letters describing their tactics to overcome these difficulties. Jacob was helped by a very able officer, Mark Norman, who, after being severely wounded, had become an Assistant Military Secretary in the War Cabinet Office; when despatched to Washington on liaison duties, Norman reported with great acumen on the tangled activities of the Combined Munitions Assignment Board. Eventually, in order to obtain urgent decisions, Lyttleton, the Minister of Production, flew with Jacob to Washington.

At a naval air station on the Potomac, they met the Prime Minister with Ismay and the CIGS. Churchill hoped that by discussion with Roosevelt and the United States Chiefs of Staff, final decisions would be obtained on joint operations for 1942–43.

Jacob joined Ismay in the Prime Minister's entourage, and then was engaged in a series of meetings of the Combined Chiefs of Staff from 19 June to 25 June, designed to clarify Anglo-American strategic policy for 1942 and early 1943.

On 20 June, the Prime Minister gave Jacob a note for the President which he was ordered to give also to Brooke, Dill and Ismay. It emphasised that heavy sinkings at sea constituted the greatest and most immediate danger for Britain. Churchill went on to say that BOLERO, the build-up of American forces in Britain for a cross-channel assault, was continuing, together with arrangements for operation SLEDGEHAMMER, a landing much favoured by the Americans of six to eight divisions in France in September 1942. However, no British military authority had been able to make a plan which offered any chance of success for SLEDGEHAMMER in September, unless the Germans became utterly demoralised, of which there was no likelihood. Churchill asked whether the Americans had such a plan? If SLEDGEHAMMER was not possible in 1942, should not the British and Americans prepare some other offensive operation to gain advantages and, directly or indirectly, take weight off Russia? He then put forward that GYMNAST, the operation in North Africa previously discussed but ruled out by the Combined Chiefs of Staff that morning, should be studied once again. Plans were therefore prepared for GYMNAST.

On 21 June, telegrams reached a meeting of the President, the Prime Minister, General Marshall, Brooke, the CIGS and General Ismay, which told of the fall of Tobruk and the grave situation in the Western Desert as a whole.

The reaction of the President was generous and immediate: what could they do to help? As a result, much study was given to the possible move of a US armoured division to the Middle East. However, when the full implications of this had emerged four days later, Marshall suggested that, instead of the division, 300 Sherman tanks and 100 self-propelled guns should be shipped by fast vessel to Suez. This met with general approval and was subsequently confirmed by the Prime Minister and the President.

On 26 June 1942 Jacob flew back to England with the CIGS. Inevitably the disaster in the Middle East dominated their thoughts. Their American friends viewed the future with alarm. Dykes, very sorry to see Jacob go, wrote in his diary: 'It has been great fun having him here these three weeks and I shall miss him a lot. [*On 30 June*] We are still drawing back in Egypt. The US, particularly the President, very windy, and fear Rommel may capture Alex and Cairo in 96 hours.'[1] Both in North West Europe and in North Africa the possibility of early offensive action was now remote. Moreover, firm agreement with the Americans on combined strategy for 1942 had not yet been achieved, and Stalin was pressing for an Anglo-American landing in France. Churchill had countered this by suggesting an assault on Norway, which many of his advisers considered impracticable.

On 18 July, Marshall, King and Hopkins arrived in London to press for SLEDGEHAMMER to relieve pressure on Russia; but Churchill at Chequers with the Chiefs of Staff and Mountbatten firmly decided that same evening that an enlarged GYMNAST with a landing as far East as Algiers was the only feasible operation. Further argument between the Allies ensued, but fortunately the President agreed to compromise, and accepted the British proposal of an enlarged Anglo-American GYMNAST, now to be named TORCH. It was to be carried out in the autumn of 1942 under an American supreme commander, General Eisenhower.

Roosevelt, in a letter to Churchill, spoke of this moment as a turning point in the whole war, as indeed it was. Plans for American and British forces to land at the Western end of the Mediterranean were now urgently pressed ahead. But Brooke, the CIGS, had another urgent task in view: a visit to GHQ Middle East in Cairo and to Eighth Army in the Desert to find out what lay behind the disasters which had occurred in the sole theatre where British forces were actively engaged. As early as 15 July, he had tactfully seized an opportunity to obtain permission to leave London and visit Egypt while Churchill was in a good mood sitting in the Downing Street garden in the evening sunshine. But on 30 July, just before he was due to leave, he discovered that the Prime Minister had decided to go too, and to extend the trip to Moscow to see Stalin.

Jacob was to have a particularly important role in this crucial visit. Fortuitously, his habitual self-confidence had been reinforced by a confidential report which Ismay had written three weeks earlier. It read as follows:

> '... It is very difficult to define Colonel Jacob's duties beyond saying that he holds a key position in the Office of the Ministry of Defence, and that he has carried an increasingly heavy load of responsibilities with outstanding success. His work brings him into regular personal contact with the Prime Minister, other Ministers of State and the Chiefs of Staff, who have one and all spoken in the highest terms of his exceptional capabilities. There have, indeed, been applications from many quarters for his services, but the Prime Minister has issued express orders that he is not to be transferred from his present appointment.
>
> Colonel Jacob has an exceptionally quick, clear and decisive mind, coupled with the gift of expression both in speech and writing. He is exceptionally quick to seize the essential features of a complicated situation and to reach a sound judgement upon them. His reports and appreciations are models of what such papers should be. He has the capability to work long hours at high speed without loss of accuracy or efficiency, and even in the worst moments of the war, I have never known him ruffled.
>
> Colonel Jacob has a human, helpful personality, is universally liked and respected, and is physically very tough. Although I cannot speak from personal experience, I am sure he would be just as good in the field as he is on the staff.
>
> To sum up, I have no hesitation in saying that Colonel Jacob is an altogether exceptional officer in every way, and that as a staff officer he is one of the best in the Army.'

The Prime Minister's visit to Cairo, Teheran and Moscow, exhausting in its intensity and marked by high drama, would be productive of some of the most important decisions of the war.

Jacob's diary begins on 30 July 1942:

> On Thursday morning, General Ismay came into my room and warned me that the Prime Minister had made up his mind to visit the Middle East, and that I was to go with him. The probable starting time would be the very next morning. The General said he had hoped to persuade the Prime Minister to take him, but this the Prime Minister refused to do, saying that he would be required to hold the fort at home. Considerable consultation then followed, with the Cabinet and with the Prime Minister's doctor, but although the risks of the journey would obviously be great, and the heat of Egypt not good for the Prime Minister's health, no-one had the strength of mind to resist. Accordingly at 8.55 pm on Saturday 1 August, there foregathered at Paddington, No 4 Platform, the party which consisted of:

The Prime Minister
Sir Alexander Cadogan
Sir Charles Wilson (later Lord Moran)
Mr Rowan (later Sir Leslie Rowan: private secretary)
Commander Thompson (PM's Flag Lieutenant)
Inspector Thomson (detective)
Sawyers (PM's valet)
Kinna (PM's stenographer)
CSM Marshall (Royal Military Police)
Myself

Monday, 3 August

After a completely uneventful journey, we landed at Gibraltar at 8.30 am, and were taken to the Governor's House, where the Prime Minister had already arrived. The Governor General, Mason-Macfarlane, seemed in excellent form, and the atmosphere seemed to be good . . . we took off at 6 pm and landed at 8.30 in the morning at landing ground No 224, 25 kilometres north-west of Cairo on the Alexandria road. We were greeted by Air Chief Marshal Tedder, the Minister of State, Sir Miles Lampson, General Corbett (the CGS) and other officers. I was greeted by Arthur Rucker and Cornwall-Jones, who told me that they had arranged for me to stay with them at their flat. After a bath and breakfast, I motored round to the Embassy, where the Prime Minister had arrived. He got to work almost at once, and spent the morning interviewing Mr Casey, the Minister of State, and Air Chief Marshal Tedder.

The Embassy is exactly as in peacetime, complete with Lady Lampson and the baby, and is certainly a very pleasant place to stay, with its enormous verandas and lovely lawn leading down to the Nile. In addition to the Prime Minister, General Sir Alan Brooke, the CIGS, was also staying at the Embassy, and Field Marshal Smuts arrived about lunchtime, having flown at great speed from the Cape. The party was to be completed by the arrival of General Wavell the following day . . .

Having seen that the Prime Minister was well engaged, I went round to GHQ, where Cornwall-Jones has his office, looking in on the way at the office of the Minister of State, separated by only a few hundred yards from each other. Accordingly, I decided to take up my position with Cornwall-Jones. The first thing to do was to collect some staff to handle the telegram traffic, and this was quickly done with the help of Arthur and Cornwall-Jones . . . .

After lunch, the Prime Minister had a talk to Field Marshal Smuts, and then went to his usual rest. At 4 o'clock, General Auchinleck arrived from 8th Army Headquarters and had an hour with CIGS before they both saw the Prime Minister at 5.30. The Prime Minister did little or no business for the rest of the evening, so we all got reasonably early to bed.

Thursday, 4 August

This morning, the Prime Minister saw General Corbett, the CGS, and talked to Smuts and others. Meanwhile, the Commander-in-Chief had a meeting, which lasted the whole morning, on the situation in the Middle East, with particular reference to the possible development of a threat in North Persia, and the measures which should be taken to meet it.

General Wavell arrived shortly before lunch, having flown from India; he was accompanied by General Winterton, his DCGS, and General Kirby, his Director of Staff Duties, both friends of mine, with whom I had a number of talks.

I spent the morning on my usual business, looking after telegrams, and seeing various friends at GHQ. One of these was Pete Rees, now a Major General, and commanding the Cairo Bridgehead. I saw a good deal of him, and heard his account of the recent battles. He had originally commanded a brigade in the 4th Indian Division at Sidi Barrani and Keren [*Abyssinia*], during which time he had received a bar to his DSO. He was then given command of 10 Indian Division in Iraq, which had been brought over to the Western Desert at the opening of the Gazala battle. It had come into action, and had heavy losses, but it had never fought as a division. Brigades had been taken and thrown into the fight piece-meal, and the Division had only concentrated on the Sollum position when the retreat into Egypt was starting. They had actually drawn anti-tank guns on their way into the battle, never having had them before! After the fall of Tobruk, Pete was rung up in the morning by General Gott from Corps Head-quarters, who told him that his Division must hold the Sollum-Capuzzo position for 72 hours. A conversation ensued, which had to be somewhat garbled owing to the fact that it was on an open telephone line. Pete explained to Gott that his Division had been considerably knocked about, had only just concentrated on an incomplete position, and he was doubtful whether it would be able to hold this position for 72 hours against a full scale attack. Gott said he would come up to the Divisional Headquarters shortly.

Some six hours later, General Gott arrived, and handed Pete a piece of paper, telling him to read it. This stated shortly, that Pete Rees did not possess the necessary resolution and firmness for his task, and ordered him to hand over his division immediately. Pete was naturally flabbergasted, but Gott, who appeared somewhat overwrought, was immovable. So Pete had to go. The whole incident was certainly rather extraordinary, especially when one knew that Gott had, in his pocket at the time, later orders to the effect that the Sollum position should be thinned out forthwith, and should not be held against serious attack. There was a good deal of feeling about all this, which seemed to be typical of a number of incidents which had happened recently. Pete's case had come before General Auchinleck, who had recommended that he should be given a division in India. In the meantime, he had given him command of the Cairo Bridgehead.

I felt very sorry for Pete, knowing him so well, and realising what a tiger of a chap he actually is. However, there was nothing to be done, and he had to accept the situation.

At 6 pm the Prime Minister held a meeting with Field Marshal Smuts, the Minister of State, CIGS, General Wavell, General Auchinleck, Admiral Harwood and Air Chief Marshal Tedder. We met in the Prime Minister's study at a round table. The main object of the meeting was to consider the future policy in the Middle East, in the light of decisions recently taken in London.

The Prime Minister gave the meeting a full account of the recent discussions in London, when General Marshall and Admiral King were over, and of the arguments which had led up to the conclusion that we should abandon 'SLEDGEHAMMER' and go for 'TORCH'. Having given his account, the Prime Minister asked for the views of all those present. They were unanimously in favour of the course of action which had been adopted, though General Wavell expressed anxiety that the build-up of the Eastern Fleet and of the Air Striking force in India would be unduly delayed.

Discussion then turned on the situation in the Caucasus, and in the Western Desert. It was soon clear that it would be hard to come to any definite conclusions until we could form a better idea of the likelihood of a German threat to North Persia developing this year. The Prime Minister expressed his intention of finding out from Stalin what Russian forces were disposed to hold the Caucasus, and what their prospects were. After visiting Moscow, he would return to Cairo and final decisions could be taken.

The meeting dispersed to dinner. The Prime Minister went to bed early for him, as he was to make a very early start the next morning for a visit to the Western Desert.

Wednesday, 5 August

The Prime Minister, accompanied by Sir Charles Wilson and Commander Thompson, left the Embassy shortly before 6 am, and motored to Heliopolis, where they got into an aeroplane with General Auchinleck, and flew to Burg el Arab where there is a landing ground just south of the railway from Alexandria to the Western Desert. Cars were waiting there, and the party visited Eighth Army Tactical Headquarters, and the Headquarters of the 1 South African and 9 Australian Divisions. The Prime Minister saw a certain number of troops, and also General Gott and General Ramsden, the two Corps Commanders. He finally lunched with Air Vice Marshal Coningham before returning by air to Heliopolis. He got back to the Embassy at about 5.30 pm, having thoroughly enjoyed his day. He found the desert air most invigorating, but of course it made him much more tired than he cared to admit. After his usual rest he saw the Minister of State at 7.30 pm, after which he did very little business.

I was unfortunately prevented from going with the Prime Minister, because General Auchinleck refused to allow any more hangers-on. He was most anxious to avoid any kind of procession of cars, which might be spotted from the air. I therefore spent the day doing odd jobs, and seeing people. Among others, I saw Jock Whiteley, who was in Cairo on his way home to England. He had been BGS Eighth Army all through the recent battle, and gave a most interesting account of Tobruk, as far as events were known. He said that General Klopper, who was in command of Tobruk, was respected by the Army, but the South African staff were not of very high grade. It seems that as soon as the Germans invaded Tobruk they were able to put into effect the plan of attack which they had drawn up last November. (At that time, they were about to assault Tobruk, when they were forestalled by our attack, which had raised the siege.) The German attack developed with great rapidity. On the south-east of the perimeter it broke in, as was inevitable, considering the length of the perimeter which had to be held, and therefore the comparative weakness of the crust. This would not have mattered if the counter-attack, which had been planned and reconnoitred, had been executed according to plan. Something went wrong with the counter-attack – no-one yet knows what – and all the British tanks were knocked out before they could interfere with the German penetration. The Germans then made straight for the harbour, and also for Divisional Head-quarters, which had a most uneasy time being chased from pillar to post by German tanks.

General Klopper was in wireless touch with Headquarters Eighth Army, all through the first night, and Jock himself was almost continuously on the air talking to him, and trying to arrange that the South Africans should break out with the help of diversions from the south by troops from the Eighth Army. Finally, there was silence, for as far as Jock knows, the breakout never could be attempted, possibly on account of the fact that the Germans had captured the petrol, without which the transport could not make the distance.

When General Auchinleck had come up and taken personal command of Eighth Army, he had brought with him his DCGS (Chink) Dorman-Smith. The object of this was that Chink should deal with all the Middle East work, while General Auchinleck dealt with the Army Staff for all matters affecting their Army only. Chink being the sort of chap he is, however, it was not long before he started issuing all kinds of fantastic instructions to Eighth Army, and generally making Jock's position as BGS impossible. In the end, Jock, who was very tired, was ordered home for a change and rest, being relieved as BGS by de Guingand, the DMI, Middle East.

Thursday, 6 August

Having had numerous private conversations with the leading figures, such as the Minister of State, the Commanders-in-Chief and the CGS, and having taken counsel of Field Marshal Smuts, the Prime Minister came to his final conclusions on certain immediate steps necessary to rectify the situation in the Middle East. This evening, he accordingly drafted a long telegram to the War Cabinet, which was vetted by Field Marshal Smuts and the CIGS. This telegram was eventually sent off at 8.15 pm.

The Prime Minister's proposals were, first of all, for an immediate change in the Commander-in-Chief, Middle East, and in certain other important posts, notably CGS and DCGS. Secondly, he wanted, forthwith, to split off Persia and Iraq from the Middle East Command, and to form it into an independent Army Command. The new post thus created would be offered to General Auchinleck. The Prime Minister's motives were these. He had found a disturbing state of affairs in the Army in the Middle East. It had received a severe beating in a battle which everybody thought should have been won. The Army was bewildered, and no longer a coherent fighting machine. Some striking change was therefore required to offer a stimulus to the troops. On the other hand, the Prime Minister had a great opinion of General Auchinleck, and was most adverse to the idea that his services should be lost to the State. He felt that if General Auchinleck had been freed from the responsibility for the Levant-Caspian front, and had been able to concentrate on the Western Desert, he would have taken command when the battle broke out, instead of waiting until the situation was desperate. This might well have turned the scale and given us a victory instead of defeat. The Prime Minister was therefore determined that the best possible fighting soldier should be placed in command of the Middle East, and that he should have nothing to think of except the battle against Rommel, which he would conduct personally.

The CIGS was in agreement with the Prime Minister over the proposal to split off Persia and Iraq, though for a rather different reason. He felt that it was wrong for an area of such vital importance as Persia and Iraq to remain any longer as the Cinderella of either the Middle East or of India. He wanted someone to give it his entire attention, and to drive on the preparations so badly needed for the reception of large forces for 1943.

The CIGS and the Prime Minister did not see eye to eye on the subject of the conduct of the battle by the Commander-in-Chief, Middle East. CIGS held the orthodox view that the C-in-C, Middle East, should give general directions, but should leave the whole conduct of the battle itself to the Commander of the Eighth Army. This difference of opinion did not declare itself in the terms of the telegram sent home, on which all were agreed. General Alexander was to succeed General Auchinleck. General Corbett and General Dorman-Smith were to go, their replacements to be chosen subsequently, and General Gott was to be given command of the Eighth Army.

As the result of my own conversations with the various people of my standing, whom I met in the Middle East, I gathered a number of interesting impressions. As the result of the events of the last three months, the Army in the Middle East is in a rather bewildered state. They have just lost a big battle, which they felt they ought to have won. They are disturbed by various happenings in the Desert, and nearly everyone you talk to has a different explanation of why there was a failure. There are certain things, however, on which all agree. I can perhaps best summarise what I have learnt as follows:

(a) There is universal respect for General Auchinleck as a big man, and a strong personality. No one openly criticises him. Nevertheless, he has not created a coherent Army, and most of the criticisms and explanations which people give are directed to matters which are his immediate concern.

(b) Everyone groans over General Corbett as CGS Middle East. His shortcomings have been particularly apparent since General Auchinleck went up to command Eighth Army. GHQ has been a rudderless ship since then. General Corbett can perhaps best be described in the words of the Prime Minister, 'a very small, agreeable man, of no personality and little experience'. This is the man General Auchinleck chose above all others for CGS, and had designated as Commander of Eighth Army.

(c) Everyone regards General Dorman-Smith as a menace of the first order, and responsible for many of the evil theories which have led to such mistakes in the handling of the Army. General Auchinleck thought Dorman-Smith had a brilliant brain, and also thought he could keep him under control. In this he was quite mistaken.

(d) Our misfortunes in the Western Desert are not universally attributed to inferior equipment. In fact, one officer of the Royal Armoured Corps, of considerable experience, went so far as to say that equipment had nothing to do with the outcome of the battle. All are agreed, however, that faulty leadership and bad tactics were the principal causes of our defeat. It seems that General Auchinleck and General Ritchie, perhaps influenced by Dorman-Smith, came to the conclusion that one of the main lessons of the previous campaign (CRUSADER) was that warfare in the Desert demands great flexibility. The theory was that the Division was too unwieldy a formation, and the operations should be carried out by the Brigade Group, or the 'Battle Group' – an even smaller detachment. This theory was put into effect on a grand scale, with the result that no formation ever fought for long under the commander and staff who had trained it. Brigades were taken from their divisions and pushed into the battle piecemeal. Some cavalry regiments were even broken up, squadron by squadron, and sent up to join other regiments. The well-tried principle that the best results from artillery are obtained by its centralised control was forgotten. A good example is offered by the 10 Indian Division, which was thrust into the fight, and suffered severely, without even being commanded by its own Divisional Commander. The Army was broken into a thousand fragments. Whether or not this flexibility-run-wild was responsible, it is undoubtedly true that we showed ourselves incapable of concentrating superior force, and of utilising the whole of our resources simultaneously. This showed itself in the dismal recurrence of the same event, namely, the overrunning of brigade after brigade by an enemy in superior force, while the rest of the Army appeared powerless to assist.

For example, 1 South African Division and 50 Division took no effective part in the battle of Gazala, while the position at Bir Hacheim, and later a brigade of 50 Division itself in an isolated locality, were overwhelmed. Throughout the battle the Germans were always in superior force where the fighting was taking place.

(e) In the later stages of the battle, the co-operation between the infantry and the armoured formations deteriorated. The infantry had had heavy losses in attacks in which they had not been properly supported by the tanks. The armour had lost confidence through having been engaged on many occasions against superior enemy tanks, and through being outranged by the enemy's guns. The result of all this was that in the battle fought in July on the El Alamein front, at a time when the Italians were at the end of their tether, and the Germans were hard put to it to stop the gaps with their much reduced Panzer Divisions, our Army was unable to seize its opportunities and complete the local successes gained. The fundamental causes can undoubtedly be traced back to the faulty tactics already referred to.

(f) The effectiveness of Eighth Army was much reduced by its heterogeneous composition. The performance of the South Africans, who were individually of fine quality, was most disappointing. The Indian troops, too, were no longer of the calibre of the original 4 and 5 Indian Divisions. These were said to be the best Divisions in the Middle East, but subsequent arrivals from India were naturally of lower quality, as they consisted of many newly-raised units with officers who had not had the long experience of their own men, which is so essential with Indian troops. 50 British Division came out of the battle with flying colours, as did many other British units. The Royal Artillery, who had very heavy casualties, also had fought magnificently. Nevertheless, even making allowances for the patchy composition of the Army, there were far too many cases of units surrendering in circumstances in which in the last war they would have fought it out.

Three main causes may have accounted for this. First, the great expansion of the Army meant that formations arriving in the Middle East were very inexperienced, and there was no method by which they could be introduced gradually to the battle. In the last war, new divisions could be placed first in quiet sectors, and thus gradually worked up till they found their feet. There was no means of doing that this time, and these new formations found themselves plunged straight into a big battle. Secondly, the discipline of the Army is no longer what it used to be, and in the last resort it is discipline which counts. Thirdly, there is lacking in this war the strong incentive of a national cause. Nothing concrete has replaced the old motto, 'For King and Country'. The aims set before the people in this war are negative, and it still does not seem to have been brought home to people that it is a war for their own existence.

Finally, there is a need for new blood, and a more rapid interchange between the Middle East and home, and particularly among the Commanders. All spoke in the highest terms of 'Strafer' Gott, but he had been two years in the desert without a break, and had gone through the hardest fighting from beginning to end. His experience would have been invaluable at home, but everyone said that he would not last much longer unless he had relief from the strain. The same is true of many lesser men.

The Prime Minister's visit will have been worthwhile, if only for the stimulus which he has given to the Army, and for the new blood which he has introduced.

Friday, 7 August
[*Jacob spent the morning seeing Squadron Leader Llewellyn about their*

onward flight and in discussion with General Wavell and CIGS about the reorganisation of Middle East Command. Then he was summoned by the Prime Minister.]

I found him in his dressing gown, having just awakened from his sleep, and about to begin dictating his reply to the telegram from the War Cabinet. The latter, while generally approving the idea of drastic changes, disliked the splitting of the Command, and furthermore were most unhappy about the proposal to put Auchinleck into the new Middle East post. They felt it would be better to remove him altogether. There seemed, on the face of it, some justification for the latter view, as what in fact was to be offered to General Auchinleck was one third of his existing command. I personally felt he would not accept it. The Prime Minister wanted to know when the Middle East Command had absorbed Persia and Iraq, and what reasons were then advanced for the change. I reminded him that the change had been made on 5 January, while he was in Washington engaged in setting up the ABDA Area. The principal reason which then turned the scale was that General Wavell, who was C-in-C India, and under whose command Iraq and Persia were, was busy looking eastward to Burma, which was threatened by the Japanese, and could not give enough attention to the countries lying to the west.

CIGS then appeared, and he and the Prime Minister went through the matter again, and reaffirmed their original views. The CIGS then went off to a meeting, while the Prime Minister dictated his telegram to Kinna, myself sitting listening. The Prime Minister, as usual, strode up and down, muttering his sentences, and going through all the agony of composition. Meanwhile, Sir Sikander Hyat Khan was waiting to see him down below, and photographers, who were to take a picture of the house party, were champing the bit. About 6.30 it was done, and when it had been typed, I was sent round to get CIGS's approval while another copy was shown to Field Marshal Smuts. They changed nothing, so that at 8.15 pm I was able to hand the telegram to the Cipher Officer.

I then rushed to dine with Brian Robertson at the Continental Hotel, where we sat in the cool on the roof and had a good dinner with a band and cabaret thrown in. Brian seemed quite unchanged after eight years, and we had a most interesting talk all about the battle and our families. We parted about 11 pm, and I returned to the Embassy. I found that the bad news had just been received that 'Strafer' Gott, the Commander of the 13th Corps, had been shot down in an aircraft and killed. This unfortunate event not only meant a cruel loss to the Army, but made it necessary to reconsider matters. Gott was to have taken over Eighth Army, and so a telegram was sent straight off to ask for Montgomery to come out hot foot on the heels of Alexander.

Saturday, 8 August

At about 12.45 am, the Prime Minister began to get restive, and asked me to try to get through on the telephone to London to get the answer to our various telegrams. This we managed to do, the call coming through at 2.30 am. Meanwhile, the Prime Minister had gone to bed, in view of an early start in the morning. Unfortunately, the Cabinet were still sitting when the call came through, so that Pug, who answered, could not give me a full answer, and I had to await the signal.

Just as he was going to bed, the Prime Minister asked me to take up to General Auchinleck the next morning the letter informing him of his removal, and offering him the Persia and Iraq Command. I spent the rest of the night making arrangements for my journey to Eighth Army HQ, and waiting for the reply from home. The latter arrived at five minutes to six, just as I was completing two hours on the sofa. The Prime Minister awoke at 6.30 and came down looking for the answer, and I went up to his bedroom with it. He had postponed until 8 am the start of his tour to Kassassin, and I spent the rest of the time till then up in his room chatting to him while he had breakfast, the CIGS being present off and on.

The reply from home gave a reluctant approval, but deprecated the term 'Middle East' for the new command, as likely to cause confusion with the old. The Prime Minister accordingly renamed his proposed commands Iraq and Persia, and Middle East, and amended his letter to General Auchinleck to conform. He also telegraphed an account of his proposals to the President.

At about 8.15 the Prime Minister and his party left, and I then managed to get breakfast and shave, and at 9.20 I reached Heliopolis aerodrome. I found that I was to be sent forward to Burg el Arab aerodrome in an ancient Audax, but fortunately it turned out to be unserviceable, so they sent me in a Proctor, a nice little three-seater trainer. The pilot did not like it much because the view to the rear was practically nil, and enemy fighters are prevalent round Burg el Arab, where, indeed, Gott's aircraft was shot down. However, all went well. We followed the Delta to Amriya and then skidded along to Burg el Arab at 100 feet, landing at 11 o'clock. A car was there to meet me, and I drove to Tactical HQ, Eighth Army . . . .

On arrival, I was met by Mackinnon, the C-in-C's PA, and shown into the Chief's caravan, where he was sitting at work. I felt as if I was just going to murder an unsuspecting friend. After offering the condolences of the Prime Minister and CIGS on the death of General Gott, I handed the C-in-C the letter I had brought. He opened it and read it through two or three times in silence. He did not move a muscle, and remained outwardly calm, and in complete control of himself. He then asked me whether it was intended that Persia should be under India. I told him it was not so, the whole idea being that there should be three independent commands. We discussed this for a bit, and then he led me out into the open, and we wandered about while he cleared his mind by talking to me. He said it was a very evenly-balanced question as to whether Iraq and Persia should come under India, or under the Middle East, but that it would never work to make an independent command in those countries. He felt that sooner or later they would inevitably come under India.

He then discussed the question of whether he would accept the proposed new Command. He stated emphatically that he was not actuated by motives of pique at being turned out of his present appointment, but that he was convinced that he could not accept what was offered. He has been C-in-C, India, and C-in-C, Middle East, and now he was asked to take a position that was virtually that of one of his own Army Commanders. The fact that he was being moved would indicate to the Army that he had lost the confidence of the Government, and had failed in his task. They would regard the acceptance of the Iraq and Persia Command as a face-saving device. The Indian Army, whose Commander-in-Chief he had been, would certainly not understand the transaction. He could hardly in these circumstances retain the confidence of the troops, and by reason of his invidious position he could hardly have confidence in himself. He would thus not be a successful Commander, and the Government would do much better to let him retire into oblivion. He greatly disliked the idea of the appointment of unsuccessful Generals to other posts, and gave as instances of this the case of Lord Gort, and of General Lloyd. He had always determined, when his time came, to set his face against accepting any sop. I felt bound to say that I had never imagined that he would take up any other attitude, and that I had told CIGS this straight. Nevertheless, I knew the Prime Minister very much hoped that he would find it possible to accept the offer.

After talking and walking for about half-an-hour, we went in to lunch in the Mess, a table set under a camouflage and anti-fly net only. Lunch consisted of bully, potatoes and beetroot, biscuits and cheese and coffee. At lunch I met and had a long talk with Noel Martin, Brigadier Royal Artillery, Eighth Army. He spoke very highly of the courage, dash and flair for desert warfare of 'Strafer' Gott, but deplored the lack of good commanders. He said he wished 'Monty' were there. I could hardly tell him that his wish might be fulfilled.

After lunch, I had some further talk in the same strain with General Auchinleck, and then said 'goodbye' leaving for Burg el Arab in the car, taking Cunningham, the C-in-C's ADC with me. He was going ahead to prepare the way for the Chief, who announced his intention of returning to Cairo the next morning. The return journey was uneventful, and I was back in the Embassy before 5 pm.

The Prime Minister, it seems, had had a successful trip, and was asleep. He woke at 6 o'clock, and I had to go and recount to him as best I could what had passed between me and General Auchinleck. CIGS joined us, and I was rather surprised to find that the Prime Minister seemed to understand General Auchinleck's point of view, and his mind seemed to be veering towards putting Iraq and Persia under India. His mind is entirely fixed on the defeat of Rommel, and on getting General Alexander into complete charge of the operations in the Western Desert. He does not understand how a man can remain in Cairo while great events are occurring in the desert, and leave the conduct of them to someone else. He strode up and down declaiming on this point, and he means to have his way. 'Rommel, Rommel, Rommel, Rommel', he cried, 'What else matters but beating him. Instead of which, C-in-C, Middle East sits in Cairo attending to things which a Minister, or a Quartermaster, could deal with'. The tussle will come tomorrow, when General Alexander arrives.

I could not have admired more the way General Auchinleck received me, and his attitude throughout. A great man and fighter.

Sunday, 9 August

General Alexander arrived safely at 7.30 am this morning, and had breakfast with the Prime Minister and CIGS. The morning was spent by the Prime Minister waiting for General Auchinleck. He saw General Lindsell at noon for 20 minutes or so. The C-in-C arrived at GHQ from the Desert about noon, and saw CIGS there. At 12.30 he went with CIGS to the Embassy, and had a long interview with the Prime Minister alone. I had five minutes or so with him when he first arrived. He seemed not to have changed his mind at all since the previous day, and I gave him an account of the reception which the Prime Minister had given to my description of his attitude. I told him that on hearing that he was unwilling to accept the post offered to him, the Prime Minister's mind seemed to have moved towards handing Iraq and Persia over to India. General Auchinleck then said that this seemed to confirm an idea which had crossed his mind that the offer was made to him in the certainty that he would refuse, so that the hand-over to India could then be proceeded with, and it could be said that an appointment had been offered to him but that he had refused to accept it. I did my best to destroy this idea.

After lunch, CIGS, the C-in-C and General Alexander conferred in GHQ. At 7 pm, Alexander saw the Prime Minister, and was followed by the Minister of State. It seems that General Auchinleck retains his attitude, but the Prime Minister has asked him to take two or three days to think it over. He hopes he will come round. No announcements are to be made until Alexander has taken over, which is unlikely to be before the 12th.

Monday, 10 August

The Prime Minister spent the morning seeing the C-in-C's and AOC-in-C's War Rooms. The former is particularly well arranged and complete, and has an excellent statistical room attached.

During the morning I drafted, and got the Prime Minister to sign, a minute to the Minister of State asking him to set up the inquiry into the details of how the separation of Iraq and Persia from the Middle East could be done, particularly in the administrative field. Cornwall-Jones immediately went into action on this, and the Minister held a meeting the same afternoon to get matters in train. The Prime Minister drafted a telegram home about the arrival of General Alexander, the arrangements for him taking over, the announcements to be made, and General Auchinleck's attitude. I lunched at the Embassy, the first meal to which I had been invited although I work here all day, and even that was screwed out of them by Rowan. Apart from the Lampsons, the Prime Minister and his own staff, the guests were General Alexander and General Catroux, the latter rather a good-looking chap with iron-grey hair, spare upright figure, and intelligent face.

The Embassy keeps nearly everything going as in peace, and the Ambassador had two ADCs, an unusual thing for ambassadors but essential in Cairo. Lady Lampson looks very little older than when last I saw her in 1938, and is quite amusing. She seems completely English, at any rate in voice and outward conduct, no trace of an Italian accent. Her baby, which is only a few months old, is much in evidence on the lawn, and keeps getting photographed with Smuts, or the Prime Minister or someone. The whole place seems rather unreal with a battle going on 120 miles away.

At 5 pm the Prime Minister saw CIGS and General Lindsell and myself about the requirements of vehicles for the Army. A most inconclusive talk, for which enormous masses of figures had been sweated out by the staff. After an hour or so of this, he moved out on to the lawn, and sat chatting with CIGS, Wavell, and later the Minister of State. The rest of the day was spent feverishly packing papers, and sorting those to be left behind.

Tuesday, 11 August

We eventually took off for Teheran and Moscow at 2.15 am, CIGS, General Wavell, Air Chief Marshal Tedder, Sir Alexander Cadogan, Kremer (a Russian) and myself composing the passenger list, and Llewellyn still being Captain.

[*To complete Jacob's account of Churchill's activities in Egypt, the diary now continues at 17 August when the Prime Minister and his advisers had returned to Cairo from Moscow. The intervening six days in Teheran and Moscow are recorded in the next chapter.*]

The diary continues:

We arrived back from Moscow at Heliopolis at 11.40 am on 17 August, the Prime Minister's aircraft being about ten minutes behind ours. We motored straight to the Embassy and settled in as before . . . .

Tuesday, 18 August

[*Jacob was involved in sorting out a muddle over the synchronisation of announcements in London and Cairo about the changes in command, and in a long meeting on the split of Persia and Iraq from the Middle East. Difficulties arose over the control of the RAF in the new Persia/Iraq Command, as Wavell demanded it should rest with GHQ India, whereas maintenance was from the Egyptian Base. The Prime Minister in general favoured the return of Persia and Iraq to India, but reserved the RAF decision for himself. He directed that General Lindsell with his Committee should report on the remaining problems.*]

Wednesday, 19 August

[*After a lengthy sitting, Cornwall-Jones, with Jacob, drew up the Lindsell Committee's report.*

The Prime Minister left Cairo at 3.15 pm for a visit to the Western Desert with General Alexander.]

. . . During the day, the news of the Dieppe raid had been coming in, and when we got back to the Embassy after dinner, we found that the Prime Minister had not been able to contain himself any longer, and was ringing up from the Western Desert for news. Fortunately, a communiqué had just come in, which we were able to give, and later a signal from home arrived. Apparently all had gone well with the Prime Minister during the day, and he was spending a very pleasant evening in the desert at Eighth Army Headquarters where General Montgomery had taken over.

Brian Horrocks arrived from England it seems, yesterday, and whizzed through Cairo on his way to the desert, where he is taking over the 13th Corps. I was delighted to hear this, but very sorry I had missed him as he went through Cairo.

Thursday, 20 August

I spent the morning seeing General Lindsell and Harriman over the development of the Persian railway, discussions on which had begun in Teheran. I lunched with Mr Kirk, the American Minister; Kirk is a tall, exceedingly smart-looking man, of the type so familiar to the English public in American films, who usually appears as the high-class lawyer, with the small moustache and the perfect suit. He is a very rich man, and keeps this big house in Cairo merely for his friends to stay at, and have lunch. He himself lives in another house at Mena . . . I found him extremely entertaining to talk to.

The Prime Minister arrived back at 6.30 pm, having thoroughly enjoyed his tour, and settled straight down at 7 o'clock to a meeting on the Iraq–Persian Command. The discussion once more developed into an argument about control of the Air between Wavell and CIGS on the one side, and Tedder on the other, the Prime Minister acting as referee. The meeting broke up about 8.30 with everything still undecided, but the Prime Minister announced his intention of sleeping on the question, and dictating a solution in the morning.

There is no doubt that the arrival of Alexander and Monty has already made a great difference to the atmosphere in the Army, and the Prime Minister feels very pleased about it. On his arrival back from the desert, he made one of his characteristic remarks to Rowan and myself. He said how sorry he was that we had not been able to go with him on his tour, but he hoped that we would go up ourselves another day, and the Commander-in-Chief himself had said how glad he would be to see us. It is so likely that we should be able to go off for a hike like that, leaving him high and dry with nobody to serve up the news and look after all his business. However, he means it all very well!

Nevertheless, despite a very exhausting day in the desert, the Prime Minister's vitality had been unabated at dinner. Sir Alexander Cadogan later described the scene:

> 'He held forth the whole of dinner, ragging everyone. Sir Charles Wilson, his 'Personal Physician', is one of his principal butts. To Winston's delight, poor CW fell ill of the usual local tummy complaint, and Winston now goes about saying to everyone 'Sir Charles has been a terrible anxiety to us the whole time, but I hope we'll get him through!' Last night at dinner, Winston held forth to the whole table on medicine, psychology etc. (all Sir Charles' subjects) and worked himself up to a terrific disquisition. I suspect (and I inferred from Sir Charles' expression) that it was pretty good nonsense. And I think Winston must have had an inkling of that too, as he ended up 'My God! I do have to work hard to teach that chap his job!'[2]

Friday, 21 August

I was sent for about 8.30 this morning, and found the Prime Minister dictating a telegram home containing his solution of the Iraq–Persia problem. He had decided to set up an independent command forthwith, and to put Jumbo Wilson in as Commander-in-Chief. Tedder had won the battle over the Air Force . . . .

The Prime Minister told me to arrange for the Director of Military Operations and the Deputy Director of Military Intelligence to come and see him at 5.30 that afternoon, to discuss the relative strengths of the Eighth Army and Axis forces in the Western Desert. Just to make things easier, he then asked McCreery, the new CGS, and Lindsell to come around at the same time. I spent the afternoon straightening matters out, and in the end we had them all bringing their figures. We then spent a happy couple of hours at the good old pastime of whittling away the enemy's strength on paper. In the end, the Prime Minister was satisfied that he had got a fair comparison of men, vehicles, weapons, and so forth, and it was generally agreed that, taking one thing and another into account, we were about fifty-fifty with the enemy in the Western Desert.

The Prime Minister asked McCreery which armoured forces he would rather have, the enemy's or our own; and McCreery stated definitely that he would rather have ours. The position seems to be that, whereas the enemy has superiority in tank and anti-tank gun power, we have superiority in numbers, the two about cancelling each other out.

Saturday, 22 August
[*The Prime Minister visited the Tura Caves, now turned into RAF workshops, motored to Heliopolis, inspected heavy bombers at Abu Sueir and saw 51 Division, newly arrived in Egypt. Jacob drafted telegrams about the Persian Railway, a directive from the CIGS to the Cs-in-C Middle East, Persia and Iraq, and a signal to London about a public announcement.*]

At 6.15, the Prime Minister saw General Anders [*Commander-in-Chief Polish Forces in the Soviet Union and Middle East*] and Jumbo Wilson, together. The meeting was conducted in French, which the Prime Minister insists on talking whenever he gets the opportunity. He does not talk very fast, and he has not a very large vocabulary, nor can his accent be said to be exactly Parisian; nevertheless, he manages to hold his own all right, and I found no difficulty in taking the record of the meeting. Jumbo's French is about on a par with that of the Prime Minister. We managed to steer the Prime Minister off any discussion of equipment for the Poles. He contented himself by saying he would go into the question with General Sikorski when he got home, and that he would intervene with Stalin when he thought the time was propitious. General Anders seemed fairly satisfied, and departed for Teheran.

After this meeting, a telegram arrived from London, saying that the War Cabinet were delighted with the Prime Minister's solution of the Iraq–Persia business. This pleased the Prime Minister very much, and he marched up and down his bedroom, saying that he knew all along that he had laid a very good egg that morning.

This evening we completed all our plans for our home departure the following day. Everything had to be kept most secret, and all the arrangements for further visits to the troops by the Prime Minister continued to be made, so that very few people knew that he was actually going. This was necessary, because the news of the Moscow visit, and the communiqué drawn up in Moscow had been released, so that the enemy might well be waiting for his return.

Sunday, 23 August

We spent the morning doing all the last minute jobs. The Prime Minister seemed full of beans, and thoroughly satisfied with everything that had happened. There is no doubt that he can look back upon an extremely successful job of work in the Middle East.

We drove out once more to Landing Ground 224, threading our way through the usual mass of transport moving on the L of C. As we were on our way, General Alexander whistled past us on his way to the Front, and flying the Union Jack. We got to the aerodrome about 5 o'clock. All went well and without a hitch. At five minutes past seven, the Prime Minister's aircraft took off, with a squadron of Kittyhawks keeping guard overhead. We followed at 7.30 – our passengers being CIGS, Cadogan, Dunphie, Kinna, Llewellyn, and myself.

Monday, 24 August

We were awakened at about 5.30 in the morning, and told to put on our oxygen masks, as we were going up to 14,000 feet to make certain of clearing the mountains in Algeria and Spanish Morocco.

All went well until we were roughly opposite Land's End. The cloud then increased, and there was an electric storm which caused sparks all over the wireless apparatus when the trailing aerial was let down. The wireless operator found it impossible to communicate with any of the stations that he tried, so we had to rely entirely on navigation by dead reckoning. We came right down to 1,000 feet, and were still in a thick fog, so no landfall in Ireland was possible. We were all wondering what would happen next, and we watched the course. When the navigator thought we were about over the south coast of Ireland, he turned east and flew for some time in that direction, sometimes low, and sometimes high, but without any break in the cloud. He then turned north again, so as to be quite sure that he would be over England and not France.

At last, at 8 pm, when the sun was getting uncomfortably low, a break appeared in the clouds, and we saw land below us in the form of a coastline running south-west and north-east. We were then herded into the bomb bay, which was the usual procedure before landing, so as to get the weight distributed right, and very soon after we touched ground safely in the gathering dusk, at Lyneham.

Mrs Churchill and CAS were on the aerodrome to meet the Prime Minister, and in a very short time we found ourselves comfortably installed in the special train on the way to London.

We then had a jolly good dinner, and arrived at Paddington at about 11 pm. There was a herd of cameramen and flashlights on the platform, and the usual ugly rush, in which the members of the Cabinet struggled to meet the Prime Minister. I watched the reception for a moment or two, and then collected my luggage, which was all handy, and got away in the car with Jo.

It was astonishing to think it was only three weeks since we had left England. We had certainly covered the ground – about 14,000 miles, or 70 hours flying. I do not think any of us realised until the next few days how tired we were.

This visit by Churchill and Brooke to the Middle East theatre was not only timely in stabilising a phase of tragic disaster but, more important, was decisive in providing new and better commanders. Alexander and Montgomery, enjoying added resources, including the Sherman tanks and self-propelled guns sent from the United States, would soon achieve a series of victories by which German and Italian forces would eventually be decisively defeated. After the defeat of Rommel at Alam Halfa, Montgomery's battle of Alamein was rightly hailed as the 'end of the beginning'; and by 30 November 1942, with Allied forces successfully landed in operation TORCH, the entire situation in North Africa and the Mediterranean would be radically changed.

Jacob's contribution to the visit had been threefold. First, with his usual efficiency he had carried out his routine task of reducing to recorded decisions the output of a multitude of meetings and informal discussions, and ensuring that action followed. Second, he had taken on the unusual task of assessing the malaise which had permeated the Eighth Army, and discussing it with Churchill. His analysis, though not accepted later by all those who had been to Agheila and back in 'the Benghazi Handicap', was shrewd, well-balanced, and profound. Third, he had had the distasteful task of delivering to Auchinleck Churchill's fateful letter removing him from his command, and then bringing back to the Prime Minister the General's reaction. He had discharged this unwelcome duty with sympathy and tact.

8

Conferring with Stalin

Churchill's crucial meetings with Stalin in Moscow were sandwiched into his Egyptian visit in the period 11–17 August 1942. Having installed Alexander in Cairo, and Montgomery as Commander Eighth Army, and made decisions about command in Persia and Iraq, the Prime Minister turned his attention to his relationship with Stalin. He decided to break his journey to Moscow at Teheran, where decisions could conveniently be taken about the running of the Persian Railway, the only communication open by land with the Russian armies.

He and his party took off from Landing Ground 224 in Egypt at 2.15 am on Tuesday, 11 August 1942. He was greatly concerned about Stalin's reaction to the unpleasant but inevitable decision that there would be no cross-channel assault in 1942. Churchill also hoped to obtain a frank and comprehensive report on the Soviet Army's situation on their main front, and on their measures to oppose the German thrust towards the Caucasus. To underline the solidarity of the Anglo-American Alliance he had arranged with Roosevelt that his special representative, Averell Harriman should accompany the British party. Finally in the hope of generating comradeship with Stalin he would acquaint him with the plans for operation TORCH, due to start in early November.

Jacob's diary begins:

Tuesday, 11 August
    The party had been swelled by the addition of Mr Harriman, General Maxwell, General Spalding, General Wavell, Air Chief Marshal Tedder, and their Staff officers. The intention was to arrive at Teheran at 7.30 am, and then go straight on to Moscow, arriving before dark. There was a miscalculation, however, of the

132

time of start from Cairo. It seems that somebody had said to the Prime Minister that he ought to see the sun rising over something or other at Baghdad. The Prime Minister said he thought that would be good, and the start was adjusted accordingly. Unfortunately, the Prime Minister had no idea that this was being done, or that it would delay the arrival at Teheran. We did not fetch up until 8.30 am, which meant that we had not enough time to get on to Moscow before dark.

On arrival at Teheran, we were met by the British Minister, Sir Reeder Bullard, General Fraser, the Military Attaché, and other officers, and taken straight to the British Legation . . . . By 9.30 we were sitting down to the sort of breakfast that no one in England had seen for years.

The Prime Minister was annoyed to find that his plan had been upset, and vented his wrath on Tommy, who was responsible for the arrangements. There was much discussion as to what we should do. One possibility was to fly on to Kuibyshev, and spend the night there . . . but after much argument, the conclusion was reached that nothing would be gained by going to Kuibyshev, as we still could not get to Moscow until the following day. Moreover, the rest at Teheran would do the Prime Minister good . . . .

After tea we had a meeting at which Harriman and General Spalding expounded their views on the development of the Persian Railway. Brigadier Rhodes, who is in charge of the Railway, had come up to Teheran to meet the Prime Minister.

[*The Americans claimed that the development of the railway was not going ahead fast enough and suggested that the project be handed over to them, backed by their greater resources. However, the PM foresaw the possibility of friction if a British force were to be dependent on a main artery controlled by the United States.*

During the meeting, the Persian Prime Minister called on the PM; their short discussion appeared to be limited to the hooting of cars outside the Legation: the noise had not assisted the PM's concentration. After dinner, the conversation turned on the training of engine-drivers. Brigadier Rhodes complained that the personnel sent out to him from England were not of a very high standard, and that to drive a main line train in the UK required fifteen years' experience; this was greeted with scorn by the PM, who also enjoyed pulling the leg of Harriman, the American railroad King.

Before retiring, the PM proposed that he should sleep at the Summer Legation and suggested that his bed, after dismantling, be taken up by car and re-erected. Needless to say, this suggestion was not adopted.

The party, with the PM's aircraft leading, took off at 6.30 am on 12 August. In Jacob's plane, piloted by a Russian, were 'the four great beasts', namely CIGS, Wavell, Tedder and Cadogan. Unfortunately they were delayed due to engine trouble, and did not reach Moscow until 7.45 pm on 13 August, where they found that the PM, on the previous evening, had already had one meeting with Stalin.

For this meeting in the Kremlin, the PM had been accompanied by the Ambassador, Sir Archibald Clark Kerr, and Mr Dunlop who acted as interpreter. Jacob learnt that the PM had made a careful plan of campaign for this first talk, and had adhered to it skilfully.]

The diary continues:

He had had to explain to Stalin why it was we could not open a Second Front in Europe in 1942. We had, of course, made no promise to do so, though we had, along with the Americans, made a public declaration that we intended to open a Second Front, without specifying when. For some reason or other, the Russians were firmly under the impression that we were going to do it in 1942 and were feeling that we had broken our word. The Prime Minister intended to explain quite frankly what the situation was, and to hold out no false hopes, and to warn Stalin that we might not even be able to continue sending convoys to North Russia in view of the loss entailed. Having painted the picture in its blackest colours, the Prime Minister intended to say to Stalin that it might interest him to know what he did intend to do, even though it might not be of such direct interest to the Russians as the opening of the Second Front. The Prime Minister would then tell Stalin about TORCH.

I was told that the interview went off exactly according to plan: Stalin, having been plunged deeper and deeper into gloom, pricked up his ears very quickly when TORCH was explained to him, and was very quick to grasp the significance of the operation, and the advantages which would accrue to the Allied cause from its success. The interview ended on a cordial note.

Thursday, 13 August

Having settled into State Villa No 7, I found the Prime Minister ready for dinner, and he walked up and down the drive with me, telling me what had happened with the meeting with Stalin the previous evening. He seemed in good spirits, and not a bit tired. He said there was to be a meeting with Stalin at 11 pm that night, but he did not intend to go over the whole ground again. He wanted simply to introduce CIGS and the others to Stalin, and after a few general remarks, to suggest that the Military Staffs should proceed to examine in more detail the matters which he had discussed with Stalin the previous evening in general terms.

We finally sat down to dinner at 9.15, Harriman, CIGS, Wavell, Tedder, and Cadogan being present. Harriman was staying with the American Ambassador . . . . After dinner, we all set off in a procession of cars to go to the Kremlin.

It was a dark night, and Moscow is completely blacked out. No headlights are allowed on cars, so that we crawled along at a very slow pace. As a result, we were half an hour late for the meeting. We eventually arrived at one of the gates of the Kremlin, where we were carefully examined through the window of the car, and were then admitted through a medieval archway. We had not driven far inside before we drew up at an entrance door where we got out of the car, and were led upstairs, and along passages, until we found ourselves in a small ante-room where there was the most extraordinary man sitting at a desk. The room was very strongly lit, half-panelled in pale wood, with furniture of the same colour. The man at the desk was about five feet high, dressed in a bluish-grey tunic and trousers, and had a completely shaven head and a round flabby face. His companion in the room was by contrast a cheerful-looking tough in Army uniform, presumably a member of the GPU troops. The little bald-headed man was either Stalin's Secretary or his valet, as in the subsequent meeting, whenever Stalin rang the bell, he bounced in, and received orders in the most obsequious fashion.

The Prime Minister, CIGS, Wavell, Tedder, and Cadogan, together with Dunlop, the Interpreter, were immediately admitted through the doorway which led into Stalin's room, while Tommy, Inspector Thompson, and myself, were shown into another adjoining room, where we waited, accompanied by a Russian with whom we were totally unable to conduct any conversation. The little 'Bald Head' was having a frightful time trying to make out, from a list he had, who actually had arrived. We found it very difficult to help him, because his efforts at pronouncing the various names were so ludicrous that we could not recognise any of them. As they were all written down in Russian characters, it was no good looking at the list. However, he eventually seemed satisfied, and we sat down and prepared to pass a few hours as best we could, doing nothing.

After about ten minutes, however, a name was called which I eventually recognised as my own, and I was ushered into Stalin's room, where I found a meeting had started, and the Prime Minister wanted me to make the record. The room, very brightly lit, was about 40 feet long and 15 feet wide, with two long tables running down each side. Stalin's desk was on the right-hand side at the far end, facing down the room, which was very bare, with the usual light coloured panelling on the lower half of the walls. There were only three pictures: one of Lenin making a speech, one of Lenin sitting at his desk, and one of Karl Marx. Another door behind the desk was open, and appeared to lead into a kind of map room, where there was an enormous globe. The meeting was taking place at the left hand of the two long tables. Stalin was lounging in a chair sideways to the table at the head, and was puffing a large, curly, pipe. On his left was Dunlop, the interpreter, then came the Prime Minister, then CIGS, then Wavell and then Tedder. On the opposite side, at Stalin's right, was Pavlov, the Russian interpreter, then Molotov, then Harriman and then Cadogan. I took my seat next to Cadogan.

I found things were not going too well. The Prime Minister's scheme had evidently miscarried, and a desultory argument about the possibility of a Second Front and similar matters, was proceeding. Stalin appeared quite at home, and made his remarks in a very low, gentle, voice, with an occasional gesture of the right hand, and never looked the Prime Minister in the face. The interpreting was done from Russian into English by Pavlov, and from English into Russian by Dunlop – an unfortunate arrangement. I naturally could not judge whether Dunlop was speaking good Russian, but Pavlov's English was crude in the extreme. Stalin was coming out with all kinds of insulting remarks, but one could not really tell whether they were being faithfully put across by Pavlov, because his vocabularly was limited.

After a time, during which Stalin was suggesting that we were not prepared to operate on the Continent because we were frightened of the Germans, the Prime Minister made an impassioned speech, in which he said the object of his visit was to try to establish real comradeship between himself and Stalin; he expressed his disappointment that Stalin should apparently not believe the sincerity of his statements, and distrust his motives. Before Dunlop translated this statement, the Prime Minister told him to repeat it in English, to make certain that he had got it right. This

Dunlop began to do, but it was soon clear that he had not got it correctly. This disconcerted the Prime Minister, and he asked me to tell Dunlop what it was that he had really said. This illustrates how difficult it is to conduct these extremely ticklish negotiations with the aid of indifferent interpreters.

The conversation continued without anything being achieved for some time, and then Stalin changed the subject, and began to talk about some new weapon the Russians had, which seemed to be a special kind of mortar. He suggested that we might like to see these in action, and he asked that we should give them any details of any new weapons which we ourselves had developed. This all seemed very irrelevant, but the Prime Minister welcomed his proposals, and it was arranged that there should be a demonstration the following day. Stalin then invited the Prime Minister to dine with him the following evening, after which the meeting began to break up.

At this stage, the Prime Minister asked Stalin what the situation was in the Caucasus. Stalin rang the bell, and told 'Bald Head' to fetch something. This turned out to be a very good relief model of the whole Caucasus area; and with the help of this, Stalin explained what the strength of the Russian forces was, and where they intended to stop the enemy. He said that they had 25 Divisions in the Caucasus, and that their main line of defence ran along the foothills on the western half of the front, and then along the river Terech, which runs rather to the north of the mountains on the eastern half of the front. He expressed complete confidence in the situation, and said that the Russians were quite prepared to meet attempts at landing at Batum, or even an attack through Turkey.

We all shook hands with Stalin, and left the Kremlin about 12.45 am. We drove back to our villa, and Harriman came with us. He and the Prime Minister and I sat discussing the meeting. The Prime Minister was decidedly upset. He thought that at the meeting the previous evening he had got over the worst of his fences, and had established good relations with Stalin. Now it appeared that the impression he had made had been dissipated, and that Stalin was turning nasty. The Prime Minister said that he had very nearly refused the invitation to dinner, as he felt that the dinner would be the end of the visit, and that nothing so far had been achieved. Apparently, at the beginning of the meeting, before I came into the room, Stalin had handed a paper to the

Prime Minister, which expressed, in very bald language, the Russian viewpoint. This was that we had fallen down on all our promises, not only as regards the Second Front, but also in the matter of delivering equipment to Russia. Harriman comforted the Prime Minister by telling him that exactly the same tactics had been employed by the Russians at the time of his previous visit with Lord Beaverbrook. Stalin had begun in a friendly manner, had then turned on the heat, as it were, but had finally come round completely. He suggested that the explanation was probably that Stalin had to adopt an uncompromising attitude at one stage of the negotiations, in order to satisfy his own people. Harriman suggested that if another meeting could be arranged, all would end well. It had at least been arranged that the soldiers should meet, and go into more detail on the Second Front and related topics, something might come out of this. We eventually got to bed at 3 am.

Friday, 14 August

The Prime Minister spent the morning seeing Cadogan and Clark Kerr, and dictated a reply to Stalin's aide memoire. He also sent off a masterly telegram to London, giving an account of the meeting. CIGS, Wavell and Tedder arrived at the villa at noon to talk over the situation, and Harriman and Admiral Stanley, the American Ambassador, came to lunch. After lunch, the Prime Minister had a rest, and I did the minutes of the previous night's meeting. Meanwhile, CIGS and the others went off to see the mortar demonstration.

We arrived at the Kremlin for the dinner at 9 pm. Once more we were admitted as if into a medieval castle, and entered a door which faced a magnificent flight of stairs. Having mounted these, we passed through great corridors and halls, including the one in which the Supreme Soviet meets. This is a very large hall, with a fine dais and rostrum at the end, and desks like those used by schoolboys filling the room. Finally, we found ourselves in a really magnificent room, with square marble pillars panelled with bright green malachite. The walls were panelled in shot silk, the great folding doors were gilded, and beautifully carved, and dinner was laid out at one large table and three smaller ones. The guests were assembled in an ante-room adjoining, which had a lovely curved painted ceiling. The furniture throughout was of Empire style, and the whole thing was said to date from the days of the Empress Catherine.

Immediately we arrived, the party moved into dinner, headed by Stalin dressed, as usual, in his little lilac-coloured tunic, buttoned up to the neck, his cotton trousers stuffed into long boots. He has rather a shambling walk, and it was extraordinary to see this little peasant, who would have not looked at all out of place in a country lane with a pickaxe over his shoulder, calmly sitting down to a banquet in these magnificent halls.

I found myself sitting between a member of the Russian Foreign Office, whose name I could not discover, and Captain Duncan, the American Naval Attaché, at one of the three smaller tables. I was almost exactly opposite Stalin, and behind Molotov who faced him. The Prime Minister was at Stalin's right hand, with Pavlov next door to interpret. Harriman was on Stalin's left. There must have been about one hundred people present, including all the leading Generals not actually engaged at the front, and various Commissars, with a good sprinkling of Americans. We had barely sat down, before Molotov sprang to his feet and proposed the Prime Minister's health in a very short speech. Pavlov translated the speech, and then we drank the toast. The Prime Minister replied, and proposed Stalin's health. Stalin then proposed the President's health, linking it with that of Mr Harriman: and so it went on. Every five minutes throughout the dinner we were drinking somebody's health. The interesting thing on this occasion was that a large number of the toasts were proposed by Stalin, who toasted all his Generals and Admirals in turn, starting with Voroshilov, Shaposhnikov, the Chief of Staff, Voronov, the Commander of their Artillery, and proceeding through the chief Airmen, the chief Admirals and so on. Each time he proposed a health, Stalin made a speech of three or four sentences, and then wandered round the table, clinking glasses with the men whose health he had proposed, and cracking jokes with Molotov and others, all in the most informal and self-possessed manner.

Meanwhile, the Prime Minister was left rather high and dry, with no one to talk to; and one could see that this was not the kind of party which appealed to him at all. All this time we were steadily eating our way through towards the soup, which arrived after about one and a half hour's steady going . . . .

We finally rose from the table about 12.30 am and went into the next room for coffee and liqueurs. The Prime Minister perked up a bit when photographs were taken of him sitting with Stalin on sofas, but when it was suggested to him that he might like to see a film, he threw his hand in, and came away. This broke up the party, and we left the Kremlin about 1 am. Stalin walked all the way down with the Prime Minister, and shook hands with us all as we went out of the front door. This, it seems, is a most unusual occurrence. We were thankful to get to bed at 1.30 in the morning.

Saturday, 15 August

I was sent for at 9 am by the Prime Minister. He had been reading through my record of the meeting with Stalin on the Wednesday evening, and forming second thoughts about what had taken place. He felt that perhaps he had been unduly depressed, and that Stalin had perhaps not meant to be as insulting as he had at first thought. I suggested to him that he certainly ought to have another meeting with Stalin alone, and that as so much turned on the efficiency of the interpreters we should fit him out with one of the members of the British Military Mission, whom I knew to be bilingual. The Prime Minister received this suggestion favourably, and a meeting was accordingly arranged for 7 o'clock that evening. In the meanwhile, the Prime Minister saw the CIGS, General Wavell and Air Chief Marshal Tedder at 11 am for a short talk, before they went to meet the Russian soldiers at noon.

Soon after 11.30 the CIGS and the others left the villa by car for No 17 Spiridonievka and I went with them; we picked up Major Birse, the interpreter of whom I had spoken to the Prime Minister, and arrived at our destination just on noon. General Maxwell and General Bradley, the United States Military Representatives, arrived about twenty minutes late, as they had not been warned.

The meeting began with a very clear account by the CIGS of the various projects which had been considered by ourselves and by the Americans for operations in Europe, and of the conclusions to which we had come after long discussion. Marshal Voroshilov and Marshal Shaposhnikov then gave their views on the formation of a Second Front, commenting at the same time on the statement the CIGS had made. Their remarks showed only too clearly how totally unable the Russians are to appreciate the nature of large scale operations across the sea. They began by saying that they were not in a position to go into the details of shipping and thus begged the question from the start. They then suggested that we should immediately move all the divisions now in England and land them in France, preferably at Cherbourg. They felt that air cover for the operations could easily be provided if we seized the Channel Islands and they seemed to imagine that, having seized these islands, we could immediately operate a large number of fighters from them and give air cover on an adequate scale. They quoted Malta and Leningrad as examples of what could be done from a small area. They did not appear to be able to see the difference between operating from an island where we had been established for years and where heavy defences had been built up, and operating from a base just captured from the enemy where there are no adequate ports to land heavy material. The argument continued until finally the CIGS told them that the Americans and ourselves had come to very definite conclusions on this subject and were not prepared to alter them. Whereupon Marshal Voroshilov said that he could not, of course, press us any further. The Russians might think our conclusions were wrong, but they would have to accept them, as we must be the judge of what we were able to do.

CIGS then asked whether the Russians could give their views on the situation in the Caucasus. In reply to this, Voroshilov said that the Russians were only authorised to discuss the Second Front. In his turn he asked the CIGS whether he could give any details about TORCH. CIGS countered this by saying that he was not authorised to do so. General Wavell then returned to the charge and asked whether Voroshilov could not get permission from his Government to discuss the Caucasus, which was of such great interest to him as Commander-in-Chief, India. Voroshilov undertook to try this, and to let us know the result.

The meeting then broke up, and we had a very good fork lunch in an adjoining room. It was by then 2.15 and we got away about 2.45. The atmosphere at lunch was very friendly, though conversation as usual, was difficult through lack of interpreters.

Immediately after lunch, I went back to the Villa to report progress to the Prime Minister, who was going off to his rest. I then did the minutes of the morning's meeting, and waited for news from the Russians as to whether or not there was to be a meeting on the Caucasus.

At about half past five, we got a message to say that the meeting would be resumed at 6.30, and we accordingly reassembled in the same place. The Russians began by asking what aspect of the

Caucasus was of interest to us. CIGS said that we were concerned as to the safety of the supply route to Russia through Persia, and also that we were interested in the rate of the German advance, which affected the rate at which we would have to build up our own forces in Persia. Voroshilov expressed complete confidence in the ability of the Russians to hold the Caucasus, and repeated the information which Stalin had given the Prime Minister at the meeting on Wednesday. He then enquired about the air assistance which the Prime Minister had mentioned. CIGS told him that the proposal for sending British air forces to the Caucasus was entirely dependent upon the outcome of other operations in the Middle East, but that we were most anxious to get ahead with reconnaissance and preparations so that if and when the air forces became available, there would be no delay in bringing them into action.

[*This statement led to an argument, but the Russians eventually agreed that Air Officers should be sent to Moscow, subject to Stalin's approval. The Americans said that they might also be able to provide air forces.*]

As we stood up to go, Voroshilov said he wanted to make a statement off the record. This turned out to be a final plea in favour of the Second Front. He expressed his conviction that if we could act in Europe this year, the defeat of the Germans would be assured. We then shook hands all round most cordially and departed.

I went back to the Villa, and found that the Prime Minister had gone off, according to plan, for his meeting with Stalin at 7 pm. He had taken Birse with him, as arranged, and was to have a private meeting.

At about 8 o'clock, General Anders turned up, having been invited to dinner by the Prime Minister. General Anders is the Commander-in-Chief of all the Polish forces in Russia and the Middle East. He is a tall, good-looking man, though his appearance is rather marred by the fact that he shaves his head. He had been a distinguished soldier in the last war, and when the Russians had walked into the Eastern side of Poland in 1939, Anders had been taken prisoner, and like all the rest of the Poles in Russian hands, had been treated disgracefully.

He was very anxious to see the Prime Minister, in order to tell him of the difficulties which the Polish Embassy has been having with the Russian Government. It seems that the Poles had set up a good organisation in Russia for collecting their nationals, and for giving them relief. Suddenly, the Russians had arrested the leading members of their organisation, and adopted an uncompromising attitude in the subsequent negotiations. The Poles were naturally very upset, and General Anders wanted the Prime Minister to intervene. I believe the other side of the story is that the Poles had in their organisation certain agents who had been told to compile lists of those Poles who could not be trusted, and that these agents had been behaving indiscreetly, collected data about the Russians who had been unfriendly to the Poles. The Russians found out all about this, and naturally objected. There certainly is no love lost between the Poles and the Russians. The Poles dislike the Germans, but they loathe the Russians with a far deadlier hatred. According to General Anders, there is not a single man in Russia whose word can be trusted. He told us the most harrowing tales of the treatment of his people. 8,000 of his best officers had been put in a concentration camp in 1939; today, they had all vanished without a trace. When asked about them, Stalin said that perhaps they had run away somewhere, but he apparently had made no efforts to clear up the mystery. We found in Teheran that the Poles who are now being evacuated from Russia, both soldiers and families, have spread the most fearful tales about the Russians. These tales, of course, get to the ears of the Russians, who are in occupation of Northern Persia, and thus add fuel to the flames. General Anders speaks no English, but fluent French and German.

Sir Archibald Clark Kerr, our Ambassador in Moscow, came round also to dinner. At about 8.34, we decided to wait no longer, and we sat down without the Prime Minister. After dinner, Cadogan entertained Anders, and we all got on with various jobs of work. Gradually, as time passed, we wondered what to do with ourselves, and the various sofas soon became occupied by people trying to get some sleep.

Sunday, 16 August

At about 1 am, Cadogan was sent for from the Kremlin, in order to polish off a joint communiqué which was to be issued after the Prime Minister left, and the rest of us resumed our vigil. At last, at 3.15 am, the Prime Minister returned. He saw General Anders for a few minutes, and invited him to come to Cairo for fuller discussions. General Anders then left, and the Prime Minister had a bath.

While he was dressing, I went in to talk to him, and he lay down on a sofa and gave Clark Kerr and myself some account of his conversation. It seems that after he had talked with Stalin for an hour or so, in a comparatively formal manner, Stalin had asked him if this would be the last occasion on which he would be seeing him. The Prime Minister said that he intended to leave at dawn. Stalin then asked him whether he was engaged that evening. The Prime Minister said he was quite free, so Stalin suggested that they should adjourn to his flat in the Kremlin, and have a drink. The Prime Minister agreed, and there he met Stalin's daughter. The drink developed into dinner, and some time during the night Stalin suggested that Molotov should join them. Cadogan was then sent for, and the communiqué was finally squared up. After seven hours together, the Prime Minister and Stalin parted on excellent terms – Stalin giving orders that Molotov was to see the Prime Minister off in his aeroplane.

The Prime Minister was very tired, and lay talking with his eyes shut. Nevertheless he was very satisfied with the way things had gone, and felt that his visit had turned out a great success.

I found out later that the two men had had a very frank talk on all kinds of aspects of the war. Birse, the Interpreter, had done very well, and apparently had taken Stalin's fancy. The Prime Minister really felt that he had established with Stalin a personal relationship of the same kind as he had already built up with President Roosevelt.

Looking back on the visit, I think that it is very doubtful whether more could possibly have been achieved. Certainly, no one but the Prime Minister could have got so far with Stalin, in the sense that we understand friendship. The thing that impressed me most about Stalin was his complete self-possession and detachment. He was absolutely master of the situation at all times, and appeared to be cold and calculating. He had a gentle voice, which he never raised, and his eyes were shrewd and crafty. He had a well-developed sense of humour, though his smile gave one the impression that it would be chiefly exercised in a cruel way. All his life he had been a revolutionary, fighting for his own position. He would have his closest associate shot without the smallest compunction, if he calculated that it was necessary. How could such a man make friends! I should say that to make friends with Stalin would be equivalent to making friends with a python ... The Prime Minister's relationship with Stalin would be close and personal only as long as Stalin thought that his own interests would be served thereby.

It came on to rain during the night, and after having breakfast at 3.45 am, we left at 4.30, followed by the Prime Minister. We drove down to the same aerodrome at which we had arrived, and found four Liberators drawn up, ready to start. A guard of honour of about 70 men was drawn up opposite the Prime Minister's aeroplane and British and American flags were displayed on the approach road. The usual crowd of cameramen was waiting, and a number of officials had assembled to see the Prime Minister off. The 'four great beasts' and I soon got into our aeroplane, leaving the Prime Minister to deal with the official send-off; and at 5.25 am we took off.

We went up to 12,000 feet to cross the Elburz Mountains, and landed at Teheran at 3 o'clock in the afternoon. The Prime Minister went to bed early, in view of his previous exertions.

On the following morning we arrived in Heliopolis at 11.40, the Prime Minister's aircraft being ten minutes behind ours. We motored straight down to the Embassy, and settled ourselves in the same manner as before.

The Moscow communiqué was a masterpiece, particularly for consumption on the home front. The fact that the Prime Minister and Stalin had discussed all the problems, and reached agreement, made it quite impossible for any dangerous Second-Front agitation to be manufactured in England, and certainly before the visit there had seemed every likelihood of this happening.

So ended the Prime Minister's gruelling visit to Persia and the Soviet Union which had lasted a week. It was a remarkable achievement for a man of sixty-seven. To illustrate his perky mood on the way home: frustrated by security restrictions at Gibraltar confining him to Government House, he had offered to disguise himself either as an Egyptian demi-mondaine or as an American suffering from toothache!

As a feat of war-direction among three allies, the entire journey had been a triumph: the course of the war had been set. Britain and the United States with TORCH and the Eighth Army's campaign would drive the Germans from North Africa and free the Mediterranean to allied shipping. Aid to Russia would continue through the Northern convoys and the Persian railway. Bombing of German cities would be increased and, when feasible, the final act would be an Anglo-American cross-channel assault in NW Europe.

Jacob, unaccompanied on this trip by Ismay, had played a leading part in supporting the Prime Minister's critical activities both in North Africa and in Moscow. He had been much more than a competent member of the Defence Secretariat: he had been Churchill's personal right-hand man. Particularly in Moscow, he had quietly influenced events, while maintaining under considerable pressure his characteristic cool efficiency. Gleams of ironic humour appear in the diary and reflect marked self-confidence.

Seventeen days after the Prime Minister had returned to England on 24 August 1942, despite his immense preoccupations, he minuted the Secretary of State for War as follows:

PRIME MINISTER'S
PERSONAL   *PERSONAL MINUTE*

SECRETARY OF STATE FOR WAR
GENERAL ISMAY

SERIAL NO M365/2

I am much impressed by the work and bearing of Colonel EIC Jacob, RE. He showed marked ability and competence when he accompanied me during my recent visit to the Middle East and Moscow.

I consider that the position which he holds and the duties which he discharges in my Defence Office should carry with them the rank of Brigadier, and I should be glad if arrangements could be made for Colonel Jacob to be promoted to that rank. I do not contemplate being able to release him from his present duties for other service.[1]

11 September 1942   WSC

On 15 September 1942 Jacob was duly promoted Acting Brigadier. The last sentence of the Prime Minister's Minute was to have a decisive effect on his chosen career.

PLATE 18.
Churchill and
Stalin after the
banquet in the
Kremlin, August
1942 (Note:
Signed by Stalin)
(*Jacob papers*).

PLATE 19. Churchill in the garden of the Cairo Embassy with the Lampson's baby (*IWM*).

PLATE 20. Casablanca Conference 1943. The British Delegation. (*Back row, L–R*) Thompson (detective), Thompson (Flag lieutenant), Dykes, Alexander, Mountbatten, Ismay, Leathers, Macmillan, Rowan and Jacob. (*Front row, L–R*) Portal, Pound, Churchill, Dill and Brooke (*US Air Force photo*).

PLATE 21. Casablanca. The United States Delegation. (*Back row, L–R*) Harry Hopkins, Arnold, Somervell and Averill Harriman. (*Front row, L–R*) Marshall, Roosevelt and King (*IWM*).

Plate 22. Churchill (in his 'dragon' dressing gown) with Eisenhower and Alexander (*IWM*).

Plate 23. Churchill with President Inonu and Marshal Chakmak, Adana, Turkey (*IWM*).

PLATE 24. Jacob broadcasting to Europe and the United States from San Francisco on the first anniversary of OVERLORD D–Day, 6 June 1945 (*Voice of America*).

PLATE 25. At the San Francisco Conference with Sir Alexander Cadogan, May 1945 (*UN Secretariat photo*).

9

Planning for Victory

On Jacob's return to London in August 1942, after Churchill's successful activities in Egypt, Teheran and Moscow, it may have seemed that the strategic intentions of the United States and Britain had once again been firmly resolved, and that Stalin's incessant demand for a Second Front had temporarily been satisfied. But divergences of view between the President and the Prime Minister and, more markedly, between the Chiefs of Staff of the United States and of Britain began to surface once more.

Despite the presence in London of General Eisenhower, the confirmed overall commander for TORCH, and of General Clark, both of whom were eager to press on with their preparations for the TORCH landings, it was not until 3 September that Roosevelt accepted the British proposal that the objective of Algiers should be added to those of Oran and Casablanca, and that the date of TORCH be finally agreed as 8 November, 1942. Meanwhile Stalin, with vast Soviet forces still under great pressure from the Wehrmacht, reasserted his demand for an Anglo-American landing in Europe to relieve the critical situation of the Soviet Army. Churchill himself once again insisted on promoting JUPITER, the proposed attack on Norway, designed to reduce the heavy losses on convoys to Russia; this operation in his view would fill the anticipated gap in offensive action between TORCH in late 1942 and ROUND-UP in North-West Europe in 1943, and it was not until late October that he reluctantly accepted the advice of Mountbatten, Chief of Combined Operations, that JUPITER was not a practical proposition in the winter of 1942–43. In the minds of many of the Americans, JUPITER had an unpleasant resemblance to Churchill's Dardanelles adventure of World War I; moreover, the United States Chiefs of Staff seemed to be giving way to their recurrent obsession that the Mediterranean theatre was a trap in which large American forces would be bottled up by the closure of the Straits of Gibraltar, following a German thrust into Spain.

After Montgomery's victories at Alam Halfa and Alamein and, later, the successful landings of operation TORCH, Churchill's plans for 1943 envisaged not only the capture of Sicily and Sardinia after French North Africa had been secured, but also a catalogue of action which included attacks on Italy or even Southern France, pressure to bring Turkey into the war, operations over land with the Russians into the Balkans, coupled with the immobilisation of large enemy forces in Northern France by means of continuous preparations to invade. This ambitious programme appealed neither to the British Chiefs of Staff nor to their United States counterparts, but nevertheless had some attractions for President Roosevelt.

On 3 December 1942, Churchill, intent upon providing maximum relief to the Russians, proposed definite targets which included: the clearance of the North African shore by the end of January 1943, the occupation of Sardinia by the end of March, together with operations to bring Turkey into the war; while in the United Kingdom, preparations for ROUND-UP were to be completed by the end of July, leading to a cross-Channel assault in August or September 1943.

When this plan was being considered by the Chiefs of Staff, Portal announced to Churchill's surprise that the US Chiefs of Staff had withdrawn large resources to the Pacific on the assumption that an offensive movement from North Africa into the Continent was not intended for 1943; moreover, Brooke then expressed grave doubts about the possibility of entering the Continent from the United Kingdom as early as 1943 in sufficient strength to overcome German resistance. In view of these uncertainties, Churchill decided to press for a Three-Power Conference with Roosevelt and Stalin.

Meanwhile, Eisenhower's offensive towards Tunis was disrupted by German counter-attacks, and the anticipated timings of the North African operations were then seriously delayed. Despite successful developments on the Russian front, Stalin announced that he could not leave the Soviet Union, but that meanwhile he was awaiting an indication of Churchill's intentions about a Second Front in Europe in the Spring of 1943. Eventually it was agreed with President Roosevelt to have an Anglo-American Conference at Casablanca, and Jacob, now a Brigadier, was sent to North Africa on Christmas Day 1942 to prepare a Conference there, code-named SYMBOL, in consultation with Eisenhower and his Chief of Staff, Bedell Smith.

Then, having obtained a situation report from Lieutenant Colonel William Stirling, who had served with him in London and was now on Eisenhower's staff, he flew to Algiers on 27 December. He quickly got in touch with Stirling, who took him to Allied Force Headquarters in Algiers where he met Eisenhower and Bedell Smith, also Whiteley and other British friends. Next day, in Casablanca he explained his requirements to General Keyes, deputy to General Patton, who was sick. For security reasons, no mention was made of the Prime Minister (code-named Air Commodore Frankland) nor of the President (Admiral Q). A young American officer who had met Jacob at the aerodrome had suggested the use of the Hotel Anfa, and this Jacob found to be admirably suited for the Conference Centre, together with spacious villas for Churchill and Roosevelt, 'the Emperors of the East and West' as Macmillan was to call them. Jacob purposely did not reconnoitre Marrakech, Churchill's favourite choice for the conference, so that the Prime Minister would be given no loophole to move there, where difficulties over communications would have been insuperable. A headquarters ship of the Royal Navy, HMS *Bulolo*, was to be stationed in Casablanca harbour to provide world-wide communications and additional staff accommodation.

Jacob's diary entry reads:

Tuesday, 29 December
The following morning, I saw General Patton, and left with him a note of what we required, and how I suggested that our requirements would be met at the Anfa Hotel and in the surrounding villas. We then returned to Algiers in the same aircraft that had brought us down. I was very interested to meet General Patton, about whose qualities as a 'Fire-eater', stories from many sources are in circulation. He is certainly a magnificent-looking man. Well over six feet, with white hair, but evidently very fit and tough with an exceedingly cold grey eye. I told him the complete story which, however, he had already guessed; and he undertook to see all arrangements were made. He himself occupies a magnificent villa not far from the Anfa Hotel, and he offered to turn out of it and place it at our disposal. I asked him not to do that, but to keep accommodation in reserve for General Eisenhower, or anyone else of that kind who might visit the place during the conference.

We got back to Algiers after another very cold flight, and landed about 4.30 pm. I immediately saw Bedell Smith, and told him what we had done, and we sent off cables to London and Washington setting out our proposals and asking for approval.

[*On 30 December, Jacob, awaiting acceptance in London of his recom-mendations, visited Allied Forces Headquarters and talked to all the principal British Staff Officers as well as to Eisenhower and Bedell Smith. He gained an impression of 'restless confusion', although he was told there was no Anglo-American friction. The difficulties of a joint headquarters of two nations were obvious, and some even doubted whether a combined Allied Staff was a practical arrangement.*]

He commented in his diary:

A most disturbing factor in the whole affair is the existence of General Clark as Deputy Commander-in-Chief. General Clark is a most ambitious man, able and active, with a strong personality. He imposes himself in the most extraordinary way on the Com-mander-in-Chief. He does not work through the Staff, but goes round in all directions issuing direct orders. This makes the posi-tion of the Chief of Staff quite impossible, and causes immense irritation throughout the branches. Most US Officers are terrified of him, and he has all along been the evil genius of the Force. His personal ambition leads him to an anti-British attitude because he is eager to get command of the forces in Tunisia. Thus he tends to belittle the doings of the First Army, and sows dissension between British and French. The effect of General Clark's activities is such that it would be wrong to judge the working of Allied HQ until it is allowed to settle down in his absence. When, if ever, he goes to take command of the Fifth Army, a great improvement may be found, and it will not be only the British officers who will heave a sigh of relief.

The fact that General Clark has been allowed to occupy the position he has made for himself, and to create such havoc, is a reflection on the Commander-in-Chief. Though a man of decisive mind in immediate issues, General Eisenhower is far too easily swayed and diverted to be a great Commander-in-Chief. He has certainly had to grapple with a baffling political situation, and his downright and honest character has been of great value in that task. Nevertheless his lack of experience of high command, and his naturally exuberant temperament prevent him from preserv-ing a steady course towards a selected goal. Sudden and frequent changes of plan, often made without the knowledge of those members of the staff who ought to know, increase the general chaos. There is a lack of dignity about the HQ, an air of aimless bustle, a constant clustering of hangers-on and visitors, and at the same time an amateur flavour which makes one wonder how anything ever gets done.

The political situation when I arrived was that Admiral Darlan had been assassinated, and General Giraud had been unanimously elected as his successor. The funeral was over, and the assassin had been shot. Mr Hull had made a statement, and General Marshall had sent a message of welcome to General Giraud. There was a complete silence from London. General Eisenhower and Admiral Cunningham were very disturbed about this. Both General Nogues and M. Boisson had been to see the latter, and had expressed their desire for co-operation. But from their remarks, and from other sources, not to mention Axis broadcasts, it was clear that the French in North Africa were beginning to think that there was a split between the US and British Governments; the former backing Giraud, the latter backing de Gaulle. Admiral Cunningham and Mack (his Foreign Office adviser) felt themselves in a very difficult situation, because they had no idea what the policy of HMG might be. The former, as the senior British Officer here, was looked to for a lead, but could say nothing. French suspicion in North Africa is very strong that nothing will satisfy the British Government except the installation of de Gaulle in supreme authority.

In the course of the afternoon, a telegram came in from London saying that the proposed arrangements were accepted, and telling me to return immediately.

I had a final interview with Admiral Cunningham, whose main preoccupation was the lack of any knowledge of the policy of the British Government in the situation created by the murder of Admiral Darlan, although, of course, he was constantly coming into contact with the French leaders, who discussed matters freely with him as the senior British representative in North Africa. General Eisenhower also consulted him on everything; it made it very awkward for him if he were kept in complete ignorance of the views of the British Government on matters which were of such burning interest to those with whom he came in contact every day.

The news had just been received of the appointment of Mr Macmillan as British representative at Allied Force HQ, and everyone felt that this would relieve the situation and put an end to the existing uncertainty and doubt.

Another matter which was exercising the Admiral's mind very much was the relations between the Free French Navy and the North African French Navy, and in particular the activities of the Free French in Gibraltar. It was always difficult to disentangle the truth from the tissue of lies told by both sides, but there was small doubt that all kinds of underhand methods were being employed by the Free French to win over any North African seaman putting into Gibraltar.

The whole French situation, apparently so simple, was bristling with minor difficulties. It was obvious that the unity of all Frenchmen was the aim to be achieved as soon as possible, and all shades of Frenchmen were agreed in theory on the subject. Unfortunately, there are so many in both factions who are frightened that their own positions will be in danger if they unite, that every kind of obstacle is constantly being placed in the way of a rational solution. Fortunately it is a matter which the French themselves must solve; nevertheless, the political situation in North Africa is of such importance to the successful conduct of military operations that one cannot allow things to drift for ever. Above all, it is essential that the French in North Africa should not gain the impression that the American and British Governments are at cross-purposes and are running different policies.

General Eisenhower, who had not been very well recently, and had been very depressed by the events following Darlan's murder and the constant tricky negotiations with the French, invited me to a New Year's Eve dinner party at his villa. I found myself the only Englishman present, the other guests being General Clark, General Smith, General Hughes (Hartle's Chief of Staff), Colonel Davies (the Adjutant General), Butcher and Lee (the two Aides) and six American girls, some of them nurses and some on the staff at Allied Forces Headquarters.

We had an excellent fork dinner, after which I thought it advisable to make a little speech with the object of cheering up General Eisenhower. He had such an exhuberant and emotional temperament that he goes up and down very easily, and a small thing like this might well have a large effect in restoring his self-confidence. I rather think that I achieved my object, and we certainly had a very jolly evening. I was introduced into a game which is widespread in America, but which I had never met before, namely,

Crap-dice. I must say that I did not fully understand the rules, even by the end of the evening, but I had beginner's luck. Ike himself played bridge, and I joined in the last two rubbers; he finished the evening at 1.30 am by calling and making a grand slam vulnerable, which put the seal on his happiness.

Friday, 1 January 1943

I left for Gibraltar next morning in General Spaatz's Fortress. We took off at 1 o'clock, and landed at Gibraltar, after a perfect flight in brilliant sunshine, three hours later. I went straight to Government House, where I found that Macmillan had arrived on his way through Gibraltar to Algiers. After ten, he and I settled down with the Governor for a full discussion of the situation in Algiers.

I feel sure Macmillan will be a great success, and it is very fortunate that the Prime Minister overcame the President's objections to his appointment.

Lord Gort was also present on his way back to England for medical treatment. In his usual impetuous way he had taken a hand in putting out a petrol fire, and had burnt his leg badly; he also had a rather irksome sore on his lip which would not heal, and altogether did not look very well. He was due to go on in a Hudson in the middle of the night, so I suggested that he should come with me in the Fortress.

Saturday, 2 January

He fell in with this scheme, and we had a very good flight to Fort Reath in Cornwall. We had a minor excitement, when two JU 88s came to investigate us. However, one short burst from the rear-gunner made them sheer off.

From Fort Reath, a Flamingo took us in very bumpy weather to Hendon, and I found myself back in the office at 5.30 pm, very dirty, tired and unshaven. I was immediately greeted with the news that I was to set out for Chequers at once; so, having given a short account of the proceedings to Jo, off I went, and arrived at Chequers at five minutes to eight. I was not allowed to go off and have a bath, but was told that the Prime Minister was waiting anxiously to see me. I found him in bed, having just awakened from his sleep, and he kept me for half an hour while I told him as well as I could all about the situation in Algeria, and the arrangements at Casablanca. He was very interested in everything, and appeared pleased with the arrangements proposed, though he was obviously still hankering after Marrakech.

We had dinner followed as usual by a film, which finished at 1 am. To my surprise, he then said to me that I must be tired, and had better go to bed – and, what is more, he went off to bed himself. However, General Weeks and General Galloway, who were also guests, kept me up talking till 2.30 am, by which time I was quite ready for a sleep.

Sunday, 3 January

On my return to the office, I found that good progress had been made with the preparations for the Conference, and that an advance party was ready to sail for Casablanca on Monday night. I was horrified at the size of it. The Chiefs of Staff had decided not only to take their Directors of Plans but also John Kennedy (Director Military Operations and Plans), Jack Slessor (Assistant Chief of Air Staff (Plans)) and a number of staff officers besides. Then, of course, there were all the PAs, the clerical staff, the cypher staff and the Royal Marine guard and orderlies – a pretty formidable total. . . .

Great precautions had to be taken to try and prevent it becoming known that the Prime Minister was going. The getting ready of Liberator No 504 was a pretty good clue, but it was given out that Harriman and Leathers were going to Dakar for a shipping conference, and that the Prime Minister had lent them his aircraft. It seems that the security measures taken were very successful, and it was never known widely that the Prime Minister had gone to Casablanca, even though it was soon suspected that he had left the country. It was thought he had gone to Washington. . . . .

Monday, 11 January

On Monday afternoon it was learnt that the weather was unsuitable, so our departure was put off for twenty-four hours. I was very glad, as I was anxious that the advance party should have enough time to get everything ready. Our headquarters ship, *Bulolo* had arrived all right, and preparations were proceeding smoothly. But I knew there was none too much time.

Tuesday, 12 January

On Tuesday the news was that the weather was going to be all right for Liberators, but the swell at Gibraltar would prevent the Clipper from landing. A hurried change of plan became necessary.

Wednesday, 13 January
   After an excellent flight, we made a perfect landfall precisely over Casablanca, and landed at Mediouna at 10.45 am. William Stirling had made a fine job of the arrangements; and I found I was sharing a room in the hotel with Vivian Dykes, who had arrived with Field Marshal Dill and the Americans. The latter, apart from the President, Hopkins, and his entourage of gunmen and thugs who were to arrive later, consisted of General Marshall, Admiral King, General Arnold, General Somervell, Admiral Cooke (Director of Plans in the Navy Department), Brigadier General Wedemeyer (Army Planner), Brigadier General Deane (Joint Secretary of the Combined Chiefs of Staff), Commander Libby (Admiral King's aide) and Captain McCarthy (General Marshall's aide). Admiral Leahy had been taken ill at Trinidad, and had gone back to Washington. This was the entire party. They had come in two of their enormous new transport aircraft, C 54s; they must have rattled like peas in drums!
   Of course, arrangements had been made locally for an American clerical staff, but what was completely lacking in the American party was any kind of staff who could tackle the problems which were bound to arise in the course of the conversations, and to produce detailed solutions for the Chiefs of Staff. When the US Chiefs saw how the land lay, and the size of our party, they went out into the highways and byways of North Africa and scraped together some sort of staff. They were lucky to find Colonel Hull on the spot. He had spent several months last year working with our JPS in London, so he knew the ropes. They got hold of one or two others, but both they and we were handicapped all the way through by their lack of staff, and nearly every paper produced during the Conference had to be the work of our people with little or no help from the Americans.
   The Prime Minister was delighted with his villa except on the morning after we arrived, when he asked Sawyers to prepare his bath at about 11 am. The hot water system at his villa was not very good, being rather like an under-engined car. Several people had had baths that morning, so that by 11 o'clock the water was cold. You might have thought the end of the world had come. Everyone was sent for in turn, all were fools, and finally the Prime

Minister said he would not stay a moment longer, and would move into the hotel or go to Marrakech. However, after lunch had had its mellowing influence, the excitement died down. Plumbers were assembled from all directions, and somehow or other the water was kept hot in future. Fortunately, the weather was uniformly good, so we heard no more about moving elsewhere. The President, too, seemed quite pleased with his surroundings.

The villa occupied by the Directors of Plans created a sensation, and was for some time like a honey-pot in the neighbourhood of a swarm of bees. It was found to contain a large library of decidedly doubtful books. True, they were all in French which made it difficult for some; but many of them were profusely illustrated, in a most artistic style, which helped. For some time we despaired of any work being done in that villa, but after a bit the excitement died down; and although one might often see a Planner in some corner laboriously ploughing through a gem from the library, generally speaking the work was not impeded. What is more, the library was handed back complete when the party left.

At 4.30 pm on the first afternoon the British Chiefs of Staff met Field Marshal Dill to get his advice on how best to tackle the Agenda, and incidentally the Americans. Before we had left London, we had exchanged telegrams with Washington so as to fix an Agenda. Actually it contained a list of every topic under the sun, but the most important thing was to get settled in broad outline our combined strategy for 1943, and then to decide exactly how to carry it out.

Sir John Dill explained that the main factors which loomed large in American eyes were first a general fear of commitments in the Mediterranean, and second, a suspicion that we did not understand the Pacific problem and would not put our backs into the work there once Germany had been defeated. Thus, although the Americans were honestly of the opinion that Germany was the primary enemy, they did not quite see how to deal with her, especially as they felt there were great and urgent tasks to be done in Burma and the Pacific. To arrive at a clear policy would be made no easier by the lack of common ground between the US Navy and Army. Apparently, the operations in the Pacific are planned exclusively by the Navy Department, who in their turn leave the rest of the world to the War Department. There is little or no collusion, so that the allocation of resources, as between the Pacific and the rest of the world, is inevitably a hit and miss affair, or perhaps one could better describe it as a game of grab. The Navy have their ships and the Army have theirs. The Navy control the landing craft, so that the Army finds it difficult to squeeze out what they want for their own projects. On the other hand, the Navy is apt to find itself in difficulty on the logistical side of their Pacific operations, as they often do not bring the Army into the picture early enough. This happened at Guadalcanal, where the US Marines were thrown ashore, and then it was found that there was no follow-up, no maintenance organisation, and no transport. The Army was then called in to help – very nearly too late.

The discussion with the Field Marshal was continued at 6 pm with the Prime Minister. His view was clear. He wanted to take plenty of time. Full discussion, no impatience – the dripping of water on a stone. In the meanwhile he would be working on the President, and in ten days or a fortnight everything would fall into place. He also made no secret of the fact that he was out to get agreement on a programme of operations for 1943 which the military people might well think beyond their capacity, but which he felt was the least that could be thought worthy of two Great Powers. He wanted the cleansing of the North African coast to be followed by the capture of Sicily. He wanted the reconquest of Burma, and he wanted the invasion of Northern France, on a moderate scale perhaps. Operations in the Pacific should not be such as to prevent the fulfilment of his programme. . . .

Thursday, 14–Monday, 18 January

Five days of hard slogging. The Combined Chiefs of Staff met as a rule twice a day. They worked on no set programme, but talked over the war from every angle, and fetched out into the open all their thoughts and argued them out. The Pacific was the first main topic. Our Chiefs felt that they knew so little of what was really going on in the Pacific, of what the US Navy planned to do, and of the amount of resources that these plans would absorb, that some enlightenment would be valuable. They also felt that 'Uncle Ernie' (Admiral King) would take a less jaundiced view of the rest of the world if he had been able to shoot his line about the Pacific. General Marshall, too, who has, and always has had, a strong feeling for China, was full of ideas about Burma, which it would be desirable to bring out into the light of day. Uncle Ernie was quite ready to subscribe to the theory that Germany was the primary enemy, the mainspring of the enemy's machine. He felt, however, that this did not necessarily mean that it was essential to defeat Germany first. It might be better to knock out the weaker brethren before finally tackling the main enemy. In any case, it was essential that sufficient force should be applied against Japan, not only to prevent her regaining the initiative, but also to prevent her building up so strong a position as to become almost unbeatable. He thought that in round figures, and as a rough guiding concept, 25 per cent of the Allied resources should be devoted to the Japanese war.

These views were discussed exhaustively. Our Chiefs did not like the percentage idea, even as a rough guide or concept. They felt that the right way of estimating the amount of effort which must be devoted to fighting Japan would be to state what situation it would be desirable to establish in the Pacific in 1943. For example, should Burma be reconquered? Or should we have to take Rabaul? Need we go for the Marshall Islands? Having decided on what position must be attained, then we could work out what forces would be necessary to do the job. Everything else could then be concentrated against Germany. The danger was that it might be found that the resources required to do what the US Navy thought to be essential in the Pacific would be so large as to hamstring all operations elsewhere. There would be no difficulty about troops or aircraft. The crux would be escort vessels and landing craft, both of which would be necessary in large numbers for any operations which we might want to undertake against Germany or Italy. After a good deal of discussion, the Combined Planners were instructed to examine this proposition, and make recommendations as to the 'situation which we wish to establish in the Eastern theatre (Pacific and Burma) in 1943, and what forces will be necessary to establish the situation' . . . .

The Combined Planners, who consisted virtually of our JPS with an occasional bit of sour help from Cooke and Wedemeyer, had a pretty stiff task over this problem. The data could only be produced by Cooke, who alone knew the full facts of the Pacific. They soon found that Cooke had no intention of studying the problem in abstract, impartially, so as to arrive at the ideal solution. He took the view that the Pacific was a US theatre, and that it was nobody else's business what was done there. Anyway, the US Navy had made their plans for 1943, and did not intend to alter them. He was quite prepared to say what they were, but he would not go into detail on the resources they required. All he would say was that the operations could be done with the resources allocated to the Pacific, in which he included everything earmarked but still in the USA. Cooke's attitude, of course, quite spoilt the fundamental idea of the enquiry which the British Chiefs of Staff had suggested. This was that the resources required for the Pacific should be cut down so as to ensure sufficient resources for the war against Germany. In other words, the Japanese war was really to be a minimum detachment from the main task. The US attitude defeated this conception, and we had therefore to fall back on an alternative, namely to interest the US Navy in a Mediterranean or other European operation, and to get Uncle Ernie to promise to produce his share of the resources for carrying it out. We could, we felt, rely on him fulfilling such a promise, and this would force him to make the necessary adjustments as between the European and Pacific theatres.

It should not be imagined that the US plans for the Pacific were thought by our Planners to be unsound. Far from it. We, too, were anxious to reconquer Burma and reopen the Burma road. What our people felt, however, was that there was a real danger of our biting off more than we could chew. We might then find ourselves halfway through the year in a position to carry out none of the too many operations which we had started to undertake. We should be short everywhere.

The Pacific having been thoroughly talked over, and the Planners having been set to work on their study, the discussion moved over to the war against Germany. We believed that the feeling of the US Army was that much as they wanted to prosecute the war against Germany, they did not quite see how it was to be done. They were uncertain of the possibility of an invasion of Northern France, but they had a deep suspicion of the Mediterranean as a kind of dark hole, into which one entered at one's peril . . .

General Marshall realised inwardly that perhaps these fears were a bit exaggerated, and that the British view that there was little or no fear of German action in Spain might be right. Certainly we had been right over TORCH. So the conversion of General Marshall to a Mediterranean strategy was not likely to be difficult. The main opposition would be from Wedemeyer, but he could be overruled. Uncle Ernie might be difficult, of course, but steady pressure might succeed even with him.

A great deal of thought had been given to our strategy before our delegation ever left for Casablanca, and our views were definite, at any rate so far as the Mediterranean versus Northern Europe was concerned. The arguments in favour of exploiting success in North Africa by attacking 'the under-belly of the Axis' were, it seemed to us, overwhelming. The more one looked at Northern France, the less one liked it, with the forces likely to be available in 1943 in the United Kingdom. These forces would be small for a 'Second Front', and the rate at which they could be put ashore was severely limited by the lack of landing craft. The United States had ceased to send any to the United Kingdom when TORCH took the field. They had said that they were not prepared to place an army, with landing craft to match, into the United Kingdom just to sit there 'on spec'. Only when a specific operation was in view would they resume the flow. This was, of course, an extremely short-sighted policy, because the flow could not be built up in a day, and many months would be needed to send over and finally polish up an amphibious force to take on the powerful opposition across the Channel. The result was that for across Channel operations in 1943, only small forces could be assembled in time.

On the other hand, the effect of being thrown violently out of Africa would be shattering for the Italians. Their vitals would be exposed to attack, and what is more, the amount of help which the Germans could give them would be strictly limited by the lack of communications and German commitments elsewhere. The main army of occupation in the Balkans was Italian. If we could cause Italy to collapse, Germany would be faced with a hard choice. Either she must let Italy go, or else abandon the Balkans. She could not possibly find garrisons for both. A crushing blow at Italy might thus have far-reaching results. Furthermore, very large Allied forces were available in North Africa and the Middle East, forces inured to battle, and accustomed to victory. The removal of the threat to the Causasus meant that not only the Eighth but the Ninth and Tenth Armies would be freed for action. The whole Middle East and North African air forces could be concentrated for battle. It only remained to decide how these great forces could best be employed.

There were two main possibilities. The first was Sicily. It might be defended by as many as eight divisions, backed by a powerful German Air Force. On the other hand, Malta, now fully recharged, stood a mere 70 miles away as an ideal advance base for the attack on Sicily. Great forces would be necessary to ensure success in the assault, and these could not be got ready and launched in a moment. Two or three months would be wanted even after Tunis had been cleared.

The second alternative was Sardinia, which could be assaulted simultaneously with the Dodecanese, and could be followed by Corsica. It was known that there were no Germans in Sardinia. The port of Cagliari in the South was the only one of value in the island. There were comparatively few aerodromes. Smaller forces would be required for the assault, which could be launched sooner. The Middle East forces would not be required to co-operate against Sardinia, and would thus be free to pursue their own line up the Aegean, menacing the Balkans and encouraging Turkey.

Which course to adopt? There were a number of conflicting currents of thought which affected the decision, and stirred up mud which clouded the clear water of reason. The British Joint Planning Staff (JPS) after much study were strongly in favour of Sardinia: their reasons were:

> (a) The operation could be launched earlier, in fact very soon after Tunis was cleared, and could be done direct from the United Kingdom.
>
> (b) Particularly if followed by the rapid occupation of Corsica, the vitals of Italy and the South of France would be laid bare to fighter-escorted raids by day. The capture of Sardinia would thus produce a more crushing effect on Italy than would the capture of Sicily.
>
> (c) If the capture of Sardinia produced the effect they expected, then Sicily might fall an easy prey soon after. Meanwhile, the simultaneous move towards the Aegean would be most valuable.
>
> (d) Sicily would strain our resources to the limit, and might even be a failure. It was the obvious frontal attack for which the enemy would be well prepared.

The JPS did their best, both in London and in Casablanca, to press their view on the Chiefs of Staff. They did not succeed. CAS was undecided in his mind, but always felt that the aerodromes of Sardinia and Corsica were not sufficiently numerous, or good enough, to allow us to reap much benefit from the occupation of these islands. Mountbatten strongly supported the JPS, but cut little ice. His invariable habit of butting in on detail, in the middle of discussion of matters of large principle, had destroyed any influence he might have in the Committee. The First Sea Lord was for Sicily, if the Americans would produce the necessary Naval forces to augment ours to the desired amount. He did not think much of Sardinia. Better air cover could be given to the operations against Sicily from Tunisia and Malta than could be given by aircraft-carriers to the landings in Sardinia. The occupation of Sicily would facilitate the passage of ships through the Mediterranean. The decisive factor in the Committee was the view of CIGS. He had carefully studied the plans for the two operations, and he had come to the conclusion that Sicily was the better bet of the two. He was convinced in this mind that as fast as we went into the South of Sardinia, enemy reinforcements would pour into the North. He foresaw a long and difficult campaign to master the island, by which time the chance of taking Corsica easily would have gone. On the other hand, the plan for taking Sicily would ensure the quick fall of the island. Reinforcements could only come in through Messina, out of which only two coast roads led, and these could easily be blocked. These ideas fixed themselves firmly in his mind, and nothing would shake him. Being a very obstinate man, further argument only annoyed him, and he became more rabidly against Sardinia, and in favour of Sicily.

[*The Prime Minister agreed with CIGS though for different reasons. The capture of Sardinia had been mooted ever since Italy had come into the war, but it had never been viewed with much favour, though the conditions now were very different. Sicily had always been the glittering prize; the Prime Minister had to take account of the size of the projected operation, since it would have to be represented to Stalin as very big. He favoured large, spectacular events, and he bounded straight to the conclusion that the only worthwhile objective was Sicily. He could not for a moment be brought to consider 'that piddling operation' – the capture of Sardinia. He proposed to get over one of the main objections, the delay between clearing Tunisia and launching the assault, by saying that somehow or other the assault must be made earlier. Also he thought that, 'by saying so loudly enough', the Dodecanese might be fitted in very soon after Sicily. As, in addition, he wanted Burma in the autumn, and an attack on Northern France in the summer, 'he was indulging to the full in his pastime of having his cake and eating it.'*]

The Prime Minister and the CIGS being at one, their influence was decisive. The task was therefore to sell Sicily to the US Chiefs of Staff: it did not prove very hard, as they too disparaged

Sardinia. They had no alternative to the Mediterranean as a theatre in which to engage Germany on a large scale in 1943, and as the President followed the Prime Minister's thinking, it was not long before everyone accepted Sicily. . . . By the afternoon of 18 January, a document was drawn up giving the broad outline of the proposed strategy for 1943, and this was approved at a meeting that evening with the President and the Prime Minister. The CIGS had then to get down to brass tacks, and the second stage of the Conference began.

[*With the arrival of visitors, Eisenhower, Alexander and Tedder, other problems came up: the co-ordination of air forces in the Middle East and north Africa, and the timing of the capture of Sfax bearing in mind Eighth Army's logistic problems. Alexander's advice to postpone the operation was accepted by Eisenhower.*

The Prime Minister and the President were both intent on reconciling Giraud and de Gaulle and they decided to invite them both to Casablanca. Giraud readily accepted, but de Gaulle impertinently refused; however, after 'a devastating message from the Prime Minister', he appeared. He behaved in a maddening manner and nothing was achieved.]

The Secretariat had a busy time, but fortunately we had come well staffed. Dumbie and Deane did most of the Combined Chiefs meetings, though Lance Grove and I sometimes lent a hand. I did the meetings at which the Prime Minister saw our Chiefs, and Lance did ordinary COS meetings. Deane and I together did the meetings with the President and the Prime Minister. We rarely had more than one or, at the most, two meetings to cope with in one day. The only person who came badly out of the business was Deane. The US party had come so poorly staffed that he had no help. In fact he himself was nearly not brought at all! The result was that he had to do the United States' COS Meetings as well as his share of the Combined COS, and of President and Prime Minister meetings. As he was a comparative amateur at the game in any case, he did not have too easy a time. . . .

Dumbie and I had the greatest fun together. We used to go to bed pretty late, of course, and spent quite a time chattering and comparing notes as we slowly undressed. We were called by our Marine, Handy, about 7.30 am, and often got him to bring us down toast and butter and coffee and oranges so that we could eat a leisurely breakfast in our room. We used in this way to spend a pleasant couple of hours talking and slowly getting ready for the business of the day. He had lost none of his wit and humour, and was the most entertaining companion it is possible to imagine. We saw absolutely eye to eye on nearly all subjects, and were real half-sections, with our private jokes and shared experiences. Dumbie was a splendid mimic, and the Conference gave him fresh fields in which to work. We had great fun over the CIGS whose birdlike aspect, and fast clipped speech, lent themselves to caricature. I have never met a man who so tumbles over himself in speaking. He is incapable of reading aloud intelligibly. He cannot make his brain move slowly enough to fit his speech or his reading, especially when his interest is strongly engaged. All this, together with his constant habit when talking of shooting his tongue out and round his lips with the speed of a chameleon, made him an easy prey to Dumbie's imitative wit.

Another joke we shared was the American use of the phrase 'it is believed'. When they begin a sentence with these words, you can be sure they will follow them with a statement which takes one's breath away with its inaccuracy. . . . This became a catchword between Dumbie and myself and, much to his joy, I managed to work an 'it is believed' into the final report of the work of the Conference.

The first two or three days of the Conference were enlivened by the bellows, as of a wounded buffalo, of the Prime Minister for more news. It so happened that there was not much going on in the great world at the time. But a can of petrol was poured on the flames of the Prime Minister's wrath by the fact that he got no detailed account of the big raid on Berlin, which took place on the night of January 16/17, until about 6 pm on the 17th. There were various technical hitches to account for the delay, but the Prime Minister despatched a series of 'winged words' to the Private Office, to Jo Hollis, demanding more information and blasting them for their failure to keep him informed. The result was such a stream of stuff, much of it of little importance, of course, but sufficient to keep him quiet. The news of the raid on Berlin the next night came pouring out in a flood of telegrams from everyone, from the Secretary of State for Air downwards; he always does his best to suck up, and also fervently presses forward the merits of the RAF. However, the fury died down, and the sun came out again.

Tuesday, 19–Saturday, 23 January

This period of five days marks the second stage of the Con-

ference. Having cleared the undergrowth, as it were, the ground
could now be marked out in detail. An Agenda to cover all outstanding points was drawn up, and the work on each distributed.
For example, the Planners were instructed to prepare certain
papers; Lord Leathers and General Somervell agreed to study
certain shipping questions; CAS with Arnold, Tedder and Eaker
(to succeed Spaatz in command of the US Air Forces in the
United Kingdom) was to study the co-ordination of air command,
and bombing policy. The reorganisation of the North African
Command was gone into in private huddles between the various
Chiefs of Staff, the Field Marshal often acting as go-between and
general lubricator. Meetings of the Combined Chiefs took place
twice a day as before, and the Agenda was steadily ploughed
through.

The remarkable thing about it all was that the gradual education of the Americans to our way of thinking was found to have
proceeded even farther than we had thought possible. The bene-
ficial results of holding such a conference for so long a period and
on a neutral pitch made themselves clearly manifest. Everyone in
these circumstances is freed from the irksome routine of his office,
and there is nothing to distract attention from the work in hand. If
the Conference is held in Washington or London, the home team
are unable to strike themselves off duty, so as to give undivided
attention to the Conference . . . . Except for formal meetings, and
formal meals, there is little contact. At Casablanca it was quite
different. Everyone fed, slept, and worked in the same building or
group of buildings. British and Americans met round the bar,
went for walks down to the beach together, and sat about in each
other's rooms in the evenings. Mutual respect and understanding
ripen in such surroundings, especially when the weather is lovely,
the accommodation is good, and food and drink and smokes are
unlimited and free.

Whatever may be the truth of the matter, the fact remains that
by the end of the Conference, when I came to write the final
document indicating the decisions taken and the agreement
reached on all the separate matters dealt with, I found that if I
had written down before I came what I hoped that the conclusions would be, I could never have written anything so sweeping,
so comprehensive, and so favourable to our ideas. On thinking it
over, I do believe that this was not an unreasonable result. After
all, we were not two business opponents making a deal in which

one was bound to profit at the other's expense. We were partners, trying to hammer out a common line of action. We British came to the Conference with more experience, with a much more complete and competent team, and having much more thoroughly thrashed out the possibilities. They came probably without any serious attempt having been made between Navy and Army to come to an agreed view. Divided, they naturally fell to our combined front.

The character of General Marshall, and also that of Admiral King, has a bearing on the matter. General Marshall is a man of great integrity, young for his age (63?), and ready to be convinced. An organiser of armies perhaps, but unaccustomed to thinking out problems of world strategy: more interested in the brass tacks of a particular problem, such as how to keep China in the war, than in the rather more abstract question of how the war in its broadest sense should be fought. His ideas were formed in the last war, when he was on Pershing's staff, and saw much of inter-allied affairs through the rigid spectacles of his chief. The impressions he then formed seem to have remained vividly alive, and his strategical views seem to go little beyond the idea that, sooner or later, there must be a large American army established in a Western front. As long as this project remains unattainable, he seems to be prepared to accept anyone else's view as to our correct strategy, confining his attention to more limited if more obvious concrete affairs. He and the Field Marshal see eye to eye on most matters, and have a great respect and friendship for each other. This is a most fortunate thing, especially as Dill sees clearly Marshall's limitations in strategical thought, and can therefore act as an unobtrusive guide and leader.

Admiral King is hard to weigh up; he seems to wear a protective covering of horn, which it is hard to penetrate. He gives the impression of being exceeding narrow-minded, and to be always on the look-out for slights or attempts 'to put something over' on him. He is secretive, and I should say treats his staff stiffly and at times tyrannically. His manners are good as a rule, but he is angular and formal, and finds it difficult if not impossible really to unbend. I am convinced, however, that there is much more to him than appears on the surface, and that if one could get beneath the horn shell, one would be surprised at what one would find beneath. However, as things are, it is very difficult to get very far with King in discussion. The outcome of the Casablanca Conference was therefore all the more surprising. The Admiral expressed himself at the end as most delighted with the results, and he evidently felt that he had been given a really good hearing and that he himself had been brought to take a new and wider view of the war, which he welcomed.

The Americans are quick to size up people. And they either take to you or they reject you wholeheartedly. When they take to you, they make no bones about it; they go the whole hog. Thus they had already taken Dill to their bosoms, and of course Dumbie. At the Conference, they were captured by Portal, and I think Alexander. I should say that they regarded the Whale as a spent force. They were a bit uncertain about CIGS. They are always a bit suspicious of being 'out-smarted'. They like transparent honesty, and not too much mental superiority; I think CIGS's extremely definite views, ultra-swift speech and, at times, impatience, made them keep wondering whether he was not putting something over on them. Nevertheless, I personally thought CIGS handled the Conference on the whole remarkably well. He certainly put his back into it, and was exhausted by the finish.

The Americans put their money on Portal. They would accept him as Commander-in-Chief over everything. They would put all the Allied Air Forces from Iceland to Bombay under his control. His great asset is his unshakeable honesty of thought and deed. They know he knows his stuff, and they trust him one hundred per cent.

A good example of the Field Marshal's tact was provided at the Combined Chiefs of Staff meeting on the afternoon of 19 January when General Giraud was present. He had been invited as a complimentary gesture, and General Marshall and the other US and British Chiefs of Staff each made a little speech to which Giraud listened in rather a frigid attitude, making to each a short reply. Finally, Dill's turn came. He spoke shortly and simply. He recalled the services that General Giraud had given to France, and rejoiced that Giraud was once more free to lead France to victory. Giraud's face lighted up. He in turn recalled the close co-operation between the French and British Armies in 1940, and welcomed the fresh opportunity for working together which had now arisen. Then he said, 'In September 1940, I was in a German prison-camp. I said to the German Generals who came to see me that they had lost the war because they had failed to defeat England. I could not prophesy how long the war would last, but I told them that they could never win, and that sooner or later the USA would come to the help of Great Britain. Then they asked me to sign a paper to the effect that I would not attempt to escape in the period of exercise each day when we were allowed outside. I said I would not sign any paper in German. "Ah", they said, "you are thinking of escaping like you did in 1915?" I said that my thoughts were my own affair. They were my jailers, I was their prisoner. It was their duty to guard me, it was mine to escape. We would see who would do his duty best. Well, it took me a year, but here I am.'

This little speech, given in such a spirited way, delighted everyone, and the Chiefs of Staff all round the table burst into applause. The meeting then ended on this most satisfactory note, largely brought about by the Field Marshal knowing what to say and how to say it.

The Prime Minister was fortunately kept fairly occupied by political matters, and the delicate situation between de Gaulle and Giraud. The President, too, took a day off in the middle of the week to go and review some US troops. The Chiefs of Staff were thus left in comparative peace to pursue their studies and discussions. There was a gradual crescendo as the days passed, and it became known that the President wished to depart on Saturday. We had no less than six meetings of various kinds on Friday, 22 January, not to mention a series of photographic sessions on various days .... Finally all was done on Saturday, and the meeting with the President and Prime Minister was fixed for 5.30 that evening (23 January). This was actually the third meeting of the full session – what the Prime Minister called 'the plenum'. They took place in the dining room of Villa No 2, with every door and window fast shut and with the central heating full on. The two great men went through the final report paragraph by paragraph, and heartily approved it all, subject to certain modifications which were subsequently drafted as amendments. With these incorporated, the document represented the result of the ten day Conference, and was a pretty comprehensive statement of the aims and intentions of the Allies in 1943. The final acts in the drama took the form of telegrams to Uncle Joe Stalin, and to the Generalissimo Chiang-Kai-Shek, and a letter from the President and the Prime Minister addressed to the Combined Chiefs of Staff approving their work but pressing for a speeding up and increasing of the magnitude of the measures planned. A final 'prod', in fact.

[*The final report of the Conference, agreed by the Combined Chiefs of Staff, and by the President and Prime Minister, can be briefly summarised as follows:*

The first charge on resources remained the defeat of the U-boat. Maximum supplies must be sent to Russia.

Operations in the European theatre would be carried out to defeat Germany in 1943 with maximum forces.

The main offensive in the Mediterranean would be to occupy Sicily, thus making more secure the Mediterranean line of communications, relieving pressure on the Russian Front, and increasing pressure on Italy. Steps would be taken so that Turkey could be enlisted as an ally.

The main offensive in the United Kingdom would be the air offensive against the German war effort; also such limited offensive operations as might be practicable, and the assembling of the strongest force possible to re-enter the Continent when German resistance weakened.

Pressure would be maintained against Japan, leading to a full-scale offensive as soon as Germany was defeated. Operations would be kept within such limits as not to jeopardise any favourable opportunity for the decisive defeat of Germany in 1943. Plans and preparations would be made in 1943 to recapture Burma, and for operations against the Marshalls and Carolines if time and resources allowed without prejudice to the recapture of Burma.

On the political front, there was the declaration of unconditional surrender.]

Jacob continues:

The Prime Minister had of course been making all kinds of wonderful plans for himself. He could do nothing until the President was safely packed off home in his monster aircraft (another C.54). There was the usual uncertainty about final movements, but at last, on Saturday, it became known that the Prime Minister and the President would leave Casablanca about noon on Sunday, and would motor to Marrakech (about 120 miles) having a picnic lunch on the way. They would stay the night at Ken Pender's villa, and the President would leave for Bathurst on his way home first thing on Monday morning.

Sunday, 24 January

The party gradually dissolved during the morning, and it was exactly like breaking up at the end of term. Each aeroplane party left the hotel in cars, with their luggage, and we said goodbye as if we were separating for the holidays. The air of abandonment in the hotel gave the same impression. Dumbie was one of the first to leave, and I said goodbye to him in front of the hotel. He had decided to return to Washington via England so as to pick up the latest news in London and take a few days' leave. The Field Marshal was going on to India and Chungking with Somervell and Arnold, and General Marshall and Admiral King were calling at Algiers on their way home, so Dumbie could afford a few days. He had, however, to go to Algiers with the rest of the party on his way to England. I little thought when we parted that it would be for ever.

The death of Brigadier 'Dumbie' Dykes on 30 January in an aeroplane disaster on the Welsh coast was not only a great loss to the British Army and to the cause of Anglo-American military co-operation, but was a personal tragedy for Jacob. Dumbie, senior by nine months, had followed a professional path in the Royal Engineers almost identical to that of Jacob, including a few months' active service in World War I, followed by Waziristan, Cambridge, Aldershot and, as a contemporary, at the Staff College. He had joined the Secretariat of the CID ahead of Ian Jacob, who had then succeeded him. After serving as an instructor at the Staff College, Dumbie had been recalled to the Secretariat of the War Cabinet in 1939. He had left in 1940 to take command of a Field Company which he had reformed after its virtual destruction at St Valery. Returning to the War Office, he had soon become Director of Plans. After a special assignment with Colonel Donovan of the USA, he with Jacob had accompanied the Prime Minister to the Atlantic Conference in 1941; and at the Washington Conference in December of that year he had been selected as the British member of the Anglo-American Secretariat of the Combined Chiefs of Staff, working with Brigadier General Bedell Smith. This had been a particularly happy and successful combination, in which Dykes had obtained the complete confidence of the American Chiefs, as well as the admiration of Field Marshal Sir John Dill. Dyke's death caused consternation amongst his friends and colleagues in London and Washington. He was posthumously awarded the American Distinguished Service Medal, never before awarded to an Englishman.

Jacob, while admiring Dumbie's outstanding ability, had relished his effervescent personality; their happy comradeship had often provided relief to the many pressures of their common work. In a letter to

Cecil from Casablanca just two weeks before Dumbie's death he had written:

> Everything in the garden is lovely and I have marked this down as one of the spots for a post-war holiday. Business fairly brisk, but nothing excessive. All the world is present or coming. . . . I have Dumbie as a stable companion, so chins wag well.

Later, on 2 February, dining with Cornwall-Jones and other friends in Cairo, he would hear by telephone of Dumbie's death. That night in his diary he wrote:

> C-J and I felt as if we had been stunned: the loss of Dumbie can never quite be made good in my mind, even though eventually the Service, and our office in particular, will manage to repair the gap which has been torn in their framework. We were so closely tuned together: our minds moved as one, and each time we met, the association seemed to have become closer. The news will also have been heart-breaking to Pug, Jo and Lawrence, who were so intimately linked with him too. I never thought the death of a friend could be so bitter.

On that same night he wrote to his wife:

> It is an awful blow, and I keep thinking of it all the time. He was my best friend, and we had such a marvellous time together, with one continual flow of jokes and laughter. It really is a tragedy and I cannot believe he has really gone.

Sir Alan Brooke in Cairo ruled that the news be kept from the Prime Minister at the time, as he was about to embark on another hazardous journey by air, with Jacob once again at his right hand.

10

On the Conference Circuit Again

The Prime Minister, well-satisfied with the achievements of the Casablanca Conference, and confident that Sicily would be occupied in the summer of 1943, now directed his tireless energies to other affairs in the Mediterranean. After a short holiday in Marrakech, where he would paint a picture of sunset on the Atlas Mountains – his sole picture throughout the war – he would set to work on a project, long cherished in his mind: to create a situation in which the Turks – those good fighters in his first World War – might be induced to throw in their lot with Britain and America.

As far back as November 1942, chiding the British Joint Planners, as was his wont, for their 'negative' attitude, he had instructed them that it would be most regrettable if no more use were made of the success of Alamein and Torch than the capture of Sicily and Sardinia; amongst other objectives he had then proposed operations to bring in Turkey and thrust overland into the Balkans.

Jacob, in Casablanca, was to be heavily involved now in a visit by Churchill to Turkey. The entry in his diary reads:

Saturday, 23 January
The Prime Minister's plans were still not firm, but he was anxious to go to Cairo, and later to Tripoli. His big project, however, was a visit to Turkey: the time had come to cash in on the Russian victories and the favourable turn of events in the Mediterranean, and nail Turkey to the mast. He had no intention of trying to force Turkey into the war, but he felt that a talk between himself and the Turkish President would show the world clearly which way the wind was blowing. He proposed to build up

172

Turkey's strength so that later she could either come in, or else, if things took an unfavourable turn, defend herself. He accordingly telegraphed home asking the Cabinet to forward to Turkey a request for a meeting, possibly in secret at Cyprus.

The Cabinet, however, advised by the Foreign Office, jibbed violently. They produced all kinds of arguments against such a meeting. The Prime Minister would be rebuffed; the time was not ripe; the Turks would think we were trying to compromise them, and to get them into the war; and so on.

The Prime Minister was furious and contemptuous, and returned immediately to the charge. He also got the President to send a message, to accompany the Prime Minister's own, reinforcing a request for a meeting. The Cabinet were asked to think again, and to transmit the Prime Minister's and the President's messages at once. The Cabinet naturally had to comply, and might well have done so the first time. The delay meant that no answer could be got before the Prime Minister left Casablanca.

The Prime Minister had decided to take CIGS with him to Cairo and beyond, and also that I should go with him, rather than Pug, who he decided ought to go home to get on with the many tasks arising from the Conference. I arranged therefore to fly to Marrakech on Sunday afternoon with William Stirling, Leslie Rowan, and some of the Prime Minister's household, so as to get there well before the picnic party. However, I had a busy morning first. I was sent for by the Prime Minister at 9 am. I found him in bed in his room upstairs with the windows tight shut, the heating full on, dictating and having breakfast by turns. A draft communiqué which the President had sent him over was the business in hand, and he was busy redrafting it. He wanted me to check it over, and see that all the names and titles were correct – 'Wigs by Clarkson' was his expression for what he wanted filled in and checked.

[*For many years, 'Wigs by Clarkson' had usually appeared as a credit at the end of theatre programmes; the catchphrase, when used by Churchill, meant that the text was to be cleaned up and any necessary details included.*]

The Prime Minister in bed in the mornings reminds me in an extraordinary way of my grandmother, who in her later years had the same rather slothful physical habits, and slow movements, combined with the extremely masterful brain demanding continual employment, and a constant stream of helpers, servants etc round her. She used to sit in bed having breakfast, while also writing a note to someone in the parish, ordering the meals for the day, telling me to get on my bicycle to fetch something from the butcher, and keeping her husband, who was aching to get on with his duties in the parish, hanging around for last injunctions.

The Prime Minister is much the same. Sawyers brings the breakfast; then Kinna is called to take something down; meanwhile the bell is rung for the Private Secretary on duty who is asked for news, and told to summon someone, say CIGS or Pug. Then it is the candle for lighting cigars that is wanted. Then someone must get Hopkins on the phone. All this while the Prime Minister is half sitting, half lying, in his bed, breathing rather stertorously, and surrounded by papers.

On this morning there was none too much time to spare, as the communiqué had to be ready, and the PM dressed and round at Villa No 2 by 12.30 for the press conference. As soon as I had checked up the facts, and Kinna had retyped the communiqué, I was sent round to No 2 to get Hopkins's agreement. I arrived to find everyone in their bedrooms as usual, and the drawing room occupied by Murphy, who was working away at a table in the centre of the room. The public announcements about Giraud's meeting with de Gaulle were being hatched out. I was taken up to Hopkins's room, and although it was already 10 am, and the sun was shining brightly, I found him in his dressing gown, with the curtains closely drawn, and a veritable pigsty around him. The tumbled bed had beside it on the floor a bowl full of half-smoked cigarettes. Books, papers, cigarettes were scattered everywhere, as also were clothes. We sat down side by side on the bed, and went through the communiqué, Hopkins making some very sensible alterations. You cannot get away from the fact that Hopkins has a striking personality concealed inside a miserable physique. The 'disused prawn' has a great heart, complete honesty of purpose, and a toughness which enables him to triumph over his weak body.

Our business was soon done, and I nipped back to Villa No 3. The Prime Minister accepted the corrections, and all was now clear for the production of the final version.

It had been my intention to fly with CIGS and others in an aircraft leaving at 11 o'clock, but the Prime Minister would not hear of it, and I had to hang about until he had himself gone. I said my farewells to everyone, and then sat myself down with Sir Charles Wilson to enjoy the sunshine until lunch. At 1.15 we set out for Mediouna, and had an uneventful trip, though we noticed that the Americans, who do not believe in half measures, had a soldier posted every hundred yards the entire way, with Bofors guns at intervals. We flew straight to Marrakech, and were met by William Stirling, who had come earlier. He took us off to the Vice-Consul's villa, where the Prime Minister and his personal staff were to stay. . . . A similar suite was set aside for the President. After looking round and settling various matters, I did not wait for the party to arrive from their picnic, but went off with William Stirling to the Mamounia Hotel where we were to stay. The CIGS and Boyle, his Staff Officer, were also there, and we joined them.

After a quiet dinner, at which we had some quite good red wine of the country, we were glad to get early to bed.

Monday, 25 January

I woke in time to see the dawn rising on the Atlas. William Stirling and I had breakfast in bed, drinking in the lovely view and the peacefulness of the scene. At 9.15 the summons came for me and the CIGS, who was having his breakfast; so I left a message for him, and went down to the villa. I found that the President had already left, and the PM was sitting up in bed planning to leave the same evening. We had been afraid that this would happen, the difficulty being that no warning had gone to Cairo. The PM had refused to allow us to send one. The Ambassador in Cairo would only hear twelve hours or so before the Prime Minister was due to arrive, which was rather unfair. The resultant 'flap' would tend to upset secrecy. However, the PM was adamant; the only point requiring confirmation was the suitability of the weather, and Van der Kloete, the Prime Minister's pilot, confirmed that this would present no bar.

The Prime Minister and the President had been very naughty the night before. They had arrived from their picnic at about 6 pm. They had two important tasks outstanding; one was the telegram to Uncle Joe, and the other was the telegram to Chiang Kai-Shek. If they had settled down to these at once, they could have got them off before dinner and could have enjoyed the rest of the evening with untroubled minds. Not a bit of it. They dawdled about till dinner time, sat for hours over dinner, and finally got down to business at midnight. However, they managed to dispose of their telegrams, and eventually got to bed. The PM apparently got up to see the President off at the aerodrome about 8 am, and stepped out of his car to say goodbye dressed in a wonderful padded dressing gown with dragons all over it, and was still wearing this when I saw him in bed later. It seemed to fit in very well with the decoration of the room.

[*In the morning, Jacob and the CIGS drove into the Atlas mountains, while the Prime Minister did some painting.*]

At 5.30 we left for the aerodrome, driving on the way through a magnificent grove of olives in which we were told there were 12,000 trees, large ones too. A fabulous revenue for someone. The PM arrived sometime after us, but we took off in succession about 6.30. The PM had purposely arranged to start early so that we could see the sunset on the mountains. Certainly the colours were wonderful, the most striking spectacle just after we had crossed the range. The sun was then just below our horizon, and filled the sky and the top of the hills with a blood-red glow.

We touched down at 7.10 am and the Prime Minister arrived five minutes later. Mr Casey, Lord Moyne, General Alexander, Air Chief Marshal Sholto Douglas (who recently had succeeded Tedder as AOC-in-C, Middle East) were all there to meet us, with a flock of cars. No time was wasted and I soon found myself driving into Cairo.

It was a lovely morning when we arrived – the Egyptian cold weather was at its best. With the Army 1500 miles away, instead of 150, things were changed. However, Cairo itself appeared no different, nor the Embassy when we reached it at breakfast time. We all had breakfast with the Lampsons who greeted us warmly, the PM having a whisky and soda, and glorying in it! I then went round to Cornwall-Jones' flat. I found him well, and everything ready for me as usual. I even had the same car and driver; so I immediately fell into the old routine, and set myself up in C-J's office in GHQ.

Little or no business was done today. The Prime Minister's main preoccupation was the French Squadron at Alexandria, which he was determined should no longer be permitted to remain there inactive and drawing rations and pay from us to maintain them in shameful sloth. At 4.30 pm we had a meeting in the C-in-C's War Room with the Commanders-in-Chief to discuss action. Harwood favoured letting sleeping dogs lie. Admiral Godfroy, the Frenchman, had worked himself in the course of nearly three years into such a peculiar frame of mind, that if any pressure were put on him, he would scuttle his ships, which, it seemed, he thought was the most honourable course to adopt. However, the Prime Minister was all against letting things be, and telegraphed off home making proposals for stopping the Frenchmen's pay and food and thus forcing the issue.

Wednesday, 27 January

I went into the Embassy after breakfast. The weather was perfect. C-J and I walked in across Gezireh along the first fairway, and across the Kasr-el-Nil bridge. The PM slept until 10 am, a most unusual event, probably indicating a very late session the night before at bezique. I went up to him with the telegrams that had come in during the night containing the answer of the Turkish Government to his message suggesting a meeting. In spite of the fears and gloomy prophesies of the Foreign Office, the reply was entirely favourable. The Turkish President said that he was quite ready to meet Churchill either openly or secretly, but preferably at Ankara. Failing Ankara, he would come by train to any point in Turkey that the Prime Minister might select, or if secrecy was essential, he would send his Prime Minister to meet Churchill in Cyprus. He himself could not leave Turkey without various constitutional formalities.

The Prime Minister was delighted. 'This is big stuff!' he kept saying. He read and re-read the telegrams, and was obviously not unhappy at the thought of how right he had been and how wrong the Cabinet and their advisers had proved. Tommy and I talked to him while he had his breakfast, making suggestions for the journey. The obvious question was whether our Liberators could land anywhere in Turkey at this time of year. A meeting in Ankara was ruled out not only on security grounds, but also that a flight to Ankara would mean crossing the Taurus Mountains, a very doubtful proposition at this time of year. The PM had an enormous breakfast consisting of 2 eggs, ham and chicken, coffee toast, butter and marmalade, 2 oranges, and a glass of orange juice as well. He had a different bedroom this time, and lay in a gauze anti-mosquito cage into which there was only room for one or two people to squeeze at a time. After breakfast we left him to read the papers, which contained the news of the Casablanca Conference, while we went to examine ways and means with Air Marshal Drummond.

[27 and 28 January were spent by the Prime Minister on a number of topics: the role of Alexander, as deputy to Eisenhower, in co-ordinating the

actions of Eighth and First Armies: the appointment of Wilson to succeed Alexander in Cairo, and the selection of a successor to Wilson in Baghdad: the onset of planning for HUSKY, (the invasion of Sicily) and the contribution of Middle East Command to that operation: the speedy clearance of Tripoli harbour: the problem of the French Fleet: and lastly the possibility of re-uniting Middle East Command with Persia and Iraq, which the PM favoured and the CIGS opposed. Jacob was kept busy writing up the minutes.]

Friday, 29 January

Most of this day was spent in preparations for the trip to Turkey. Commanders-in-Chief had had a brief prepared by the JPS, and we had a long meeting to go through it and consider the present position, and how best we could help the Turks, and what action we should want them to take. CIGS was in the Chair. During the meeting a long paper dictated by the PM arrived bit by bit, hot from the typewriter, for the Commanders-in-Chief to check. It proved to be a statement for the Turks, from which the Prime Minister proposed to speak when he met President Inonu. It dealt mainly with Turkey's position in the scheme of things, with the situations which might arise to involve Turkey in the war, and what we would do both to prepare for these situations and also to meet them. The Commanders-in-Chief made a few alterations, and the paper was then taken by CIGS to go through with the Prime Minister.

It had been agreed with the Turks that the meeting should be held near Adana, in trains to be provided by them, there being a suitable airfield on which our Liberators could land. We were to arrive on Saturday, 30 January, and stay probably 24 hours. All arrangements were to be made by the Turks. Group Captain Hudleston (an Air Staff Officer) would get in touch with the Turks and act as a kind of advance party. However, bad weather prevented them getting beyond Beirut today. The Ambassador (Sir H. Knatchbull-Hugessen) and the Military and Air Attachés in Ankara (Major General Arnold and Air Vice Marshal George) were to accompany the Turkish party, and to bring the necessary interpreters. Communications would be by our own W/T set to Cairo, and thence to London.

Saturday, 30 January

At 7 am, having picked up Peter Loxley of the Foreign Office, who had arrived the previous day with Cadogan from England, we motored together out to Landing Ground 224. The passenger list was as follows: General Alexander, General Wilson, General Lindsell, Air Marshal Drummond, Commodore Dundas, Mr Loxley (of the Foreign Office), Mr Kinna; and myself.

We were met on the tarmac at Adana airport, by Arnold (the Military Attaché), George (the Air Attaché), Helm (Counsellor at the Embassy), Falla (Secretary of the Embassy), and by our advanced party. They were in a fair state of excitement, having only succeeded in making the aerodrome by the skin of their teeth. It seems that the two trains, one of Presidential train, and one a special made up to take our party, had arrived during the night at the place where the meeting was to be, a loop-line at a spot about three quarters of an hour slow steaming away from Adana. It had been arranged that our train was to move off and come to Adana station in time to embark the members of our party, except the Prime Minister who was to be taken to a neighbouring level crossing where he would be whisked on board the train which would pause for the purpose. However, the train was late, and Helm and Co, finding that there was no sign of action, had grabbed an engine and coach and induced the driver to bring them on in advance. They had just managed to arrive as we were circling the aerodrome, and so were still a bit agitated when we alighted. They were relieved to find that there was still an hour before the Prime Minister was due.

[*Some complicated manoeuvres then took place and, in the nick of time, the special train arrived just ahead of the Prime Minister. Eventually, all were assembled in the train, which steamed away westwards.*]

Hugessen greeted us with the news that the Germans evidently had got to hear of the meeting and had already rung up the Turkish Foreign Ministry to enquire whether this meant that the Turks had come down on our side of the fence. However, the Turks were not in the least disturbed by this, and were quite prepared to snap their fingers at the Boche. This was a further proof, if one were needed, of the changed outlook of the Turkish Government. We were a bit worried about security, but the Turkish arrangements appeared very thorough, and we did not propose to stay long. It is not easy to lay on an efficient assassination at very short notice, at an out-of-the-way place, when the authorities are on the look out . . . .

The Turkish Prime Minister (M Sarajoglu) and the Foreign

Minister (M Numan) were rather nondescript people, obviously delighted with the whole affair, and having none of the pomposity of ministers in some countries. They put on no airs, and the arrival was more like a family welcoming a relation than an official reception. No one stood on his dignity. The same friendly spirit pervaded the train. We were soon down to an excellent lunch, the bigwigs with the Ministers in a special saloon, and the rest of us in the ordinary restaurant car. After lunch we arrived at the loop-line, and were gently backed down it until our tail joined the tail of the Presidential train, and we formed one long string of coaches. The President's saloon was only separated from the Prime Minister's by the Ambassador's coach, and all three had saloons suitable for meetings.

The PM met President Inonu when the two trains linked. The latter was in a small saloon which formed part of his private coach. Marshal Chakmak was there, and our Generals were introduced, followed by the more junior members of our party.

The PM was conducting proceedings in French, and made the necessary introductions. When my turn came, he said that I was the '*fils du Maréchal Jacob*', and then turning to Marshal Chakmak he said: '*Vous savez. Aux Indes.*' Chakmak looked pretty blank, but bowed politely! All the time the Press were doing their best to insert themselves and to take photographs, until finally the saloon resembled the Black Hole of Calcutta. However, everything comes to an end at last, and the PM and the President decided that there should be a formal meeting of the two delegations forthwith. We accordingly adjourned to the large saloon. The PM stayed behind a bit alone with the President, and then they joined us.

It had been decided that the proceedings should be conducted in French and English, and Falla was installed as our interpreter. His French was extremely good. So when the PM arrived, we told him of this arrangement. The PM then produced the paper which he had prepared in Cairo, and proceeded to read it to the Turks. After he had said the first two or three sentences in English, he paused, and Falla translated. However, the Prime Minister evidently thought that this procedure would be too tedious, and perhaps he also felt that he could give better emphasis to the appropriate passages if he did the whole thing himself. Whatever his motive was, he launched himself into French, translating on the spot what he had written in his paper. This amounted to doing orally, with no time for thought or preparation, a long unseen into French – no small task. The PM's French is fairly fluent, and he was rarely stuck for a word. But of course he could make only a literal translation, and his accent is almost pure English. The result was therefore completely intelligible to all the English present, even if they had no knowledge of the language beyond what they had learnt at school; but the Turks could only have formed a very hazy idea of what the whole thing was about. The PM waded resolutely on, and came out at the far end bloody but unbowed. It was really quite a *tour de force*! Peculiar though it all was, I do not think anyone felt like laughing. They could not help admiring his determination and self-possession. The Turks were much too polite to express any surprise or amusement.

At the end of the PM's speech, the President thanked him, and said that there were evidently two matters for discussion. One, the circumstances in which Turkey might become involved in the war – a political question. The second, what could be done to prepare for the situation – a military question. He therefore suggested that he and the PM with their political advisers should go apart and talk about the first question, leaving the Military representatives to discuss the second. This was done, and we got down to business straight away, CIGS taking the chair opposite Marshal Chakmak. Meanwhile, Loxley, Helm, and Falla got down to making a translation of the PM's speech into French for the Turks. . . .

The CIGS fortunately speaks perfect French, at his usual lightening speed, having been brought up in Pau, where his father had had a house. The Marshal was pretty poor at French, but he had on his one hand his nephew, the head of the Turkish Air Force, and on the other M Surayya Anderiman, the Secretary-General of the Turkish Foreign Office, both of whom spoke French perfectly. Everyone else understood sufficiently well, so that the only drag on the proceedings was caused by the efforts made by the Marshal's supporters to make him understand the knotty points, and occasionally by the huddles over figures which kept occurring on the Turkish side.

The greater part of the discussions were about the material which we could supply to the Turks. Their oriental nature showed in the keenness with which they entered into this aspect of the business, which was the only thing they were really interested in. They asked no questions at all about the progress of the war, nor did they try to find out what had been decided at Casablanca. But from little things we picked up here and there, it is evident that they are convinced that Germany's days are numbered, and that their main preoccupation is the state of Europe following or during the German collapse, and what Russia may do. It was this that made them so ready to agree to this meeting. They wanted to be sure of our support if Russia turned nasty. They were a bit apprehensive that the PM would come with proposals for their immediate entry into the war. When they found that he had no intention of trying to push them along, they heaved a sigh of relief and entered wholeheartedly into the fun. Everywhere there were smiles, and, of course, demands for material assistance on the largest scale.

However, CIGS handled them very well, and declined to go into detail on the spot. He also pressed them hard on the side of their obligation to improve their communications, to train their men in the use and maintenance of mechanical equipment, and to make the greatest possible use of our help. Everything went along well, and after the meeting I was able to draft some conclusions which we could consider the following morning and polish up as necessary. These would form the military outcome of the conversations, and be the basis on which future progress would be made. For example, one of the conclusions was for the acceptance in Ankara of a British Military Staff to study properly the Turkish communications and their capacity, so as to decide what forces could be maintained in the event of war, and to plan the improvement of facilities so that these forces could be augmented. Agreement on this conclusion would pave the way for General Lindsell and his staff to get really down to the Turkish problem, which they had never been able to do before. The Turks have always tried to exclude foreign influence, remembering as they do the domineering attitude of the Germans in the last war. So it will be very satisfactory if we can take a good step forward in collaboration. Without our help, the Turkish communications will make no progress, and traffic in war will be chaotic.

Apparently the political talks went well, and at 9.30 pm we had dinner. Loxley, Martin and I had ours in the Turkish coach with Anderiman. He is a most interesting man who talks excellent English, as well as French, and we had a very pleasant dinner. We broke up somewhere about midnight, and went along the train to find the PM sitting in a small saloon, into which nearly all our party were also wedged, all drinking whisky. The atmosphere was appalling. The PM was in excellent form, and it looked as if he might be there all night; however, wiser councils prevailed, and we were able to totter off to our sleeping cars at 1 am.

Anderiman's conversation at dinner was interesting. His main theme was the great responsibility which would lie on the British after the war. He seemed to regard us as the only bulwark against chaos, and although he did not say it, against Russia.

Sunday, 31 January

I awoke at 8 o'clock after an excellent sleep. The wagon-lit was I suppose, one of those normally employed on the Taurus express, belonging to the Wagon Lit Company, and was comfortable and clean. I found no travelling companions. After breakfast, I arranged for Loxley and Co to translate into French the conclusions I had drafted the previous night. I got CIGS's approval and then took the draft into the Prime Minister, who was lying in bed in his coach, the walls of which all round him were hung with red silk. He too had been busy, and had dictated a paper on political subjects, dealing with some of the post-war fears of the Turks. He called it 'Morning Thoughts', and later gave a copy to the President. At 11.45, the PM met the President, and the military people also met. The draft conclusions were examined and approved with certain amendments, and the business concluded with complimentary speeches and general satisfaction.

The next forty-eight hours at Adana were to be marked by order, counter-order and pandemonium. The Prime Minister's first intention was to go to Cyprus to visit his Regiment, the 4th Hussars, accompanied by the CIGS. The entourage was to be sent off direct to Cairo. Churchill then changed his mind, and decided he must fly straight to Cairo in order to send off important telegrams to President Roosevelt, the War Cabinet and others, with a report of the Adana talks. After a farewell lunch with the Turks, accompanied in Jacob's words with much 'back-slapping and expressions of *d'accord*', there was a helter-skelter rush to land at Cairo before dark.

Unfortunately the Prime Minister's plane was manoeuvred off the edge of the runway, and a wheel became hopelessly bogged down in the mud. Jacob, being in the delightful position of the person who was in no way responsible for the occurrence, or for putting it right, relished the ensuing pandemonium in which the Prime Minister played an active part equipped with a 'rakish homburg hat and a large cigar'. The spectacle ended with the Turkish Guard of Honour tugging at the wheel with a rope which, as anticipated, broke 'before the wheel so much as trembled'.

The Prime Minister, recognising it was now too late to get to Cairo, decided once more on Cyprus with a change of aircraft. The entourage, after discussion, decided to stay in Turkey; and after a fond farewell to President Inonu 'who was most charming and might have been saying goodbye to his dearest friends', bedded down in a railway coach now marooned in a siding. Jacob commented that 'things now fell back into normal Turkish style – no water to wash or shave, and a most peculiar breakfast, cooked by a dishevelled hunchback'.

However, they eventually reached Cairo on 1 February, where the Prime Minister later joined them from Cyprus. Jacob, who had been unable to write his reports at Adana, immediately got to work on the minutes of the two important meetings. He commented, perhaps over-optimistically on the outcome, for it was not until 1945 that Turkey declared war on Germany and Japan.

The diary continues:

> Looking back on the Turkish visit, I feel that it was outstand-ingly successful, and a real triumph for the Prime Minister, who had undertaken it against all the advice of the experts. Fur-thermore, the meeting was the most friendly of all the many international meetings I have attended. There was none of that atmosphere of each side being out to try and prove its case, and get its views adopted. Once the Turks realised tht we had not come to try and force them into the war forthwith, their attitude was not only cordial, but natural and homely. The President was a charming man, white-haired and rather deaf, but alert and intelligent. Sarajoglu and Numan were not very striking per-sonalities, and I did not see enough of them to form any opinion of their quality. Marshal Chakmak struck me as a fairly command-ing personality, although not very lively or agile-minded. The Turks were incorrigibly behind the times, and are unlikely ever to catch up, now that they no longer have Mustapha Kemal to drive them along. However, they are stubborn and loyal, and not easily frightened. They have stood firm throughout the war and will act when they think wise. They certainly will not act until they feel sure of being on a certainty.

After dinner at the Cairo Embassy with the Lampsons, enlivened by Churchill's recollections of Omdurman, they took off for Tripoli, on 3 February. At headquarters Eighth Army, where the officers were being addressed by Churchill, Jacob once again met Brian Robertson, who was about to be promoted Major General. He also met Kirkman, the Brigadier Royal Artillery, whose guns had played such a successful part in the Alamein battle.

Kirkman had succeeded Martin, Jacob's colleague in the War Office in 1934. It was Martin who had suggested to Jacob, on his previous visit to Eighth Army, that they needed someone like Montgomery to put them back on their feet again. Ironically, when Montgomery did arrive, he had taken one look at Martin, and decided he needed 'new blood' in the vital post of head gunner, who would be required to organise concentrated artillery fire and not fritter it away in battle groups. He put this to Brigadier Maxwell, the senior gunner at GHQ, who had responded: 'But Noel Martin is a splendid fellow: he played golf in the Walker Cup!' Montgomery replied: 'This isn't golf', and very soon both Maxwell and Martin were relieved.

Jacob, with the Prime Minister and CIGS, witnessed Eighth Army's ceremonial parade in Tripoli. Like all those present he was much moved:

'The sun shone down in a cloudless sky, and the Union Jack floated from a staff set up over an archway on the upper part of the ruined castle, an armed sentry standing outlined in the archway. All around were veterans of the Eighth Army, standing in the last city of Mussolini's Empire. No wonder the tears rolled down the Prime Minister's cheeks as he took the salute, with General Alexander and General Montgomery standing beside him. It was an occasion that made all the disappointments, hardships and setbacks of the Middle East campaign seem to be robbed of their sting. The bitter moment in the White House, when Tobruk fell, was swallowed up in the joy of the morning in Tripoli.

[*After the parade, Montgomery and Freyberg greeted Jacob, both having known his father, the Field Marshal. Later that day a telegram from London arrived, warning of plots to intercept the Prime Minister's plane at Algiers, and begging him not to go there but to go straight to Gibraltar or Marrakech.*]

Leslie Rowan and I saw the Prime Minister who had gone to bed in his caravan. He was very scornful of the whole affair, and I agreed with him.

The Prime Minister thought Gib much more risky than Algiers.

At Gib the landing ground is in full view of the Spaniards, and nothing would be easier than to turn a machine gun on the Prime Minister's plane as it took off. 'Commando' is well marked, and well advertised. At Algiers, the aerodrome is well away from the town, and a closed car would rapidly convey the Prime Minister to the Admiral's villa. No one would know he was there until he had gone. CIGS backed the PM, so it was decided to make no change in the plans which had been made for visiting Algiers for a few hours on his way home.

[*Taking off for Algiers from Castel Benito, Jacob overheard a classic comment from Churchill.*]

He related it thus:

It was not long before the PM joined us, and after a drink all round, produced of course by Sawyers from the bowels of the bomb-bay, he decided to go to bed, where Sir Charles had already preceded him. It was quite a business for Sawyers to hoist him into his perch and undress him. At one stage I heard Sawyers say: 'You are sitting on your hot water bottle. That isn't at all a good idea'. To which the PM replied 'Idea? It isn't an idea, it's a coincidence.'

[*They landed at Algiers on 5 February, and were met by Eisenhower, AB Cunningham and William Stirling, and were given breakfast in the Admiral's villa. 'ABC himself is an excellent host, and treats everyone the same, which is nice.'*]

Jacob's diary continues:

After lunch I went down to AFHQ to see my various friends, 'Beetle' Smith, Jock Whiteley, Mockler Ferryman, General Gale, and so on. Meanwhile, the Prime Minister was dealing with French political matters ... I found things much as usual at Allied Force Headquarters though there was much relief over the absence of Clark, who had, at last, been disposed of as GOC 5th Army at Ouida. Beetle himself seemed relieved, and able to take a much firmer grip of things.

[*Eventually, on 6 February, after another day's delay due to engine trouble, they flew off to England.*]

The PM sat opposite to me, and it seemed that his mind was thinking of crashes. He said: 'It would be a pity to have to go out in the middle of such an interesting drama without seeing the end. But it wouldn't be a bad moment to leave. It is a straight run in now, and even the Cabinet could manage it!'

On 8 February 1943, Jacob returned to routine work in Whitehall. Having spent many weeks involved with major strategy in the company of world leaders, he would now have to concentrate on problems of 'nuts and bolts', over the whole field in which the Prime Minister's restless and exacting mind would range.

(Typically, a Churchill minute to Bridges and Jacob in April 1943 demanded investigation of thicker tank armour, the development of a heavy tank, and of an amphibious tank with a 'galosh' to take it across the Channel, and the substitution of a 95 mm tank howitzer for the American 75 mm gun.)

However, a more exciting prospect soon opened when the Prime Minister and the President agreed to confer once more, and Washington was chosen for the meeting. An urgent question was the next move after the capture of Sicily. The British were determined to move into Italy to knock Hitler's unenthusiastic ally out of the war and clear the Mediterranean shipping lane, but the Americans were as yet unconvinced. Another question was the extent of future operations in the Burma-China theatre. The Americans were dubious whether the British War Cabinet intended to pursue that campaign with the requisite energy and resources. The Prime Minister agreed that the time had come to make a long-term plan for the defeat of Japan.

A large British delegation was assembled and took passage in the liner Queen Mary, arriving in the United States on 11 May 1943. Jacob accompanied General Ismay from the Defence Office and, with the American Brigadier General JR Deane, now a Secretary from the Combined Chiefs of Staff, recorded the meetings of the President and the Prime Minister. Jacob kept no diary of this conference, codenamed TRIDENT, but in a letter to his wife, written immediately after arrival, he commented that 'Master' had been delighted with the sumptuous arrangements in the Queen Mary. There had been meetings throughout the voyage, and he had dined once with 'Master' and had enjoyed a most interesting evening. On arrival in America he was saddened that there was no Dumbie Dykes to greet him, but he had been cheered by the luxury of his suite in the Statler Hotel in Washington – a double bedroom with bath and shower and a drawing room. However, 'they had not made much progress with their work as yet, and it was much harder to thrash things out in Washington than in an isolated spot like Casablanca. There were too many competing interests – lunches, dinners, visiting Dominion Ministers, and so on and, of course, the normal preoccupations of the Missions there.'

A few days later, he dined with Sir Robert Sinclair and with Bedell Smith who had come from Algiers. At a dinner with Brigadier 'Dixie' Redman, Dykes's successor, he had been reminded sadly once again of Vivian's irrepressible humour and vivacity. On 18 May the British Ambassador, Lord Halifax, had asked him to dine to meet the Windsors, in a small party. Afterwards Jacob wrote to his wife that 'the Duchess was very smartly dressed but not very becomingly, I thought. I came to the conclusion that she is a very ordinary American woman! He looked just the same, though far less nervy. We had a very pleasant evening, discussing the French collapse, and things like that. I talked to him a lot, and he remembered all about my father without any prompting. . . .'

When the great men went off for a spree at Williamsburg, Jacob had a lazy morning in his 'suite', reading the hundred page newspapers and writing letters. The papers told him how the Americans had 'cleaned up Tunisia'; also about 'a girl who kept a pet crocodile' how hobbies 'relax clubwomen', how 'boys hail return of crew-cuts' and what was 'ultra chic for a little chick'. So Cecil would see 'that all sides of his nature were well taken care of'.

At the conference, the discussions of the professionals were intense and at times acrimonious. The Americans, although still divided amongst themselves, were unimpressed by the idea of exploiting success in Sicily by invading Italy, principally because of its possible effect on an early cross-Channel operation. The British stand was that they would contemplate a cross-Channel operation only when the conditions were right, i.e. in terms of German strength, a sufficient number of battle-tried British and American divisions, command of the air and sufficient landing craft and specialist paraphernalia for an opposed landing. They now considered that such conditions could not be attained until 1944. Meanwhile TORCH, after a shaky start, had been a success, and had inflicted heavy losses on the Germans. On the critical question of the Mediterranean versus cross-Channel priority, the final decision of the conference bore every mark of a compromise: agreement was reached on the exploitation of HUSKY so as to knock Italy out of the war and contain the maximum number of enemy divisions, using all available forces up to 1 November 1943. Thereafter, a decision on which of the various operations should be adopted would be reserved for the Combined Chiefs of Staff.

Churchill, frustrated by this conclusion, decided to fly with Marshall to Algiers to confer with Eisenhower and his Commanders in order to obtain a firm decision to follow up HUSKY by an immediate invasion of Italy. Jacob accompanied the party, which left the United States on 26 May. Eventually, the Prime Minister obtained the decision he wanted. A further success for Churchill was the decision that development of the atom bomb should be a joint enterprise with the Americans.

HUSKY was launched on 10 July and completed, later than had been hoped, on 17 August.

However, before that successful outcome, yet another Conference was arranged, this time at Ottawa, and Jacob set sail once more on 5 August. The Prime Minister had Mrs Churchill with him as well as Junior Officer Mary Churchill. There were two unusual additions to the party: Wing Commander Guy Gibson VC, the 'dam buster' and Brigadier Orde Wingate, the 'Chindit' leader. They were to be shown off to the Americans; Gibson was to be given a rest from active operations, and Wingate would be called on to explain his operational technique.

The most important item on the agenda for the Ottawa Conference, code named QUADRANT, was an outline plan for the cross-Channel assault in 1944, now named OVERLORD, which had been produced by a special joint planning staff located in London under Lieutenant General FE Morgan and designated COSSAC (Chief of Staff, Supreme Allied Commander). Next in importance was the Far East theatre.

Jacob, two days out from Britain in the *Queen Mary*, wrote to Cecil:

> I saw Master for the first time this morning about 8.45 am, he was lying in bed smoking a cigar as long as a trombone and brooding over South East Asia. He had a bedtable in front of him and two thick sorbo pads on either side of it, presumably to save his forearms when he rests them on the edge of the table when reading papers. He questioned me on various points, and then I got away to breakfast. I am dining with him tonight.
>
> We have among other interesting people on board, Wingate who led the Long Range Penetration Groups in Burma last winter. He arrived home by air one day before we left and dined at No 10. The PM told him to come with us, and asked about his wife. Wingate said he had not seen her yet, so the PM said she was to come along too. She was taken off a train and conveyed to the ship. Neither of them have any clothes at all, except what they stood up in.
>
> Wingate had his Indian hot-weather uniform, and has now borrowed a dark blue serge overall suit from the Captain. He is a most interesting study – deep set eyes, beaky nose, rather fanatical looking, and I should say single-minded, and without much sense of humour: a sort of modern Gordon.
>
> Our routine is much as usual. Chiefs of Staff meeting 10.30 am. Not much after lunch; perhaps a meeting with the PM after tea. We had one last night, and then I dined with him. I sat next to Mrs C, who is very nice to talk to . . . the PM

is in very good form, and was discussing the battle of Ramillies, Wendell Wilkie, Sicily and all kinds of topics. . . .'

Later from the Chateau Frontenac Hotel, which had been taken over for the Conference:

> I love this place and we must come here after the war. There is a splendid promenade outside the hotel, a sort of platform of wood about a quarter of a mile long, parallel to the river down below. We go out whenever possible and 'pace the quarterdeck, and admire the view. . . . Things are very hectic as usual. . . .' At noon, off I went to 'the Citadel' (residence of the Governor General) to meet the PM. At 2.30 pm the Combined Chiefs met, and then again at 5.30. The latter all met the President and the PM again at the Citadel. . . . They have made it very gay here. Every night after dinner a band plays on the promenade, and I believe there is dancing. Miss Wallace (Jacob's secretary) and Co seem to have a pretty good time when they can get off, which isn't often, I fear.

In other letters, a strain of optimism, if not over-optimism appears: 'the news from the battle fronts was good'; Italy was searching for an armistice; the 'Russians roaring through Kharkov' and 'the Boche nearing the end'. Ismay was sick and off duty for some days, so Jacob, once again, was Churchill's right-hand man. Frequently, he had conferred with 'Master' in his cabin, and in his bedroom, as well as more formally at the conference table; the relationship by now was very close and relaxed, and the Prime Minister relied heavily on Jacob's excellent memory, keen efficiency and sound judgement. As Junior Officer Mary Churchill was to comment forty years later: 'Ian Jacob understood my father'.

The Conference ended on 24 August, a week after Sicily had been occupied and the Italians had sued for peace. Jacob reported to Hollis who was 'minding the shop' in Whitehall: 'I cannot see that what has been decided takes us much beyond TRIDENT. However, I think much suspicion has been dissipated. They realise we are not bluffing on OVERLORD, and there has been a much more realistic approach to Burma operations. . . .'

However, the decisions, if not stupendous in Jacob's eyes, were important: they were first, that OVERLORD should take place in the early summer of 1944, if conditions, as defined, were met. Second, a campaign in Italy would be pursued as far North as the line Pisa-Ancona. Third, a South East Asia Command was set up with Mountbatten as Supreme Commander. Fourth, the French Committee of National Liberation was formally recognised. Fifth, agreement was reached on important issues concerning the atom bomb. Last, following a protest from Stalin over the peace negotiations with the Italians,

it was accepted that the USSR should participate in armistice negotiations in Western Europe. They also invited Stalin to a tripartite
meeting: the Soviet leader, aware now that victory was on the horizon,
proposed it be held in Teheran.

At the conclusion of QUADRANT, Jacob, with most of the staff,
returned by air to England, leaving the Prime Minister with Ismay
and some other members of the delegation to return in the battleship
Renown. Admiral Pound, the undaunted 'Whale', who earlier
appeared to have had a breakdown, never left his cabin, and died on
21 October, being succeeded by Admiral Sir Andrew Cunningham.

When Jacob returned once more to Whitehall, he looked forward
with satisfaction to a period of stability, although his 'Master' was still
intent on further conferences overseas, which would soon lead to a
breakdown in his health at Carthage. It was just over two years since
Jacob had first set forth with Churchill by battleship to Placentia Bay
and, in that period, he had visited Washington three times, as well as
Egypt, Persia, the Soviet Union, Morocco, Turkey, Tripolitania,
Algeria and Canada. In those two years, he had spent 145 days in
major conferences overseas, where the demands, both mental and
physical, had been considerable. Travel by sea had been luxurious
except for seasickness, but by air, the journeys had been uncomfortable and often hazardous. It was fortunate that his mental resilience
was matched by physical toughness. He fully realised that the strain
on the Prime Minister at the age of sixty-nine was incomparably
greater.

The experience gained was unique. Even before 1941, he had
accumulated a wide knowledge of the workings of the British governmental machine. During those 145 days he had been able to contrast
it with the American, Russian and Canadian equivalents, and
throughout had watched the highest operators in international affairs
deploying their techniques of advocacy and negotiation. From the
diaries, it is clear that he rated the British operators as the most
convincing and adroit, partly, no doubt, because, thanks to his tactful
persuasion, they had been compelled to review and unify their positions before engaging in debate. Little escaped his critical eye.

The winter of 1943/44 was now to be dominated by a flood of
executive action linked to the preparations and build-up for OVER-
LORD, the cross-Channel invasion, destined to be the beginning of
the final act of the war in Europe.

11

The Road to Victory

By September 1943, Jacob was back in London after QUADRANT. Although OVERLORD, still optimistically scheduled for the following May, dominated military planning, hesitations over priorities between the Mediterranean theatre and North-West Europe lingered on, particularly when the withdrawal of landing craft and divisions from the Italian theatre had to be carried out despite Alexander's protestations and Churchill's reluctance. Further debate ensued at the Cairo Conferences in late November and early December; another meeting with Stalin at Teheran failed to resolve the Polish question, but Stalin's keen acknowledgment of ANVIL, which the Americans also favoured, gave added priority to that unrewarding operation.

Jacob was not required to attend those Conferences, but was kept busy in London on routine work. With the appointment of Eisenhower to command OVERLORD, announced on 6 December 1943, responsibility for the cross-Channel assault fell decisively upon COSSAC. Thus Jacob's attention was now focused increasingly on postwar problems, and on many extraneous but vital matters such as defence against flying bombs.

One of his responsibilities was the CROSSBOW Committee, which was charged with analysing intelligence regarding Hitler's secret weapons, and with developing counter-measures. As a result of meagre and conflicting intelligence reports, the Chiefs of Staff had first studied the problem in April; the CROSSBOW Committee had then been set up by the Prime Minister at a meeting attended by Duncan Sandys, with Eden, Lyttleton, Morrison, Cripps, Professor Lindemann, Crow, a rocket expert, and the Chiefs of Staff. Duncan Sandys was then charged with running the Committee. It was decided that a definite threat existed and that, Peenemunde, which was known to have been visited by Hitler in June, should be bombed. A heavy attack had been carried out on 17 August.

Later, there was much controversy in the committee between Lindemann on the one hand and the technical experts on the other as to whether the 'V' weapon was a pilotless aircraft or a rocket with, as some experts surmised, a 10-ton warhead. In their lengthy search for an agreed decision, the pragmatic conclusions of the Professor proved to be much nearer the truth than those of the multitudinous experts. The VI, a pilotless aircraft, was the first to arrive, and the long range ballistic rocket, the V2, came later with a warhead of only 1 ton.

Jacob referred to the disputations of the CROSSBOW Sessions as 'Elijah and the prophets of Baal'. As a boy, he had been well grounded in such biblical stories by Granny Isabella. It must be said however that to resolve the question 'How long halt ye between two opinions', the children of Israel, having viewed the heavenly fire 'consuming the burnt sacrifice, the wood and stones and licking up the water in the trench' despite a fourfold dousing with water, had a simpler decision to make than the Committee members searching amidst the gleanings of MI6 agents, Enigma reports and air photographs, for Hitler's secret weapon.[1]

On 8 June 1944 two days after the launching of OVERLORD, the name of Brigadier Jacob appeared again in the Honours List, this time as a Companion of the Order of the Bath (CB), an unusually high honour for one who, though aged 44, was still a Brigadier.

In August, Churchill decided to visit the Mediterranean theatre once again, assuming the security disguise of 'Colonel Kent', and taking with him a smaller entourage than usual but including Jacob. The Prime Minister intended to encourage Wilson and Alexander and their Commanders, from whom so much had been withdrawn for ANVIL (later named DRAGOON), which was about to be launched. He also intended to meet Tito, to be summoned from the island of Vis, where he was under British protection, and the Greek Prime Minister Papandreou, whose return to Athens after German withdrawal could now be foreseen. There was also the problem of the status of Italy, which was no longer an enemy nor yet a fully-fledged ally.

OVERLORD having been successfully launched in June, there was the glimmer of a holiday atmosphere throughout this Italian journey, strongly reflected in Jacob's letters to his wife. After a stop in Algiers, the party moved on to the Villa Rivalta overlooking the Bay of Naples, the residence of General 'Jumbo' Wilson who has succeeded Eisenhower as Supreme Commander in the Mediterranean. With him was Pierson Dixon, Eden's Principal Private Secretary.

Jacob recorded in a letter to his wife:

> Yesterday, we went off after the PM had conferred with Tito to bathe on the island of Ischia . . . in the launch which belonged to Prince Umberto and had been taken over by C-in-C Mediterranean. It was simply glorious. . . . The PM went in stark, and swam and floated majestically. To-day the PM took lunch over to Capri. I went off to do some business with James Gammell (Wilson's Chief of Staff). The HQ is at a place called Caserta in a vast palace which was intended when built to outdo Versailles. It was later a sort of Fascist Cranwell.

The official business of the day had been concerned with political discussions with Tito and Dr Subasic, the Ban of Croatia. Tito had been a guest at dinner, confined, despite the heat, in his gold-laced 'straight jacket'.

On the next day, Jacob accompanied Churchill to Corsica by air in order to observe from HMS *Largs* the DRAGOON landings between Toulon and Nice. The PM returned to Naples on 16 August and after a useful discussion on Greece, prompted by Enigma decrypts, which always reached the PM wherever he was located, he demanded that, to outwit the Communists, preparations should be made for a British Military expedition to Greece as soon as the Germans had withdrawn. More bathing followed in the Bay of Naples.

On the next day, they set off for Alexander's headquarters in order to observe the Cassino battlefield and move on, as was hoped, to the front line near Florence. Jacob commented in a letter dated 18 August to his wife:

> This place, where we arrived yesterday is heavenly. We are in a charming villa 1000 feet up . . . I have seen a lot of friends: Jumbo, James Gammell . . . and tonight I shall see Brian Robertson . . . I am very well, and so is Master . . .

Then returning once more to the Villa Rivalta, he wrote:

> I had a lovely early night last night away from Master, and before dinner had a nice walk in the hills with James Gammell . . . Master is well, and I think, has benefited. He is getting very slow, and one hears the same talk over and over again on subjects on which he feels deeply. It is different to get him down to humdrum affairs.

[*Since verbal persuasion by staff officers was not acceptable to Churchill, the normal method of expediting business was by typewritten note which, with the aid of the duty private secretary, was placed 'top of the box'. Nevertheless, this device did not always succeed.*]

Jacob continued:

> 'We are all thrilled with the news from the North. The German armies in France West of the Seine are completely destroyed, and Paris will be ours anyday we want it. I think the days of the doodle-bug are numbered. The battle in Southern France is a walk-over, and I don't think there will be a German in the

country a month from now. If they try to stay, they will be destroyed . . . I shall get home on our Wedding Day. We must celebrate on 27 September, by which time I think London will be free.'

Two days later he flew to Rome and stayed with Sir Noel and Lady Charles at the British Embassy:

'A most enormous mansion, very florid with great staircases . . . all ornately decorated: it is only gradually being reopened. The Charles' are trying to move into something more up-to-date and less showy. He is our High Commissioner on the Advisory Council for Italy, an Ambassador in rank. She looks too good to be true: very much done up, very smart with hair dyed a rather nice blue-white, and terrifically haughty – but rather nice and amusing I should think if you got to know her.

Yesterday we had M Papandreuo to dinner – the Greek PM. The Greeks are thrilled at meeting Churchill in Rome of all places, the capital of the despised Italians, who attacked Greece in such a disgraceful manner.'

After high level meetings concerned largely with future developments in Greece, the party flew home on 28 August. Although much serious business had been done, faithfully recorded either by Pierson-Dixon or Jacob, for Churchill it had been a period of refreshment lightened by the prospect of victory, and heartened by the greetings of devoted soldiers on the battle fronts he had visited. Jacob had shared his Master's enjoyment. Five days after reaching London the Prime Minister dictated the following Minute:

Secretary of State for War

Brigadier Jacob, as one of my right-hand men in the Defence Office, bears responsibilities which are fully equal to those of most Major Generals. He has discharged these responsibilities with unfailing success, and I should like to see him promoted to Major General forthwith.

I should be glad if you would take the necessary action.

WSC
2.9.44

While Jacob had been in Italy with the Prime Minister, the subject of the post-war World Organisation had been considered at a Conference at Dumbarton Oaks by the United States, Britain, the Soviet Union and China, resulting in the creation of the United Nations Organisation. Jacob was not involved at that stage, but would be called on to play an important part in the subsequent Conference at San Francisco in 1945. Nor was he involved in the Second Quebec Conference (OCTAGON), attended by Ismay, which was concerned principally with British participation alongside the United States in the war against Japan.

However, in October, he was required to visit Moscow once more with the Prime Minister. He kept no diary of that meeting, code-named TOLSTOY, but his letters to his wife describe the great change in atmosphere, caused presumably by Anglo-American military successes in North-West Europe combined with victories by the Soviet Union on the Eastern Front. The imminent prospect of Germany's defeat had brought a change in Stalin, and his attitude to his allies was no longer grudging and suspicious; the prospect that the map of Europe looked like changing in favour of the Soviet Union must also have given him great satisfaction.

Churchill, accompanied by Eden and Averill Harriman, arrived with Jacob in Moscow on 9 October 1944. The main topics for discussion were the Soviet's contribution to the war against Japan, a resolution of the Polish question which, once again, was not achieved, and an agreement with the Soviet Union over the political future of the Balkan countries and the roles to be played by the Soviet Union and Britain in these developments.

It was in discussing the latter, that Churchill produced his startling 'half-sheet of paper', with suggested percentage figures defining Russian and British spheres of influence in Romania, Greece, Yugoslavia, Hungary and Bulgaria. Surprisingly, or with hindsight perhaps inevitably, Stalin took his blue pencil, made a tick on it, and passed it back to Churchill across the table.

The Prime Minister at the time commented that it might be thought cynical to bargain over the fate of millions of people in such a crude offhand manner. Jacob, however, took a more rigid view, and after reading his official record, he wrote to Bridges in London:

> I have sidelined certain passages which seem most inappropriate for a record of this importance. Stalin and Roosevelt would probably prefer to have no record at all, as these notes would give the impression to historians that these very important discussions were conducted in a most unfitting manner.

Bridges agreed to deletion.[2]

Churchill subsequently explained to the War Cabinet that his percentages were intended only as a guide. Nevertheless, in Volume VI of his *History of the Second World War*, published in 1953, he expatiated at some length on the bargain struck with Stalin. He obviously took pride in his crude approach, which had been so successful in reaching agreement with the Russian dictator across the table.[3] After the war, however, the bargain was not observed faithfully in practice, and *force majeure* prevailed, with disastrous political consequences, which would persist for forty-five years.

After farewell scenes of great cordiality, the Prime Minister's party left Moscow on 20 October. At Cairo and Naples there were further discussions with Mountbatten, Wilson, Alexander, Mark Clark and Macmillan, and they reached London on 22 October. Immediately on the next day the Prime Minister started to push forward yet another meeting between Roosevelt, himself and Stalin, which had already been delayed for some months. This was to be the Yalta Meeting, code-named Argonaut.

After the great successes of the Soviet Armies on the Eastern front, which had carried them forward into East Prussia and Silesia, and on the West the progress of OVERLORD which had now reached the frontiers of Germany, there was an optimistic expectation that victory might be achieved in 1944 despite the onset of winter. Thus it was essential that the future shape of post-war Europe, including the festering problem of Poland, be urgently discussed with Stalin. Moreover, with the prospect of victory in sight, further attempts must be made to agree on a future peace-keeping organisation, despite the partial failure of previous discussions at Dumbarton Oaks.

Early in January 1945, Hitler's last offensive through the Ardennes had been dealt with, and preparations for the Yalta Conference were pressed ahead; both Ismay and Jacob were to attend. Churchill had hoped that a full preliminary conference with the Americans could take place in Malta, but he had to be satisfied with a meeting there of the Combined Chiefs of Staff, and on 29 January 1945: the decision was taken to reinforce Eisenhower's thrust towards the Rhine with six divisions from Alexander's forces in Italy, thus finally discarding Churchill's option of a thrust towards Vienna.

The sharp controversy between Eisenhower and Montgomery over the necessity for a Land Forces Commander was also on the agenda. Bedell Smith, now Eisenhower's Chief of Staff, usually a very diplomatic operator, took a very strong line, making it clear that any support given to Montgomery's plea would result in the resignation of Eisenhower.

Later President Roosevelt, observed by all to be looking very frail, arrived at Malta by warship, ready for the onward flight to Yalta, and by 3 February, the large British and American delegations had arrived after a six hour drive from Saki aerodrome over tortuous roads recently repaired by the Soviet Army. Jacob was delighted by the impressive mountainous scenery. Despite efforts made by the Russians to repair the wanton damage and destruction left by the retreating German Army, the living accommodation for the staffs was still most primitive. Jacob's description to his wife was ... 'living in a mixture of grandeur and squalor: conservatories, banqueting halls, five-course meals but practically no baths, or even basins, no mirrors and a shocking paucity of "usual offices". We sleep in droves like prep school boys in dormitories. The "highest nobs", however, were comfortably housed in the Vorontzov Villa. As to the Conference, he doubted whether they would achieve much: "it would be all politics".'

The political decisions at Yalta covered the post-war occupation and control of Germany, reparations, a declaration on liberated Europe, and an agreement on the setting up of a broad-based provisional Polish Government of national unity, to include Poles abroad. It was this agreement that was subsequently violated by Stalin.

Jacob, the realist, and never one to be swept onwards by euphoria, had expected little from Yalta. It was clear that Roosevelt, near to death, had decided to play an independent hand rather than confront Stalin with an united Anglo-American position; moreover in declaring in advance his date of departure he had given Stalin the major tactical advantage of playing out time on agenda items on which he was not disposed to reach agreement.

The tragic result of Yalta was the imposition, backed by force, of Marxist-Leninist ideology throughout Eastern Europe. The Western world was to live through more than forty years of Cold War, before Churchill's perception that the unnatural division of Europe would eventually create powerful grievances in the Soviet Satellite States was vindicated in 1989 by the advent of opposition to Communism in Czechoslovakia, Hungary, Poland, Romania, Bulgaria and East Germany, while in Afghanistan the expansionist policies of the Soviet Empire were reversed. As Churchill had said to Stalin at dinner at Yalta: 'The eagle should permit the small birds to sing ...'[4] After 45 years they were in full song.

A final item in the conclusions of Yalta, which was to prove more hopeful for mankind, was the agreement to hold a conference of fifty nations at San Francisco on 25 April 1945, to establish a United Nations Organisation to keep the peace of the world. Jacob attended that Conference, accompanying Eden, Attlee, Sir Alexander Cadogan and others as the Military Representative of the United Kingdom. He found the task uncongenial, and confessed to his mother in a letter dated 2 May that he was bored by the proceedings.

> There was so little real military interest, and the general atmosphere was so different from the vital war conferences when something concrete was being done ... I could not derive great satisfaction from all the political haggling and the

welter of words and the vapourings of the South American republics, and the clouds of Press photographers and the artificial hotel life . . . I do wish I was in London in these exciting days. . . . .

Earlier he had commented:

> Squads of dagoes debouch from every train and aeroplane . . . the newspapers here barely mention England or the British Armies . . . they are very much more critical of Russia than ours. There are some very outspoken articles about Poland and the Russian actions there and in South East Europe . . . The Russians will find the atmosphere very hostile, and the Americans and ourselves will find it very difficult to keep up any sort of impression of an united front with them, unless they are ready to be more accommodating.

The formal opening of the Conference took place in the San Francisco Opera House, and drew from Jacob a description. He went on:

> At the Second Plenary Session there were speeches by Stettinius, Soong, Molotov and Eden. Eden made an excellent speech and quite wiped the floor with the others. His speech was the first that was not to be simply the reading of a rather dull lecture; and the first breath of life was injected into the Conference when he spoke. He got a great ovation.

On the days following 'there was a flood of orating, since the leader of nearly every one of the 49 delegations is determined to get his resounding ideas given to the world' . . . 'The Russians have refused to agree to the structure of committees, together with the list of chairmen as proposed by the Americans, until the participation of the Ukrainian White Russian delegations (who, we suspect, are at present lurking in the hold of a Russian ship, which is in harbour here) has been agreed . . . The dagoes want to trade Argentinian participation for White Russian and Ukrainian.' 'There is unlimited scope for jiggery pokery behind the scenes, but that doesn't concern me, thank God.'

Jacob himself was concerned in the work of three Committees: Enforcement, Regional arrangements and Territorial Trusteeship.

Disillusioned with the character of the Conference:

> 'It is quite cured me of any desire to take on a job in any international organisation after the war . . . the absurdity of having to pay attention to the voices of 49 countries on every topic, on most of which they know nothing and can contribute less.'

> 'However, one must not despair', he wrote to his wife three days before VE day; but it is absolutely maddening to be taking part in this tom-foolery at a time when the Germans are beaten, and when we ought to be enjoying the celebrations in London. What a victory! Thank God the end has come so quickly before

either John or William goes to sea in home waters. I imagine the U-boats are finished too, though nothing has been said about that yet.'

'Monty has got full credit here and a local paper had a full-sized portrait of him yesterday. And now the future is bound up with one word – Russia.'

Although the work of the Conference, except for an occasional crisis, was undemanding, social life was hectic and enjoyable: two cocktail parties every night, with dinner and luncheon engagements, provided opportunities to meet American delegates, and also Eden, Halifax and Attlee who, to Jacob's surprise, would become Prime Minister on 26 July. Jacob gave parties to his international colleagues, played high-class golf with American friends, and enjoyed superb Symphony concerts. He was also invited to speak to an audience of 400 at the San Francisco Rotary Club. He was introduced as 'one of the greatest military brains in Europe', and had a great success speaking on 'The Anglo-American conduct of the War'.

Although, as the faithful untiring envoy, Jacob was absent from London when Victory in Europe was celebrated on 8 May, he was well informed a fortnight later by letters from Hollis and Mark Norman of the Defence Office. Hollis wrote on 24 May:

> Thank you for your letter. The whole party sounds like Bedlam, and I am sure you will be glad when it is over. It is not a very cheerful prospect for the future. . . .
>
> The day before VE Day was declared, the Headmaster gave the Chiefs of Staff a lunch at No 10. It was really rather nice of him, and we had some photographs on the lawn afterwards. During lunch, our host said what a pity it was that you were away, as you would have of course been invited. So you see you were not forgotten. . . .

After mentioning the celebrations, Hollis continued:

> As we rather anticipated, the end of the German war has brought in its train a spate of problems and difficulties . . . All the Zone business and the Control Commission arrangements are now in the fore, and are not panning out quite as smoothly as we hoped. I am purposely being guarded in what I say in this letter.
>
> I think Mark Norman has sent you a copy of the very generously worded mark of appreciation which the Chiefs of Staff handed out to us last week. In case he did not, I send you a copy. They had drafted it themselves, and there was much whispering and exchanges of slips of paper between them during the previous three days, which puzzled us considerably.
>
> The Election is a bore, as it means that business, which has already been clogged at the top, will now become stifled with exasperating delays obtaining decisions.
>
> It is very difficult to forecast what will happen on 5 July. I have a sneaking suspicion that neither side are all that keen to get in, but it would of course, be a very bad thing if we lost the Old Man's hand on the steering wheel just now.

Mark Norman's letter, in more racy vein from a thirty-five year old amateur soldier, set the scene as follows:

> ... I am afraid I am way behind with my correspondence to you, but the enclosed papers I think should make up for everything. You will see that the period of gestation between VE Day and the delivery of this COS baby was nine days, but this is pretty good going for three cold fish of that ilk. It was a magnificently kept plot – quite unknown to Ismay and the others – and the ceremony at the Chiefs of Staff meeting, I am told, was charged with emotion. Altogether everyone is very pleased about it.
>
> The end of the war in Europe has, of course, brought us its inevitable troubles. The PM has at once taken an intense interest in everything to do with Germany, and as he knows absolutely nothing about it, he has shot off a series of minutes and telegrams which have caused the greatest dismay and confusion. As a result, we have returned to the charge for getting some organisation in this Office, parallel to the Chiefs of Staff, to deal with civil affairs on the Continent, and Bridges, after agreement with Ismay, has raised this with the PM who has tentatively agreed that there should be a day-to-day or thereabouts meeting between Grigg (in the Chair), and some Minister from the Foreign Office, Cherwell, plus high-powered representatives from one or two other Departments such as the Treasury and the Ministry of Production. He has also said that you should be both Member and Secretary of this Organisation in the same way that Ismay is of the COS, and you will be his representative.
>
> I suppose the American papers give you some news of the end of the Coalition; it is taken for granted today, although no announcement about a dissolution has yet been made. Under the circumstances it is very difficult to get any Ministerial decisions on any subject at all, and I suppose this difficulty will remain, at any rate for big issues, until after the General Election. ...
>
> San Francisco has had a full Press here and there has been a spate of very long official telegrams from the UK Delegation ... people here seem to think that something very useful is being hammered out with pain and anguish, and that all your labours are likely to be crowned with a good measure of success. You will have to explain it to us all when you come back. ...

The Chiefs of Staff's 'baby' (in Norman's phrase), read as follows:

EXPRESSION OF APPRECIATION BY THE CHIEFS OF STAFF TO THE DEFENCE OFFICE AND THE CHIEFS OF STAFF SECRETARIAT

We would like to place on record our deep appreciation of the help we have received throughout the German war from General Ismay, and from General Hollis, General Jacob and the other members of the Chiefs of Staff Secretariat and Defence Office. If the machinery of the High Command has worked smoothly and swiftly, and if the presentation of military advice to Ministers has been clear and effective, this has been largely due to their sound judgement and outstanding ability. Moreover, the resourcefulness with which they have met the host of intricate problems which inevitably arise in the conduct of a world war by widely separated allies has constantly shown itself to be of the greatest value. We would like to express our gratitude for the great debt we owe to them.

C Alan Brooke
C Portal
Andrew Cunningham

On 6 June 1945, the anniversary of OVERLORD D-Day, Jacob delivered in San Francisco a broadcast which was received throughout America and in Europe, through the facilities of the 'Voice of America', The Chief of the New York Special Events Section in San Francisco commented that he was 'impressed and moved by your message, not only in the reading, but in its actual delivery.'

The message, phrased adroitly to emphasise the British contribution without upsetting the susceptibilities of the Americans, went as follows:

Today we are commemorating D-day, a day which has a special significance for us all, and for none more than for us in Great Britain. It marked the beginning of the final phase of the grand assault on Germany. It marked the dawn of the day of liberation for the oppressed peoples of Europe. It marked for England two things – the return to the continent almost exactly four years after we were driven out of Dunkirk, and the beginning of the end of the menace which had hung over the country for that long period with the enemy only 25 miles away. That menace had various aspects, from the threat of invasion to the actuality of bombardment by aircraft, by flying bomb, by rocket, and by long range artillery. It gained a sharper edge from the progress of scientific invention, and it demonstrated what the future may hold for us all unless we prevent it.

Finally, D-day afforded the opportunity – long awaited, for the deployment of the great Anglo-American armies which had been patiently built up for that day, and for the final test between the armed forces of freedom and of tyranny.

It is worth trying to recapture for a moment the air of tense expectation which came to a climax on this day a year ago in England. For months, the whole of the Southern part of the country had been turned into a vast base from which two million men were to cross the Channel. Great camps and transit areas, huge depots, parks of tanks, vehicles and guns, mountains of ammunition, grew and spread throughout the countryside. Ports and dockyards all round the coast resounded to the noise of activity on landing aircraft, on Mulberries, and on all the special engines of amphibious war. Great fleets of aircraft roared out daily and nightly across the Channel, while an ever growing force of fighters and bombers assembled on the airfields of the South coast. Everyone knew that the liberation of Europe was about to begin, that the task would be hard and costly, and that the great bolt, once shot, could not be withdrawn and shot again. This was the supreme moment of the war.

The Allied forces did not fail. Eleven months from that moment, Germany lay in complete defeat.

The lessons of that great day a year ago have a special meaning for us in the war against Japan. We can look forward with confidence to a similar day – let us hope not far distant – which will as successfully mark the start of the final phase in that struggle as D-day did in the struggle against Germany

For us in San Francisco we can draw special encouragement from the events of a year ago. By the exercise of the same determination, the same self-sacrifice, and the same single-mindedness that characterised those who launched and carried through the great operation which began on D-day, we too can lay the foundations for a future which will vindicate the sacrifices of the United Nations in the terrible struggle from which we hope shortly to emerge.

Jacob had planned to return from San Francisco to London via Seattle, Victoria, Vancouver, Banff, Calgary, Ottawa and Montreal where many friends were eager to entertain him, but the trip was vetoed and he was told to fly home as soon as possible. 'Coming events' he supposed. He rejoined Cecil and the boys on 10 June 1945.

Forty-five years later, it would be apparent that the United Nations Organisation, whose chaotic birth pangs he had assisted, had achieved more for the peace of the world than the cynics at San Francisco had expected.

On returning to London, Jacob found that preparations for a General Election were in full swing, demanding full attention from the Prime Minister and his colleagues. Another conference was looming, this time in Potsdam; and the post-war occupation and control of Germany, with which Jacob had been concerned since the setting up of the European Advisory Commission, was an important item on the agenda. Agreement was reached at Potsdam on creating an Allied Control Council for Germany, and a Council for Foreign Ministers to draft peace treaties. Despite Churchill's objections, territory in East

Germany was 'provisionally' allocated to Poland. Ismay was in attendance on Churchill, and Jacob paid only a short visit.

*   *   *

On 14 August, Japan capitulated unconditionally after the bombing of Hiroshima and Nagasaki.

Jacob's next assignment, in November 1945, was to accompany the new Prime Minister, Attlee, to the United States and Canada for a tripartite meeting to agree measures for the control of atomic weapons. This was to lead in January 1946 to the establishment by the General Assembly of the United Nations of the Atomic Energy Commission. The party was to include Sir John Anderson, Sir John Cockcroft, and Sir Roger Makins, Ambassador in Washington.

Jacob knew Attlee well, having oberved him as an effective senior minister in Churchill's War Cabinet. But inevitably he compared him to his old 'Master' and, in his diary of the visit, on which Attlee addressed both the United States Congress and the Canadian House of Commons, he showed anxiety about his Chief's performance, as 'he was "quite incapable of any oratory" . . . He had neither a commanding figure nor a resounding voice: it tends to go up and becomes almost squeaky at times . . .'

Jacob's anxiety was not altogether groundless: the United States was cruelly critical of Attlee's address. A headline in the *Washington Daily News* on 14 November 1945 read: 'Clem tosses a mean cliché: in 30,000 words he broke platitude record'. However, Jacob's personal relations with Attlee were warm, as he found that the Prime Minister did not 'stand on his dignity'.

The principals at the Conference, President Truman, Prime Minister Mackenzie King, and Mr Attlee, with Lord Halifax and Sir John Anderson, had two private sessions on the Presidential yacht, as the result of which an American draft appeared which in Jacob's words contained certain new ideas which had not been mentioned in the previous discussions. The principal one was a proposal for a Commission to be set up by UNO to arrange for the exchange of scientific information, to make proposals for the elimination or control of atomic and other major weapons, and for inspection etc. This all seemed to raise those very ideas, Jacob commented, which we regarded as so objectionable in London. Control, inspection, elimination: impossible conceptions which could only lead to international friction, and advantage to the aggressor.' Jacob with Roger Makins and others then set to work 'to make a redraft which would contain some of the American verbiage, but would eliminate the dangerous ideas.'

Further discussions and re-drafting followed, and eventually Sir John Anderson, Mr Pearson, the Canadian Ambassador to the USA, and Dr Vannevar Bush, the atomic bomb expert, were charged with the task of preparing a final agreed statement. In Jacob's view this still contained 'the objectional terms' previously noted. However, forty-five years later, he would find the impossible conceptions of control and inspection being realistically negotiated between the United States and the Soviet Union, and a start being made on elimination. Perhaps American idealism had been preferable to British caution.

His conclusions were summarised in his diary:

> Looking back on it all I find I enjoyed the visit enormously, but I do not feel any satisfaction with the outcome. I do not like the declaration that was eventually signed by the three in Washington, and I do not feel that something good has been accomplished as one usually felt after a war-time conference. I played a very small part in the result. I was not present at the international discussions. I did my best in British meetings and in drafting British drafts to get across what I took to be the views of the people at home, but these views were overridden in the end by the Americans. The whole of the discussions were in my opinion mishandled. On our arrival it was clear that neither the Americans nor the Canadians had any clearly defined idea of how to deal with the atomic bomb. We had some ideas, though they could only with difficulty be made into convincing proposals. The only sensible thing to do, was for the Big Three to get together, as they did on the yacht, and to continue steadily to meet *with their advisers present*, until they had come to a real agreement on the principles at stake and on the policy to be expressed. Once they had done this, they could have instructed a team of officials from the three parties to draft a declaration to give effect to the agreed principles and policy.
>
> As it was, after an inconclusive discussion on the yacht, the three big men parted with no clear idea of the next step, and each side began independently drafting . . . The two drafts showed that ideas were far from being harmonised. Then the publicity factor began to come into play. The President was afraid of keeping

things dark much longer, and wanted to rush out a declaration . . .
Silence had so far been maintained in the White House, and the
Press were becoming restive, particularly as some rather
unfortunate 'background information' had been given to the Press
. . . by No 10. Mr Attlee managed to stave things off for a short
time, but the President insisted on . . . announcing the declaration
at 11 am on Thursday. This gave far too little time for the final
hammering out of the draft and for any careful study of what it
contained. Moreover, it turned Mr Attlee's consultation with the
Cabinet into a farce. Once the tyranny of publicity had taken
charge, nothing could have stopped the declaration going out at
11 am without a first-class sensation. If the Cabinet had disap-
proved of it, and the PM had had to ask for a postponement . . .
rumours of all kinds would have sprouted and flourished.

Thus are things of first-class importance dealt with in modern
times. A declaration that may decide our future is rushed through
like a cup-tie result. . . . I personally think the PM should have
refused to be rushed, and should have insisted on a better procedure. However, I can't help thinking that if Winston had been
doing the job he would have in the first place have arrived in
Washington with a cut and dried idea, and he would then have
laid careful siege to the President so as to get his idea accepted,
and would have drafted the declaration himself in his incompar-
able language. However, times and people change. The world
does not seem unduly critical of the declaration, but it remains to
be seen how the Russians will take it. They have said nothing. No
doubt they are thinking hard, and we shall see the result of their
thought in January when UNO meets.

In a letter to his mother Jacob, having told the same tale, ended:

'It would never have done for "the dook"! If our late boss had been here, things
would have been fixed up very differently. The subject is enough to baffle the
stoutest intellect, and I feel pretty dubious about the result.' As usual the social
side of the visit was interesting, including a dinner at the White House, and
another with Mackenzie King, Prime Minister of Canada.

After twelve days in the United States and Canada, Jacob was back
in London on 20 November 1945. Three weeks later, he was called
upon to accompany Mr Bevin, the Foreign Secretary, to Moscow. The
party, fourteen in number, included Cadogan, Campbell, Pierson
Dixon, Sterndale Bennett, and Hayter of the Foreign Office. On the
afternoon of 14 December they landed at Gatow airport in Berlin, and

Jacob and Cadogan were taken to the house of Brian Robertson, now the Deputy Military Governor of the British Zone of Germany. William Strang, political adviser to Montgomery, the Military Governor, gave a dinner party attended by Bevin, Robertson, Cadogan, Macall (Bevin's doctor) Sir Percy Mills (head of the Economic Division of the Control Commission) and others. Jacob noted that 'the presence of Sappers is most noticeable'. There were four at the table, four more at Control Commission headquarters and three others elsewhere in important positions.

Jacob noted in his diary on 14 December 1945:

> I gathered in conversation before and at dinner that relations with the Russians just now are very good, at any rate on the level of the Co-ordinating Committee. Brian told me that Zhukov was quite sheepish when he tabled his memorandum accusing us of fostering a large German Army in our Zone. It was pretty evident that it was done on orders from Moscow. William told me that, as far as we can tell there is no sign of a German underground, or resistance movement in our Zone, though there are slight indications in the American Zone. Politically, the Germans are still quite apathetic. The mere effort to exist at all takes up all their time.
>
> On 15 December, the party arrived in Moscow. There was some doubt about what to wear on arrival. Whether to put on, as it were, the whole armour of God, furry boots, fur-lined coats, jerseys, fur caps, and gauntlets, or whether to take a chance and wear a reasonable coat, and hat. The majority went the whole hog, and there was a wonderful variety of fur caps.
>
> Vyshinsky and others met us, and Harriman and several Dominion Ministers were there, and the usual bunch of photographers. Colonel Gimson, Irish Guards, whom I had last met on the *Neuralia* in 1938 when he was adjutant and we were going to Egypt, met me and took me off without delay to the Embassy. The Embassy staff, whom I gradually met, consisted of Roberts, Grosthwaite, Watson, Tomkins, and Paddy Bolton the Ambassador's Private Secretary.

On Sunday, 16 December, the first meeting of the three Foreign Ministers took place in the building in Spiridonevka Street, named by Jacob from previous visits as 'the Spirited Donkey'.

> Molotov is accompanied at the table by Pavlov (the interpreter),

Gusev (Ambassador in London), Vyshinski (Vice-Commissar for Foreign Affairs), Melek (late Ambassador in Tokyo) and Tsarapkin (the head of the American section of the Foreign Office). Byrnes is accompanied by Bohlen, who also interprets, Harriman, Ben Cohen, and either Vincent or Dr Mathews according to whether Far Eastern or European affairs are under discussion. Bevin has Macafie (interpreter) Clark Kerr, Cadogan, and either Ronald Campbell or Sterndale Bennett or another adviser according to the subject. Everyone else sits behind, or waits outside if not required.

Discussion at the first meeting concerned principally the Agenda. Whenever either we or the Americans suggest anything for the Agenda that the Russians don't like, or don't want to discuss, the Russians make a counter-suggestion by putting forward some item that they know will annoy us, such as the 'withdrawal of British troops from Greece,' or the 'situation in Indonesia,' or some offence they allege we or the Americans are committing in Germany. But this means they secure the cancellation of the offending item. On this occasion the withdrawal of British troops from Greece, the withdrawal of all troops from Persia, and the withdrawal of American troops from China were all taken off the Agenda after discussion, and relegated to informal meetings, probably bi-lateral, and apart from the main meetings. The Agenda was finally settled, and we adjourned at 6.45 pm. We were then led to a well stocked buffet. I spoke to Dr Conant, the President of Harvard University, who is the American atom-bomb adviser on this party, and who seems a very intelligent, quiet, and straightforward man.

That night Jacob wrote to his mother: 'I feel I shall largely waste my time here. It is difficult being a sort of nebulous military adviser to being Secretary as I always used to be at the Military Conferences. There one was never finished. Now one hangs about.' The diary for Monday, 17 December, starts:

I had breakfast in my room this morning. Dead fish and doubt-ful baked eggs. This morning we received a fresh paper from the Americans containing their proposals for a memorandum, to be circulated to the three, on the setting up of a Commission on Atomic Energy. It consisted of a covering memorandum and the draft of a document containing the constitution and terms of reference of the proposed commission. Campbell and I worked together on the American draft, and prepared our comments. We got these agreed by Cadogan, and arranged to go over to the American Embassy to discuss them with Conant and Cohen after lunch. This S of S was to see Byrnes at the same time.

The main points on which our views differed from those of the Americans were:

(a) They proposed that the Commission should report to the Assembly, while we consider that it should report to the Security Council. As Bevin put it, the Council should be regarded, in all matters having a security implication, as the Cabinet, and the Assembly as the Parliament.

(b) We favour the retention of the conception of a gradual advance from step to step by the Commission, as confidence is built up and as reciprocity is secured. The American draft omitted this idea, which figured in paragraph 8 of the original declaration by Truman, Attlee, and Mackenzie King.

There were some other minor amendments we wanted to propose. There were two matters of machinery which were important. In the first place, we felt that as we were signatories with the Americans of the declaration, it would be best for us to adopt a common line in Moscow, and thus that any paper put in by the Americans should be agreed with us beforehand. Secondly, we knew that Ministers were to meet in London tomorrow, Tuesday, to discuss a previous American draft. Consideration of these two points led us to conclude that the Americans should be asked to hold their paper and not to circulate it until Wednesday at the earliest so that we could telegraph home the new draft and get London's views. So the S of S said he would impress this on Conant.

We duly had our talk after lunch. We were not able to convince Cohen about either of our points; he seemed to have a very woolly idea of the hard facts of UNO and the Russian attitude to it, and both he and Conant being doubtful about the procedure by stages. However, we deployed all the arguments, and asked them to hold the paper.

The S of S in his interview also had not much success on the first point, but Byrnes too agreed to discuss the matter further and to hold his paper in the meanwhile.

We then went off to the 4 o'clock meeting, but it didn't last long. Each item on the Agenda was raised, and there was always one of the three who stated he was not ready to discuss the item.

We soon adjourned. I drafted a telegram home explaining what had happened on the atomic paper, and after dinner in the Embassy Mess, we went to an early bed.

On Tuesday, 18 December, Jacob lunched with Frank Roberts (the No 2 in the Embassy) 'a dapper, friendly man with a reputation for efficiency' . . .

'The other guests were Cadogan, Bullard, Campbell, M Alphand who is head of the economic side of the French FO and is here temporarily on a mission to discuss certain problems with the Russians; General and Madame Catroux (he is the French Ambassador here), M van Breugel-Douglas and his wife (he is of partly Scottish ancestry, and is the Dutch Minister here), and Miss McBride, the S of S's stenographer. M Alphand is a very good mimic, and at the end of lunch after some pressure, he gave us a wonderful imitation of a meeting of the Council of Foreign Ministers.

We got back from lunch shortly before it was necessary to go to the four o'clock meeting. The first item on the Agenda was how to get the Council of Foreign Ministers on its legs again. This involved the production of a formula to govern the making of the peace treaties with the satellites, which was what the Council had broken on in London. The Americans and the Russians had put forward drafts. The latter was a complete return to the position taken up in London.

No concession of any kind was made. A very good discussion took place, in which Byrnes and Bevin pressed Molotov very hard without making the least impression. Finally Byrnes conceded two points to Molotov, and urged the latter to concede the third to him. Molotov's only reply was that there was no question of concession, because the matter was settled in Potsdam by the heads of States, and the Soviet draft only gave effect to that decision. In other words, the Soviet is always right. However, the meeting ended on Molotov undertaking to consider the matter.

Just as we were breaking up, Byrnes suddenly handed round a paper which proved to be the Memorandum on the Atomic Energy Commission. One despairs at times of the American way of doing business. They had departed from their undertaking to hold the paper till Wednesday without a word of warning. We found that they had incorporated our comparatively minor amendments, but neither of the two main points. When taken to task they looked pained and pleaded a misunderstanding. Even if they had given no undertaking, common courtesy would have demanded that they should tell us beforehand that they were going to circulate a paper which had been the subject of discussion and amendment between us. However, there was nothing to be done but telegraph to London and tell them. This we did after dinner in the Mess, and then Hayter and I went to the Bolshoi for the last two acts of *Prince Igor*. I was a little disappointed . . .

At noon on 19 December the Secretary of State went off to have an informal talk with Byrnes and Molotov . . . At 5 we went to the next official meeting of the three, which was pretty abortive. One or other of them found himself unready to discuss each item that came up, so we adjourned soon after 6 pm. This was fortunate as it enabled me to get off to the Bolshoi theatre with Gimson to see *Giselle*. I had seen the first act done at the gala performance given for Mr Churchill in October 1944. with Lepschinskaya in the name part, and had enjoyed it enormously. This time I was able to see both acts, and Ulanova the première ballerina from Leningrad who is said to be the best in Russia, even beating Lepschinskaya and Semonova. Having now seen all three, I agree with this verdict. The principal male dancer, Sergrev, was excellent too, and they danced together with complete unison and certainty.

The daily meeting on Thursday, 20 December, took place at 3 pm so as to clear the decks for a cocktail party by Mme Molotov. Before the meeting I worked on the subject of the atom bomb, a telegram having come in from London giving the views of the Cabinet on the American draft. Byrnes had already tabled the draft, but we had a little meeting with Cohen and Conant to tell them something of the views of London. The main point of decision is whether the Atomic Commission should be made answerable to the Assembly or to the Security Council. Byrnes has come out in his paper for the former, and so has London, though Bevin has been given latitude to agree to the latter if it is necessary for the purpose of getting Russian agreement. Another point is the instruction to the Commission to proceed by stages in its work, as confidence is built up. This was one of the main foundations of the declaration issued at Washington, and London is anxious to retain it in any proposal which is to be laid before the Assembly in January. The Americans have omitted it in their draft, partly I think through sheer ineptitude and lack of organisation in their delegation, and partly because Conant was not anxious to perpetuate the reference to the survey of raw materials.

Today's meeting of the three touched on most of the items on the Agenda, but did not succeed in carrying any of them much further. The Russians seem to find it impossible to admit to being convinced by argument on any point. The only way to bring them round is to be equally adamant, but there are frequent signs that Byrnes is quite prepared to sell us, if by doing so he can get something out of Molotov. It is awful to think that the foreign policy of a great country like the USA should be in the hands of a shanty Irishman from Carolina, advised by a rather vague visionary like Cohen.

Uncle Joe arrived back in Moscow yesterday, and Bevin had an interview with him in the Kremlin last night. He is reported to be in excellent health, and was friendly. Of course, he gave nothing away.

A preliminary informal meeting between the three had been arranged for 2.30 pm at which a Soviet paper on policy in Germany was to be dicussed. We were not prepared to discuss this in the absence of France at the formal meetings. We arrived at the Donkey at 4, and found the meeting still in progress.

At 6.30 the meeting broke up and we returned to the Embassy. Good progress has been made, and the items on the Control of Japan, on Korea, and on the making of peace treaties with the satellites have been agreed. There remain Persia, Romanian and Bulgarian Governments, and the Atom. The Russians have also put in two offensive papers on alleged German forces kept in being in the British Zones in Germany and Austria. These must be dealt with.

I had a chat with the S of S before dinner in which he told me his views on the future of defence. He is against combining the Services, but in favour of a single budget supervised by the Minister of Defence. He regards the rivalry lower down between the Services as healthy. I think there is no doubt that he is right, in spite of the fact that we see in today's summary of news that President Truman has sent a message to Congress asking them to authorise the combination of the War and Navy Departments into a single Department of Defence.

The Foreign Ministers met at noon today in the Kremlin in Molotov's study. The reason for the new meeting was that it was supposed to be informal and not attended by 'experts'. Campbell,

Ward, Sterndale Bennett, Hayter and I therefore sat outside in the ante-room. The meeting made no progress and broke up at 2.30 pm, by which time the pangs of hunger were pretty sharp.

A visit to Lenin's tomb was quickly over, and we were taken on to the Donkey for a further meeting at which the American proposal for the setting up of a Commission under UNO to deal with the atom was at last discussed. The Soviet Delegation expressed their agreement with the proposal and agreed to join in sponsoring it, but, as we expected, came out strongly in favour of the Commission being placed squarely under the Security Council, and not under the Assembly as suggested by Byrnes. After a short discussion we adjourned, and the British and American officials got together to consider the matter. We drafted certain amendments which would produce a compromise providing for the reports of the Commission to go in the first instance to the Security Council, but leaving the actual allegiance of the Commission somewhat vague. These amendments were prepared for Bevin and Byrnes to discuss later in the evening.

On 23 December there was another meeting at noon in the Kremlin during which various formulas were proposed which would meet the Soviet view without violating our principles. One cannot ever get Molotov to give way to a compromise at a meeting, but when he ends by saying that he will study the matter further it generally means that he will come round at the next meeting after consulting Uncle Joe in the interval.

At 7.30 pm we went to the Bolshoi Theatre where there was a special performance of Prokofiev's new ballet *Cinderella*, with Lepechinskaya in the part of Cinderella. We were all guests, and the three Foreign Secretaries sat regally in the centre box. There was quite an assemblage of the Diplomatic Corps and Russian officials and their wives, and the usual clapping took place when the three men entered and the orchestra struck up the three National Anthems. Byrnes radiated false bonhomie, putting his arm round Molotov's shoulder. There was a similar performance at the end, and Bevin wiped Byrnes' eye by giving the clenched fist salute, which brought the house down! All in very doubtful taste, I fear, but perhaps understandable.

After an uneventful morning on Monday, 24 December, we repaired to the Donkey where the formal meeting of the three was resumed at 3 pm. The Commission on atomic energy went through pretty much as drafted in our final amendments, and in a form which should be entirely satisfactory to London. For all practical purposes, the Commission is to be under the Security Council, though sufficient of a loophole is left to satisfy all but the most ardent supporters of the Assembly. All that remains now to be squared up is Persia, and Romania and Bulgaria.

Mr Bevin then left for the Kremlin for an interview with Stalin, while we returned to the Embassy to get ready for the Kremlin banquet. This took place at 8. The British who attended were Mr Bevin, Sir A Clark-Kerr, Cadogan, Campbell, Dr McCall, Dixon, Roberts, Sterndale Bennett, Bullard, Macafie (interpreter) and myself. On arrival, we mounted the great staircase and were shown into the room directly facing us at the top, where we were asked to wait as the S of S was still with Stalin.

We were first joined by the cow-like Gusev, and then by the Americans. After a few minutes delay we were led through the great hall with 2,500 desks where the Supreme Soviet meets, to the room of the order of St Catherine where dinner was laid out in its usual place. We joined the Russians in the adjoining room and shook hands. After a bit Stalin arrived and shook hands all round, and we went in to dinner. Apart from Stalin and Molotov there were present Beria, Malinkov, Kaganovitch, Mikoyan, General Antonov, Admiral Kuzhetsov, Zhdanov, and a number of lesser lights. I found myself sitting between Roberts and a Russian whose name I never discovered, but who is head of Tass, the Soviet news agency. Fortunately he spoke French, having spent four years in Paris between 1925 and 1940.

Stalin looked well, but aged. His hair is greyer and thin, and his expression is less alert and animated. His smile is no longer so genial, if crafty, but is more the leer of an old man. However, he seems quite on the spot still, and I do not think there is any failing of his powers.

We had a good dinner with the usual toasts, and rose at about 10 o'clock. We went into the next room for coffee, and I had a talk with General Antonov. I gave him greetings from our Chiefs of Staff, which he cordially reciprocated. He expressed interest to Colonel Kelly and myself about the American proposals for amalgamation of the Services. I told him an enquiry was in progress in England. I asked him about the Military Staff Committee, and he said our note on the subject was being studied, it having reached him the day before.

It has been hard to realise that this is Christmas Day. The

morning was much as usual, with not a great deal to do. I lunched with the Roberts. They very kindly organised a fork lunch for about 24 people in their flat. The only foreigners present were Dr Conant, M Alphand, and M & Mme Charpentier from the French Embassy. After lunch, a party of us went by arrangement to look round the Kremlin.

At 4 pm we moved on to the Donkey for the next meeting, which was to be an 'informal' one. It began a bit late, but it made up for this, by its length. The Foreign Ministers sat almost continuously till 10 pm. Occasionally Bob Dixon, or the Ambassador came out to ask for information.

At 10 pm the Ambassador came out and said he was going to abandon the business and go home, knowing that about 150 hungry guests had been waiting since 9 pm for the buffet Christmas dinner that he was giving in the Embassy. A general *sauve qui peut* took place, and the experts followed his example. Bevin and Cadogan and Dixon were not long behind us, and we soon drowned our sorrows in turkey and champagne cup.

Wednesday, 26 December, was a quiet morning, but a pretty feverish afternoon and evening for the Foreign Secretary. My work came pretty well to an end with drafting a rude counterblast to an insulting paper in which the Russians accused us of resuscitating a German Army in the British Zone in Austria, and I took little or no part in the evening's affairs after dinner. The Atom Commission proposal went through without difficulty, but we got no change out of the Russians about Persia. Mr Bevin felt very concerned about this, and at one moment he asked for another interview with Stalin. But Molotov then seemed to be coming round to a more accommodating frame of mind, and proceedings continued. However, finally Molotov refused to agree to any arrangement over Persia, and Bevin was faced with the choice of accepting the situation, or of refusing to sign the remainder of the agreements unless there was one about Persia. Realising that Byrnes would almost certainly fail to support him, and would proceed to sign without him, Bevin chose the first alternative, hoping to continue the struggle over Persia through the diplomatic channel after the Conference.

Endless time was taken over the final stages of drafting the communiqué and harmonising the English and Russian texts of the agreements, and it was about 4 pm when the documents were finally signed. Byrnes was determined to leave in the morning, and this impatience naturally suited the Russians who had only to stonewall to be sure that Byrnes would be bound to give in. Byrnes was somewhat the worse for wear tonight, but he had his way, finished a rather botched job, and was able to leave as planned. Mr Bevin rather wisely decided to rest for 24 hours.

Jacob had much admired the way in which Bevin, lacking any formal education, had coped successfully with the complex agenda of the conference.

Thursday, 27 December, was spent in 'finishing up and squaring off' and on the following afternoon the party landed at Northolt. Once again, Jacob had had to spend Christmas away from his family on official duties: this time seven months after the war in Europe had ceased.

12

A Second Career

Early in the following year, 1946, Jacob received from the American Ambassador in London the award of the United States Legion of Merit, degree of Commander. The citation, signed by President Truman, referred to his 'wise council and unfailing devotion to the common cause'. He was now 46 years old, and he felt it was time to consider his future. After eight exciting and rewarding years in the Cabinet Office, he could not see much point in staying on there: it was one thing to serve Churchill in wartime but quite another to serve Attlee in peacetime. Moreover General Ismay, to whom he was devoted, and many of the friends and colleagues who had made up that close-knit team would be moving on to other appointments: life would never be the same again.

His first move was to find out what prospects he might have in the Army, and accordingly he sought an interview with General Wemyss, the Military Secretary. The advice given was depressing, but did not come as a surprise: having spent the entire war in the centre of government, and not having served with troops at all, the indications were that there was little chance of progressing up the ladder of the General Staff and command. The Military Secretary told him that he was about to be promoted substantive Major General from his temporary rank, and that he might be appointed to one of the less active directorates in the War Office. Jacob was in no way taken aback by this: modest as always about his own achievements, he felt that he had no claim to a more prominent appointment, as his strictly military experience had ended in Egypt in 1938. He decided that he must keep his eyes open for some opportunity outside the Army, and was confident that he would fall on his feet. His personal philosophy was never to look back.

If that official view of a brilliant officer's future may seem today to be too narrow-minded and short-sighted, it must be remembered that there was a surplus of talented officers of his age who had been successful in battle, and were also being considered for appointments that might lead to further advancement. Nevertheless Jacob's future career outside the Army would show that he was very versatile, and with his experience at the centre of government and on the international scene, and his acute analytical mind, he had much to offer.

The first proposal for employment came from Spedan Lewis, the founder and head of the John Lewis partnership. Jacob's name had been suggested by Lieutenant General Sir Charles King – the 'Monarch' King of the Royal Military Academy's teaching staff – who was now a director. But Jacob did not fancy becoming a personnel specialist, which was Lewis' intention. Soon afterwards, he was invited to meet Mr Haley, the Director General of the BBC, and was asked whether he would join the BBC as Controller of European Services. His name had been put forward by Sir Ivone Kirkpatrick, who in the war had been seconded from the Foreign Office to become Controller, and had now returned to his department.

Jacob accepted in March 1946. Although the management of broadcasting was a field unknown to him, his wartime experience was relevant; he had held a unique position from which to observe the development of international relations, and had been closely involved with the British Foreign Office in handling questions where the interests of defence and of foreign affairs were both involved. In addition, he had acquired a large circle of influential friends and foreign acquaintances, and had had intimate contact with representatives of the United States and of the Soviet Union, from two American Presidents and Stalin downwards. Rightly, he felt he was fitted for the duty of directing the voice of Britain in what was rapidly becoming the 'Cold War'. The fierce political warfare of the war years might be giving place now to a more measured form of broadcasting, but the task would still be of national importance.

In the interval between accepting the job at the BBC and his actual retirement, Jacob was sent to Egypt as the military member of Lord Stansgate's mission: their task was to negotiate a new treaty with the Egyptian Government. It was an interesting experience, but fruitless because of irreconcilable differences over the future of the Sudan and disagreements over the disposal of the military base, built up in Egypt during the war years. Jacob took the view that the base should be written off, handing over to the Egyptians anything of use to them, and that the British Government should announce the intention to withdraw completely from Egypt, including the Canal Zone, to which there was no foreseeable external threat. He was confident that Egypt would then invite Britain to keep a small garrison on the Canal, and mutual goodwill would prevail. However, the British Government did not accept this view and, under the uninspiring leadership of Lord Stansgate, the negotiations resulted in the withdrawal of British Forces from Cairo to the Canal Zone.

Jacob spent about three weeks in Cairo, and returned home before the rest of the delegation, as there was nothing military in the negotiations that could not be left to the local Commanders-in-Chief to deal with. Soon afterwards, he learnt that the War Office, hearing that he proposed to retire on 30 June, had cancelled his promotion to Major General. This made little difference, as he was given the honorary rank of major general on retirement, and his pension would not have been increased. It amounted to the sum of £645 a year, (equivalent to about £8,000 pa in 1988). So, on 30 June 1946, Jacob retired after twenty-eight years' service in the Army, and went off with his wife and friends to spend a month's leave in Scotland before starting a second career.

In July, fresh from his holiday, he joined the BBC at Bush House to take up the appointment of Controller of the Corporation's radio broadcasting service to Europe. He was answerable to Haley, now Sir William. Haley was a complex character. He had had a brilliant career in journalism, but was shy and reserved. He was an ardent supporter of Reith's policies of providing programmes of the highest quality, while resisting all forms of governmental pressure. Jacob soon established harmonious relations with him, based on mutual respect.

The European Service had received many tributes from its users during the war. In 1944 Bidault, the French Foreign Minister, had written 'It is thanks to you, dear familiar voices, that our minds stayed free while our limbs were bound'.[1] Leon Blum, throughout the war a prisoner in German hands, went so far as to compare the voice of the BBC to a Beethoven symphony. Leaders in the recently liberated countries had unanimously declared that, without the BBC's transmissions, it would not have been possible to organise and retain resistance to Nazi occupation. Jacob had first hand evidence of the BBC's standing when he had visited Norway in May, and had received a rapturous reception.

Whereas, at the outbreak of war, the Service had been finding its feet in only half a dozen languages, now it had developed into the largest, most sophisticated, and above all, the most trusted, foreign language radio service in the world. The temporary staff of journalists, civil servants, actors, dons and professional broadcasters, producers and politicians, who had been gathered under the roof of Bush House, represented a remarkable aggregation of talent. However, with the cessation of hostilities there was a natural drop in all overseas audiences. Liberated European nations re-established their domestic services, free from either a Nazi or Quisling grip, and continental broadcasters and politicians in exile returned to their homelands, where freedom reigned once more. Universities reclaimed their dons and newspapers their foreign correspondents. Moreover, the newly established United Nations Radio Department, with its offers of tax-free posts in an unrationed community, exercised a strong attraction on those who had served in Britain through years of austerity tempered by danger. By the end of 1945, it had seemed to many in London that the BBC's European Service was disintegrating. Such was the scene that was to confront Jacob on arrival.

In July 1946, the Government issued a White Paper defining the policies to be followed. The Corporation should remain independent in the preparation of programmes for countries overseas, though it should obtain from the Government Departments concerned such information about conditions in those countries, and the Government's policies towards them as would permit it to plan its programmes in the national interest.

In the White Paper, it was recognised that Bush House broadcasts could not hope to keep the audiences that they had enjoyed during the war, but it was declared: 'The European Service retains a large audience, and friends of this country on the Continent are anxious that it shall continue. Moreover there are clear indications, at present, that the other Powers intend to continue to use the broadcasting medium to put their point of view before the European audience, and we cannot afford to let the British viewpoint go by default'.[2]

Jacob's own view of the policy which the European Service should follow was issued within a month of his joining Bush House. 'The spread of truth and the full ventilation of facts are highly desirable in themselves . . . Britain has to struggle against calumny and insidious propaganda of a different way of thinking. Our part in counteracting this is not by refuting it, but by seizing and retaining the initiative . . .[3] It may be asked whether this implies that we are to conduct political warfare. The answer is that the BBC itself is not conducting anything. It is a mirror held to reflect the view and activities of the British people. When, as now, the British people are engaged in a struggle to maintain their existence and way of life in the face of a campaign of propaganda and subversive activity, openly designed to overthrow them, we must not in any way shrink from giving full expression to the British view, and to assist by all means in our power the national effort. Only in this way shall we be framing our programmes in the national interest'.[4]

He firmly rejected the notion that items of news should be suppressed because they were inconvenient from a short term political standpoint. Nor did he expect the heads of his language Services meekly and automatically to accept governmental direction. When they visited the Foreign Office, he declared, 'They should seek to learn all they could . . . but should not act on the guidance received without testing it by the BBC's long-term standards, referring as might be necessary to him.'

There were few people in Whitehall who had as comprehensive an understanding of the international scene as Jacob; and although now retired from government service, he still retained many friends in military and diplomatic circles, and was still clothed in authority, particularly as his brilliant service throughout the war had just been recognised by a Knighthood in the Birthday Honours List of 1946. It was not surprising that his predecessor in the European Service, Ivone Kirkpatrick, who had now been transferred by the Foreign Office to the Control Commission for Germany, and Haley the Director General both spoke of him as 'the ideal man' to manage the European Service.

It soon became apparent that his intellectual capacity fully matched the requirement of the new assignment, but initially some doubt may have been felt whether he had the ability to lead an unfamiliar organisation of such diverse personalities in a period of declining morale. Responsibility for commanding an enterprise had not rested directly on his shoulders since his military career before the war. Moreover, throughout his service as one of Churchill's trio, his instinct to lead had had to be suppressed. It had been said of Ismay that he was 'the man with the oil can': it might equally have been said of his assistant, Jacob, who had inherited from his father – that self-effacing Field Marshal – the family trait of modesty. Now, no longer oiling the wheels, he was to be the driver of a most unusual train operating in the full glare of national publicity.

However, very soon any doubts about his suitability were dispelled. One of the 'old hands' Harman Grisewood, who was occupying an important position, commented: 'the BBC was lucky to attract Jacob.

I wasn't in his class'.[5] The official history of the BBC recorded that 'Jacob did much to strengthen the BBC's position on all fronts, and from the start his presence was strongly felt'.[6] Two immediate tasks faced him. One was to arrest the seepage of talented staff from Bush House: this was largely a question of reviving morale. The other was to prevent further cuts in the grant-in-aid, which funded the BBC's broadcasts abroad.

Jacob's early grounding in military leadership, together with a recognition that he needed to learn quickly how broadcasting worked, soon solved the first problem. He made himself visible and approachable. He did not retreat behind the Controller's office door, but regularly went to studios and newsrooms to see the polyglot operation in action. A sense of post-war purpose was soon established, and the search for jobs away from Bush House was largely abandoned.

In December 1947 his responsibilities were increased by an important reorganisation, which was carried out by Haley, to whom Jacob as Controller of European Services had made proposals. After his many years in Whitehall, he had observed in the BBC some lack of logic in their organisation, evidenced by an excessive number of subordinates reporting to one superior. To remedy this defect, Haley introduced a Board of Management consisting of four directors:

Sir Noel Ashbridge: Technical Services
BE Nicholls: Home Broadcasting
Major General Sir Ian Jacob: Overseas Service
Air Chief Marshal Sir Norman Bottomley: Administration

Under Jacob, the European division was administratively merged with the Overseas division, which broadcast to Commonwealth countries and others not in Europe. The reorganisation gave additional prominence to Jacob's activities, and developed his relations with the Governors, to whose meetings he would be invited by the Director General when an item in his field of responsibility was to be discussed.

In that same month, he took part in an event in sharp contrast to his new career: this was a dinner given by Churchill at 28 Hyde Park Gate for General Marshall. The other British guests were the three former Chiefs of Staff, Lord Alanbrooke as he had now become, Cunningham and Portal, with Anthony Eden and Hollis. For Jacob it was a nostalgic evening, at which old memories of 'hot' war and present problems of 'Cold War' generated a lively discussion.

Although encouraged by talking over these issues with many old

PLATE 26. The Stansgate Mission. Cairo 1946. Viscount Stansgate with (*left*) General Sir Bernard Paget and (*right*) Major General Sir Ian Jacob (*Jacob papers*).

PLATE 27. Sir Ian Jacob, Controller of European Services BBC, with Czech film star Dr Lili Hodacova (*BBC*).

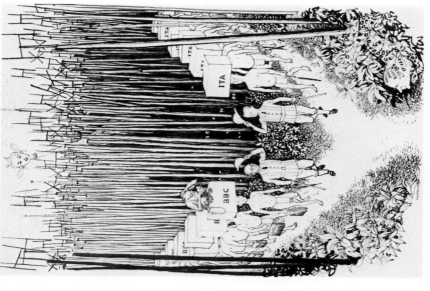

PLATE 29. 'Sir Ian Jacob, I presume?'. The BBC, led by
Sir Ian Jacob meet their competitor, The Independent
Television Authority, led by Sir Kenneth Clark, in the
television jungle (*Punch*).

PLATE 28. Jacob, elected President of the European Broadcasting Union, at
his Conference in Torquay 1950 (*BBC*).

PLATE 30. Receiving the Marquess of Salisbury at Bush House (*BBC*).

PLATE 31. Answering questions on broadcasting at a special meeting of the 'Asian Club' (*BBC*).

PLATE 32. M Gabriel Delauney, Director General of *Radiodiffusion et Télévision Française* is greeted by Sir Alexander Cadogan and Jacob in 1957 (*BBC*).

PLATE 33. Jacob attends a rehearsal of Montgomery's Television programme 'Command in Battle' in 1958. (*Right*) The producer, Michael Bowen (*BBC*).

PLATE 34. As President of the European Broadcasting Union, Jacob has an audience with Pope John XXIII on 'broadcasting for schools', Rome 7 December 1961 (*Felici*).

PLATE 35. Some members of the Covent Garden Market Authority, 16 January 1967. (*L–R*) Sir Alex Maxwell, Ian Jacob, W Balch, Sir Henry Hardman and Sir Thomas Yates (*Terence Wilson Ltd*).

PLATE 36. Some Board Members of Fison's Ltd. (*L–R*) Jacob, Paul Hodgkin and Sir John Carmichael (*Picture Coverage Ltd*).

PLATE 37. Ian and Cecil with grandson Nicholas

PLATE 38. Sir Ian and Lady Jacob in retirement at the Red House (*BBC*).

friends, Jacob, always a realist, was in no doubt that his second problem, obviating further cuts in the grant-in-aid, would entail a long, hard battle with the Treasury. After the strain of the war years, it was a period of great financial stringency for the nation. The grant was sponsored annually by the Foreign, Dominions and Colonial Offices, but was at the ultimate mercy of the Treasury, which funded the BBC's broadcasts abroad, in contrast to the licence-fee system, which was the financial basis of its domestic broadcasting in peacetime. Thus the Government controlled the scale and range of the European operation as it had done in the war, although it was not responsible for the content of the broadcasts.

It was already clear to Jacob's colleagues that he would fight skilfully and vigorously to gain the resources needed for the Overseas programme. Moreover, those who were charged at that uncertain time with planning their programmes in harmony with the national interest began to realise how fortunate they were in obtaining Jacob's shrewd guidance on the interpretation of British foreign policy and the defence policy associated with it. This backdrop, to which their broadcasts had to relate, was ill-defined and undergoing rapid change. In 1946, the military threat against which post-war defence was to be organised was far from clear, and there was great uncertainty as to the value to be placed on potential allies in Europe. As to Britain's war-time ally, the Soviet Union, the illusion in some quarters that there was little cause for anxiety about the post-war attitude of its people, provided they were cultivated as friends, had only recently been dispelled by unscrupulous Soviet actions in Eastern Europe, which had begun to undermine the Yalta agreements. A further imponderable lay in the potentialities of the new weapons of mass destruction; although these had been under study for some years, an official assessment had not yet been reached. Hence it was not until 1947 that an approved defence strategy was agreed by Prime Minister Attlee. Although the Soviet Union was at last identified as the potential enemy, the reality of the Cold War, which had been adumbrated by Churchill in his Fulton speech in March 1946, was still not acknowledged.

Nevertheless, the vital importance of the Overseas Service, and hence the requirement for adequate funds, fully recognised by Jacob, would soon be emphasised by the stark reality of the Cold War as it intensified in the next three years. The treatment of news and current affairs would have to be harmonised constantly with changes in the international scene, such as the Czech coup in February 1948, followed in March by the signing of the Brussels Treaty, and the ratification by Congress of Marshall Aid. In June 1948, the blockade of Berlin would be imposed by the Soviet Union, to be countered by the British-American air lift, in which General Sir Brian Robertson, Jacob's Commanding Officer of 1921, best man, and life-long friend would play a major role. In April 1949 would come the signing in Washington of the North Atlantic Treaty, and in May, the Soviet Union's lifting of the Berlin blockade.

In 1947 a change took place in governmental thinking on the policy for external broadcasting. Fortunately, and due largely to Bevin, foreign policy was still bi-partisan; and until then, it had been accepted that there was no objection to different points of view being expressed in external broadcasts. However, even before the Czech coup, the Foreign Office had decided that there was a need to establish an anti-communist publicity policy. Jacob was actively involved with the Foreign Office in shaping the new policy, and he recommended that the peoples of Eastern Europe should not be incited to subversion, but that a systematic attack on the techniques of communist propaganda should be made to give a lead to the friends of Britain in those countries: in such broadcasts, it was important to be incisive and to avoid the abstruse. As the Cold War developed, the BBC's external services reacted shrewdly and appropriately, and in some cases were able to anticipate events. Their success drew savage criticism from Moscow, and eventually the Soviet Union organised a comprehensive system of jamming. However, by a programme of cooperation with the Voice of America, the Soviet jamming system was placed under great strain, with the result that most of the BBC broadcasts got through. The scale of external broadcasts continued to increase with the introduction of additional languages, and by 1949 Britain was broadcasting 687 hours a week as against the 214 hours of the USA, and the 434 hours of the Soviet Union. Nevertheless cuts in the grant-in-aid had continually to be resisted and not every battle was won. Jacob did not hesitate to argue his case with Lord Salisbury, the Lord Privy Seal, having first mobilised the support of the Chiefs of Staff.

He would cite the effect of cuts on operations, such as the abandonment of broadcasting to certain large areas of the world, for example North and South America, and the restriction of broadcasting to Europe to the period from 1600 to 2400 hours GMT. Moreover, he would argue, such cuts would also be very damaging to the relevant staffs of the BBC, who would assume that the value of their work was not appreciated, and would look for employment elsewhere. Broadcasting was not something that could be turned on and off like a tap. In the ten years leading up to 1949, their operations had won great prestige and a remarkable standing for the BBC – their programmes were rebroadcast in 65 countries, and their news bulletins had won an unequalled reputation in the world. The BBC's world-wide audience and its reputation for truth and quality had been built up slowly and laboriously: once sacrificed, they would be very hard to restore.

In fighting the Treasury for adequate resources, Jacob had an ally in Bevin, the Foreign Secretary; but Churchill, his old master, now on the Opposition benches, having relinquished the levers of power, had an attitude to broadcasting which was peculiar. He was still in occasional touch with Jacob, and had written to him in 1948 to tell him that he had heard that the Czechs, after the coup, had listened to the BBC more diligently even than in the war, but that there was a feeling that the best use of that great opportunity was not being made – to which comment Jacob reacted with alacrity.

However, after extensive observation of his old master, Jacob had come to the conclusion that he had never really understood or absorbed the idea of public relations; certainly, during the war, he had never attached much importance to organisations such as the Ministry of Information. His attitude could be summed up in a sentence heard more than once by Jacob 'if something is needed, I will make a speech'. This attitude seemed to have been influenced by a conviction that the BBC in the 1930s had been unjust and wrong-headed in keeping him off the air on matters on which he had felt strongly, such as the future of India and the rise of Hitler.

On one occasion, Jacob, as Controller of European Services, wrote to Churchill asking him if he would like to make a broadcast to Europe on a big issue which was topical at the time: he was informed by the Private Secretary that 'when Mr Churchill deemed the moment opportune, he would broadcast'. In other words he would again 'make a speech'!

Throughout their association, Jacob had found that Churchill was chary of broadcasting in all its forms. He thought it was a dangerous development, because out of that box in the English-man's sitting room came things over which he had no control.[7]

From 1949 onwards, Haley the Director General brought Jacob increasingly into international discussion in Europe on the allocation of wavelengths and the possible exchange of programmes. A succession of conferences led eventually to the establishment of the European Broadcasting Union (EBU) and later to the technical system known as 'Eurovision'. Jacob's diplomatic skill and his experience in international conferences during the war were invaluable in developing this field which, in 1946, was in a highly confused state.

The history of programme exchange may be traced back to 1926, when the *Union Internationale de Radio-diffusion* (UIR) was founded, with headquarters in Geneva. During the war, the organisation had fallen under German influence and censorship, and in 1945 there was a general desire among the victors to create a new organisation. However, the British Foreign Office, represented by Ivone Kirkpatrick, pressed for a new international body under the aegis of the United Nations; Kirkpatrick was prepared nevertheless to allow UIR to continue, provided it dealt with purely technical questions.

A conference held in Brussels in 1946 had resulted in the founding of the *Organisation Internationale de Radio-diffusion* (OIR), which the BBC and several other corporations declined to join. As a result, the UIR continued its existence. At a subsequent conference in Geneva, the UIR agreed, as did the new OIR, to dissolve, if a new world broadcasting organisation were to come into being. There were further conferences at Atlantic City in 1947 and at Copenhagen in 1948. Meanwhile, the Soviet Union had adopted an unacceptable stand over voting procedures, and had caused great difficulties; the continued existence of the OIR and the UIR further complicated the discussions. Yet another conference, held in Stresa in 1949, again failed to reach agreement with the OIR, and the BBC then resolved to set up an alternative Broadcasting Union within Europe. At a preparatory conference in Paris in 1949, the BBC was asked to convene a further conference in 1950 of all the broadcasting organisations of countries in the European Zone, which were members of the International Telecommunication Union (ITU), to form a new Union.

Jacob, by now in charge, decided to hold the conference outside London, and chose the Imperial Hotel in Torquay to mitigate wartime austerity still in force. He was elected as President, with Belgian and Swiss Vice-Presidents, and he continued in that office until his retirement from the BBC many years later. Although agreement was reached at Torquay on the constitution of the European Broadcasting Union, a programme committee was not established until three years later. In addition to radio, exchanges of television programmes followed, with the result that Eurovision, supported by technical improvements, developed most successfully. Many of the legal problems and those concerned with copyright were solved amicably, and negotiations were facilitated on big sporting promotions such as the Olympic Games and the World Cup. The BBC, which was by far the biggest organisation in the European Zone, had a lot to offer; and the other countries, which sometimes had peculiar diffi- culties – for instance the Latin races disagreeing with the Scandinavians – were happy to collaborate with the BBC in an atmo- sphere that was generally harmonious. In the EBU – a fine example of international co-operation – Jacob made many friends over the next ten years, who greatly admired the incisiveness, friendliness and diplomatic skills of their President. When he retired in 1960, the international staff of the EBU in Geneva made a presentation to him 'as a small mark of our gratitude for the sympathy and kindness you have shown us during the years you have been in office'.

Although leading the Overseas Service was a full-time job, Jacob's links with Whitehall at this period remained close, and involved him in many extraneous activities. In 1946, Ralph Ingersoll's book *Top Secret* was published, giving, from an American standpoint, a con- troversial view of the British contribution to victory. Jacob, having been asked by the Editor of *The Economist* to review the book, wrote four articles published anonymously to put the record straight. Mont- gomery asked *The Economist* for the name of the author: they met at a dinner given by Attlee in honour of General Eisenhower, and the CIGS told Jacob that the articles were 'excellent'.

Jacob also became an active member of the Council of the Royal Institute of International Affairs, Chatham House, and later its Vice- Chairman; he also joined the panel of Service advisers to Sir James Butler, the chief military historian of the war, and continued in that role for more than thirty years. In 1950, he was asked by Sir George Turner, the Permanent-Under-Secretary of State in the War Office, to lead a committee charged with studying the organisation of that department. His most radical proposal was that the civil branches of the War Office, concerned primarily with finance, should be integrated with their military colleagues, sharing with them the responsibility for efficiency as well as economy, and helping in the preparation of policy. Although this recommendation was pigeon- holed by the then PUS, it was adopted after his retirement.

In October 1951, the Conservative Party returned to power; Churchill once again became Prime Minister, and assumed the title of Minister of Defence as he had done in wartime. Jacob was asked to take on an inquiry into the organisation of NATO.[8] The Treaty Organisation had been in force for a couple of years, and had various offices established in Paris and Washington, but the Cabinet was not satisfied that these, and their location, had been sensibly arranged. In his reply Jacob informed the Prime Minister that the BBC had agreed to his absenting himself for six weeks to do the job. He set to work and consulted many people in London and Paris, in particular Averell Harriman, who was in Paris on behalf of the President engaged chiefly with the furtherance of the Marshall Plan and with NATO. Jacob completed his task in six weeks, and sent his report[9] to the Prime Minister, but before that there was a further development.

One day he was called to No 10, expecting that the Prime Minister wanted to hear how he was getting on with his NATO study. However, this was not what the PM wanted. When he was ushered into the Cabinet Room, where Churchill was sitting in his familiar spot at the big table with his back to the fire-place, the Prime Minister said: 'Jacob you must come back'. Jacob was startled. However, he said he would do whatever the Prime Minister thought he should do. Churchill then told him he was dissatisfied with his staff in the Ministry of Defence, and that Jacob should go and see Sir Norman Brook, who had succeeded Bridges as Secretary to the Cabinet, and Brook would make all the necessary arrangements for his return.

This peculiar arrangement presented some difficulties to the official mind. Jacob had left the Army and to bring him back now, particularly in a rank above that with which he had retired, was without precedent. However, the Prime Minister, unable to pull back Ismay, who was now Secretary of State for Commonwealth Relations, persisted in his endeavour to get Jacob. George Mallaby, a shrewd observer, then in the Cabinet Office, commented:

> Churchill liked Jacob and he was used to him. He liked his strong and lucid intellect, his grasp of detail, his air of unruffled and unhasting efficiency. He admired, perhaps, Ian Jacob's character, so utterly different from his own, the stoic calm, the absolute self-control, the mistrust of exaggerated and excessive emotion, nothing too much of anything. Of course the Prime Minister won. Everything was arranged.[10]

Jacob went round to see Norman Brook, who told him that the idea was that he should take the places of both Sir Harold Parker, the PUS, and Lieutenant General Sir Kenneth McLean, the Chief Staff Officer. It was thought that there was not work for two people, and it would be sensible to combine the jobs in one man who knew the Prime Minister's methods. Whether he should come back as a soldier or a civil servant had yet to be worked out. The PM wrote to Haley, and asked him to give Jacob leave of absence for a year while he returned to the Ministry. Several days passed in exploring various plans with the Cabinet Office and the Treasury and, in due course, it began to appear impracticable for Jacob to replace both the civil and military heads. So the proposal was narrowed down to the simpler one that he should supersede McLean as Chief Staff Officer to the Minister of Defence. Meanwhile, nothing was said to either Parker or McLean.

The arrangements were nearing completion when there appeared in the newspapers a statement that the Prime Minister was shortly to visit Washington and Ottawa for consultations, and a list was given of those officials who were to accompany him. This included McLean's name. When the Prime Minister saw this, he said to Brook that it would be very humiliating for the change to be made at once and for McLean to be removed from the Washington party: all arrangements had better be put in abeyance until the party had returned. So nothing was said and Jacob relaxed.

In early January 1952, the Prime Minister and his entourage arrived home and Jacob was summoned. Churchill said: 'You will be very interested to know who I am going to appoint as Minister of Defence.' Jacob agreed; and the Prime Minister said: 'Alex'. Jacob was not at all pleased to hear this, as he held strongly to the view that soldiers, however eminent, made very bad ministers. There were numerous examples to be cited in many countries; the whole training of an official or of an officer was entirely at variance with the road that a successful politician must follow. Even as Minister of Defence, and with the Prime Minister behind him, Jacob thought it would be very doubtful whether a Field Marshal, in the House of Lords too, could successfully carry conviction to his colleagues and to Parliament on the merits of Government policy.

The Prime Minister continued by saying that it would be a month or so before Alexander, who was just giving up as Governor General of Canada, would be available to take up his new appointment, and clearly the arrangements must await his arrival: he might have other ideas. Everything was again in abeyance, and Jacob returned to his normal occupations in the BBC. In due course, Alexander arrived, and by the end of March, as Jacob had heard nothing, he assumed that the whole plan had been dropped. He rang up Norman Brook and asked if he could confirm it. Brook said that, on the contrary, the plan was now on the boil, and he must come round. This time there was no delay, and by the beginning of May, Jacob found himself on leave for a year from the BBC, restored to the active list of the Army, and given the honorary rank of Lieutenant General.

There were still people in the Cabinet Office, and in the Ministry of Defence, whom he had known in the past, but he was surprised to find how much the Military Secretariat had expanded. George Mallaby was Assistant Secretary to the Cabinet. The Chairman of the Chiefs of Staff was Field Marshal Sir William Slim, and the First Sea Lord was Admiral Sir Roderick McGrigor. Air Chief Marshal Sir John Slessor was the Chief of the Air Staff. Jacob found that they were a splendid team to work with. 'Though the First Sea Lord was not up to the weight of the others.' Slessor's only trouble was that 'he found it difficult to think without a pencil in his hand, and having had much experience as Director of Plans and in other staff jobs, he was a great drafter, which was not really the function of a Chief of Staff. However, this was a minor difficulty.'[11]

In 1970, Jacob looking back on that time recorded:

> The big problem that stood out, and has been with us ever since, was how to produce the forces required by our commitments all over the world without absorbing an undue proportion of the nation's finances.
>
> It was pretty clear that a choice would have to be made between being strong in Europe or weakening ourselves there and maintaining our contribution to forces in the Indian Ocean and South East Asia.
>
> The Conservative Government under Churchill was not prepared to face this issue, and so we went on knowing full well that we were falling slowly but steadily behind in our modernity while maintaining large forces and continuing to take our share in any trouble going. They were probably right, and the issue was still unresolved in Macmillan's day. Alexander did nothing to bring matters to a head. The estimates of the three Services continued to be a compilation of three demands, pared down separately by the Ministry and the Treasury, and not really being ruthlessly scrutinised from a point of view of a national strategy.
>
> I found Alex an enigma. No one can achieve the highest position in war without considerable qualities. His were courage of a very high order, a fine appearance, which gave him the look all over of the practical soldier, a fund of commonsense and an ability to meet and talk to everyone on level terms. This is quite a formidable list, but there seemed to be lacking the equivalent mental equipment. His thought was by no means profound, and he did not seem to have any original ideas. He did not seek to impose his thinking on the development of affairs when he became a Minister, and I couldn't help wondering about his share in the conduct of the Italian Campaign. I found him very difficult to get to know, and he always seemed to be somewhat withdrawn and detached. At the end of six months I don't think I knew him any better than at the beginning. Subsequently, I suppose we may have met half a dozen times, when he would be affable, but our lives were in quite different paths. No doubt, if I had been a different person, he would have been more forthcoming. As it was, I don't think I

have ever served closely with anyone with whom I made less impression and who made less on me. The fault, I am sure, lay with me.

I did not see a great deal of Churchill during this period, though from time to time I was summoned either to his flat in No 10 or to Chartwell. I remember a visit to Chartwell, when we had lunch and then fed the goldfish, but at which it was impossible to get business done. He no longer read and mastered papers, or fired out his scintillating minutes. I thought it tragic that he should have felt it necessary to return as Prime Minister. He was hardly so, and was beginning to show his age. He could still master his resources for a big occasion, but the humdrum slog of daily business bored him. I was grateful to him for electing me to the Other Club, in 1952.

The Other Club was a unique association, which had been created by the young Winston Churchill with his friend FE Smith, the future Lord Birkenhead, in 1912. At that time, there had been a dining club called 'The Club', which brought together political opponents, but the members would not elect Churchill, who by crossing the floor of the House some years earlier had scandalised so many. The 'Other Club' was accordingly formed, with interesting rules. It was limited to 50 members, of whom not more than 25 could be members of the House of Commons. The object of the Club was to dine, and dinners were supposed to be held every fortnight when Parliament was sitting. One of the rules was that the affairs of the Club should be conducted by an Executive Committee, who should decide matters without appeal, but the membership of the Executive Committee should be 'wrapped in impenetrable mystery'.

One day lunching with Churchill, Jacob asked him some questions about the Club:

'Do you ever consult the Executive Committee?'

'I do as much as possible, but most of them are in the other world'. Churchill replied.

'Was political strife as bitter before the First War as it is now?'

'More so, because members on both sides of the House moved in the same circle, and if you changed sides, half the people in London cut you dead, and did not receive you in their houses.'

'You do not seem to have any members of the Labour Party as members except Lord Jowitt, and he was a Liberal when he was elected. How is this?'

'It is not because I don't want Labour members. It is simply because they are so boring.'[12]

Years later, Jacob summed up this episode of his career as follows:

Looking back on my time in the Ministry of Defence, I cannot help thinking that it was a foolish plan, which might have made sense if I had gone there at once in December 1951 when Churchill was himself the Minister, and if I had stayed at least a year. To go in in April, with Alexander as Minister hardly made sense, particularly as I only stayed six months. Little can be achieved by a newcomer in that time; in any case, the original situation that had caused my recall had come to an end when a new Minister was appointed. I enjoyed it, particularly as I had two such excellent Chiefs of Staff in Slim and Slessor to work with. It also provided a useful break, so that I could come back into the

BBC fresh to it all. It gave me a step in honorary rank to Lieutenant General when I left, but of course made no difference to my pension. It was thus an interlude which did no one much good.

About to leave Whitehall, Jacob, aged only fifty-three but retired from Government service for the second time, must have had his name placed high on the list of 'the great and the good', which it is said exists as a prime source of effective chairmen of governmental inquiries. The fact that he had been put forward to replace simultaneously a permanent-under-secretary and the Ministry of Defence's chief staff officer had demonstrated his great versatility and exceptional talent for administration. Although happy now to return to the BBC, his skill as an 'organisation man' would not be forgotten.

13

Director General of the BBC

The selection and appointment of Jacob as Director General – a matter for the BBC Governors – was complicated by the lien which the Prime Minister had on him as Chief Staff Officer to the Minister of Defence, and it was unfortunate for both Jacob and the BBC that six months were to elapse between Haley's decision to resign and the arrival of the new director general. Jacob had been in the Ministry of Defence only a few weeks when he had received a letter from Haley in June 1952 announcing his intention to leave the BBC and become Editor of *The Times*. The news was unexpected: Haley had only just turned fifty, and Jacob, although aware of Haley's past experience and interest in the newspaper world, had never visualised his early departure from the Corporation. Jacob himself had not thought of a future outside external broadcasting and, until then, promotion to Director General had never entered his mind.

On the following morning he had visited Churchill at No 10, on routine business, and the Prime Minister had surprised him by saying:

'I see that your Director General is going. Who will get the job?'

Jacob had replied: 'I don't know, but I suppose I have some claims to it.'

'I suppose you have', said Churchill.

From the days of Reith, the founding father of the BBC, to those of Haley, the post of Director General had been surrounded by controversy; neither the governors nor the government of the day had seemed to have defined the type of man they required. Reith had retired in 1938 and had been followed by Frederick Ogilvie, Vice-Chancellor of Queen's University, Belfast. His administration under

war conditions came under criticism, and Robert Foot, an industrialist was installed to investigate. Later Foot was appointed joint Director General with the existing deputy, Cecil Graves. In 1943 Graves
had to retire through illness, and Foot became the sole DG until the
governors, seeking to strengthen the editorial function, inserted Haley
in a new role as 'Editor-in-Chief'. When Foot decided to return to
industry, Haley was appointed Director General.

By 1952, throughout the BBC there was no doubt that Haley, by
experience and instinct a journalist, had been a very successful Director General. In selecting his successor, was a background of journalism to be a relevant qualification, or should importance be attached to
an academic background or to industrial experience? Was previous
service within the BBC a necessary qualification?

Jacob, although educated at Cambridge and highly intelligent,
could never be classified as an academic, nor had he had any personal
experience of industry or journalism. However, if when he had first
joined the BBC, the title of General had seemed to be an irrelevance,
if not a stigma, his performance as the Director of Overseas Service
had convinced many colleagues that he was a considerable asset; in
particular his ability to manipulate the levers of Whitehall had
proved of great benefit to the Corporation. His patient judgement
and powers of decision had been impressive, and he had made no
enemies within the Corporation, where personal squabbles were not
uncommon.

Haley, at a farewell gathering of senior staff, many of whom were
changing jobs, had spoken of a new Charter, [*which would appear in
August, following the Beveridge Report*] and a new era. He had said:
'Reorganisation – although not regional reorganisation – was complete, with greater devolution guaranteed. If the BBC did not resist
sponsored television, sound would be next. They must fight against
too many hours [*of transmission*] and against lowering of standards.
They must fight for all necessary outside co-operation, and for
resources. Television must not become a film industry: it must remain
civilised and adult.'[1]

Jacob was still at the Ministry of Defence but, if present, might
have been daunted at the turmoil amongst senior appointments and
the simultaneous changes in the Governing Board. Sir Alexander
Cadogan, the recently retired head of the Foreign Office, aged sixty-
eight, had take over on 1 August 1952, before Jacob's arrival. The
conjunction of a senior civil servant and a General at the top of the
BBC hierarchy would be greeted later with the untutored comment:

'Too many brasshats',[2] although it was difficult to visualise a perma-nent-under-secretary adopting such headgear!

Cadogan had carried enormous responsibilities throughout the war, and had received unprecedented recognition from King George VI by the award of the Order of Merit. At an interview with Church-ill, he had questioned the relevance of his qualifications, and the difficulty of coming in from outside with no knowledge of the BBC and no experience of the Board. 'There are no qualifications' said Church-ill. 'All you have to do is to be fair', 'and sensible I suppose', Cadogan added. Churchill nodded.[3]

Cadogan and Jacob knew each other well from attending Churchill at his war-time conferences, also from United Nations' business at San Francisco and from Cabinet meetings, at which both had frequently been present. He had found Jacob pleasant to deal with. 'He seems to suffer me gladly though it must waste a lot of his time putting me wise'.[4] Jacob expected that Cadogan, unlike his prede-cessor, would understand the functions of a non-executive part-time chairman.

Jacob's appointment as Director General had been recommended by the previous governors, chaired by Simon, before they had left office, and in October Jacob was invited to Cadogan's flat where Tedder, the Vice-Chairman who knew Jacob well, was also present. They offered him the job, which he accepted. Then they asked, somewhat diffidently, whether in making the public announcement they could omit any reference to his military rank. Jacob thought this an amusing suggestion 'savouring of the ostrich', but readily agreed. The announcement was made in October, but Jacob was not released until December.

The *Manchester Guardian* commented on the selection of the new Director General:

> *I must find a man, if he can be found*
> *Who is quite allergic both to sight and sound,*
> *Who has carved like me his whole career*
> *In a more exclusive diplomatic sphere,*
> *And who never, never listens to Varietee,*
> *For the new Director General of the BBC.*[5]

The Times, more serious, stressed continuity: 'Sir Ian Jacob has been chosen to safeguard and to keep fresh and contemporary the tradition of British broadcasting created by Lord Reith'. Although Reith him-self disputed this, Jacob would have agreed with it, but he was also prepared for new styles, new men and new measures. Cadogan was delighted with the appointment: it was perhaps the best decision the Board had ever taken.

In 1952, under the new Charter, the Board had been increased from 7 to 8 members including, for the first time, national governors for Scotland, Wales and Northern Ireland. The members were Lord Tedder, Lord Clydesmuir (Scotland) Lord Macdonald (Wales), Sir Henry Mulholland, (Northern Ireland), Professor Barbara Wootton, IAR Stedeford Lady Rhys Williams and Sir Philip Morris.

Jacob took up his duties on 1 December 1952 at Broadcasting House. He was already aware from newspaper comment and parliamentary debates that the future of the Corporation which he was to manage was clouded. The seeds of controversy over the constitution of the BBC, far from dormant since the end of the war, had been given hothouse propagation by the long drawn-out processes of the Beveridge Committee and the Parliamentary debates which had followed. The External Services, of which Jacob had then been director, officially were exempted from giving evidence, as they were funded by the Government: nevertheless Beveridge, whose reputation as the author of the Social Security Plan, stood very high, had summoned him to appear. A BBC colleague later described the event:

In answer to a series of probing questions, designed to expose error in Jacob's management, he had given polite, monosyllabic replies, and had then withdrawn. Outside he had muttered: 'Silly old man'! His colleague, in tentative reproof, had countered with: 'But, you know, he is very clever.' 'He is a silly old man', repeated Jacob with even greater conviction.

In the public mind, the principal doubts about the constitution and management of the BBC were, first, whether the power derived from a position of monopoly was being abused; this idea had been publicly dramatised by phrases such as 'the canker of monopoly complacency'; secondly, whether the administration of personnel was being properly carried out, devoid of favouritism, and thirdly whether tax-payers and licence holders were getting value for money.

The BBC had been incorporated by Royal Charter in 1927, and new amended charters had then been issued at ten-year intervals, prompting Haley to remark in 1948 that there was probably no other organisation in the country which was pulled up by its roots every ten years, and was so uncertain of its future. Notwithstanding root disturbance, in 1949 Beveridge's Broadcasting Committee had begun its comprehensive inquiry; resulting more than a year later in two massive volumes of 327 and 583 pages, respectively. Beveridge was an experienced broadcaster, and had drafted most of the report himself.

The Report encompassed the entire BBC field, including listener research, regional broadcasting, the treatment of religion and of the views of minorities, sponsored radio, the financing of television and its use in cinemas, and the continuation of monopoly.

Those in the BBC who had contributed a vast amount of evidence to the enquiry had derived great satisfaction from the Committee's announcement on the main issue of monopoly. In Volume II of the Report the fundamental question was asked whether all broadcasting, including the Overseas Service and Television, should continue as the monopoly of a single corporation, to which the Committee's answer was 'yes'. However, Selwyn Lloyd, then a junior Conservative Member of Parliament, had submitted a minority report, in which he had pressed for the introduction of commercial radio and commercial television, although the BBC was to continue in being to 'set standards'.

Although the Labour Government's firm intention had been to exclude competition, action had been delayed, and after a General Election, the Conservative Government, returned to power, had introduced a vague clause opening the door to future competition. Attlee, in opposition, immediately declared that if commercial competition were introduced it would be removed by a Labour Government. Thus future policy on broadcasting became a political issue, and objective arguments carried little weight. Strong pressure was also exerted by commercial interests which foresaw great profits from advertising.

On becoming Director General, Jacob was faced with the White Paper, Cmnd 8550 of May 1952, which contained the 'Trojan Horse' clause stating 'in the expanding field of television, provision should be made to permit some element of competition when the calls on capital resources make this feasible'. Thus he had to accept loss of monopoly as a *fait accompli*; he resolved to keep clear of the political battle, and devote the efforts of the Corporation to maintaining its position, its standards and its tradition in the face of powerful commercial rivalry.

During his absence at the Ministry of Defence, Ministers in Whitehall had also been taking an interest in the External Services of the BBC. Despite his vigorous championship of their cause while Controller, the grant-in-aid had fallen sharply in real terms between 1947 and 1952, and the output from Soviet broadcasts would soon be doubled, as would those of Poland and other members of the Warsaw Pact and of the Arabic Service from Egypt. In March 1951, the *Daily Mail* had commented: 'The Voice of America booms, the Voice of Stalin roars, the Voice of Britain must whisper'. Neither the Labour Party nor the Conservatives, and certainly not Churchill, were prepared to support increased expenditure; Gaitskell had proposed a cut of 20 per cent which Jacob had described as the 'height of folly in the present international situation'. The subject became so controversial that a Cabinet Committee of Inquiry had been set up in April 1952; they had been unanimous about the importance of all Overseas information work in the Commonwealth, Europe and in the 'Cold War'. This initiative was followed by the Drogheda Committee which first met in October 1952, and eighteen months later, in its report, gave support to three objectives which Jacob, much earlier had defined as:

> To support our foreign policy
> To preserve and strengthen the Commonwealth and Europe
> To increase our trade and protect our investments overseas.[6]

Neither inquiry recommended increased expenditure, but reported that the opportunities to achieve savings were 'restricted'.

During his years with External Services, Jacob had observed the entire panorama of a new and exciting industry with a sophisticated eye. With his alert intelligence, sharpened by those vintage years with Churchill, he had to a large extent foreseen the immense potentialities of television and the need for increased resources to permit rapid development, while safeguarding high standards of output and transmission. Moreover, he was sensitive to the tensions that had evolved within the organisation: tensions between those who regarded themselves as the trustees of the Reith tradition, the old hands who viewed the newcomers, experimenting with their TV tricks, sometimes with jealous suspicion and occasionally with disdain. If the best results were to be drawn from this hotch-potch of talent, he would have to nurture morale and weld together the disparate cliques of Broadcasting House, Bush House, Lime Grove and White City. But above all, he was determined that Reith's concept of a public service, providing every sector of the population with information, education and entertainment of the highest quality, should not be undermined by insidious pressures either from Government or from sponsors and entrepreneurs without the walls.

Unlike Haley, in whom he had detected a 'puritanical streak', Jacob did not set great store on maintaining large financial reserves. Even before the success of the Coronation broadcast, which would greatly increase the BBC's revenue, he had foreseen a considerable growth in income from combined television and radio licences. Although governmental restrictions on capital expenditure were still stringent, and in such a new field future costs were uncertain, his policy was to spend money where needed; but all such expenditure, whether for capital items or for running costs, was to be met out of revenue. He did not despise economy but objected to cheeseparing.

At that time there were 15,000 people in the Corporation and Jacob, who realised from his military experience that management of them required that their leader should have a recognisable face, spent a great deal of time getting to know everybody, dealing with their problems, helping individual directors and looking to the future.

Soon after his arrival, he had established his own priorities: he would concentrate particularly on the sensitive areas of news, current affairs, education and religion, as it was in those areas that criticism from Parliament and the public was likely to be frequent and dangerous. Drama, music and variety were in the hands of competent experts, and although controversies in those departments would also arise, they were likely to be academic rather than semi-political. If any of those experts expected their General to be a Philistine, they would soon find themselves mistaken: although neither in school, university nor India had the arts played a part in his life, his subsequent activities had provided some opportunities for appreciation, particularly in the case of opera and ballet, illuminated by his experiences in Moscow.

In programmes of Variety, questions of 'good taste' would often arise, and in religious broadcasts also the element of morality would enter. Jacob, while recognising that standards in society were changing, probably for the worse, took the view that it was wrong to suppose that the BBC had 'a missionary function'; nevertheless, the Corporation should reflect the best and not the worst in current society. The function of the Governors and the Director General was to maintain a steady course without departing from reasonable standards above those generally accepted by the less moral members of society; otherwise the creative staff would feel severely restricted, and would go elsewhere. It was a tight-rope act, and he accepted that those governing the BBC would inevitably fall sometimes on one side and sometimes on the other.

On the controversial matter of relations with the government of the day, Jacob, who still had access to many politicians, set out to strengthen the normal link for day-to-day business which was with the Chief Whips. He would only use his personal card of entry very sparingly.

Politicians in general tended to be much more critical of the BBC in the nineteen-fifties than they were later. This may have been due to two factors: first, that television was evolving very rapidly towards a destination which few could foresee and of which many were apprehensive, and secondly, that few politicians at that time had mastered the art of using television; when in later years they had realised its immense potential, they were less disposed to be hostile.

The year 1953 was a particularly busy period for Jacob. Inasmuch as the Board of Management was the focus of his administration, it was there that he would have to impress his personality on his directors and engage their loyalty. The directors concerned were Lindsay Wellington, Director of Home Sound Broadcasting; Sir Norman Bottomley, Director of Administration; Harold Bishop, Director of Technical Services; Sir George Barnes, Director of Television Broadcasting; JB Clark, Director of the External Services; and Harman Grisewood, Director of the Spoken Word.

Grisewood after hearing of Jacob's appointment, had written to him saying 'he had doubts about his post and that if Jacob wanted to do away with it, or with the holder of the job, he was quite willing to be transferred'. They then met in Jacob's office and Grisewood commented:

> . . . his office (in the Ministry of Defence) was disconcertingly large and dark. The fact that he could convey so much cordiality and good humour across the cavernous gloom was all the more reassuring to me. It was not only good humour . . . there was about his manner an interesting mixture of stolidity and alterness.[7]

Jacob had then decided to install Grisewood as his 'Chief of Staff'; and although Harman would have preferred a title which could be more readily interpreted by the BBC's hierarchy, the combination proved a great success, and their friendship continued for more than thirty years.

The Management Board met weekly on Mondays, and Jacob made a point of seeing each Director separately every week, as well as by other contacts during visits to their departments. At the Board, decisions were never taken by vote; Jacob, educated by Churchill, considered that that method of operating was unsound, since it implied that some director could not in all conscience agree, and therefore should resign. It was far better to put the matter back for further discussion, and hope thereby to achieve consensus: unanimity was usually achieved.

Jacob had had opportunities of observing many great men as chairmen – Chamberlain, Churchill, Attlee, Alanbrooke, Marshall, Roosevelt and Truman, to name a few – and had himself become a skilled exponent of the technique. The secretary who took the minutes was intrigued by the Chairman's profile, from which he inferred a dual capability: from one aspect the brisk, decisive traits of a general, and from the other hints of the ruminative and judicious character of the profound thinker. There was some truth in this.

However, it soon became clear to all members of the Board that the Chairman invariably had a very clear idea of the decisions he wished to reach, but was meticulous and patient in soliciting the views of every colleague present.

Grisewood once mentioned his exasperation with a colleague who was well known for his slow elaborate manner and his clumsy exposition. Jacob commented:

> You haven't patience enough; talking to him is like going along in a slow moving train through a long dark tunnel. Even if it is still dark after the first half-hour, you must keep on believing in the light at the other end![8]

Grisewood and many others in the BBC came to admire not only the persistence but also the generosity of the new Director General in his dealings with his supporters.

During the months when the BBC's monopoly had been under discussion in Parliament and elsewhere, Jacob had initiated three or four corporate plans designed to meet the Conservative Government's objections to monopoly without wrecking the BBC. The Governors had considered them, and were prepared to put them to the Government. However, they were then told categorically that Ministers were determined on satisfying two principles: first that any alternative TV programme should not be managed by the BBC, and second, that it should be financed by advertising. The BBC, for their part, were determined to have nothing to do with advertising.

Jacob then took a step which was to have a marked influence upon the Corporation's staff. He arranged a special meeting of the Management Board to take place in a good hotel at Climping near Arundel over a working weekend. His object was to raise morale, develop good relations with his directors, and with their assistance define the policies they must follow in meeting competition. To Grisewood, the tactic was a new departure, all the more welcome because of the good living, the cocktails and the port which accompanied it; he had retained a vivid recollection of meeting Reith long ago in the canteen, when he had heard 'with alarm the Director General's stern and eloquent praise for the rites of high tea'. Now he deduced that the new Director General 'saw no reason why the enjoyment of the good things of life should be incompatible with a high sense of duty and a lot of hard work.'[9]

At the meeting, a consensus was reached that the onset of competitive television, expected by 1955, would not change the existing principles and obligations of the Corporation. They must prevent any rival capturing the mass audience, otherwise the licence fee would lose its justification. The BBC TV Service, then rudimentary, should follow the same principles, and be developed by the introduction of a News Service, already anticipated, together with facilities for experiment and training, and the extension of programme hours. The BBC's Sound and TV Services should offer to the public a complete range of programmes for selective use; close association between the departments concerned should be encouraged, and the Corporation's policies, unrestrictive as possible, should be applied uniformly to both Services.

A major question facing them was the attitude they should adopt to their commercial competitors. Should they do everything possible to help them? Or should they treat them entirely in accordance with the BBC's interests? Or should they have no truck with them because of the conflict of interest between a public service corporation and a commercially motivated organisation? There should be no concession to competitors over programmes, but collaboration over relations with unions, copyright, fees and so on should take place. Jacob's policy was that they should assess in each case where the public interest lay; there might well be instances in which collaboration with the competitor would be desirable if the future of the BBC's Services was to be safeguarded. They should not adopt 'a dog in the manger' attitude.

Jacob emphasised the importance of the sporting programmes, and the danger of losing them to a competing organisation with strong financial backing; this would inflict great damage on the Corporation. Fortunately, it was discovered later that advertisers did not much like attaching their programmes to sporting events, as these were too irregular to conform to their commercially rigid arrangements. Thus the threat was never fully developed.

Jacob, with his directors, appreciated that, contrary to the popular view, the loss of monopoly would not produce competition for better broadcasting programmes: it would generate competition for larger audiences.

This implied competition to secure the 'raw material' needed to attract larger audiences, i.e. the writers, actors, journalists and producers. As the number of such talented people could not be suddenly increased, there would be a contest for them in the labour market, and hence the level of salaries would be crucial. It was for this reason that Jacob, with some reluctance, arranged for especially generous salaries to be provided for a few key personnel to ensure they were not attracted to the competitor's camp.

During this period the BBC's position was well maintained. The Corporation had the great advantage of a long-established place in the public's mind and, although at times considerable audiences were lost, the Corporation was able to finance and maintain its output without distortion and, in the battle of the ratings, did not have to resort unduly to inferior programmes to attract large uneducated audiences. The idea of public service was safeguarded, and quality was maintained. Moreover, the existence of competitors certainly invigorated the BBC staff: the urge to cover the whole field with good imaginative programmes was more strongly felt.

In February 1953, the Governors accepted Jacob's proposal that a Ten Year Plan, covering television and sound, should be drawn up to guide the Corporation into the future. He had found that Haley, his predecessor, had felt very strongly, only eight years after the war's end, that the nation could not afford to have too many people tied up in 'unproductive' occupations, and that the twelve thousand in the BBC should be the upper limit; hence Haley had been chary of authorising more money, more staff and more equipment for a service that might expand very rapidly. In an outline statement on BBC plans, published in June 1953, Jacob laid down that the Ten Year Plan should cover communications technology as well as finance. The aim should be to bring 95 per cent of the population within effective range of the TV service. The plan would require eight stations in addition to the five already planned, an increase in the TV service of two hours per day, encouragement of experiments in colour TV, and the introduction of an alternative TV service.

Jacob's initiative, which was approved by the Governors, set in train further planning on a five year basis which, by 1958, would produce many technical improvements, including a specially built Television Centre, costing £9 m, together with a staff to operate an expanded service in two channels. It was a feat of imaginative executive direction which established BBC Television on a level with any other competitor world-wide.

Throughout the previous year, many of the Corporation's staff and their engineeers, who with the Post Office engineers had won the admiration of the Director General soon after his arrival, had been preparing for the greatest opportunity in Television that had yet arisen anywhere in the world: the Coronation of Queen Elizabeth II in Westminster Abbey. Charles Max-Muller and SJ de Lotbiniere were the men responsible for policy decisions, WH Wood was in charge of engineering, and Peter Dimmock was the television producer of the Coronation programme. The young Queen herself favoured television, and the Duke of Norfolk, as her impresario for the whole event, soon overcame his initial repugnance, and thereafter gave encouragement to the BBC.

On 2 June, the Coronation was seen live in France, The Netherlands, Germany and Belgium through Eurovision relays, and telerecordings were dispatched throughout the world: 98 per cent of viewers recorded that they were completely satisfied, and the historian Arthur Bryant called the day 'the greatest achievement in the Corporation's history'. Only in the United States were the proceedings marred by the intrusion of advertising, and the appearance at a very solemn moment of a 'charismatic' chimpanzee; this led the *Daily Sketch*'s critic to report 'Jubilation among the BBC's Chiefs', as they heard the public exclaim loudly, 'Surely that sort of thing must never happen here! For the first time since this sponsorship battle began, Sir Ian is sitting pretty, and the viewing public, I believe, is solidly behind him.' Jacob sent round a message congratulating the staff on a most notable achievement, worthy in every way of the great event that was being celebrated.

In an interview years later, Jacob with his usual modesty said:

'I had practically no hand at all in the Coronation, as it was all in train when I arrived'. But a military commander, even if he takes over just before the battle, is answerable for any disasters that may occur. In the Coronation Programme, there were no disasters. A visit by the Queen to Broadcasting House and Lime Grove in October set the seal on the BBC's triumph. At that time Jacob's distinguished war service was known only to a few; now he had become a public figure. He and his wife would have the honour of staying with the Queen at Windsor Castle a few years later.

He was also evolving his management style: with regard to the large daily output of the Corporation, he accepted that he must bear full responsibility for it, but he was not disposed to become a Censor-in-Chief. The policy he laid down was that he was to be kept informed of any programme that broke new ground and might be controversial.

Throughout those years of rapid development and major change, he gave a lead in enunciating the principles which governed their operations. Thus in 1954 he wrote:[10]

> First, they should develop to the maximum the potentialities of the medium as a means of communication. There should be a constant effort to think of new ways in which information, interest and enjoyment could be conveyed. The value of any programme resided in its contents, whether it be grave or gay, serious or trivial. But however good the content, the programme failed if no one could absorb it. The challenge to the broadcaster was perpetually there – how could the programme be made to arouse the maximum interest and enjoyment?
>
> Secondly, the BBC must try to satisfy the needs and tastes of the full range of listeners and viewers. The public was not a uniform mass of people, but a great company of individuals with an almost infinite variety of interests, inclinations, enthusiasms, dislikes and prejudices. They had to try and achieve a similar variety in the programme services they presented. To express the situation in a negative way, something would be wrong if any one individual, however representative, found that he liked all the programmes.
>
> Thirdly, the BBC in its several programme services should include all types of material that it was possible to convey by broadcasting, provided that in each field the aim would be to search constantly for the best available. Much has already been done in that way. As television got into its stride still more could be done.
>
> Fourthly, the BBC should try so to enlighten the listener and viewer that they would tend to prefer what was best. This didn't mean that they should thrust down peoples' throats what they conceived to be good for them at the expense of what they wanted. It meant that every opportunity should be taken to lay before the audience, in each field of output, examples of the highest standard so that in the process of time they would come to reject that which fell below it. Many new vistas could be opened by broadcasting, and people might be enabled to explore some of which previously they were unaware. But the aim was not so much to change tastes and interests, as to raise them to the highest level of which they were capable.
>
> Finally, the BBC should embrace the world in its operations, while remaining responsive to national needs as those become evident.

One of Jacob's principal aims was to remove constraints on the Corporation's liberty of action, particularly in the field of news and current affairs, where he continued to emphasise the importance of accuracy and impartiality; and he insisted, against opposition from local vested interests in the Corporation, that news by television and news by radio should be under single control.

One of the irksome restrictions on the handling of political news was the so-called 'fourteen day rule', which had been enshrined in an Aide Memoire of 1947. Originally, the rule had been established in wartime by the then governors to protect the Corporation from what they regarded as an abuse of power by the Coalition Government; but, ironically, it had become a rod for the BBC's back, because it was used to veto discussions on important topical issues. The Aide Memoire had defined complicated rules about controversial party political broadcasts, and it contained the direction that:

> No broadcasts arranged by the BBC, other than the normal reporting of Parliamentary proceedings, are to take place on any question while it is the subject of discussion in either House.

This paragraph created difficulties, and in July 1948 Government and Opposition agreed with the BBC that it should be interpreted as:

> (a) The BBC will not have discussions or *ex parte* statements on any issues for a period of a fortnight before they are debated in either House:
> (b) While matters are subjects of legislation, MPs will not be used in such discussions.[11]

The object of the 'fourteen day' constraint was to maintain the supremacy of Parliament and prevent debates on the air becoming a substitute for those in the House.

Following a meeting in March 1953 between the political parties and the BBC, led by Jacob, the Governors asked that the rule be withdrawn, as it was unnecessarily restrictive and very much criticised. However, the leaders of the parties, including Churchill, strongly disagreed, and Cadogan was requested to drop his suggestion. In 1954, the BBC returned to the attack, demanding that the rule, if maintained, should be incorporated in the Corporation's licence, but once again at a meeting attended by Cadogan and Jacob, the Postmaster General disagreed. The dispute continued throughout 1954, the BBC using in argument the contrasting freedom afforded to the Press, but without avail. In July 1955, Dr Hill, the Postmaster General, with the support of both political parties, issued a regulation formally preventing the broadcasting of any discussion on issues about to be debated in either House of Parliament for a period of a fortnight before debates. By this time the restriction had been openly discussed and criticised in the national Press, but Churchill continued to stand his ground while some newspapers urged the BBC to 'do its duty', and ignore the regulation. In November 1955, an inconclusive debate took place in the House: this was followed by the setting up of a Select Committee, and finally the Postmaster General's directive was revoked for an experimental period of six months. It was finally disposed of by Prime Minister Macmillan in July 1957. By this time Jacob no longer had to fight the battle for freedom alone, but had enlisted a powerful ally in Independent Television. However, contro-versy inevitably continued as politicians discovered the power of tele-vision broadcasting and, within the BBC, techniques of production were further developed, leading to agreed codes of practice for 'party political' and 'ministerial' broadcasts and similar programmes. Jacob, pertinacious as usual, and versed in the political field, was well-qualified to fight the battle, supported by Cadogan his Chairman, and deserves credit for the abolition of the 14-day rule.

Nevertheless, despite the victory, peace and calm were short-lived. The nationalisation of the Suez Canal by Nasser on 26 July 1956 produced a situation in which the independence of the BBC was gravely threatened by disputes between the Corporation on the one hand and Eden, the Prime Minister, Gaitskell, the Leader of the Opposition, and certain Members of Parliament on the other. The fire that stoked these disputes was the profound division in the nation over the morality and wisdom of undertaking military operations against Egypt. Cadogan, at one time Eden's permanent-under-secretary and respected colleague, throughout the period of dissension was in a particularly difficult position, but staunchly defended the BBC's interests.

The Corporation sought steadfastly to preserve its reputation for political impartiality, and for truthfulness in the dissemination of news. Impartiality demanded that the agreed conventions designed to maintain balance in ministerial broadcasts, together with the right of reply, should be meticulously observed. Moreover, the BBC's repu-tation for truthfulness could not be sustained if items of home news, critical of the Government, were to be censored or distorted before they were transmitted in overseas broadcasts, addressed to those audiences which were unsympathetic to the British Government, and thereby potential enemies. It was indeed an established policy agreed by the Government, that the treatment of a news item in an overseas bulletin must never differ materially from its treatment in domestic news.

Moreover, Cadogan and Jacob took the view that with warlike operations impending, and the House of Commons recalled, Minis-ters and Opposition leaders would hardly think it desirable, even in the absence of a declaration of war, to engage through the media in party political strife; but as Jacob declared ruefully a year later:

> ... the procedures which govern political broadcasting were designed for domestic controversy of the kind that normally accompanies political life; a

national energency, where Government action was not nationally supported, presented a problem.

Eden, worn down by his attempts to lead a divided nation into war, and thwarted by the Corporation's defence of its principles, became so incensed by broadcasts which, in his view, gave comfort to the enemy and thus weakened the credibility of the threat to Nasser, that he sought to put great pressure on the BBC to 'toe the line'. Many of those in Britain whose husbands or sons were on the point of moving into battle were equally disgusted by an inflammatory broadcast by Gaitskell, in which he called for a new Prime Minister to halt the invasion and declare a ceasefire.

As evidence of Eden's pressure, Jacob, before leaving for a Commonwealth broadcasting conference in Australia, had been summoned to the Foreign Office where he was informed that one million pounds would be cut from the grant-in-aid for the BBC's External Services; but on the next day Cadogan with Jacob was able to persuade RA Butler to reduce the cut by half. However, they were not able to resist the appointment to the Corporation of a Foreign Office 'liaison officer', charged with watch-dog duties, whose prime function was to vet the BBC's news bulletins in Arabic, broadcast from Cyprus.

Eventually, with the British Government's acceptance of the United Nations' ceasefire and the withdrawal of the sick Prime Minister to recuperate in Jamaica, the BBC's problems in handling these difficult issues were temporarily laid to rest. In December, charges of political bias in the BBC were withdrawn after a Committee had found no evidence to support them.

Many Conservative Members of Parliament during the crisis had considered that undue emphasis had been given to the views of newspapers and individuals hostile to the Government, while for Labour the notorious Colonel Wigg had accused the BBC of 'indulging in Tory propaganda' and 'withholding the truth from the British people'. In the safety of the House of Commons, he had proclaimed that Jacob was 'a Tory stooge' and Cadogan 'a Foreign Office deadbeat'. The two individuals concerned were sufficiently robust to take comment from such a source as a compliment.

Jacob's views on the Suez affair were disclosed in a letter dated 26 April 1957 to the BBC's manager of the Cyprus Broadcasting Station:

Whatever may be the rights or wrongs of the decision taken by HMG, there is not the slightest doubt that the whole affair was monstrously bungled. The general muddle over broadcasting was appalling and we found, as I am sure you did, that we never knew from day to day where we stood. We can only regard it as a bad dream, and hope that people have woken up, and will act in the future in a more sensible manner.

On the twenty-first anniversary of BBC television on 27 October 1957, commemorating the first transmission of 1936, which were suspended during the war, Jacob spoke on the BBC Television Service.

Many of you will remember what it felt like to be twenty-one. It is a moment full of excitement. You're no longer a child, you've already tasted life, and the future stretches invitingly in front of you. You feel you can do anything.

We are now 21 in the BBC Television Service, and in some ways we share these feelings – but not altogether, because for a long time we have carried great responsibility as the national instrument in the most significant medium of communication of modern times.

When the BBC began its first regular transmissions from Alexandra Palace, four years ahead of anyone else in the world, I doubt if anyone realised what a tremendous force was being set in motion. There weren't many viewers, and the pioneers tried their hand at everything, and made the most of their opportunity. But long before our 21st birthday there came a change. We had to face a big question. And it wasn't only those in the BBC who had to face the question. It became a matter of importance to everyone as Television spread over the country.

On what principles should a national Television Service act?

First, it had to be a national job: it had to serve all the many kinds of people in the country, young and old, rich and poor, serious and frivolous. It had to serve Wales as much as Scotland, England as much as Northern Ireland; and it had to combine in its programmes the rich streams that flowed through all the main parts of Britain . . .

Secondly, there must be a full use of the power and possibilities of television. Entertainment was a very wide term: it included the light and the serious, the artistic and the trivial. All of them must be given in the best way that could be presented in television. The BBC must not be content to slip into a groove of repetition, or simply to serve up what could be presented elsewhere. Whether they gave an opera or variety, music or a play, a good talk or a football match, they must strive to get the highest standard of television performance and the last ounce of quality into it.

But there was more to it than that. Television had powers that no other medium possessed. In the studio and outside, it could stretch out and grasp life itself, as it was lived by people famous or unknown; they could see those who were changing the world, and the events that resulted from their action. To get these glimpses of truth, to meet these people in one's room, to follow their thoughts and to see events as they happen, this was something that perhaps only television could do.

Much had already been done. The urgent problems of the day had been constantly illustrated; they had become acquainted with countless men and women whose nature and mode of living had become alive . . .

He went on:

> How can we develop this further? by using colour? Yes, but I think there is something more significant than that, and Eurovision points the way.
>
> I believe that in the next twenty one years we are going much further afield. We cannot now watch the Queen arriving in Canada; we merely get pictures next day – we can't watch a new island rising from the oceans in the Azores. We can't watch the Olympic Games when they are held in Melbourne. But these things will become possible.
>
> In radio, we can hear the Foreign Minister of one country being questioned by several people, each of whom is in a different country. One day we shall see them all. If a satellite is launched in the Pacific, scientists here will be able to watch its departure. The world will truly be brought to us in our homes.
>
> I have said that we must do a national job, and the world itself must be the limit to our range. This great flow of ideas and activity means that we must speak to the nation, and reflect it and speak for it. This is a great task, which brings me to my third principle – responsibility.
>
> We already handle and shall increasingly handle great issues. We also deal in the many-sided life of the people, much of it lighthearted and trivial. We must be serious without being stuffy. We must be enterprising and imaginative without being heartless or insensitive to reason and honesty.
>
> Throughout we must act responsibly, with integrity and truth. We must faithfully reflect the greatness of our nation. . . .
>
> The BBC intends to act on these principles. We approach the task with a due sense of its difficulty and of its worth. We shall do our best to make the next twenty-one years of Television exciting and adventurous, and to make our service something of real value to the nation.
>
> In this way we shall gather the full fruits of the seed sown so bravely by the pioneers of twenty-one years ago.[12]

During Jacob's tenure as Director General, following this forecast, many new developments, particularly in television, took place. He took a keen interest in television for schools and fully acknowledged the creative influence of the Schools' Broadcasting Council. In his opinion, the special advisory councils, the regional ones and those for music, education, religion, appeals, agriculture and so on, could bring to bear upon the BBC a very knowledgeable influence and the Corporation would have been 'mad to operate without them'. The General Advisory Council, consisting of men and women with high reputations in their particular fields, were in a different category: they were hardly in a position to criticise or advise on any particular aspect of broadcasting brought to their attention, because the Executive knew so much more about the technicalities than they did; but their value lay in the reverse direction, in explaining to the educated public the policies and activities of the Corporation.

On 14 October 1957, the Queen made her first television broadcast;

and in February 1958 there appeared for the first time the important Medical Series, *Your Life in Their Hands*. Also in that month, Macmillan was the first Prime Minister to appear in a regular TV programme – *Press Conference*. In July, the BBC's engineers took pride in the success of their first live television programme from Africa, transmitted via Eurovision, a system which, despite some opposition from the trade unions, had developed well under Jacob's leadership. Another Eurovision success was the Coronation of Pope John XXIII. The State Opening of Parliament was first televised on 28 October 1958, and in January 1959, John Freeman's highly successful programme called *Face to Face* was first televised. On 8 October of that year, the BBC covered the General Election campaign in news broadcasts for the first time.

Throughout Jacob's tenure as Director General, he was intent on widening the scope of the Corporation's output while preventing the intrusion of items of poor taste. A selection of his replies to a variety of critics, demonstrates his fair-minded attitude in defending the BBC's judgement, independence and impartiality.[13]

On propriety in a light entertainment programme: 8 September 1955

> Mr Harding is somewhat of an eccentric and there are times when his attitude and bearing go beyond what is proper even in a light entertainment programme; but his characteristics are well known, and on balance it seems to me better to have someone who, though he may occasionally annoy and irritate, can also stimulate, rather than to fall back on a flat level of boring propriety.

On an inaccurate statement in *Any Questions*: 5 February 1957

> I am sorry that the speakers in *Any Questions* last Friday made inaccurate reference to the cadet training ship HMS *Worcester*. The first person to draw attention to the mistake was a member of our own staff who was listening to the programme, and, as you know, a correction of fact was made by the Question Master later in the programme.
>
> We have taken two further steps to put matters right: we have arranged to move the reference from the repeat broadcast which takes place today, and we have invited the Secretary of *Worcester* to write a brief letter, giving the true facts about the ship, which would then be broadcast on Thursday evening in 'Any Answers', which is the counterpart of 'Any Questions'. I very much hope he will do this. It is by far the best way of seeing that a large number of listeners clearly understand what the facts are.

On religious prejudice: 25 February 1957

> I am afraid that your mailbag shows only too clearly what ours demonstrates every day, that there are a large number of people in this country who seem to

think that everything that does not agree with their own view should be pro-hibited, and I fear that religious people are some of the worst offenders.

On impartiality in political broadcasts: 29 October 1957

In general, people notice those programmes with which they disagree, and pass by those with which they agree. This, I think, accounts for people on both sides of politics thinking that their adversaries get a larger share of the cake.

On public criticism of the BBC: 26 March 1958

A great deal of it has little foundation in reality. For the rest we always have made an occasional mistake and shall continue to do so. If we do not, it would be a sign that we were trying nothing new and adventurous.

On an unsuitable item in Children's Television: 13 November 1958

I have been looking into the matter of the On Safari programme broadcast in Children's Television on 2nd November, about which you wrote to me. I agree with you that this was not a suitable item for children and should not have been included. Perhaps the best thing I can do is to send to you the enclosed letter from the Head of the Department which explains, although it does not excuse, how this happened. Thank you for drawing my attention to it; I do most sincerely regret this lapse in the usual good standards which we try to maintain in programmes for children's viewing.

To a military friend who criticised a play: 19 January 1959

Your must forgive me if I deal rather bluntly with your criticisms, but I get rather tired of people who object to things in plays, because they don't conform to things that ought to happen. They would be damned dull if they did.

On impartiality in Broadcasting: 6 October 1959

You seem to think that I have been conducting the BBC for the last seven years without paying attention to what it does. I can assure you that the question of impartiality, which is one of the key points in the conduct of broadcasting, is bound to be the continual concern of whoever is in charge, and has certainly been mine. You say there is a large body of opinion that is convinced that the BBC is red. This remark does not surprise me in the least because there is an equally large body of opinion which is convinced that the BBC is a hide-bound organisation, 'the prop of the Establishment', and rootedly opposed to anything left wing. This is bound to be the situation of anybody who tries to steer a course down the centre.

At the end of November 1957, Cadogan aged seventy-two, had retired from the Chairmanship of the Board of Governors. With Jacob he had steered the Corporation through a challenging period of five years in which unparalleled development had taken place. On the ideals of a public service independent of the Government, on the preservation of impartiality and on maintaining the quality of output, he and his Director General had had similar views; it had been a harmonious and successful partnership.

His successor, Sir Arthur fforde, who was to remain as Chairman for seven years, came from a different background. He had been a solicitor, and a Member of the Council of the Law Society, and during the war had served as a civil servant in the Ministry of Supply and in the Treasury. He had then become Headmaster of Rugby School. Transparently honest, he was a quiet, sensitive and unobtrusive chairman, with an esoteric sense of humour and a great capacity for friendship. He quickly established with Jacob a very close relationship which was fully reciprocated.

On 27 September 1959 Jacob reached the age of sixty, and for some time past he had been considering whether he should retire. There could be no doubt in his mind that his tenure had been successful, and he had enjoyed it to the full. It was obvious to many of his colleagues that he had found the job exhilarating, and happily some of that exhilaration had passed down the line. Not one of his predecessors had continued in office to the age of sixty, the BBC's normal age of retirement; Reith and Ogilvie had retired at forty-eight, Graves and Haley at fifty-one and RW Foot at fifty-four. Jacob had done seven years as Director General, and an important consideration was the imminence of the next enquiry into broadcasting: it was looming a year or two ahead. He therefore felt that he must either stay for another five years and see the Corporation through and beyond the next enquiry, or go at once and give his successor ample time to prepare for the enquiry and the revised charter that might follow. In his view, broadcasting was a young man's job and, after the age of sixty, a Director General might find himself increasingly out of sympathy with many of the ideas that would arise from the creators of output – the young writers, journalists and producers. Rather than finding himself acting as a brake on the machine, he felt he would much prefer to cut adrift from a job which was very demanding, and seek more varied and less intensive activities. So on 31 December 1959, after a total of thirteen and half years' service Jacob retired from the BBC.

He left behind a 'last testament' entitled *The BBC: Past and Future*. Addressed to the Corporation's staff, it provided not only a summary of his stewardship, but also guidance for the future, much of which has relevance today.[14]

THE BBC: PAST AND FUTURE
Memorandum by the Director General

In July 1953 when it became evident that commercial television was certain to be introduced in one form or other the Board of Management met over a weekend to take stock of the position and to decide on measures to meet the impending competition. It is interesting to re-read the conclusions of that meeting and to see how the reality compares with what was foreseen. A paper was put to the Board of Governors at that time in which the Board of Management's conclusions were incorporated, and which ended with the following passage:

> It would be foolish to minimise the probable effect of competition on the general policy to be followed by the Corporation, even though it may not become apparent in the early stages. Much will depend upon the form taken by our competitors, on the money that they will have at their disposal, and the drive that they put behind their operations. The Corporation ought to be able to hold its own because it starts with so many advantages, but there is bound to develop a struggle for the mass audience. The Corporation can never afford to let the people of the country feel that they have no incentive to buy a licence. There will be many difficulties of detail, but we have not seen any which cannot be overcome. It is the main threat to Corporation policy which gives us the greatest concern.

There were indeed many difficulties of detail, which we have successfully overcome, but the main point at issue was whether in the face of competition we could pursue our traditional policy. Would the inevitable struggle for the audience force us to abandon our standards, our range, and our integrity? We have now had four years' experience, and during that time we have had the handicap of doing our work in Television without the freedom given by a second service. We can confidently state that we have proved that it is possible to succeed in our aims even in the face of strong competition. The only question on which there is doubt is whether the average audience that we can command, i.e. 35–40 per cent of the public who have a choice of programme, is sufficient to satisfy the claims of a national broadcasting organisation. I unhesitatingly state that it is. We would be in grave danger, in my opinion, if we had secured a 50:50 *average*, because in doing so we would have made our output indistinguishable from that of the ITV. There may be 40 per cent of the public who normally stay with the commerical programmes. There are perhaps 25 per cent who stay normally with the BBC. The remaining 35 per cent switch from one to the other. There is no doubt, however, that the significance of the 25 per cent far outweighs that of the 40 per cent. The greater part of the educated, thinking, and articulate public is numbered in the former.

In the last six years the quality of the TV output of the Corporation has steadily improved in all fields. The service had done more than keep pace with technical developments, increased resources, and greater programme allowance. It has made striking advances, and has established higher standards. It has made errors of course, but it has made fewer than might have been expected in the difficult conditions of recent years. There is nothing to fear from an analysis of the output or a comparison with what is done elsewhere in the UK or abroad.

The Sound Services have not had their due share of public attention, and have had to operate in the knowledge that their evening audiences were being steadily whittled away. They have had the satisfaction of a free run of the air in the mornings, and they have known that their many audiences, though much smaller than in the past, still derive great enjoyment from what they hear . . .

The position of the External Services has always been somewhat precarious for reasons that are well known. The annual financial battle is a recurring menace, and it has to be fought largely at second-hand and in competition with other information agencies who have the inside position. In spite of all this the standing of the BBC abroad is as high as ever, and we have no cause to fear any objective examination of our work. As a new public enquiry could only deal with a very limited aspect of our External Services, there is no need to say more, except to emphasise the importance to the Corporation of its being the instrument which represents this country on the air throughout the world.

To sum up, I would say that the Corporation is in excellent shape to face any investigation. Its policy is steady and its output is as enterprising, as wide-ranging and as imaginative as that of any other body in the world – indeed more so. It has maintained a high standard. Such criticisms as can be made of it are those which can more properly be made of the state of modern society in this country, of which inevitably a broadcasting output is the reflection.

What, then, is the danger now to be apprehended? I would explain it in this way:

Very strong forces are going to be deployed against us before the Committee of Enquiry. They will not appear as being against the

BBC or indeed against public service broadcasting, but as strong advocates of the extension of commercial Television, and of the introduction of commercial Sound broadcasting. Their opposition to us will take an indirect form, the opposing of the idea that the BBC has any need to entertain. They will seek to confine the BBC permanently to a subordinate role while opening the door to an extension of commercial operations in every field. The people who will join together to generate these forces will be those who see broadcasting merely as a means of making money, and those drawn from the manufacturing and advertising industries who see it merely as a valuable means of extending the selling mechanism of industry and commerce. These will be their basic aims though they will cloak them with talk of competition.

The problem for us is how best to defeat these forces and maintain the system of public service broadcasting and the BBC's position. It should be noted that outside the interested groups mentioned above the natural habit of mind is quite different from theirs. It takes the BBC for granted, assumes its future to be secure, and regards it as an essential stabilising element in the world of broadcasting. Men and women who have this starting point are likely to provide the membership of the Committee of Enquiry. They will at first be unaware of what is at stake. They will soon find out that the hard facts of channels, finance, and conflicts of interest demand that they examine more deeply the underlying basis of broadcasting, and it will then be for the Corporation to make its case. What the Corporation has to demonstrate is:

1. The importance of public service broadcasting (and this must be defined).
2. That the existence of a strong and independent BBC is essential if public service broadcasting is to survive.
3. That conditions must be such that the BBC can do its work effectively.
4. That the provision of the funds necessary for the BBC's work is essential and possible.

It must be brought home to the Committee that something of serious importance is at stake, and that it is not merely a question of judging between equal interests by arriving at a business-like compromise.

The definition of public service broadcasting is of crucial importance. It can hardly be put in one sentence. It is a compound of system of control, an attitude of mind, and an aim, which if successfully achieved results in a service which cannot be given by any other means. The system of control is full independence, or the maximum degree of independence that Parliament will accord. The attitude of mind is an intelligent one capable of attracting to the service the highest quality of character and intellect. The aim is to give the best and the most comprehensive service of broadcasting to the public that is possible. The motive that underlies the whole operation is a vital factor; it must not be vitiated by political or commercial considerations.

The BBC as established by its original Charter, as inspired by its founders, and as developed in subsequent renewals of its Charter, goes nearer to achieving this ideal of public service than does any organisation elsewhere in the world. It is for this reason that it has been taken as the model in so many places; that constantly foreign people – Ministers, broadcasting authorities, sociologists and others – come to study its constitution and practice; and that students flock from all countries to take part in its schools of Training. It has an unrivalled reputation throughout the world. It is the acknowledged leader among European organisations. It has achieved this position because it has been strong and independent, stable and solvent. Its services have become an accepted – indeed an essential – part of the lives of all classes of people in this country, including the most intelligent and the most humble. Nowhere else in the world has broadcasting achieved so complete a result. The contents of the *Radio Times* surpasses in range and comprehensiveness that of any other programme schedule in the world. These statements, though they may be classed as assertions, can be tested and will be found to be entirely true. They are no less true than they were 5 years or so before ITV came on the scene. They will not remain true unless certain conditions to be specified later are fulfilled.

It hardly seems necessary to argue whether or not quality and range in broadcasting are important. One has only to look at the place which broadcasting, and particularly Television, now occupies in the life of every individual to realise that these two characteristics are of paramount importance. To allow broadcasting to consist of output which is merely good enough to attract the people in their unthinking mood, and to limit its horizon to proved successes would be a grave failure. The full exploitation of the medium, the search for new capabilities, the insistence on quality in all forms of programme, and the setting of a high standard throughout – these are the marks of a first-class broadcasting service. They can only be attained by the public service system for reasons that are described below. A strong and healthy BBC is a *sine qua non* of good broadcasting.

We have all seen the evil results that flow from political control of broadcasting. When complete, political control results in mere propaganda, but even when it is partial it leads to a stifling of initiative, and the avoidance of inconvenient forms of output. It drives away those independent-minded men whose presence is so necessary to a first-class operation.

Less obvious perhaps, but no less insidious, is the effect of commercial control. The motive that inspires the service becomes clouded because success in selling goods, and thus in attracting commercial clients, becomes the overriding consideration. This confusion of motive does not arise in industry because the aims of industrial operations are themselves commercial. In broadcasting the aims diverge, and the motive that determines the supply of money dominates.

Analogies drawn from the Press are not in many respects valid, but in so far as they are valid they are not reassuring. The popular Press is driven by the need for a large advertisement revenue to subordinate all other considerations to that of large circulation. This is not conducive to quality. One sees in the controlling interests of the popular press a cynicism and a contempt for intellectual standards which everyone deplores but which no one has been able to eradicate. These same characteristics come to exist in varying degree in the control of commercial broadcasting.

I have stated above that in the last four years of competition the BBC has held its own, has maintained its standards, and has steadily improved its output. It has been able to do this mainly because its highly-skilled staff have been able to use their experience in conditions of stability, and with the backing of adequate funds secured to the Corporation with no strings attached. The financial future must be squarely faced but first let us see what other conditions are necessary to enable the BBC to carry on successful public service broadcasting. I would list these as follows:

1. No change in the unitary system. The public service instrument must not be fragmented, and must embrace Sound, Television and External Services.

   There are some who argue for the creation of another public body to conduct a third Television Service. This could only result in a fatal weakening of the resources behind public service broadcasting, and would add to the forces tending towards the degradation of output. There are others who quote the printing press, and say that there is no need to check in any way the freedom of broadcasting. They visualise a kind of free-for-all in broadcasting, with the maximum diversity of origination and control. This might be a sensible conception if there were unlimited frequencies so that anyone with the necessary backing could start a station in any chosen part of the country. The situation, however, is a different one which makes this conception impracticable. Because the number of outlets is severely restricted it has been necessary to concentrate in a few hands the control of those that exist. A few chosen instruments of broadcasting have to be created. In these circumstances it is necessary to take positive steps to ensure that the public service instrument is strong and independent enough to do a real job.

2. The independence of the BBC must be maintained intact. This point needs no elaboration.

3. If there is to be more Television, the BBC must have a second service.

There are formidable difficulties in the way of more Television. These, and how they might be surmounted, have been dealt with in the paper submitted by the Corporation to the TAC. The ability to give the viewer an alternative public service choice has always been one of the Corporation's aims. Many people regard it as a disaster that the BBC was not allowed to achieve its aim in 1955 and that commercial TV was established instead. The mistake then made cannot be rectified, but it should certainly not be enlarged.

4. The Sound broadcasting monopoly should be preserved.

It would be singularly foolish to repeat the error made in 1955 by permitting commerical radio to be introduced. This is peculiarly important because of the form it would almost certainly take – namely the proliferation of small cheap stations, with no output beyond local trivialities and gramophone records. The idea of such stations, apart from its commercial attractions, has an appeal to those who quite rightly regard the preservation of local interest as important. They point to the local newspaper. Unfortunately the financial facts of life ensure that the local station if run commercially shall be an animated juke-box. This can be seen in many parts of the world. It is much too easy to make money by broadcasting of this type to make it worth anyone's while to attempt anything better. The collapse of responsible radio of the comprehensive type built up by the BBC would be a high price to pay for the satisfaction of local money-makers. The BBC should itself develop radio, spreading its possible services to the public to the extent required by changing requirements, but preserving the quality of the output.

We come finally to the question of finance. The foundation of good broadcasting is adequate money with independence in spending it. This has been assured in the past thirty years by the licence system. The growth of licences has been steady, and as sound licences approached saturation the TV or combined licence came in. The needs of the BBC for capital and revenue expenditure, for rising costs, and for development have been met. The great merit of the licence system is that the income of the BBC is tied to an actual scale of payments by the public. The amount to be received can only be varied by the process of fixing the percentage of the licence currently in force that shall be handed over. No other system yet devised has the same degree of automatic assessment combined with direct relation to the service given. The policy of the BBC should be to preserve at all costs this highly effective system. It is only the existence of the licence system that has enabled the Corporation to maintain its remarkable degree of independence of political or commercial pressures, and to avoid undesirable forces, whether Governmental or private, from gaining a footing in its control.

Some people argue that to exclude advertisements from broadcasting is to deprive industry and the public of a service which they are entitled to have. This may or may not be so. It is certain, however, that the quickest way of ruining the BBC and bringing public service broadcasting to an end in this country would be to narrow the differences that exist between our output and practice and those of the commercial system. If these differences disappeared the *raison d'être* of the BBC would disappear too. Hence, quite apart from the likely effects on our control of our output which would follow the introduction of a commercial element into our operations, a move to seek revenue from advertising would be the height of folly. The history of the Canadian Broadcasting Corporation is an object-lesson if one were needed.

Can we be sure that the licence system will give us the necessary resources in future as it has in the past? Our present expenditure demands the whole of the present net licence revenue, and desirable developments in Sound and Television cannot now be satisfied fully by the natural growth of licence numbers. If there is to be more Television, perhaps colour, and if local Sound broadcasting is to be exploited, the licence fee will have to rise . . .

30 December 1959 IJ

Jacob's style of management and his achievements as Director General were assessed with sympathy and accuracy in a tribute written by Sir Arthur fforde, Chairman of the Governors. It was published in *Ariel*, the BBC's House Magazine, in December 1959 (Vol 4 Number 12).[15]

> It is said in *Ariel* . . . that some people are born and remain conspicuous, and others inconspicuous: but that Sir Ian belonged to a third category, those who can make themselves invisible when they wish to, but (if they wish) can also compel attention and dominate those with whom they are dealing. This was a true assessment. One might add, perhaps, that one measure of the success of this kind of person is that he very seldom needs to do the latter.
>
> Sir Ian himself has been heard to observe that 'Nobody can cover the whole waterfront'. In conversation, the brevity and conciseness of his utterances might suggest at first hearing that his duties and problems are simple and easy of solution. But to put to him any closer question about any aspect of broadcasting in any part of the world, is to discover that there is little of any waterfront, or any landfront either, about which he is uninformed, or concerning which he is without definite and considered views. If he normally chooses to remain invisible, it is partly because it is not his practice, until the need arises, to disclose his reserves. When he does so, they are ready to call for orderly and swift deployment: an extensive knowledge of facts, figures, problems and personalities, and a wide range of interests, aptitudes, recollections, and prognostications; marshalled by an energy inexhaustible yet in repose; obedient to an imperturbable and serious purpose; and enlivened by a perceptive zest for recreation as well as work.
>
> These are among the qualities which have sustained him, and through him and his colleagues have sustained the BBC, in seven years of rapid expansion, and of problems new and strange. As with his distinguished predecessors, the responsibilities of the office have steadily grown; and it is not too much to say that the quality of the production has grown in proportion. For what statistics of listeners and viewers may be able to tell, his period of office has seen an increase of combined Sound and Television licences from under 2,000,000 to over 10,000,000. . . .
>
> None of these things, Sir Ian would at once observe, happen because of one man, but it is also true that one man, in his position, could easily have produced

a situation in which they could not have happened so well. The visible achievement manifestly owes much to many people. Invisible behind them, has been his clarity of thought, patient judgement and firm decision.

In these ways Sir Ian Jacob has in the main followed and furthered the pattern set by his predecessors. But his term of office differs from theirs, partly in its extension of co-operation with other countries, notably through the European Broadcasting Union, which he initiated and over which, since 1955, he has presided: and, most clearly, in the fact that he is the first Director General who has been faced with the emergence in Television, of a competitor, in this country, and with the challenges which that development has brought to the BBC.

It is clear enough, even from this very incomplete catalogue of subjects, that to be a Director General of a round-the-clock service round the world, is to be on call, in many directions, at all times: and, active as he is, and little as we welcome his decision, none can question his right to decide that at the end of the year the time has come for him to turn to fields of action less intensive and less demanding. He takes with him the gratitude and goodwill of all who have had the good fortune to work with him and for him, in the public Service Broadcasting of the BBC.

14

'Never Look Back'

On New Year's Day 1960, Jacob's name appeared once again in the Honours List: he was promoted to Knight Grand Cross in the Order of the British Empire. He received a great number of congratulations, many from his colleagues in the BBC, some of whom would maintain their friendship with him for years to come. On the day before, he had shed his responsibilities for leading, managing and defending the Corporation, and he felt confident that under Hugh Greene it would survive with its principles intact alongside powerful competition from commercial television.

Now he could spend much more time at the Red House, the attractive focus of his life as a countryman in Suffolk.

However, his managerial talents had been quickly recognised beyond the walls of Broadcasting House, and two industrial companies had already invited him to join them as a non-executive director: the first was Electrical and Musical Industries, with Sir Joseph Lockwood as Chairman, and the second Fisons, under Lord Netherthorpe. The Boards of these and other companies soon found that Jacob's clear analytical brain, his ability to identify rapidly the root of a complicated matter, and his sound judgement, were of great value, and his association with them continued for many years.

Ever since his return from Egypt in 1938, Jacob had identified himself with Suffolk. Now, he put his name forward to stand for the County Council to which he was elected in 1960. Nine months later, he became a Justice of the Peace, in 1964 a Deputy Lieutenant, and in 1970, an alderman. He had also accepted the Chairmanship of the Army Benevolent Fund at a crucial time when the Committee was about to launch a major appeal, which in due course was crowned with success.

Although based in Suffolk, he took pains to keep in touch with many of his wartime colleagues, particularly Lord Ismay: a happy occasion was a dinner in London to mark the publication of Ismay's Memoirs. This took place on 26 September 1960, and was attended by Churchill, now aged eighty-five, as guest of honour. The other guests were General Pownall, Lord Cunningham of Hyndhope, Lord Alexander, Sir Alan Lascelles, Sir Edward Spears, Lord Portal, Sir Robert Laycock, Colin Coote, and Jock Colville.

In the autumn of 1961, he was asked to take on an unusual task: to be Chairman of the Covent Garden Market Authority, which had been set up by Act of Parliament to plan and carry out the removal of the markets from the Covent Garden site and re-establishing them in a more suitable location. The 'instrument of appointment', to run for a period of five years, was signed by Christopher Soames, Minister of Agriculture and Churchill's son-in-law. Among the Committee members was Charles Forte, whose contribution to the work of the Committee was particularly valuable.

All these new activities in commerce and in the service of the Government involved frequent visits to London. Jacob often stayed at the Army and Navy Club where he was particularly welcome because, at a critical moment in the Club's history, when its finances were in a bad way, he with some other members, had intervened successfully to prevent its closure.[1]

This unlikely event had occurred in 1957 when Jacob was still Director General of the BBC. A member of the Club had visited him in Broadcasting House to tell him that the Chairman of the Club had worked out with the Chairman of the United Services Club, the 'Senior', a scheme under which the Army and Navy Club, the 'Rag' would sell its entire freehold buildings and join up with the Senior, taking with it its funds and its possessions.

The scheme was far advanced with a purchaser already interested, and was about to be put to the membership for 'rubber stamping' by way of a referendum. It appeared that alternative schemes, by which the continuation of the Rag might be assured, had not been considered; moreover the Chairman of the Rag, who was in the property business, had handled the scheme behind closed doors from the office of his own company as a simple property deal.

The dissenting Committee member was greatly concerned that the Rag with its century-old tradition should not be absorbed by another club, and he appealed to Jacob to intervene. Jacob advised him that the only way to proceed was to lodge a demand for an Extraordinary General Meeting. Provided that the members who opposed the scheme first resigned from the Committee, as was proper, Jacob would do his best to prevent the scheme going ahead. The dissenting members, who were in the minority, duly resigned on the grounds that they disagreed with the Committee's statement that there would soon not be room for more than two Service Clubs in London; they also maintained that the Senior was already overcrowded, that the Rag's freehold, valued then at £400,000, was in jeopardy, and that to take a vote by referendum was inappropriate and dangerous. Their intention was to preserve their own Club – the Rag.

Accordingly Jacob, accompanied by two supporters, requested an Extraordinary General meeting and addressed the Committee, putting to them the simple issue: 'Did they attach primary importance to the continuance of the Rag, or would they be satisfied provided a Service Club continued to exist, no matter which?' Meanwhile, the Chairman of the Club, whose behaviour had been criticised, resigned from the Committee and from the Club. Eventually, the Extraordinary General Meeting was held on 30 April 1957 and by a vote of 386 to 158 a simple resolution, tabled by Jacob was passed:

> That no referendum relating to the amalgamation with another Club shall be sent to members until a new Committee has come into being in June and has time to reconsider the question.

This decision temporarily preserved the identity of the Club, but did not solve the problem of its economic viability. General Sir Richard Gale then became Chairman, and investigations were put in hand, leading to a decision that consideration be given to the sale for redevelopment of the Club's detached freehold sites at 46 and 47 Pall Mall, and rebuilding of the Club on the remainder of the site facing St James's Square. On the departure of General Gale to become Deputy Supreme Commander in 1958, Jacob became Chairman and, despite numerous problems – architectural, artistic, financial, legal and managerial – the membership enthusiastically approved plans for the new Club at an Extraordinary General Meeting on 28 October 1959 and authorised the sale of numbers 46 and 47 Pall Mall for the sum of £680,000, an increase of 70 per cent on the previous figure.

Jacob had been ably assisted by a number of members who had volunteered to help, including Major General GN Russell, Major General WS Cole, Colonel WLR Benyon, Major General RJ Moberly, Major General PH de Havilland, and Major General Cosmo Nevill.

On 1 October 1962, Jacob, as Chairman, laid the foundation stone

of the new Club: and on 16 June 1965, to the great regret of the
membership he resigned the Chairmanship after a span of seven
years. The history of the Army and Navy Club recorded:

> ... It was Sir Ian's hand at the helm that had steered the Club past the shoals,
> rocks and reefs, through the troubled and indeed shark-infested waters of the
> past seven years. ...

The project proved to be an outstanding success, and the
popularity and viability of the Club has continued to the present day.

In January 1963, Jacob was asked once again to carry out an
enquiry on behalf of the Government. The problem on this occasion
transcended in importance the selling and despatch of London's
flowers, fruit and vegetables: it was the central organisation of
defence, a highly controversial question which would have ramifica-
tions in Whitehall and throughout the Armed Services for more than
twenty-five years. Jacob, with his wartime experience and his recent
enquiries into the organisation of the War Office and of NATO, was
well placed to handle this problem, which had been at the back of his
mind since 1940 and, most prominently after the disastrous operations in Norway.

Moreover, alongside Ismay and Bridges, he had been a major
contributor to the Defence White Paper of 1946. The questions
before the Government at that time had included the functions of a
peace-time Prime Minister in relation to defence, the organisation of
munitions supply, the balance to be struck between the individual
Services and a central organisation, the future place of CID sub-
committees, and the impact on British defence organisation of the
United Nations, and of the United States as possessors of the atomic
bomb. They had considered three alternatives: an all-powerful Minister of Defence at the head of a Ministry which would absorb the
Service departments: a Combined General Staff on the lines of the
former German *Oberkommando der Wehrmacht* (OKW), and lastly an
independent Chairman of the Chiefs of Staff who would report
directly to the Minister of Defence. All these had been rejected as
being too extreme. Hence, in their report to Attlee, they had recommended a more modest proposal, the introduction of 'a guiding hand
to formulate a unified defence policy and to ensure regular examination of Service programmes.'

Their proposals, welcomed as an interim stage in a process of
evolution, had resulted in 1947 in the formation of a small Ministry of
Defence, headed by a Minister who was to act as the Prime Minister's

Deputy Chairman of a new Defence Committee. That Committee was to include the Service Ministers, certain key Cabinet ministers and the Chiefs of Staff. In addition, a Defence Research Policy Committee under a scientist, and a Ministerial Production Committee with a joint war production staff, were established.

Although the new Defence Minister was in a better position than the unfortunate wartime 'Minister for the Co-ordination of Defence', he was still under the disadvantage that the constitutional responsibility to Parliament of the heads of the individual Services remained unchanged. Thus, in the fields of his own responsibility, which were specified as the allocation of resources in broad outline and the establishment of a common administrative policy for the three Services, he had to proceed by persuasion, but backed by the Prime Minister. The authority of the individual Chiefs of Staff was safeguarded, and they remained fully responsible for executive action.

It was hardly surprising that this interim organisation fell short of achieving its main purpose of reconciling the conflicting financial demands of the three Services, particularly as Attlee's first Minister of Defence was AV Alexander, whose reputation in the Cabinet did not stand high. Montgomery, the CIGS, who had been riding rough-shod over his naval and air colleagues in the Chiefs of Staff Committee, had been much frustrated by their lack of enthusiasm for long-term joint planning. He had written in February 1947 to Freddie de Guingand, his wartime Chief of Staff:

> . . . the Chiefs of Staff are a useless body. We never initiate anything; we meet and deal with whatever the Secretariat put on the agenda; we resemble a Board of Directors. I would say we are a completely spineless outfit. Tedder is utterly useless as a Chairman; he sits on the fence and never gives a definite opinion on any matter.[2]

Some months before, Montgomery had contemplated asking his colleagues to agree that Jacob be brought back to Whitehall, but had discarded the idea because he thought they would suspect some ulterior motive. He had also made a revealing comment to Jacob on the ministers he had served:

> The Secretary of State has only got to do two things. He must understand and he must decide. I have served so far with three of them. The first was Lawson, and he could do neither. He was only interested in the letters he received from individuals, which he carried about stuffed in his pockets. The second was Bellenger. He could decide but he couldn't understand. The third was Shinwell. He can both understand and decide, and is thus very good.[3]

In the following year, Jacob, still an active member of the Council of the Royal Institute of International Affairs, had continued his interest in Defence, despite his employment in the BBC, and he had discussed the unification of the Services with Montgomery, the CIGS, and had written a paper, a copy of which was later given to Montgomery:

The Unification of the Services

The quality which the nation must demand of its Defence organisation is professional skill. This must take two forms. First, tactical and technical skill. Sailors must be first-rate sailors both in handling their ships and in the use of their weapons. Soldiers and airmen must be similarly adept at their respective trades. Secondly, strategical skill. This consists in the ability to look at warfare as a whole and to apply tactical and technical skill in the most effective way. What we want, therefore, is a system which will allow both forms of skill to develop to the full. If you examine the Services as they are now constituted, you will find just what we need within each Service, but not in the relationship between them. Let us take two examples.

A ship has a complement which consists very largely of special-ists. Among the junior ratings and ranks there are a few who perform general duties, but the majority are assigned to particular tasks for which they receive special training, superimposed on the basic training which all sailors are given. When you reach the top of the heirarchy on board the ship, you find the captain, a man who earlier in his career had been a specialist in gunnery, or navigation, or air, but who now takes a general view and seeks to apply the power of his ship and the various skills of all on board to the best advantage.

Similarly, in the Army, the other ranks, after basic training, join one of the arms, cavalry, artillery, infantry, etc., and stay there for their whole service. The officers, after a general educa-tion at a military college, also join their selected arm of the service. There they normally remain, except when they join offi-cers from other arms on courses, at Staff Colleges, etc., until they reach the rank of Lieutenant Colonel. Then, those who are pro-moted Colonel go on to one list. This does not mean that when a senior job requiring specialist knowledge and training has to be filled it is given to anyone on this list, regardless of his previous career. As a general rule, an officer who has spent his regimental career in the Royal Engineers would be selected to fill the post of

Chief Engineer of a Corps, and so on. But all the Commands and higher staff posts are filled impartially by taking the best man. The only proviso usually made is that the man selected must have had training at a Staff College. If you want to fill the post of Director of Plans at the War Office, or Chief of Staff of a Corps, you do not consider whether it should be filled by a Gunner or an infantryman; you choose from the list the man whose qualities and experience fit him best for the job.

These two examples are sufficient to show that each Service has developed within itself a system which provides for specialisation where it is wanted, and yet ensures overall unity in direction. The specialists are free to give their enthusiasm full rein and to press their own point of view. But they are all part of one Service, and are guided and governed by men who have graduated from the ranks of the specialist into a broader company.

If we look back before the 1914–1918 war, there were only two Services, and only on rare occasions did their operations impinge upon each other. The Navy put the Army ashore where it wanted to go, and looked after its sea communications, but thereafter the two Services fought apart. This fact was reflected right through to the highest levels of direction. The Admiralty and the War Office had few dealings with each other, and their plans for 1914 were prepared independently. It was only when war was imminent that there was some discussion in the Committee of Imperial Defence about the general plan for a war against Germany. The situation did not materially improve before the end of the war, and it was only the creation of the third Service, the RAF that led twenty three years ago to the formation of the Chiefs of Staff Committee. Since then, co-operation between the Services has slowly improved, and under pressure of 1939–45 real advances were made. But the fact remains that we have not yet achieved for the three Services in combination a system which is comparable to that which each Service has evolved for itself. The specialisation is there, it is true, but there is not that junction in the higher ranks that alone can give the strategical skill we are after. We had glimpses of the possibilities during the war when Supreme Commanders were appointed, but these have faded out and we are back with triumvirates of specialists wherever interservice affairs have to be dealt with. It is rather as if a ship was commanded by a committee consisting of a Gunnery officer, the Major of Marines and the Engineer officer, each of whom had under him one third of the crew, and each wearing a different uniform.

There are several reasons why we should not allow this situation to persist. In the first place, the tasks of the three Services are not nearly so clearly differentiated as they used to be. The Navy flies, the Air Force devotes much of its efforts to crippling the enemy's army and transporting our own, and all three Services are equally committed in an invasion. Secondly, the advance of scientific discovery has produced ideas and weapons which do not fit neatly into the picture of three separate Services. They tend to unify warlike operations, and it is more important than ever before that objective minds should examine the application of science to war. Thirdly, the nation is very hard up, and can no longer afford the luxury of duplication and the waste which comes from adding together the demands of three Services.

The first step which should and could be taken without too much difficulty can be clearly seen from the examples quoted above. We must get all officers of the rank of Commodore or equivalent and above on to one list. This step itself can be taken in stages:

> The recognition that the three Services are to become one Service by stages.
>
> The immediate creation of a Chief of Staff of the Armed Forces in place of the Chiefs of Staff Committee. He would be assisted by a staff drawn from the general list, and leading up at first to three Vice-Chiefs.
>
> The gradual evolution of the Ministry of Defence as a unification of the three Service Ministries.
>
> The abolition wherever they exist of command triumvirates, and their replacement by single commanders with unified staffs,
>
> The creation of a General List for senior officers.

These processes would begin the gradual merging of the three Services into one Service.

The ultimate layout would be:

> A single Defence Ministry, and a single Service.
>
> A Defence Council, replacing the three boards of Councils which now exist (e.g. The Second Sea Lord, the Adjutant-General, and the Air Member for Personnel would be replaced by one man).

A common uniform for the General List. Variants for specialised branches, but basically similar.

Fully specialised branches, Sea, Land, and Air, in which officers would remain up to equivalent rank of Captain RN

A Staff College structure as at present, but a more closely integrated system of schools. A Defence University to train the officer entry

A common system of administration.

February 1948

Later in that year, Jacob had been asked by the Editor of the *Sunday Times* to comment on an article by Sir James Grigg, who had been Secretary of State during the war, on the subject of the requirements of the three Services, and the need to strike a balance between them; he had responded with the following letter:

Unifying the Armed Forces
From Major General Sir Ian Jacob

Sir – Sir James Grigg raises in his article an issue of first class importance, namely the nature of our higher defence organisation. During the war, as Sir James Grigg points out, the framing of a common strategic policy, and the allocation of resources, were done by the Prime Minister and Minister of Defence working through a small Defence Committee and through the Chiefs of Staff Committee. The system worked very well; and the Services, given a lead from the top, were brought closer together than ever before. A joint staff served the Prime Minister and Chiefs of Staff. At the end of the war, the Government, after careful investigation, decided to perpetuate this arrangement, while creating a separate Minister of Defence and turning his office into a small co-ordinating ministry. The principle which was to continue was that at all levels from the Chiefs of Staff downwards the responsible officers drawn from the Service Ministries were to work together as teams. The question that arises, and about which Sir James Grigg is clearly in doubt, is whether this system really does work well enough in peace. Are we likely, if it continues, to get the best defence that we can afford, and to keep the Services close together? Will the Government get the clear and expert advice that it needs? Will the application to warfare of the great scientific advances of the modern age be studied objectively? I fear that the answer to these questions is almost certainly in the negative.

It seems certain that our whole future will depend on our condition at the outbreak of any future major war, and that the days when we had a long period after the declaration of war in which to pull ourselves together have gone. A really sound defence organisation in peace-time is therefore vital.

In war-time, when the whole resources of the nation can be called upon, and when strategy is the main preoccupation, a three-Service triumvirate can reach sound conclusions: whereas in peace-time, when the problem is the division between the Services of a small amount of money and men, each member of the team finds it incumbent on him to fight for his own Service. Prestige, rivalry, prejudice, and similar regrettable but human motives come into play, and there is not the urgency of war to compel an objective solution. There is none except the Minister of Defence to judge between rival claims. The ideal of a balanced and sound joint military view being placed before the Minister is rarely attained, and wrangles at the centre tend to spread outwards and to drive the Services apart. The nation runs a great risk of providing men and money for a defence plan, which is merely the sum of those proposals from each Service which the others judge to be comparatively harmless to their own interests.

A Radical Solution

Much depends on the quality of the Minister, and the desire and capacity of the Chiefs of Staff to set an example by sinking their Service interests in the pursuit of a really sound plan. Nor do I suggest that, given three Services to co-ordinate, the present system could be much improved. I think we have got to work towards a more radical solution.

In the White Paper on Central Organisation for Defence (Cmd 6923) issued in October 1946, there occurs the following passage:

> During the war, a unified defence policy was achieved by the assumption of executive control by the Prime Minister and the Minister of Defence. How is it to be achieved in peace? One method would be to amalgamate the three Services completely, and to place them under a single Minister of the Crown. . . . His Majesty's Government do not wholly reject this conception: it may be that at some stage in the future amalgamation might be found desirable. They have decided, however, that this is a step that could and should not be taken here and now.

I believe that the time has now come when this decision should be reconsidered.

It would be absurd to suggest that the Services could be unified by a stroke of the pen. It will be no easy matter to create 'The Armed Forces of the Crown' as a single Service. Many deep prejudices will have to be overcome, and many very real obstacles will have to be surmounted. But I do suggest that our aim should now be set as unification, and that we should deliberately move towards it. I am convinced that it is only by this final reform that we shall attain to a system of command in which modern weapons will be developed and utilised in an objective and unbiased fashion, and a defence plan framed giving the country the best value for the resources we can afford.

IAN JACOB

The pressure on Ministers to identify a 'defence requirement' as opposed to the unreconciled requirements of three separate Services became more serious as the budget for defence expenditure was reduced. Moreover with the setting up of Western European Union in 1948 and NATO in 1949, international business grew in volume, demanding that the military representatives of the nations involved speak with a single voice.

Macmillan, who was Minister of Defence for six months in 1954, complained of his lack of effective authority, and soon afterwards, Eden strengthened the powers of the Minister by giving him responsibility for the composition and balance of the Armed Forces: he also introduced a Chairman of the Chiefs of Staff in replacement of the previous Chief Staff Officer. Moreover, after the Suez crisis, Macmillan appointed Duncan Sandys, a strong personality, as Minister of Defence, and gave him specific authority to take decisions on the size, shape, organisation and disposition of the Armed Services and their equipment and supply (including defence research and development), and to decide questions of Service administration and appointments of special importance. Sandys used his powers to the full, and laid down strategic guidelines for the next five years; and, in the following year, the authority of the Minister of Defence was further strengthened: he was made responsible not for co-ordinating but for *formulating* and *applying* a unified policy. However, the Chiefs of Staff, who were responsible for single Service advice which, after co-ordination, was transmitted to the Minister of Defence, remained responsible for execution, and they retained their individual rights of access to the Minister and if necessary to the Prime Minister himself. Marshal of the Royal Air Force Sir William Dixon, a man of modesty and tact, was able as first Chief of the Defence Staff to adapt his activities to this paradoxical situation, which obviously contained the seeds of sharp controversy.

On the departure of Duncan Sandys in 1959, it became evident that the new machinery had in fact achieved little in relation to the three major problems of central control of programmes and budgets, allocation of resources for the procurement of competing weapons systems, and formulation of central defence policy. With the arrival of Mountbatten as Chief of Defence Staff in 1959, more fundamental changes in the evolutionary process would take place, and Jacob as an 'organisation guru', though in retirement, would play a prominent part in defining them.

Mountbatten's assertive attitude on integration was strongly coloured by his experience as Chief of Combined Operations in 1942, and as Supreme Allied Commander in South-East Asia in 1943. Combined operations had been a special organisation set up for a particular purpose: it did not follow that the example of its success in the last war should necessarily weigh heavily in shaping the central organisation in peace twenty years later. However, Mountbatten had succeeded in setting up unified commands in Cyprus, Aden and the Far East and the success of these organisations was cited to promote a unified solution to the problem of Whitehall. But the disappearance of these commands was already a matter of speculation, and within a short span many would, in fact, exist no more.

By contrast, the potential operations relevant for the future were the maintenance of the nuclear deterrent by sea and air, the defence of Britain, the defence of Central Europe under NATO, and the maintenance of Atlantic sea communications. The application of the principle of tri-service unification to these commitments appeared more questionable.

However, encouraged by the seeming success of his reforms, Mountbatten then produced a radical solution: the Ministry of Defence should be reorganised in unified functional departments including weapons procurement, supply, logistics and personnel administration. The CDS with his defence staff would formulate policy, and the Chiefs of Staff would lose their status as the professional heads of their Services, those functions passing to three commanders-in-chief or inspectors-general. These radical proposals produced strong opposition from all three Services. In particular, the Chiefs of Staff were united on the principle that those who contributed to the formulation of defence policies should also have a responsibility, fully evident to all, towards those men who, ultimately, would have to carry out those policies at the risk of their lives.

It was at this stage that Ismay and Jacob, as 'outside consultants', were invited on 1 January 1963 by Thorneycroft, the Defence Minister, to undertake an independent inquiry into the operation of the Ministry of Defence. Thorneycroft's action had followed a minute sent to him by Macmillan[4] with a copy to CDS, in which he had called for reforms 'to expedite major strategical decisions, simplify the higher direction of operations, unify certain functions such as communications, intelligence etc, improve the allocation of resources and the control of their use, and finally foster a common outlook among the higher ranks of the three Services.' The solutions he envisaged, based on advice he had received from Mountbatten, were a single channel of advice to the Defence Minister in respect of strategy, planning and weapons requirements, centralised direction of operations and allied functions, allocation by the Ministry of Defence of all resources and finance, and lastly the creation of a common list of all three-star officers, from which all appointments would be made by the Minister of Defence. The minute concluded that the Prime Minister rejected the suggestion that all three Services be completely integrated, on the grounds that it could only be carried through at an unacceptable cost in morale and fighting efficiency.

The Chiefs of Staff commented that they did not contemplate the integration of the three Services in the foreseeable future, and while the Services remained separate, the Chiefs of Staff must exercise personal leadership: the fighting man should not have 'a feeling of separation from those responsible for his destiny'. To expedite decisions on major strategy, they recommended that a Strategic Policy Committee should be established at the highest official level. This might not resolve every difference of view between the individual Services, but 'we see no virtue in a convention that the Chiefs of Staff should always speak with a single voice'. To assist the higher direction of operations they recommended that CDS should operate like a Supreme commander, exercising his authority through the Services' Chiefs of Staff, using a War Room which was to be provided. They considered that the processes of unifying communications and intelligence were already developing satisfactorily.

Thorneycroft, the Defence Minister, when confirming his invitation to Jacob to proceed, together with Ismay, on the inquiry, enclosed with his letter the Prime Minister's minute, with papers by Mountbatten and the Chiefs of Staff, and letters from Sir John Slessor and

Field Marshal Lord Harding. The key paragraph of Slessor's letter, which was strongly supported by Harding, read:

> In this field there is one golden principle from which I believe we depart only at our grave peril; namely that the men who advise you and the Cabinet on the strategic employment of the Armed Forces must be the same men who, as the professional heads of their own Services, would have – under the Cabinet – the final responsibility for the conduct of the operations of these Services, consequent upon the strategic advice they have tendered.[5]

Thorneycroft also sent Jacob for comment a draft of a persuasive letter to General Lord Ismay (as he had now become) who, aged 74 and not in robust health, was enjoying his retirement at his home in Worcestershire. Jacob immediately wrote to Ismay:

> ... I very much hope you will agree to do what he asks. It need not be burdensome because I can do all the talking to the people and running round, and I can nip down from time to time to see you at Wormington. The important thing is to have you behind me, because whatever comes out of all this will be accepted if it is in your name far more easily than it would be if it was simply in mine.

He then set to work immediately, taking evidence from about twenty-five ministers, civil servants and officers, and within six weeks the report of 13,000 words, written largely by him but much influenced by Ismay, was in the hands of the Minister of Defence.

The details of the reorganisation, following this Ismay/Jacob report, and introduced by a White Paper (Cmnd 2097 of 1963), have been examined by many authorities.[6] Here it will be sufficient to comment that the two major points of contention in the controversy were interrelated; they were the future responsibilities of the Chief of Staff of each Service in relation to a central organisation with increased executive powers, and the degree to which unification and functionalisation of the Services could be accomplished. Ismay and Jacob firmly rejected Mountbatten's proposal to eliminate the Chiefs of Staff, following the argument stated in Slessor's letter and elsewhere. Had they done otherwise, they would have had to face enormous opposition from all three Services and from many influential sectors of the public. However, it would in future become apparent to all, and doubtless was evident to them at the time, that safeguarding the position of the Chiefs of Staff must impede the evolution of the central organisation towards a fully integrated and functional solution. It was perhaps for this reason that, having rejected a mere adjustment of the existing system, Ismay and Jacob opted for an intermediate course which they recommended as 'a considerable and logical step' towards the final and in their view 'inevitable' aim of 'a completely integrated functionally organised Ministry of Defence, with the three Services retaining their identity in units and formations, while being fused together in their higher organisation.'[7]

In relation to integration, they went even further: they suggested that if the Government decided to adopt their recommended course, 'they would be well advised to announce that they were doing so with a view to the eventual attainment of the final aim.'

Their recommendations were well received: Montgomery, now retired, agreed wholeheartedly with their report, particularly with the ultimate aim. A historian commented some years later that:

> In 1963, Ismay and Jacob served as catalysts, and blue-printed the major reforms ahead. In 1964 Thorneycroft (the Secretary of State for Defence) and Mountbatten began to implement the blue-print. Reaching that phase of Cabinet agreement on overt plans and on legislation was a minor political miracle.[8]

Thereafter, the Central Organisation for Defence followed a somewhat erratic path, largely dependent on the political figures influencing it at various stages, but by 1974 'virtually all the changes envisaged by Mountbatten and the reformers of the early sixties were completed under Edward Heath.'[9] However, achievement of the final aim, which Ismay and Jacob had defined as 'inevitable', was still no more than a distant hope. Even by 1980, it would be stated:

> There is no intention by either political party to merge the Services or to remove the Chiefs of Staff. The Chiefs are seen by uniformed leaders, civil servants and politicians alike as significant symbols of their Services both to their subordinates and to their opposite numbers in NATO.[10]

Historians may speculate on the reasons for this paradox: perhaps Mountbatten's outdated enthusiasm for Unified Commanders overseas carried too much weight: perhaps the Ismay/Jacob single Service analogy of the 'generalist' commander directing successfully a group of 'specialist' officers in a small unit oversimplified the problem: perhaps the wholesale unification of the Canadian Armed Services (subsequently modified) which had been carried well beyond the Jacob/Ismay plan, gave the word 'integration' a bad name.

Hence the validity of Jacob's recommendation that the three Services should eventually be unified at the higher level must be questioned, if only on the grounds that forty years after he had proposed it, there seems little prospect of such unification taking place. In the 1985 reorganisation, no attempt was made to unify the Services; the heads of the three single Services remained in charge of their own Service, although included in the membership of the Defence Council, and 'the position of the Service Boards remained unchanged'.[11]

However, Jacob's intellectual contribution in 1963 must be recognised as a unique catalyst, producing changes at that time which were essential and long overdue.

In 1964, the year of Jacob's sixty-fifth birthday, there was anticipation all round the world of Churchill's ninetieth birthday; and Jacob, no longer involved in defence matters, accepted an invitation to broadcast in French a contribution to a programme about his old 'Master' transmitted on *Radiodiffusion – Télévision Française*. In July, the great old man went to the House of Commons for the last time, to be presented with a resolution recording 'the unbounded admiration and gratitude of the House for his services to Parliament, to the nation and to the world'. On 13 October, Sir Leslie and Lady Rowan were his guests at a last dinner to be held at Chartwell, and were greatly saddened by his declining health. Nevertheless, on 5 November, he was taken to dine once more with the 'Other Club' in the Savoy Hotel. Churchill himself took the Chair, and the thirty-five members attending were drawn as usual from Parliament and his circle of personal friends, of which Jacob was one.

On 30 November, Jacob sent him a birthday greeting:

'Warmest congratulations from one whose finest hours were spent in your service.'

Ian Jacob

To which a reply, one of 70,000, was received two days later:

'Thank you so much dear Ian.'

Winston

Two months later, on 24 January 1965, Churchill died: Jacob and his wife were numbered amongst the principal mourners who, with the greatest in the land, attended the funeral in St Paul's Cathedral. From his service to Churchill as a member of the 'Secret Circle', Jacob was well qualified to pronounce with admiration, affection and shrewd judgement on the personality and triumphs of his 'Master', and was often called upon to do so, notably in *Action this Day*, a book edited by Sir John Wheeler Bennett and published by Macmillan in 1968.

In the nineteen years since his first retirement from the Army, Jacob had not only won distinction in a new career at the BBC, but had repeatedly been called on by the Government to unravel complicated problems of organisation. Now the pressure would ease, allowing him more leisure to deal with family matters and his local interests. Despite great outside pressures in the past, he had always made himself readily available to help his two sons, and had been generous to them not only with financial support but also with advice drawn from a successful career of great versatility. He also took an increased interest in the whole family of Jacobs, attending weddings of distant relatives and, as head of the clan, advising and assisting any who appealed to him for help.

As the rescuer from oblivion of the Army and Navy Club, where his portrait in oils now hangs in the entrance hall, he continued to take a great interest in its prosperity and standing. On 17 February 1965, four months before handing over the Chairmanship, he presided at a very happy occasion: an evening reception for Her Majesty The Queen.

In December of that year, Lord Ismay, who had retired from the office of Secretary General of NATO, died at the age of seventy-eight. He had left Whitehall in March 1947, to become a senior member of the staff of the Viceroy of India, and later had been appointed Secretary of State for Commonwealth Relations. His death was felt keenly by Jacob, who wrote an additional obituary of his friend and mentor, which was published in *The Times* on 30 December 1965.

The passage of years made no impression on Jacob's intellect, and he continued to undertake various responsibilities for which his special experience either in Whitehall, the BBC, or commerce would be advantageous. In 1966 he became a trustee of the Imperial War Museum in succession to Field Marshal Sir Gerald Templer. In 1969 at the age of seventy he was invited to become Chairman of Burton, Son and Sanders, a big firm in Ipswich engaged in the food business; a year later it was merged with a similar firm, Matthews Holdings, and Jacob became executive Chairman of the new company. In that same year he undertook to run an appeal for funds to complete the extensions needed to convert the Parish Church of Bury St Edmunds to a Cathedral Church. He had been a 'friend of the Cathedral' for some years, and was asked to help at a critical stage when the building programme was nearly finished, but considerable sums of money were still needed to meet the cost. It was decided that the programme should be terminated at the second stage, and sufficient funds were raised to meet the commitment. On 24 July 1970, the 1100th year of commemoration of the martyrdom of St Edmund, Jacob, with seven others, was installed as a lay Canon of St Edmundsbury Cathedral.

In 1971 he was invited to be the guest speaker at the annual dinner of the Churchill Society of Canada at Edmonton, Alberta, following in the footsteps of Harding, Mountbatten, Alexander, Butler, Douglas-Home and Mark Clark. The Society had been founded with Churchill's permission, in 1964, to ensure 'that the ideals and achievements of this outstanding leader should never be forgotten by successive generations'.

On the Dinner Programme the first paragraph of a biographical note read:

> 'My debt to its members is immeasurable' were the words Sir Winston used to commend the Military Wing of the War Cabinet Secretariat, headed by General Ismay, the urbane gourmet, with General Hollis, the witty rough diamond, and . . . Sir Ian Jacob the ascetic intellectual. This fabulously efficient triumvirate fed Churchill with military facts, figures and plans. Wherever Churchill went, Sir Ian Jacob set up an office through which outgoing orders and incoming reports flowed without pause; for six years his desk and brain were the channels through which passed every secret of State, so that by 1945 few men in Britain had a better grasp of war strategy.

In September 1971, Jacob took over the Chairmanship of the Suffolk Police Authority, of which he had been a member for some years, and recently Vice Chairman. He had a profound knowledge of police problems, having been a member in 1960 of the Royal Commission on the Police, chaired by Sir Henry Willink; their recommendations, covering police constitution, status and accountability, relations with the public, handling of complaints and principles governing pay, had been accepted almost *in toto* and implemented.

On 12 November, on his way to Sherborne School, of which he was Chairman, he called on Field Marshal Montgomery, aged eighty-four. Jacob had often been involved with the Field Marshal in the past, and he felt he might call on him for a chat, perhaps for the last time. Montgomery, though resting in bed, answered Jacob's questions with his usual decisiveness. Jacob's first question was about World War I, in which Montgomery had been shot through the chest and left lying in no-man's land for six hours:

> 'The Germans nearly finished me then,' Montgomery replied, 'but they didn't!' The wound had troubled him a bit when he was young, but later on he never felt it. 'The Generals in the first war didn't really understand war, and had been too far from the troops – it was different the second time.'
>
> We then talked about the hand-over of command in the Middle East.
>
> 'I was commanding South East England, when one day I was suddenly told to go to Cairo – There Auchinleck said "if there is anything you want, or if you get into any difficulty, ring me in Cairo." I went up to the desert, and simply sent

him a message saying: "Today I have assumed command of the Eighth Army."
I do not think there was anything on which Auchinleck and I agreed. Of course I
knew nothing of the desert, but that did not matter: what you have to know is
war, and then it doesn't matter where it takes place, in deserts, or swamps, or
anywhere.'

I then asked him about Alexander:

'You know I taught Alex at the Staff College. When I was an instructor at
Camberley, Alex was a student. We didn't think he had any brains, and we were
right. I couldn't have had a better C-in-C Middle East, because he only gave me
one order: "You go into the desert and beat Rommel", and then he left me
completely alone. He was nice, I was not nice, I was nasty'.

I asked him which of his Corps Commanders was best:

'I think Oliver Leese was best. Horrocks was good, but he didn't quite know
what to do next. Oliver, however, provided I kept a thumb on him, was very
capable. Afterwards he was sent to the Far East, and then he tried to behave like
me, and that was no good. You can't pretend to be someone else, you must be
yourself. He tried to be me and was sacked.'

The Jacobs celebrated their Golden Wedding on 27 August 1974,
and their Diamond Wedding ten years later. To these happy events,
launched with great generosity, Jacob contributed the same careful
planning and attention to detail as had invariably marked his professional duties.

On 27 September 1989 he reached the age of ninety; although his
agility had been reduced, his mental vigour was quite unimpaired. On
the day after his birthday, the Board of Governors of the BBC, under
their Chairman Mr Marmaduke Hussey, gave a luncheon party at
Broadcasting House to celebrate Jacob's birthday. A large number of
previous BBC colleagues attended, as well as his friends from other
walks of life, and all concurred that it was a joyful occasion. Soon
afterwards, he attended a ceremony at Neuve Chapelle commemorating the battle in World War I in which his father had taken part.

Historians will have to search extensively to find a record of versatile service equal to that of Lieutenant General Sir Ian Jacob, late
Royal Engineers. He achieved success in many professions, and in
them certain motivations can be found which are common to all. The
first is his total commitment to the task in hand: whether in his
relations with the great war leaders, or when piloting the BBC
through a period of change, or involved in the controversies of defence
organisation, or engaged in the competitive world of commerce, his
concentration on the task in hand was invariably complete, and personal considerations were barred from his calculations. A man of
modesty, contemptuous of ostentation, he insulated himself from personal ambition, being motivated throughout by dedication to serve.

The second is objectivity: whatever might be the crisis, and he was involved in many, he never allowed emotion or fear to influence his judgement.

His intellectual ability, recognised at an early stage, fully matched the challenges which arose in his service to Churchill: and his remarkable memory, analytical skill and dexterity with words made him an excellent rapporteur; moreover those qualities were supplemented by the outlook of a historian, so that events were studied not in isolation but in a long-term perspective set in an historical context.

Another characteristic is his insight into organisation. At a personal level, this produces an unhurried orderliness in his work, which is often the envy of his friends. In a wider context, it stimulates a critical approach to the organisational structures with which he is involved, and leads to a vigorous search for improvements.

In the early years of his married life, his emphasis in the family circle was centred on achievement, which included sporting as well as academic success, but excluded frivolity; the future head of the Jacob clan appeared to some to be an unworldly idealist. Later in his official relationships in the darkest days of the war, his iron self-control compounded with stoic calm, though admired by many, was regarded by some as austere. However, with the advent of victory, naturally he became much more relaxed and extrovert; and after some years of leading the BBC, the mellowing process developed, creating warm relationships sustained for many years with a wide variety of people.

Throughout his governmental service, he sought to lubricate any rough edges which might develop between the military and civil authorities. With Vivian Dykes, he did much to foster good relations with the Americans, although the personal characteristics of many of them were so different from his own. Involved unceasingly with the great controversies of the war, he was tireless in setting up the framework of decision-making.

Hankey rightly called him 'a true son of his father'. Had he harked back to an earlier generation, he could have likened him to John Jacob, that other child of the Raj, described at the end of his tragically short life as 'one of those rare spirits who love work – good true and noble work for its own sake: despising noisy fame, which he held so cheap.'

Ian Jacob, favoured with twice that life span, achieved fame in a different sphere; but throughout a distinguished, many-sided career, he has followed the lofty tradition of his forebears, and may be paired with John Jacob as another brilliant, devoted, and trusty servant of the State.

TAILPIECE

10, Downing Street,
Whitehall.

Personal.

GENERAL JACOB.

     I am told this cipher is
your signature.   If you wish to
continue this practice, would you
kindly have your name typed underneath.

18.12.44

Chapter Notes

Chapter 1   Child of the Raj
1. Jacob family papers.
2. Lambrick, L.T. *John Jacob of Jacobabad* (Cassell, 1960), p. 6.
3. Ibid., p. 376.
4. Churchill, Winston S. *My Early Life* (Collins, 1930), p. 109.
5. Newsome, David. *A History of Wellington College* (John Murray, 1959), p. 8.
6. Viceroy's commissioned officers, in increasing order of seniority, were Jemadar, Subedar and Subedar-major.
7. 'Chota Jacob Sahib', meaning literally 'the small Jacob', can be translated colloquially as 'Jacob's son'.
8. 'burra', literally large, can be translated colloquially as 'Father Jacob'.
9. Jacob typescript.

Chapter 2   'Peace for our Time'
1. Jacob typescript.
2. Gilbert, Martin. *Winston S. Churchill*, Vol. V (Heinemann, 1976), p. 489.
3. Churchill, Winston S. *The Second World War*, Vol. I (Cassell, 1948), p. 52.
4. The future Lieutenant General Sir Frederick Browning (Commander Airborne Corps).
5. Jacob typescript. The *Mousquitiere del Duce* were Mussolini's personal guard.
6. Feiling, Keith. *Life of Neville Chamberlain* (Macmillan, 1946), p. 381.

Chapter 3   Stumbling into War
1. Wheeler-Bennett, Sir John. *Action This Day, Working with Churchill* (Macmillan, 1968), p. 196.
2. Astley, Joan Bright. *The Inner Circle* (Hutchinson, 1971), p. 60.
3. *Action This day*, op. cit., p. 51.

Chapter 4   Churchill at the Helm
1. *Action This Day*, op. cit., p. 162.
2. Jacob typescript.
3. Jacob typescript.
4. Colville, John. *The Fringes of Power*, Vol. I (Hodder and Stoughton, 1985), p. 330.
5. *The Second World War*, Vol. II, op. cit., p. 19.

Chapter 5   With Churchill to Meet Roosevelt
1. Hansard, 4 June 1940, columns 787–796.
2. Lash, Joseph P. *Roosevelt and Churchill* (Andrew Deutsch, 1977), p. 391.

3. Ibid., p. 394.
4. Ibid., p. 402.
5. Ibid., p. 402.

Chapter 6 'All in the Same Boat Now'

1. Jacob typescript.

Chapter 7 Darkest Days

1. Danchev, Alex. *Establishing the Anglo-American Alliance* (Brassey's, 1990), p. 161.
2. Dilks, David. *The Diaries of Sir Alexander Cadogan* (Cassell, 1971), p. 475.

Chapter 8 Conferring with Stalin

1. *Prime Minister's Personal Minute*, M365/2, 11 September 1941, Churchill Papers 20/67, quoted in *Winston S. Churchill*, Vol. VII, p. 206.

Chapter 9 Planning for Victory

Chapter 10 On the Conference Circuit Again

Chapter 11 The Road to Victory

1. See Kings XVIII paras 21–40.
2. Jacob note 26 October 1944, and Bridges note 8 November 1944. CAB 120/158.
3. *The Second World War*, Vol. VI, p. 198, and p. 202.
4. Charlton, Michael. *The Eagle and the Small Birds*, BBC 1984, see pp. 42–44 for an account of Jacob's attitude to Yalta post-war.

Chapter 12 A Second Career

1. Simon of Wythenshawe Lord. *The BBC from Within* (Victor Gollanz, 1953, p. 154).
2. Cmnd 6852 (1946) paras 58/60.
3. Briggs, Asa. *The History of Broadcasting in the United Kingdom*, Vol. IV, *Sound and Vision* (Oxford University Press, 1979), p. 155.
4. *The BBC From Within*, op. cit., p. 159.
5. Grisewood, Harman. *One Thing at a Time* (Hutchinson, 1968), p. 157.
6. *The History of Broadcasting in the United Kingdom*, op. cit., p. 155.
7. Jacob typescript.
8. Minute to Jacob from Prime Minister, M45 (c) 51 of 15 November 1951.
9. Secret, Inter allied organisation 41558 of December 1951.
10. Mallaby, George. *From My Level* (Hutchinson, 1965) p. 38.
11. Jacob typescript.
12. Ibid.

Chapter 13 Director General of the BBC

1. *Sound and Vision*, op. cit., p. 445.
2. Briggs, Asa. *Governing the BBC*, BBC 1979, p. 101.
3. Dilks, David. *The Diaries of Sir Alexander Cadogan* (Cassell, 1971), p. 792.
4. Ibid., p. 792.
5. *Manchester Guardian*, 26 July 1952 quoted in *Sound and Vision*, Vol. IV, pp. 450 and 451.
6. *Sound and Vision*, op. cit., p. 528.
7. Grisewood, Harman. *One Thing at a Time*, op. cit., p. 183.
8. Ibid., p. 188.
9. Ibid., p. 183.
10. BBC Written Archives: Article by DG for First Edition of *Radio Times Annual*.
11. *Broadcasting Committee Report* 1949 and *Beveridge Report* 1950/51, Appx. H.

12. BBC Written Archives: DG broadcasting in the TV Service on the 21st Anniversary.
13. BBC Written Archives.
14. Ibid.
15. Ibid.

Chapter 14 'Never Look Back'

1. Based on *History of the Army and Navy Club*, privately printed.
2. Richardson, Charles. *Send for Freddie* (William Kimber, 1987) p. 193.
3. Jacob typescript.
4. M330/62 of 9 December 1962.
5. Jacob papers.
6. For a comprehensive historical description of the higher direction of defence see Franklyn A. Johnson. *Defence by Ministry* (Duckworth, 1980).
7. *Higher Direction of Defence*. Report by Lord Ismay and Lieutenant General Sir Ian Jacob dated 20 February 1963.
8. Johnson, Franklyn A. *Defence by Ministry*, op. cit., p. 126.
9. Ibid., p. 174.
10. Ibid., p. 196.
11. Cmnd 9315 of July 1984, para. 11.

Bibliography

ASTLEY, Joan Bright. *The Inner Circle* (Hutchinson, 1971).

BRIGGS, Asa. *The History of Broadcasting in the UK*, Vol. IV (Oxford University Press, 1979).

Governing the BBC (British Broadcasting Corporation 1979).

CALLAHAN, Raymond. *Servants of the Raj* (Typescript).

CHARLTON, Michael. *The Eagle and the Small Birds* (BBC, 1984).

CHURCHILL, Winston S. *The Second World War*, Vols. I to VI (Cassell, 1948–1953).

My Early Life (Collins, 1930).

COLVILLE, John. *The Fringes of Power*, Vols. I and II (Hodder and Stoughton, 1985).

The Churchillians (Weidenfeld and Nicholson, 1981).

COOTE, Colin R. *The Other Club* (Sidgwick and Jackson, 1971).

DANCHEV, Alex. *Very Special Relationship*; Field Marshal Sir John Dill, *Establishing the Anglo-American Alliance* (Brassey's Defence Publishers, 1986 and 1990).

DILKS, David. *The Diaries of Sir Alexander Cadogan* (Cassell, 1971).

FEILING, Sir Keith. *The Life of Neville Chamberlain* (Macmillan, 1946).

FFORDE, Sir Arthur. *What is Broadcasting About?* (Privately printed, 1963).

GILBERT, Martin. *Winston S. Churchill*, Vols. V to VIII (Heinemann, 1976–1988).

GOLDIE, Grace Wyndham. *Facing the Nation, Television and Politics* (The Bodley Head, 1977).

GRISEWOOD, Harman. *One Thing at a Time* (Hutchinson, 1968).

HAMILTON, Nigel. *Monty*, Vols. I to III (Hamish Hamilton, 1981, 83, 86).

HOBKIRK, Michael D. *The Politics of Defence Budgeting* (RUSI/Macmillan, 1983/4).

HOWARD, Michael. *The Central Organisation of Defence* (RUSI, 1970).

ISMAY, General the Lord. *Memoirs* (Heinemann, 1960).

JACOB, Lieutenant General Sir Ian. *Family papers, Diaries, Typescript, BBC Transcript* (unpublished).

The Campaign of Liberation 1944–55 (*Economist*, 1946).

The High Level Conduct and Direction of World War II (*RUSI Journal*, 1956).

His Finest Hour (*Atlantic Monthly*, 1965).

Churchill and His Generals (*Listener*, 1979).

JOHNSON, Franklyn A. *Defence by Ministry* (Duckworth, 1980).

LAMBRICK, H.T. John. *Jacob of Jacobabad* (Cassell, 1960).

LASH, Joseph P. *Roosevelt and Churchill* (Andre Deutsch, 1976).

MALLABY, George. *From My Level* (Hutchinson, 1965).

MONTGOMERY, Field Marshal The Viscount. *Memoirs* (Collins, 1958).

NEWSOME, David. *A History of Wellington College* (John Murray, 1959).

SIMON OF WYTHENSHAWE, Lord. *The BBC From Within* (Victor Gollanz, 1953).

TALBOYS, R.St.C. *A Victorian School, Wellington College* (Basil Blackwell, 1943).

WHEELER-BENNETT, Sir John. *Action This Day* (Macmillan, 1968).

WYATT, Woodrow. *Distinguished for Talent* (Hutchinson, 1958).

    Confessions of an Optimist (Collins, 1985).

ZIEGLER, Philip. *Mountbatten* (Collins, 1985).

Index

Abadan 81.
ABDA (American-British-Dutch-Australian area in Pacific) 91, 92, 104, 120.
Abyssinia 22, 23.
Action this Day 278.
Adana 178, 179, 183, 184.
Addiscombe, East India Company's College 1, 2.
Aden 274.
Admiralty 38, 47, 48.
Aegean Sea 161.
Afghanistan 198.
Africa 160, 251.
Africa, North 148, 160.
Agheila 131.
Air Ministry 38, 75.
Alam Halfa 130, 148.
Alamein, see El Alamein.
Alanbrooke, Viscount, see Brooke.
Albania 37.
Aldershot 9, 17, 20, 104, 170.
Alexander, Maj Gen Sir Harold, later Field Marshal Earl Alexander of Tunis 116, 121, 123, 124, 125, 126, 127, 129, 130, 132, 163, 167, 176, 177, 179, 185, 192, 193, 194, 197, 229, 230, 231, 264, 280, 281.
Alexander, A.V. later Earl of Hillsborough 267.
Alexandria 22, 23, 24, 26, 109.
Algeria 153, 191.
Algiers 109, 147, 149, 153, 170, 185, 186, 188, 193.
Ali Dost, Subedar 9, 15.
Allied Control Commission (Germany) 200, 203, 207, 221.
Allied Control Council 203.
Alphand. M 210, 215.

America, see United States.
American-British-Dutch-Australian Command (ABDA) 65.
Anderiman, Surayya 181, 182, 183.
Anders, Lt Gen Wlazdyslaw 128, 142, 143.
Anderson, Sir John, later Viscount Waverley 204, 205.
Ankara 177, 182.
Antonov, Gen A.I (USSR) 214.
Anvil 192, 193.
ARCADIA, (Washington Conference) 84, 104.
Archangel 44, 82, 104.
Ardennes 147.
Argentia 66.
Argentinian Delegation to UNO 199.
ARGONAUT (Yalta Conference) 197.
Ariel 261.
Arkansas U.S.S. 67.
ARMIES
   British.
      First 150, 178.
      Eighth 107, 109, 114, 115, 116, 117, 118, 121, 122, 126, 128, 178, 185, 281.
      Ninth 145, 160.
      Tenth 160.
   United States.
      Fifth 150, 186.
   Soviet.
      Armies 82, 147, 197.
Army and Navy Club 46, 264, 279.
Army Benevolent Fund 263.
Arnold, Gen H.H. (US Army) 68, 72, 90, 154, 165, 170.
Arnold, Maj Gen, Mil Attaché 178, 179.
Arundel 241.
Ashbridge, Sir Noel 222.
Asoka, Moghul Emperor 1.

Astley, Joan Bright   31.
Athenia S.S.   39.
Athens   193.
Atlantic, battle of   69, 76.
Atlantic Charter   71, 75, 76, 80.
Atlantic City   226.
Atlantic Committee   51.
Atlantic Meeting (RIVIERA)   62–81, 95,
   105, 107, 170.
Atlas Mountains   172, 175.
Atom Bomb   189, 190, 205, 211, 212.
Atomic Energy Commission   204, 208, 209,
   210, 211, 215.
Attlee, Clement   64, 81, 107, 198, 200, 204,
   206, 209, 217, 223, 227, 241, 267.
Auchinleck, Gen, later Field Marshal Sir
   Claude   58, 74, 82, 104, 107, 113, 114,
   115, 116, 117, 120, 121, 122, 123, 124,
   125, 131, 281.
Augusta U.S.S.   60, 67, 68.
Australia   23, 69, 94, 248.
Australian Government   92, 93.
Austria   21, 23.
Azores   74, 76, 86, 250.

Baal   193.
Baghdad   133, 178.
Baillie-Stewart, Captain   38.
Balkans   57, 82, 148, 160, 161, 172, 196.
Baltimore and Ohio Railroad   88.
Baluch Regiment   3.
Bandoeng, Java   93.
Banff, Canada   203.
Bannu, Pakistan   13.
Barnes, (Sir) George   240.
Bathurst, West Africa   169.
BATTALIONS.
   2nd Battalion Grenadier Guards   23.
   3rd Battalion Coldstream Guards   24.
BATTLEAXE operation   58, 60,
Batum   137.
British Broadcasting Corporation,
   BBC   233, 281.
   Alexandra Palace   249.
   Broadcasting House   236, 238, 244, 281.
   Bush House   219, 220, 222, 238.
   Lime Grove   238, 244.
   White City   238.
   European Service   219, 220, 221.
   Home Service   86.
   Overseas Service   227, 234, 237.
   Television   237, 242, 249, 250.
   General Advisory Council   250.

Beardell, Capt (US Navy)   89.
Beaverbrook, Baron   52, 73, 75, 76, 82, 84,
   85, 86, 87, 98, 102, 103, 104, 138.
Bedell-Smith, Gen Walter (US Army)   148,
   149, 152, 170, 186, 188, 197.
Beirut   178.
Belgium   244.
Bellairs, Rear Admiral R M   60.
Bellenger, F   267.
Bengal Army   2.
Benghazi   57, 107.
Bennett, Sir John Wheeler   278.
Bennett, Sterndale   206, 208, 213, 214.
Benyon, Col. W.L.R.   265.
Berchtesgarten   25.
Berlin   164, 206, 224.
Bermuda   86.
Beveridge, Sir William, later Lord   236.
Beveridge Committee   236.
Bevin, Ernest   206, 207, 209, 210, 211, 212,
   213, 214, 215, 216, 224, 225.
Bidault, George   219.
Bikaner, India   10.
Bir Hacheim   118.
Birse, Maj A.H.   140, 142, 144.
Bishop, (Sir) Harold   240.
Bismarck, German battleship   62, 73, 83.
Blood, Gen Sir Bindon   17.
Blum, Leon   219.
Boer War   9.
Bohemia   36.
Bohlen, Charles E (US State Dept)   208.
Boisson, Pierre   151.
BOLERO: Assembly of troops in U K for
   cross-channel assault   106, 188.
Bolshoi Theatre   108, 211, 213.
Bombay   15.
Bombay Artillery   1, 2.
Bombay Native Infantry   1.
Bombay Presidency   1, 2.
Bonnet, Georges   33.
Bottomley, Air Chief Marshal Sir
   Norman   222, 240.
Boyle, Lt Col   175.
Brand, Hon R.H. later Lord   98.
Brandon, Suffolk   5, 6.
Brazil   74.
Brest   106.
Breughel-Douglas, van   210.
Bridges, Sir Edward later Lord   24, 29, 33,
   46, 187, 196, 201, 228, 266.
BRIMSTONE: codename, operation into
   Sardinia   32, 33, 37, 38, 40.

Britain 5, 34, 79, 147, 196, 238.
British Army 33, 38, 41, 54.
British Expeditionary Force BEF 42, 53.
British Red Cross Society 46.
British Supply Council 98, 102.
Brook, (Sir) Norman, later Lord Normanbrook 228, 229.
Brooke, Gen Sir Alan, later Field Marshal Viscount Alanbrooke 104, 105, 108, 109, 111, 114, 171, 222, 241.
Brooks, Brigadier (Canal Brigade) Plate 8.
Brown, Francis, Private Secretary to Mr Churchill 91, 101.
Browning, Lt Gen Sir Frederick 'Boy' 22, 23.
Brownjohn, Gen Sir Neville 18.
Brussels 226.
Bryant, Sir Arthur 244.
Bulgaria 57, 196, 212, 214.
Bullard, Sir Reader 133, 210, 214.
Bullitt, William C 96.
Bulolo HMS 149, 154.
Bundy, Col (US Army) 68, 71, 72.
Burgh-el-Arab, Egypt 114, 121, 122, 123.
Burgin, Leslie, Minister 41.
Burgis, Lawrence, Civil Servant 61, 171.
Burma 120, 156, 157, 158, 162, 169, 187.
Burma Road 159.
Burns, Gen (US Army) 68.
Burton Son & Sanders Ltd 279.
Bush, Dr Vannevar 205.
Butcher, Capt Harry (US Navy) 152.
Butler, (Sir) James 227.
Byrnes, James, US Senator 208, 209, 210, 211, 213, 215, 216.

Cabinet, British 20, 32, 110, 121, 186, 206, 211, 227, 228.
Cabinet Committee on Manpower 51.
Cabinet Committee on BBC 238.
Cabinet Office 19, 51, 52, 217, 229, 230.
Cabinet, United States 95.
Cadogan, Sir Alexander 60, 61, 63, 68, 71, 111, 125, 127, 129, 134, 135, 136, 138, 143, 144, 179, 198, 206, 207, 208, 209, 210, 214, 215, 234, 235, 246, 247, 252.
Cadogan, Lady 61.
Cagliari 161.
Cairo 22, 24, 109, 110, 111, 112, 114, 123, 125, 126, 143, 171, 172, 173, 176, 178, 183, 184, 192, 197, 219, 280.
Caldwell, Bishop Robert 5.

Calgary 203.
Cambridge 15, 170, 234.
Campbell, Sir Ronald 206, 208, 210, 212, 214.
Canada 191, 204, 250.
Canadian Armed Services 277.
Canary Isles 74.
Cape Town 83.
Capri 194.
Caroline Islands 169.
Carthage 191.
Casablanca 147, 148, 149, 153, 154, 155, 159, 161, 165, 172, 173, 187.
Casablanca Conference: SYMBOL 148, 177.
Caserta, Palace of 194.
Casey, Richard, later Baron, Minister of State, Middle East 111, 113, 114, 124, 125, 176.
Catalina flying boats 78.
Catroux, Gen, French 125, 210.
Caucasus 107, 113, 114, 132, 137, 141, 142, 160.
Ceylon 107.
Chakmak, Marshal, Turkey 180, 181, 184.
Chaman, Baluchistan 3.
Chamberlain, Sir Austen 21.
Chamberlain, Sir Neville 25, 33, 35, 36, 37, 38, 40, 41, 45, 51, 241.
Channel, English 160, 202.
Channel Islands 141.
Charles, Sir Noel 195.
Charpentier, Monsieur 215.
Chartwell 231.
Chateau Frontenac Hotel, Ottawa 190.
Chatfield, Admiral of the Fleet Lord 35, 41.
Chatham 15, 17.
Chequers 61, 82, 109, 153.
Cherbourg 106, 141.
Cherwell, Lord, see Lindemann.
Chesapeake Bay 87.
Chiang-Kai-Shek, Generalissimo 168, 175.
Chiefs of Staff British 30, 31, 33, 38, 39, 40, 47, 48, 50, 51, 52, 54, 60, 63, 64, 65, 66, 67, 68, 71, 72, 76, 78, 81, 84, 85, 86, 87, 92, 99, 101, 102, 103, 105, 109, 147, 148, 154, 155, 156, 158, 159, 161, 167, 192, 200, 214, 224, 267, 273, 275, 277.
Chiefs of Staff United States 69, 71, 88, 90, 97, 99, 102, 103, 107, 108, 147, 148, 155, 162, 163, 167.
Chiefs of Staff Committee 28, 32, 34, 47, 48, 51, 104, 105, 270, 271.

Chief of Naval Staff, see First Sea Lord.

Chief of the Imperial General Staff   28, 61,
    65, 68, 69, 71, 72, 73, 74, 108, 109, 112,
    113, 115, 116, 120, 121, 122, 123, 125,
    128, 129, 134, 135, 136, 138, 140, 141,
    142, 162, 163, 164, 167, 173, 174, 175,
    176, 178, 181, 182, 183, 185, 186.

Chief of the Air Staff   61, 90, 91, 130, 161,
    165.

Chief of Defence Staff   273, 274, 275.

Chief of the General Staff, India   9, 10.

Chief Whips   239.

China   157, 166, 187.

Chunking   170.

Churchill, Sir Winston   3, 4, 20, 21, 26, 35,
    36, becomes First Lord of the
    Admiralty   38–41, seeks to impart
    drive over entire war effort   42, his
    reaction to the crisis in Norway   43–44,
    becomes Prime Minister   45–47, issues
    minutes: 'Action this day',   48, 49,
    handles the crisis of the German
    breakthrough in NW Europe   49. Flies
    to Paris to confer with M.
    Reynaud   50. Establishes his regime
    including his afternoon sleep   50.
    Galvanises the Chiefs of Staff
    Committee   51. Sets up his research
    department under Major Jefferis
    RE   52. His technique in
    argument   53, is briefed by Lt Gen
    Pownall on the Dunkirk
    evacuation   53, deals with French
    request for more fighter squadrons   54,
    proposes that support be sent to Greece
    by withdrawals from Middle East
    Command   57. Replaces Wavell, C in
    C Middle East, with Auchinleck   58.
    Builds a relationship with President
    Roosevelt   59. Decides to confer with
    Roosevelt at Placentia Bay,
    Newfoundland   60, and embarks in
    HMS Prince of Wales for Conference
    RIVIERA   62–76. Visits garrisons in
    Iceland and returns to London   77–79.
    Learns of Japanese attack at Pearl
    Harbour   82; embarks on HMS Duke of
    York to confer with Roosevelt in
    Washington: Conference
    ARCADIA   84–104. Appoints General
    Sir Alan Brooke as CIGS to succeed
    Gen Dill, who is assigned to
    Washington   105. Defeats a vote of
    censure in the House of
    Commons   107. Flies to Washington
    for further discussions on Anglo-
    American strategy   108. In London,
    obtains American agreement for the
    launch of Operation TORCH   109.
    Decides to visit the Middle East
    Command and Teheran, and confer
    with Stalin in Moscow, Operation
    BRACELET   110–146. Appoints
    General Alexander C in C Middle East
    Command   116, and General
    Montgomery Commander Eighth
    Army   121. Flies to Casablanca for
    conference with Roosevelt and
    Combined Chiefs of Staff,
    (SYMBOL)   155–169. Enjoys a
    holiday in Marrakesh   175–176. Flies
    via Cairo to Turkey for a conference
    with President Inonu   176–184. Visits
    Cairo, and attends Eighth Army's
    parade at Tripoli   184–185. Returns to
    London and sails to Washington in
    Queen Mary for a conference with
    President Roosevelt and Combined
    Chiefs of Staff (TRIDENT)   187. Sails
    for Canada in Queen Mary for a
    conference with President Roosevelt,
    Mackenzie King and Combined Chiefs
    of Staff (QUADRANT)   189–191. Flies
    to Italy to confer with General
    Alexander and observe landings in
    South of France (DRAGOON)   193–
    195. Flies to Moscow accompanied by
    Averell Harriman to confer with Stalin
    on defeat of Japan, and post-war
    problems in Europe (TOLSTOY)
    196–197. Flies to Yalta for conference
    with President Roosevelt and Stalin on
    post-war problems (ARGONAUT)
    197. Gives a dinner at Hyde Park Gate
    for General Marshall, the war-time
    Chiefs of Staff, Eden, Hollis and
    Jacob   222. Comments to Jacob, now
    in the BBC, on the overrunning of
    Czechoslovakia   225. Returns to power
    as Prime Minister and invites Jacob to
    return to his service   228. Discusses
    The Other Club with Jacob   231.
    Attends a dinner to mark the
    publication of Ismay's Memoirs   264.
    Receives a tribute of admiration and
    gratitude at the House of Commons and

takes the Chair at a dinner of The
Other Club 278. Dies on 24 January
1965 278.
Churchill, Clementine, later Baroness
Spencer-Churchill 130, 189.
Churchill, Mary, L/Bombardier A T S, later
Baroness Soames 85, 189.
Churchill's Research Dept 52.
Citadel, Ottawa 190.
Clark J B 240.
Cinderella, ballet by Prokofiev 213.
Clark, Gen Mark Wayne 147, 150, 152,
186, 197, 280.
Clark-Kerr, Sir Archibald later Baron
Inverchapel 134, 138, 143, 144, 208.
Clemenceau, Georges 10.
Climping, Sussex 241.
Clydesmuir, Lord 236.
Cockcroft, Sir John 204.
Cohen, Benjamin 208, 209, 211, 212.
Cold War 198, 215, 222, 223, 224.
Cole, Maj Gen W.S. 265.
Coleridge, R.D.C Capt Royal Navy, later
Baron 88, 94.
Colville, Sir John 31, 35, 264.
Combined Chiefs of Staff 90, 93, 97, 104,
107, 108, 157, 163, 167, 168, 170, 187,
188, 190, 197.
Committee of Imperial Defence, C I D 19,
20, 21, 24, 25, 27, 28, 29, 30, 32, 33, 34,
37, 38, 39.
COMPASS operation (Western Desert) 57.
Conant, Dr 208, 209, 211, 212, 215.
Congress of the United States 80, 81, 204.
Coningham, Air Vice Marshal later Air
Marshal Sir Arthur 114.
Convoys, Atlantic 77, 78, 82.
Convoys, to the Soviet Union 145, 147.
Cooke, Director of Plans U S Navy 154,
158.
Coote, Sir Colin 264.
Copenhagen 226.
Corbett, Lt Gen T.W. 111, 112, 116, 117.
Cornwall-Jones, Brigadier A.T. 111, 112,
124, 126, 171, 176.
Corps 13th 126.
Coronation of H M Queen Elizabeth
II 238, 244.
Corsica 161, 194.
COSSAC 189, 192.
Council of Foreign Ministers 203, 210.
Covent Garden Market Authority 264.
Cranwell, R A F Cadet College 194.

Crete 57, 58, 74.
Cripps, Sir Stafford 107, 192.
CROSSBOW Committee 192, 193.
Crow, Dr 192.
CRUSADER, Auchinleck's offensive 82,
107, 117.
Cunningham, Admiral Sir Andrew, later
Viscount Cunningham of
Hyndhope 151, 186, 191, 222, 264.
Cunningham, Captain (A D C) 123.
Curacoa H M S 62.
Curtin, John, Prime Minister Australia 92,
93.
Cyprus 177, 183, 184, 191, 248, 274.
Cyrenaica 22, 57.
Czechoslovakia 25, 36, 198.

D-day 202, 203.
Daily Mail 239.
Daily Sketch 244.
Dakar 154.
Dardanelles 147.
Darlan, Admiral Jean Francois 151, 152.
Dartmouth Royal Naval College 94, 106.
Davies, Col (U S Army) 152.
Dean, M.J. (Sir) Maurice 84.
Deane, Maj Gen John R., (U S Army) 155,
163, 187.
Defence Committee 51, 53, 54.
Defence Registry 48.
de Gaulle, Gen Charles 151, 163, 168, 174.
de Guingand, Brigadier later Maj Gen Sir
Francis 267.
de Havilland, Maj Gen P.H. 265.
Delhi 9, 10, 11.
de Lotbiniere, S.J. 244.
De Pree, Maj Gen Hugo 17.
Derby, Earl of 7, 20.
Deutsche Afrika Korps 57.
Dickson, Air Commodore W., later Marshal
of the Royal Air Force Sir William 84,
86, 273.
Dieppe Raid 126.
Dill, Field Marshal, Sir John 18, 20, 50,
84, 98, 102, 103, 104, 105, 108, 155,
166, 167, 170.
Dimmock, Peter 244.
DIVISIONS.
British.
50th 118, 119.
Australian.
9th Australian 114.

DIVISIONS (*cont.*)
South Africa.
1st South African 114, 118.
Indian.
Meerut Division 6, 16.
4th Indian 112, 119.
5th Indian 119.
10th Indian 112, 118.
Dixon, (Sir) Pierson 193, 195, 206, 214, 215.
Dodecanese Islands 161, 162.
Donovan, Col William (US Army) 96, 170.
Dominion Governments 93.
Dorman-Smith, Brigadier E.E. 115, 116, 117.
Dorsetshire HMS 62.
Douglas, Air Chief Marshal (Sir) Sholto 176.
Douglas-Home, Lord Home of the Hirsel 280.
Dowding, Air Marshal Sir Hugh 54.
Downing Street, No 10 39, 47, 60, 231.
DRAGOON, operation: landings in South of France, later called ANVIL 193, 194.
Drogheda Committee 238.
Drummond, Air Marshal 177, 179.
Duff Cooper, Alfred, later Viscount Norwich 21.
Duke of York HMS 84, 85, 104.
Dumbarton Oaks 195, 197.
Duncan, Admiral (US Navy) 139.
Duncan-Sandys, Lord 192, 273, 274.
Dundas, Commodore RN 179.
Dunkirk 53, 54, 59, 105, 202.
Dunlop, Major, Interpreter in Moscow 134, 135, 136, 137.
Dunphie, Peter 129, 136, 137.
Dutch East Indies 107.
Dutch Government 92, 93.
Dykes, Vyvian Lt Col, later Brigadier, 'Dumbie' 25, 28, 60, 61, 67, 68, 71, 74, 77, 84, 96, 97, 107, 109, 155, 163, 164, 167, 170, 171, 187, 188, 282.
Dyson (Sir) George 7.

Eaker, Gen Ira C (US Air Force) 165.
East India Company 1.
Economist, journal 227.
Eden, Sir Anthony, later Earl of Avon 45, 192, 193, 196, 198, 199, 222, 247, 248, 273.

Edmonton, Alberta, Canada 280.
Egypt 21, 22, 23, 26, 58, 109, 110, 112, 125, 147, 191, 207, 217, 218, 219, 237, 247, 263.
Eisenhower, Gen Dwight D. 109, 147, 148, 149, 150, 151, 152, 163, 177, 186, 188, 192, 193, 197, 227.
El Agheila 57.
El Alamein 18, 118, 130, 148, 172, 185.
Elburz Mountains, Persia 145.
Electrical and Musical Industries (EMI) 263.
Elijah and the prophets of Baal 193.
Engineers 2.
England 15, 101, 104, 153, 202.
Enigma decrypts Ultra 193, 194.
Esher Committee 27.
Europe 23, 25, 202, 203, 224.
European Advisory Commission 203.
European Broadcasting Union EBU 225, 226.
Eurovision 226, 244, 251.
Euryalus HMS 62.

Falla, Paul, Secretary at Ankara Embassy 179, 180, 181.
Far East theatre of war 65, 69, 86, 92, 93, 106, 189, 274, 281.
fforde, Sir Arthur 253, 261.
Field Companies RE.
3 Field Company 11, 13.
12 Field Company 17.
First Sea Lord 61, 65, 68, 69, 71, 72, 84, 85, 87, 162.
Fisons Ltd 263.
Florida 101.
Foch, Generalissimo Ferdinand 17, 91.
Focke-Wulf aircraft 78.
Foot, Robert 234, 253.
Foreign Office 52, 173, 221, 224, 248.
Forte, Sir Charles, later Lord 264.
Fourteen day rule 245, 246.
France 10, 16, 37, 51, 83, 109, 148, 157, 160, 161, 162, 194.
Fraser, Gen 133.
Freeman, John 251.
Freeman, Air Chief Marshal Sir W. Plate 13.
French Army 33.
French Committee of National Liberation 190.
French Navy 152, 176, 178.

French North Africa 148.
Fraser, Peter, PM New Zealand 93.
Fraser, Gen, Mil Attache Persia 133.
Freyberg, Lt Gen Sir Bernard, later
  Lord 185.

Gaitskell, Hugh 247, 248.
Gale, Gen Sir Richard 265.
Gale, Gen Sir Humphry 186.
Galloway, Lt Gen Sir Alexander 154.
Gammell, Lt Gen Sir James 194.
Gazala 104, 107, 112.
Geneva 226, 227.
George, Air Vice Marshal 178, 179.
Germany (Germans) 4, 9, 21, 26, 33, 36,
  38, 69, 76, 79, 82, 157, 158, 159, 169,
  184, 198, 201, 203, 244.
German Army 33, 118, 147, 194, 197.
German Navy 37, 39.
Gezireh, Cairo 177.
Gibraltar 86, 111, 145, 148, 152, 153, 154,
  185, 186.
Gibson, Wing Comd Guy 189.
Gimson, Colonel T.W., Irish Guards 207,
  211.
Giraud, Gen Henri 151, 163, 167, 168, 174.
Gizelle: Russian ballet 211.
Godfroy, Vice Admiral, Rénée 176.
Goodenough, Commander RN 67.
Gott, Lt Gen W.H.E. 112, 113, 114, 117,
  119, 121, 122, 123.
Gordon of Khartoum 189.
Gort, Gen Lord 34, 40, 122, 153.
Gourock, Scotland 85.
Graves, Cecil 234, 253.
Greece 37, 57, 58, 74, 194, 195, 196.
Greene, (Sir) Hugh Carleton 263.
Grigg, Sir James 201, 271.
Grisewood, Harman 221, 240, 241.
Grove, Maj Lance 163.
Guadalcanal 157.
Gulf of Bosnia 105.
Gusev, USSR Ambassador, London 207,
  214.
GYMNAST operation 106, 108, 109.

Haley, Sir William 218, 219, 221, 222, 225,
  229, 233, 234, 236, 238, 253.
Halifax, later Earl of 33, 34, 91, 188, 204.
Hankey, Sir Maurice, later 1st Baron 19,
  20, 24, 28, 45, 90, 282.
Hampton Roads 87, 88.

Harcourt, Captain RN 85.
Harding, Gilbert 251.
Harding, Field Marshal Lord 21, 276, 280.
Harriman, W. Averell 71, 82, 84, 85, 126,
  132, 133, 135, 136, 137, 138, 139, 154,
  196, 207, 208, 227.
Harris, Marshal of the Royal Air Force 98.
Hartle, Gen Russell P. (US Army) 152.
Harwood, Admiral Sir Henry 113, 176.
Hayter, Sir William 206, 211, 213.
Hazara Pioneers 9, 15.
Heath, Edward 277.
Helm, Counsellor, Ankara 179, 181.
Hill, Mrs, stenographer 85.
Hill, Dr, Postmaster General 246.
Himalayas 10.
Hiroshima, Japan 204.
History of the Second World War
  (Churchill) 196.
Hitler, Adolf 16, 23, 25, 26, 36, 44, 59, 60,
  81, 106, 192, 197, 225.
Hoare, Sir Samuel 34.
Holland 33.
Hollis, Col, later Gen Sir Leslie 29, 31, 36,
  39, 51, 56, 60, 61, 63, 68, 75, 84, 85, 86,
  88, 91, 94, 99, 100, 101, 103, 104, 153,
  164, 171, 190, 200, 201, 222, 280.
Hong Kong 104.
Hopetoun Dormitory, Wellington
  College 7, 17.
Hopkins, Harry L. 60, 62, 64, 74, 79, 96,
  102, 103, 109, 155, 174.
Hore-Belisha, Leslie 32, 33, 37, 41.
Horrocks, Lt Gen Sir Brian 18, 126, 281.
House of Commons, British 59, 231, 246,
  248, 278.
House of Commons, Canadian 204.
House of Lords 3, 229.
Hudleston, Gp Capt, later Air Chief
  Marshal Sir Edmund 178.
Hughes, Maj Gen (US Army) 152.
Hull, Cordell 151.
Hull, Colonel (US Army) 155.
Hungary 196, 198.
Hunstanton, Norfolk 6.
Hurricane, aircraft 78.
HUSKY, operation in Sicily 178, 188, 189.
Hussey, Marmaduke 281.
Hussars, 4th 4, 183.
Hyderabad, battle 2.

Iceland 78.

Idak, Waziristan 13.
Imperial War Museum   279.
Inchcape, Earl of   20.
Independent television   247.
India   1, 2, 5, 9, 10, 16, 23, 58, 69, 112,
     113, 116, 119, 120, 123, 124, 141, 170,
     225.
Indian Ocean   69, 106.
Indo-China   83.
Indomitable HMS   83.
Indus River   1, 2.
Ingersoll, Ralph   227.
Inonu, President of Turkey   178, 180, 181,
     183, 184.
Inskip, Sir Thomas (later Viscount
     Caldecote)   30, 35, 36, 37.
International Telecommunication Union,
     ITU   226.
Iran see Persia.
Iraq   116, 120, 122, 123, 124, 178.
Ironside, Field Marshal Lord   27, 49, 50,
     87, 104, 105.
Ismay, Col H.L. 'Pug', later General
     Lord   24, 25, 29, 31, 33, 39, 45, 46, 47,
     48, 49, 50, 55, 56, 61, 82, 105, 108, 110,
     121, 146, 171, 173, 174, 181, 190, 191,
     195, 199, 201, 204, 217, 221, 228, 264,
     265, 275, 276, 277, 279, 280.
Italy   22, 26, 36, 148, 158, 160, 161, 169,
     187, 188, 189, 190, 193, 194, 197.
Italian Forces   57, 118.
Italian Somaliland   22.

Jacob, Aileen   3.
Jacob, Lt Col Arthur le Grand   15.
Jacob, Cecil, Lady   16, 24, 46, 106, 188, 189,
     203.
Jacob, Sir Claud William Field Marshal   3,
     20, 45.
Jacob, Edward of Faversham   1.
Jacob, Edward Ian Claud, Lt Gen Sir Ian.
     Childhood and boyhood   1–8; joins the
     Royal Engineers   9; in India; sees active
     service on the NW Frontier   9–15;
     returns to England and enters King's
     College, Cambridge   16–17; instructor
     at the Royal Military Academy,
     Woolwich   17; his comments on the
     Staff College, Camberley   19; serves as
     Garrison Engineer, Aldershot and then
     in the War Office operations
     directorate   20; to Egypt as brigade-
     major Canal Brigade   21–24; meets
     Hankey and Ismay in UK and becomes
     military assistant secretary of the
     Committee of Imperial Defence   24; his
     criticisms of Churchill as First
     Lord   41–43; Churchill becomes Prime
     Minister, and Jacob joins Ismay and
     Hollis in the 'Secret Circle'   45; his
     comments on Churchill as PM   46; his
     appreciation of Ismay   49; applies to
     return to regimental duty, but is refused
     in the national interest   56;
     accompanies Churchill to meet President
     Roosevelt in Placentia Bay   59–80; his
     views on United States' reaction to
     Britain at war   73; after Pearl Harbour,
     accompanies Churchill for another visit
     with President Roosevelt   81–104;
     comments on US machinery of
     Government   95–97. Accompanies
     Oliver Lyttelton to USA and attends
     meetings of Combined Chiefs of
     Staff   108. Accompanies Churchill to
     Cairo; reports on condition of Eighth
     Army; carries PM's letter of dismissal to
     Auchinleck   110–131; with Churchill to
     Teheran and Moscow to confer with
     Stalin   132–145. Impressions of
     Stalin   144. Organises conference at
     Casablanca for Churchill and President
     Roosevelt   149–171; accompanies
     Churchill to Turkey and Tripoli   178–
     186; attends TRIDENT conference in
     Washington   187–188, and
     QUADRANT conference in
     Ottawa   189–191; accompanies
     Churchill to the Italian Front   193–195;
     accompanies Churchill to Moscow
     (TOLSTOY)   196; attends conference
     at Yalta (ARGONAUT)   197–198; as
     UK Military Advisor attends conference
     on United Nations at San
     Francisco   198–200; his broadcast from
     San Francisco   202, 203; attends
     Potsdam Conference (TERMINAL)
     203; accompanies Prime Minister Attlee
     to USA and Canada for discussions on
     atomic weapons   204–206; accompanies
     Foreign Secretary Bevin to
     Moscow   207–216; goes to Egypt as
     UK Military Adviser to Stansgate
     Commission   218, 219; retires from the
     Army, and becomes Controller of

European Services of the BBC 219; gives Churchill's reaction to broadcasting 225; is released temporarily by the BBC to be Chief Staff Officer to Alexander as Minister of Defence and becomes Deputy Secretary of the Cabinet 228; returns to the BBC and becomes Director General 233; his reaction to commercial competition 237, 242; his management priorities 239; his ten year development plan 243; broadcasting the Coronation 244; his definition of guiding principles 245; his reaction to the 'fourteen day rule' 246; the BBC and Suez 247; his guiding principles for Television 249, 250; his reactions to complaints against the BBC 251, 252; 'The BBC: Past and Future' 254, 261; A tribute from Sir Arthur fforde, Chairman of the Governors 261, 262; resigns from the BBC at the age of sixty and takes up new interests in Suffolk 263; prevents the demise of the Army and Navy Club 264–266; is invited by the Minister of Defence to report on the central organisation of defence 266–277; attends funeral of Sir Winston Churchill 278; installed as Lay Canon of St Edmundsbury Cathedral 279; guest of honour at the Churchill Society banquet at Calgary, Canada 280; celebrates his diamond wedding 281; attends ninetieth birthday luncheon at the BBC 281; his achievements 281, 282.

Jacob, Rev George 1, 2.
Jacob, George le Grand 1, 2.
Jacob, Herbert 1.
Jacob, John (of Sextries) 1.
Jacob, John (of Sind) 1, 2, 3, 5.
Jacob, John Claud 17, 22, 40, 106, 200.
Jacob, Pauline, Lady 3, 4.
Jacob, Stephen Long 1.
Jacob, Sir Swinton 10.
Jacob, William 1.
Jacob, William le Grand 17, 22, 40, 106, 200.
Jacobabad, Pakistan 1, 2, 3.
Jaipur 10.
Jamaica 148.
Japan 69, 74, 82, 83, 84, 106, 107, 120, 158, 169, 184, 195, 196, 203, 204, 212.

Jefferis, Maj M.R., later Sir Millis 13, 52.
Jews 22.
Joint War Production Staff 51.
Joint Staff Mission 75.
Jones, Mr, Personal assistant to Hollis 100, 101.
Jowitt, Lord 231.
JUPITER, operation planned for Norway 106, 147.

Kaganovitch, Lazar Moiseyvitch Soviet Commissar 214.
Kanghur, Pakistan 2.
Kelly, Col US Army 214.
Kennedy, Maj Gen Sir John 154.
Keyes, Gen (US) 149.
Keren, Abyssinia 112.
Kharkov 190.
Khyber Pass 11.
Kiel Canal 39.
Kilindini 83.
King George V HMS 62, 85.
King George VI 45, 60, 79, 235.
King, Maj Gen Sir Charles 17, 218.
King, Admiral Ernest J (US Navy) 67, 68, 72, 97, 98, 102, 103, 109, 113, 155, 157, 159, 166, 170.
King, Mackenzie, Prime Minister, Canada 204, 206, 209.
King's College, Cambridge 16, 18.
Kinna, Patrick 'Peter', stenographer 111, 120, 129, 174, 179.
Kirby, Maj Gen S.W. 112.
Kirk, Alexander, US Minister, Cairo 126.
Kirkman, Gen Sir Sidney 18, 185.
Kirkpatrick, Sir Ivone 218, 221, 226.
Klopper, Maj Gen (South African) 114, 115.
Knatchbull-Hugessen, Sir Hughe 178, 179.
Knox, Frank, US politician 91, 99.
Korea 212.
Kremer, Soviet liaison officer 125.
Kuibyshev, USSR 133.
Kurram Valley, Pakistan 11.
Kuznetsov, Admiral USSR 214.

Labour Party 231.
La Guardia, Mayor of New York 90.
Lahore 11.
Lambe, Captain, later Admiral of the Fleet, Sir Charles 84, 86.

Lampson, Sir Miles 27, 111, 125, 176, 184.
Lampson, Lady 111, 125, 176, 184.
Largs HMS 194.
Larmour, Edward 8.
Lascelles, Sir Alan 264.
Lawson, John James 267.
Laycock, Sir Robert 264.
Layton, Sir Walter 59.
Leach, Captain J.C. (RN) 63.
Leahy, Admiral William D., (US Navy) 155.
Leathers, Lord 154, 165.
Lee, Col Raymond E. (later Brig Gen) 89, 152.
Leese, Gen Sir Oliver 281.
Lend-lease 96, 102.
Lenin, portrait in Kremlin 136.
Leningrad 141.
Lepschinskaya (Russian ballet dancer) 211, 213.
Levant-Caspian front 116.
Lewis, John Spedan 218.
Libby, Commander, Aide to Admiral King 155.
Libya 86.
Lindemann, Professor Frederick later Viscount Cherwell 21, 52, 60, 64, 65, 71, 75, 95, 192, 193, 201.
Lindsell, Lt Gen Sir Wilfred 124, 125, 126, 128, 179, 182.
Llewellyn, Sqn Ldr RAF 119, 125, 129.
Lloyd George 28.
Lloyd, John Selwyn (later Baron) 237.
Lockwood, Sir Joseph 263.
London 6, 40, 75, 83, 93, 104, 109, 113, 126, 138, 147, 150, 165, 195, 211, 214.
Londonderry, Marquess of 21.
Loxley, Peter (Foreign Office) 178, 179, 181, 182, 183.
Luftwaffe 21, 54.
Lyttleton, Oliver (later Lord Chandos) 107, 108, 192.

Macafie, Ernest Bevin's Russian interpreter 208, 214.
Macall, Dr 207, 214.
Macarthy, Maj, Aide to Gen Marshall 155.
Macready, Gen (Sir) Gordon 19, 20, 84, 85, 88.
McCreery, Gen Sir Richard 128.
Macdonald, Lord 236.
Macdonald, Ramsay 21.

McGrigor, Admiral Sir Roderick 230.
Mack, Foreign Office advisor 151.
Mackinnon, Capt Angus 122.
McLean, Lt Gen Sir Kenneth 228, 229.
Macmillan, Harold, later Earl of Stockton 149, 151, 153, 197, 230, 246, 250, 273, 275.
Macmillan, Publishers 278.
McMullen, Maj Gen Sir Donald 88.
Macnair, Lt Gen Lesley J (US Army) 91.
Mahsud Tribe, Pakistan 11.
Makins, Sir Roger, later Baron Sherfield 204.
Malaya 23, 83, 84, 86.
Malenkov, Georgi M (Politburo) 214.
Mallaby, Sir George 228, 230.
Malta 107, 141, 160, 162, 197.
Mamounia Hotel 175.
Manchester Guardian 235.
Manila 99.
Marines, see United States Marines.
Marrakech 149, 154, 156, 169, 172, 173, 175, 185.
Marx, Karl: portrait in Kremlin 136.
Marshall, C.S.M Royal Military Police 111.
Marshall, Gen George C. 59, 68, 69, 71, 72, 73, 74, 76, 89, 90, 91, 92, 98, 100, 102, 103, 105, 108, 109, 113, 155, 157, 159, 166, 167, 170, 188, 222, 241.
Marshall Aid 224, 228.
Marshall Islands 158, 169.
Martin, (Sir) John 60, 94, 101, 182.
Martin, Brig G. Noel 20, 122, 185.
Marylebone Station 61.
Mason-Mcfarlane, Gen Sir Noel 64, 111.
Mathews, Dr, US State Dept 208.
Matthews Holdings Ltd 279.
Maude, Maj 87.
Max-Muller, Charles 244.
Maxwell, Brig, Royal Artillery 185.
Maxwell, Mrs Wendy 190.
Mediterranean 22, 145, 147, 156, 159, 162, 169, 172, 187, 193.
Medouina, Morocco 175.
Melek, Commissar 208.
Menzies, Sir Robert (Australia) 93.
Mesopotamia 10.
Messina 162.
MI6 193.
Miani, battle 2.
Middle East 69, 78, 82, 83, 94, 108, 109, 110, 112, 113, 115, 116, 117, 119, 129, 142, 160, 280.

Middle East Command 22, 24, 109, 120, 173, 281.
Mikoyan, Anastas Ivanovich Commissar 214.
Mills, Sir Percy, later Lord 207.
Minister for the Coordination of Defence 30, 41, 267.
Minister of Defence 47, 48, 229, 273, 275.
Minister of State for Middle East, see Casey
Ministry of Aircraft Production 75.
Ministry of Defence 228, 230, 231, 240, 270, 275.
Ministry of Information 225.
Ministry of Labour 52.
Ministry of Production 52, 201.
Ministry of Supply 37, 41, 59, 75, 253.
Mir Din Subedar 9.
Moascar 21, 22, 24, 25, 26.
Moberly, Maj Gen R.J. 265.
Mockley, Ferryman, Brig E.E. 186
Molotov, Vyacheslav 136, 139, 144, 199, 201, 210, 211, 212, 213, 214, 215.
Monnet, Jean 97, 98, 103.
Mons, battle of 7.
Montgomery, Field Marshal, Viscount 18, 19, 23, 121, 123, 126, 127, 130, 132, 148, 185, 197, 200, 207, 227, 267, 277, 280.
Montreal 203.
Moore, Gen (US Army) 91.
Moran, Lord, see Sir Charles Wilson.
Moravia 36.
Morgan, Maj Gen Sir Frederick 189.
Morocco 191.
Morris, Sir Philip 236.
Morrison, Herbert, later Baron 192.
Morton, Sir Desmond 55, 95.
Moscow 38, 39, 74, 81, 109, 110, 114, 125, 129, 132, 135, 145, 146, 147, 195, 196, 197, 206, 207, 209, 212, 224, 239.
Mountbatten, Lord Louis, later Admiral of the Fleet, Earl 109, 147, 161, 190, 197, 274, 275, 277, 280.
Mousquitiere del Duce 24.
Moyne, Viscount 176.
Mulberry, artificial harbour 202.
Mulholland, Sir Henry 236.
Munich 25, 29, 35.
Munitions Assignment Board 51.
Murmansk 81.
Murphy, Robert (US) 174.
Mussolini 22, 26, 33, 185.
Mustapha Kemal 184.
Mutiny, Indian 1.

Nagasaki, Japan 204.
Napier, Field Marshal Lord 10.
Napier, Robert John 10.
Naples 193, 194, 197.
Narvik 74.
Nasser, Gamal Abdel 247, 248.
Nazi 220.
Nelson 66.
Netherlands 244.
Netherthorpe, Lord 263.
New Zealand 23, 69.
Nevill, Maj Gen Cosmo 265.
Newall, Marshal of the Royal Air Force Sir Cyril 34, 84, 87, 105.
Newfoundland 60, 73, 77.
Nice 194.
Nicholls, B.E. 222.
Nicholson, Major, later General Sir Cameron 17, 18.
Nogues, General Auguste 151.
Norfolk, the Duke of 244.
Norfolk, Virginia 88.
Norman, Mark Richard 107, 108, 200.
North Africa 57, 104, 145, 146, 152, 157.
North Atlantic Treaty Organisation, NATO 224, 227, 228, 273, 274, 277.
Northern Ireland 104.
North West Frontier, India 2, 4, 7.
Norway 109, 147, 266.
Norwegian Campaign 43, 46.
Numan, Foreign Minister Turkey 180, 184.

O'Connor, Lt Gen (Sir) Richard 57.
OCTAGON, Second Quebec Conference 195.
Ogilvie, Sir Frederick 233, 253.
OGPU, Soviet Security Service 135.
OKW, Oberkommando der Wehrmacht 266.
Olympic Games 227, 250.
Omdurman, battle of 184.
Oran 147.
Order of the Bath 193.
Order of the British Empire 221, 263.
Organisation internationale de radio-diffusion 226.
Other Club 231, 278.
Ottawa 92, 101, 203, 229.
Ouida 186.
Ovington Court 46, 55.
OVERLORD: assault on NW Europe 189, 190, 191, 192, 193, 197, 202.

Pacific theatre 74, 83, 84, 104, 148, 156, 157, 158, 159.
PAIC, Persia and Iraq Command 121, 127, 128.
Pakistan 1.
Palestine 22.
Papandreou, Prime Minister Greece 193, 195.
Parker, Sir Harold 228, 229.
Paris 9, 33, 50, 54, 226, 227.
Parkinson, Sir Cosmo 29, 38.
Paschendaele 32.
Patton, Gen George S. (US) 149.
Pau, France 181.
Pavlov, Vladimir, interpreter 136, 139, 207.
Pearson, Lester, Canada 215.
Pearl Harbour 82.
Peck, Sir John 55.
Peenemunde 192.
Pender, Kenneth, Vice Consul 169.
Pershing, US General in World War I 91, 166.
Persia 82, 104, 107, 112, 114, 116, 120, 122, 123, 124, 142, 145, 178, 191, 212, 214, 215.
Persian Gulf 23.
Persian Prime Minister 133.
Persian railway 126, 128, 133, 145.
Peshawar 11, 13.
Philippines 69.
Phillips, Rear Admiral Tom 84.
Pim, Capt (Sir) Richard 62.
Phoebus (USA) 88.
Pisa-Ancona Line 190.
Placentia Bay, Newfoundland 60, 63, 66, 73, 191.
Poland 36, 38, 39, 40, 142, 197, 198, 199, 204, 237.
Poles 142, 143.
Pollock Medal 9.
Pope John XXIII 251.
Portal, Marshal of the Royal Air Force Charles, Viscount of Hungerford 84, 148, 167, 222, 264.
Port Said 27.
Post-War Committee for Europe 51.
Potomac river 87, 108.
Potsdam 203, 210.
Pound, Admiral of the Fleet, Sir Dudley 34, 75, 83, 84, 191.
Pownall, Lt Gen Sir Henry 53, 264.
Prince Igor, opera by Borodin 211.
Prince of Wales HMS 60, 62, 67, 68, 71, 83, 85.

Prokofiev, Sergei 213.
Prussia 197.
Purvis, Arthur B. 59.

QUADRANT: First Quebec Conference 189–191, 192.
Quebec 195.
Queen Elizabeth II 244, 250, 279.
Queen Mary, Cunard steamship 187.
Quetta, Pakistan 1, 3.
Quisling, Vidkun Norwegian fascist 220.

Rabaul 158.
Raj, British Indian Empire 1, 4, 5, 9.
Ram Rup Singh, Subedar 10, 14.
Ramillies, battle of 190.
Ramsden, Maj Gen W.H. 114.
Razani, Waziristan 12, (map), 13, 14.
Razmak, Waziristan 11, 12, 13, 14.
Redman, Brigadier, later Lt Gen Sir Harold 188.
Rees, Maj Gen T.W. 'Pete' 18, 112, 113.
Reith, Lord 219, 233, 235, 238, 241, 253.
Renown HMS 191.
Repulse HMS 83
Reynaud, Paul 50, 54.
Rhine 52.
Rhineland 23.
Rhodes, Brigadier 133.
Ribbentrop, Joachim von 38.
Ritchie, Maj Gen N.M., later Gen Sir Neil 117.
Roberts, (Sir) Frank 207, 210, 214, 215.
Roberts, Ouvry, later Gen Sir 16, 17.
Robertson, Field Marshal Sir William 10.
Robertson, Maj Sir Brian, later Gen Lord Robertson of Oakridge 10, 14, 15, 16, 120, 185, 207, 224.
Romania 57, 196, 198, 212, 214.
Rome 33, 195.
Rommel, Gen Erwin, later Field Marshal 57, 58, 107, 109, 116, 123, 130, 281.
Roorkee, India 9.
Roosevelt, President Franklin Delano 59, 60, 62, 63, 64, 65, 67, 70, 71, 72, 74, 76, 79, 81, 82, 83, 87, 88, 89, 91, 92, 93, 95, 96, 98, 99, 100, 101, 102, 103, 105, 108, 109, 121, 139, 144, 147, 148, 153, 155, 156, 163, 168, 169, 173, 175, 183, 187, 190, 196, 197, 198, 241.

Roosevelt, Franklin junior 70.
Rottingdean School 40.
ROUND-UP: Assault on NW Europe later
OVERLORD 147, 148.
Rowan, (Sir) Leslie 111, 125, 127, 173, 185,
278.
Royal Air Force 21, 24, 28, 39, 41, 126, 164.
Royal Armoured Corps 117.
Royal Artillery 22, 119.
Royal Commission on the Police 280.
Royal Engineers 6, 7, 9, 17, 20, 24, 207,
281.
Royal Institute of International Affairs 227.
Royal Marines 65, 154.
Royal Military Academy, Woolwich 8, 9,
17, 18.
Royal Navy 6, 83.
Rugby School 253.
Rucker, Sir Arthur 111, 112.
Russell, Maj Gen W.N. 265.
Russia, Russians, see Soviet Union.

Saint Paul's Cathedral 278.
St Valery 170.
Saki, aerodrome (Yalta) 197.
Salazar, Dr (Azores) 76.
Salisbury, Lord 224.
Salter, (Sir) Arthur 98.
San Francisco 195, 198, 200, 201, 202, 203.
Sappers: see Royal Engineers.
Sappers and Miners: King George Vth's
Own Bengal 9, 10.
Saraçoglu Sukru, Prime Minister
Turkey 179, 184.
Sardinia 148, 161, 162, 163, 172.
Sawyers, Churchill's valet 111, 155, 174,
186.
Scapa Flow 87.
Schofield, Capt, later Vice Admiral
Brian 67.
Scotland 219.
Scrabster, Scotland 62.
Seal, (Sir) Eric 55.
Seattle 203.
Second Front 82, 134, 138, 140, 141, 142,
145, 147, 148, 160.
Sedan 50.
Self, (Sir) Henry 102, 103.
Semonova, Russian ballet dancer 211.
Sergrev, Russian ballet dancer 211.
Shaposhnikov, Gen Soviet Army 139, 140.
Sfax, Tunisia 163.

Sherborne School 40, 106, 280.
Sherman, Commander (US Navy) 72.
Sherman tanks (from USA) 109, 130.
Shinwell, Emanuel, later Baron 267.
Sicily 148, 157, 160, 161, 163, 169, 172, 187,
188, 190.
Sidi Barrani 112.
Sidi Rezegh 104.
Sikander, Hyat Khan, Sir 120.
Sikorski, Gen Wladyslaw 128.
Silesia 197.
Simeonova, Russian ballet dancer 211.
Simla, India 10, 15.
Simon, Sir John 34.
Simon, Ernest, later Baron of
Wythenshawe 235.
Simpson, Mrs Wallis 22.
Simpson, Gen Sir Frank 18.
Sinclair, Sir Robert, later Lord 188.
Sind, Pakistan 1, 2.
Sind Irregular Forces 3.
Sind Irregular Horse 3.
SLEDGEHAMMER: Plan for landing in
NW Europe 106, 108, 109, 113.
Slessor, Air Vice Marshal John, later
Marshal of the Royal Air Force Sir
John 18, 154, 230, 231, 275.
Slim, Field Marshal Sir William, later
Viscount 230, 231.
Smuts, Field Marshal 111, 112, 113, 115,
120, 125.
Soames, Sir Christopher 264.
Soames, Baroness see Churchill, Mary.
Sollum 112, 113.
Somervell, Gen (US Army) 90, 155, 165, 170.
Soong, Dr T.V. 199.
South American Republics 199.
Southampton 27.
South East Asia Command 190.
South East Asia theatre 189.
Soviet Army, see under Armies.
Soviet broadcasts 237.
Soviet Union 38, 58, 59, 60, 74, 81, 106,
109, 145, 148, 169, 183, 190, 191, 196,
199, 205, 206, 207, 208, 218, 223, 224,
226.
Spaatz, Gen Carl (US Air Force) 153, 165.
Spain 33, 74, 148, 159.
Spalding, Gen (US Army) 132, 133.
Spears, Maj Gen Sir Edward 264.
Spectator 3.
Staff College, Camberley 17, 18, 19, 28, 34,
104, 170.

Stalin, Joseph Generalissimo 74, 82, 109, 114, 128, 132, 134, 135, 136, 137, 138, 139, 140, 142, 143, 144, 145, 147, 148, 155, 162, 168, 175, 190, 191, 192, 196, 197, 198, 212, 213, 214, 215, 218, 238.

Stanley, Admiral, US Ambassador Moscow 138.

Stansgate, Lord 218, 219.

Stark, Admiral Harold R. (US Navy) 67, 68, 69, 71, 72, 89, 97.

Statler Hotel, Washington 187.

Stedeford, Sir Ivan 236.

Stettinius, Edward R. jnr 199.

Stimson, Henry L. 91, 100.

Stirling, Lt Col William, later Gen Sir William 94, 149, 173, 175, 186.

Strang, Sir William, later Lord 207.

Stresa 226.

Subasic, Dr Ban of Croatia 194.

Sudan 218.

Sudetan Germans 25, 26.

Suez Canal 4, 22, 109, 219, 247, 248.

Suffolk 263.

Suffolk Police Authority 280.

Sukkur Dam 1.

SUPER GYMNAST, operation 104.

Supreme War Council 36, 38.

SYMBOL: see Casablanca Conference.

Tamil language 5.

Tank Parliament 51.

Tass, Soviet News Agency 38, 214.

Taurus mountains 177.

Tedder, Air Marshal Sir Arthur, later Marshal of the Royal Air Force, Lord 111, 113, 125, 127, 132, 134, 135, 136, 138, 140, 163, 165, 235, 236, 267.

Teheran 110, 125, 128, 132, 133, 143, 145, 147, 191, 192.

Templer, Field Marshal Sir Gerald 21, 279.

Ten Year Rule 20.

Terech river, Caucacus 137.

Tal, Pakistan 13, 14.

The Times 235, 279.

Thomson, Inspector 60, 111.

Thompson, Commander RN 60, 62, 101, 111, 114, 133.

Thorney, Peter, later Lord 277.

Thornton, Group Captain W. 88.

Thrace 105.

Tibet 10.

Tinnevelly 5.

Tirpitz , German battleship 64.

Tito, Josip Broz 193, 194.

Tobruk, Libya 82, 108, 112, 114, 185.

TOLSTOY: Conference in Moscow 196.

TORCH operation: Allied landings in Western Mediterranean 104, 109, 113, 130, 132, 134, 141, 145, 147, 148, 159, 160, 172, 188.

Torquay 226.

Toulon 194.

Treasury 223, 225, 229, 253.

Treaty of Brussels (WEU) 224.

Treherne, Maj Gen Sir Francis 28.

Treherne, Cecil Bisset, see Lady Cecil Jacob.

TRIDENT: codename for Second Washington Conference 187, 190.

Trincomalee 83.

Tripoli 82, 172, 178, 184, 185.

Tripolitania 57, 191.

Truman, President Harry S. 204, 205, 206, 209, 212, 217, 241.

Tsarapkin, Soviet commissar 208.

Tunis 82, 148, 161.

Tunisia 150, 162, 188.

Turkey 57, 137, 148, 161, 169, 172, 177, 178, 181, 184, 191.

Turkish Government 179.

Turner, (Sir) George 227.

Turner, Rear Admiral (US Navy) 68, 69, 71, 72, 89, 97.

Tuscaloosa USS 67, 68.

Union internationale de radio-diffusion UIR 226.

U-boats 37, 39, 86, 169, 200.

Ukrainian delegation to UNO 199.

Ultra, see Enigma.

Umberto, Crown Prince of Italy 194.

United Kingdom 160, 161, 169.

United Nations Organisation 104, 195, 198, 203, 204, 206, 213.

United Nations Radio Department 220.

United States Air Force 76, 77, 142.

United States of America 52, 54, 59, 66, 74, 82, 106, 107, 130, 147, 204, 205, 218, 244.

United States Army 69, 73, 74, 76, 77, 79, 90, 156, 159.

United States Forces 101.

United States Government 89, 97.

United States Legion of Merit 217.

United States Marines   67, 70, 157.
United States Navy/Fleet   69, 73, 74, 76, 79, 82, 90, 91, 156, 158.
Urdu   10.
USSR, see Soviet Union.

V 1 pilotless aircraft, 'doodle-bug'   193, 194.
V 2 ballistic rocket   193.
Vancouver, Canada   203.
Van der Kloete, Sqn Ldr   175.
Variety programmes   239.
Vaughan, Dr   7, 8.
Venice   24.
Versailles Conference   10.
Vice Chief of the Air Staff   68, 71, 72.
Viceroy of India   279.
Victoria   203.
Vienna   197.
Villa Rivalta, Naples   193.
Vincent (US)   208.
Vis Island, Adriatic   193.
Voice of America, broadcasting corporation   202, 224, 238.
Vorontzov Villa, Yalta   198.
Voroshilov, Marshal K.E.   139, 140, 141, 142.
Vyshinski, Andrei   207, 208.

Wales   2.
Wallace, Miss, see Mrs Maxwell.
Wana, Pakistan   11.
War Cabinet   38, 39, 40, 44, 46, 48, 50, 79, 92, 107, 108, 115, 120, 128, 170, 183, 196, 204.
War Office   20, 38, 170, 219.
Ward, Sir John   213.
Warsaw Pact   237.
Washington   59, 76, 84, 87, 88, 89, 92, 93, 98, 99, 101, 105, 108, 120, 150, 165, 170, 187, 191, 205, 227, 229.
Washington Conference, ARCADIA   84, 105, 106, 170.
Washington Daily News   204.
Watson, Brigadier-General (US Army)   89.
Wavell, Gen Sir A., later Field Marshal Earl   57, 58, 74, 92, 93, 104, 111, 112, 113, 120, 125, 132, 134, 135, 136, 138, 140, 141.
Wazir, tribesmen   12.

Waziristan   11, 13, 18, 170.
Waziristan Circular Road   11, 52.
Wedemeyer, Maj Gen Albert C. (US Army)   155, 158, 159.
Weeks, Gen Sir Ronald   154.
Wellington College   7, 17.
Wellington, Sir Lindsay   240.
Wells, Sumner   67, 70, 74.
Wemyss, Gen Sir Colville   217.
Wendover, station for Chequers   61.
Western Desert   113, 114, 116, 117, 123, 126.
Western Desert Force   57.
Western European Union   273.
White House, Washington   87, 88, 91, 96, 100, 101, 103, 185, 206.
Whiteley, Maj Gen later Gen Sir John, 'Jock'   114, 115, 149, 186.
White Papers   237, 272, 276.
White Russian delegation to UNO   199.
Wigg, Col George, later Baron   248.
Wilkie, Wendell   190.
Williams, Lady Rhys   236.
Williamsburg   188.
Willink, Sir Henry   280.
Wilson, Sir Charles, later Lord Moran   101, 111, 114, 127, 174, 186.
Wilson, Gen Sir Henry, 'Jumbo', later Field Marshal Lord   18, 127, 128, 178, 179, 193, 194, 197.
Wilson, Morris   98.
Winant, US Ambassador   82, 84.
Windsor, Duke of, previously King Edward VIII   22, 188.
Windsor, Duchess of, see Mrs Wallis Simpson.
Wingate, Brigadier Orde   189.
Winterton, Maj Gen (Sir) John   112.
Wood, Sir Kingsley   41.
Wood, R.H.   244.
Woodbridge, Suffolk   16, 28, 39, 46, 55, 106.
Wootton, Professor Barbara, later Baroness   236.
Worcester HMS   251.
World Cup (football) '227.
World War I   147, 280, 281.
Wright, Capt (US Navy)   67.
Wyatt, Mrs Eliza (Isabella)   5, 17, 193.
Wyatt, Lt Col Ernest   15.
Wyatt, Rev J.L.   5.
Wyatt, Pauline, later Lady (Claud) Jacob   3.

Yalta Conference, ARGONAUT   197, 198,
    223.
Ypres Salient   8.
Yugoslavia   57, 58, 196.

Zhdanov, Andrei (Party Secretary)   214.
Zhob Valley, Baluchistan   3.
Zhukov, Marshal Georgi K.   207.

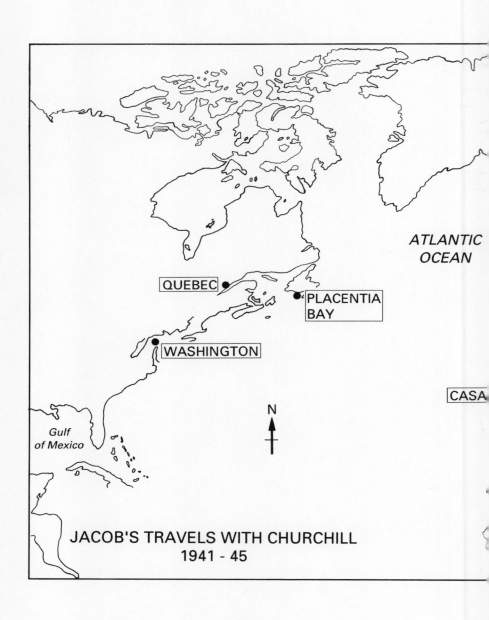

ATLANTIC
OCEAN

QUEBEC •

• PLACENTIA
BAY

• WASHINGTON

CASA

N

Gulf
of Mexico

JACOB'S TRAVELS WITH CHURCHILL
1941 - 45